The
Interpretation
of Music

The Interpretation of Music

Philosophical Essays

Edited
with an Introduction by
Michael Krausz

CLARENDON PRESS · OXFORD

Oxford University Press, Walton Street, Oxford OX2 6DP
Oxford New York
Athens Auckland Bangkok Bombay
Calcutta Cape Town Dar es Salaam Delhi
Florence Hong Kong Istanbul Karachi
Kuala Lumpur Madras Madrid Melbourne
Mexico City Nairobi Paris Singapore
Taipei Tokyo Toronto
and associated companies in
Berlin Ibadan

Oxford is a trade mark of Oxford University Press

Published in the United States by
Oxford University Press Inc., New York

First published 1993
First issued in paperback 1995

British Library Cataloguing in Publication Data
Data available

Library of Congress Cataloging in Publication Data
The Interpretation of music: philosophical essays/edited with an
introduction by Michael Krausz.
Includes index.
1. Music—Philosophy and aesthetics.   I. Krausz, Michael.
ML3845.I62 1992   781'.1—dc20   92-16508
ISBN 0-19-823958-0
ISBN 0-19-823550-X (Pbk)

Printed in Great Britain
on acid-free paper by
Bookcraft (Bath) Ltd
Midsomer Norton, Avon

Contents

IV

V

VI

Notes on Contributors

F. M. BERENSON is part-time tutor in philosophy at Birkbeck College, University of London, Department of Adult Studies. She was holder of the Distinguished Scholar in Humanities Woman's Chair at Marquette University in Milwaukee. She is the author of numerous publications, including *Understanding Persons*.

BOJAN BUJIC is a University Lecturer in Music and a Fellow of Magdalen College, Oxford. His research interests include the history of music of late medieval and Renaissance Italy, and aesthetics of music, especially German thought of the nineteenth and early twentieth centuries. Among his recent publications are *Music in European Thought 1850–1912*, and essays on various aspects of Italian literature and music in the fifteenth and sixteenth centuries.

MARK DEBELLIS is Assistant Professor of Music at Columbia University. He received his Ph.D. in philosophy from Princeton University in 1988. He is currently writing a book about music and conceptualization.

LYDIA GOEHR is Assistant Professor of Philosophy at Wesleyan University, Connecticut. She is the author of *The Imaginary Museum of Musical Works: An Essay in the Philosophy of Music*.

ROM HARRÉ is a Fellow of Linacre College, Oxford, and Professor of Psychology, Georgetown University, Washington, DC. His publications include *Varieties of Realism*, *Pronouns and People* (with P. Mühlhäusler), and most recently *Physical Being*, a study of the role of the body in human life.

GÖRAN HERMERÉN has been Professor of Philosophy at Lund University, Sweden, since 1975, and since 1988 he has served as President of the International Association of Aesthetics. His previous books include *Representation and Meaning in the Visual Arts*, *Influence in Art and Literature*, *Aspects of Aesthetics*, *The Nature of Aesthetic Qualities*, and *Art, Reason, and Tradition*. He has also published papers in scholarly journals and co-edited several anthologies in aesthetics.

JOANNA HODGE studied for her doctorate in philosophy at Wolfson College, Oxford, and in Germany. She is now a senior Lecturer in Philosophy at Manchester Polytechnic. She works in the post-Kantian philosophical tradition and is finishing a study of Heidegger and ethics.

MICHAEL KRAUSZ is Milton C. Nahm Professor of Philosophy at Bryn Mawr College, and is Chairman of the Greater Philadelphia Philosophy Consortium. He is the author of *Rightness and Reasons: Interpretation in Cultural Practices* (forthcoming), and has edited volumes on the philosophy of R. G. Collingwood, creativity, relativism, and rationality. A former violin student of Josef Gingold, Krausz founded and was associate artistic director of the Philadelphia Chamber Orchestra.

ROBERT KRAUT is Associate Professor of Philosophy at Ohio State University. His primary interests are metaphysics and the philosophy of language. He is also a working jazz guitarist.

JERROLD LEVINSON is Professor of Philosophy at the University of Maryland, College Park. He is the author of a collection of essays, *Music, Art, and Metaphysics*, and is currently at work on a monograph about musical comprehension.

JOSEPH MARGOLIS is currently Laura H. Carnell Professor of Philosophy at Temple University, Philadelphia. He is the author of more than twenty-five books, including the trilogy *The Persistence of Reality*, comprising three books: *Pragmatism without Foundations, Science without Unity,* and *Texts without Referents*. His latest book is *The Truth about Relativism*.

ROBERT L. MARTIN is Assistant Dean of Humanities and Adjunct Associate Professor of Philosophy at UCLA. He was cellist of the Sequoia String Quartet from 1975 to 1985, and is currently producer of the Los Angeles chamber music series, *Music for Mischa*.

DIANA RAFFMAN is an Assistant Professor of Philosophy at Ohio State University. She is the author of *Language, Music, and Mind* (forthcoming), which addresses the problem of ineffable musical knowledge.

JAMES ROSS, Professor of Philosophy at the University of Pennsylvania, has recently written on cognitive voluntarism as replacement for evidentialism, on semantic contagion as an account of diversity of meaning, and is presently completing a book, *Truth and Impossibility*.

ROGER SCRUTON is Professor of Aesthetics at Birkbeck College, University of London, and author of numerous books, the latest being *Francesca* (a novel), and *A Dove Descending and Other Stories*. He is currently writing a study of Wagner's *Ring*.

FRANK SIBLEY read PPE at Oxford. Between 1949 and 1964 he taught philosophy at Yale, Iowa, Michigan, and Cornell universities. From 1964 to 1988 he was Professor of Philosophy at Lancaster University where he is now Professor Emeritus.

FRANCIS SPARSHOTT is University Professor Emeritus at the University of Toronto. His writings include *The Theory of the Arts, Off the Ground: First Steps to a Philosophical Consideration of the Dance,* and the article on 'Aesthetics of Music' in *The New Grove's Dictionary of Music and Musicians*.

J. O. URMSON is Emeritus Professor of Philosophy at Stanford University and Emeritus Fellow at Corpus Christi College, Oxford. He is the author of *Philosophical Analysis, The Emotive Theory of Ethics, Berkeley, Aristotle's Ethics,* and *The Greek Philosophical Vocabulary*.

KENDALL WALTON is Professor of Philosophy at the University of Michigan. He is the author of *Mimesis as Make-Believe: On the Foundations of the Representational Arts*, and many papers on aesthetics, including the aesthetics of music.

Introduction

MICHAEL KRAUSZ

In the opening bars of his Symphony No. 3, Johannes Brahms indicates 'Allegro vivace'. How fast is allegro vivace? He indicates that the winds should play 'forte'. How loud is forte? At the third bar Brahms indicates 'passionato' for the first and second violins. How should this passage be played? These sorts of questions preoccupy serious musical performers. They are questions of interpretation.

While musicians are engaged in the details of performing particular musical works, philosophers of music enquire into the presuppositions of the practice of musical interpretation. Yet there is a dialectical relationship between the practice of musical interpretation and philosophizing about it. Characteristically, interpreters of music entertain philosophical views (however inchoate) about musical interpretation. And philosophers of music—by taking certain cases as salient and describing them in certain ways—reveal their musical biases (however inchoate). For example, an interpreter's decision whether to play one or another version of a piece, whether he should make certain cuts, whether he should use one instrument or another, whether he should emphasize certain elements and de-emphasize others, in part depends upon certain philosophical convictions. How he deals with these sorts of decisions will involve his view on what a musical work is—for example, on whether it is fully embodied in a score, on how strictly all markings should be respected, on what pertinence historical research has to his performances, on how decisive is the role of a historical or reconstructed composer, and so on. In short, discourse about musical interpretation should be informed at both the practical and philosophical levels. This collection of essays by philosophers of music is offered as a contribution to one side of that dialectic relationship.

The very idea of interpretation in general and musical interpretation in particular is 'open' in that it eludes strictly formulable rules of application. Just as the notion of musical interpretation varies with interpretation in other cultural practices (such as visual art, literature, history, ethnography, etc.), it varies as well between musical practices within the history of music. These considerations point to the implausibility of any essentialist theory of interpretation, in which necessary and sufficient conditions for its application are ahistorically mandated. Such a theory would close an open concept. The implausibility of an essentialist theory of musical interpretation is reinforced by the fact that music itself is not a natural kind. That is, what any given musical practice takes as music in a historically defined context, should not be countenanced as the privileged nature of real music as such, as if there were one ahistorical authentic pure nature of music to start with. Correspondingly, the idea of music changes in its history, and there are no philosophical grounds for affirming that any one idea of music, entrenched within a certain musical practice in its history, captures an enduring and historically fixed phenomenon. This does not mean, though, that there are no appropriate procedures or conventions for the reasonable application of the idea of musical interpretation.

Indeed, the openness and historicity of the idea of interpretation reveals a general condition about salient concepts of culture, and in this respect appropriate modes of theorizing about interpretation in music may serve as a template for the analytic discourse of culture. While our concerns are specific to music, the present contributions may inform cultural discourse generally.

Given its central place in musical practice, we should clarify the notion of musical interpretation to the degree it will admit, and in so doing we should distinguish it from, and show its relation to, such associated notions as performances, scores, and works of music, among others.

Both Göran Hermerén and Jerrold Levinson distinguish interpretation in the performance sense from the interpretation of critics of literature. Hermerén proposes that the distinction can be drawn on the basis of the aims to which respective interpretations are put, and this approach helps to understand the 'process-result' ambiguity in the idea of interpretation. Also, Hermerén discusses the conditions under which an interpretation is an interpretation of a given work. In turn, Levinson distinguishes the interpretation of a performer from that of a music critic. He holds further that not every performance where a work is 'realized' embodies a performance interpretation. Some performances do not represent a set of considered choices. Levinson outlines the dialectical development of performance interpretations and critical interpretations in a musician's experience.

For analytic purposes, one may distinguish an interpretation from its object. But interpretative activities may also constitute their objects, as when, for example, as a consequence of considered choices based upon what one takes the meaning of a work of music to be, it is performed one way rather than another. The objects of musical interpretation are neither logically nor phenomenologically fully separable from interpretation.

Frances Berenson emphasizes that in addition to the performer and the music critic, the listening audience interprets. Listening, as opposed to hearing, involves interpreting. The fact that audiences take a critical stance toward a performance implies that they are also engaged in interpretation. Listening to music is an intentional activity, and this fact helps us see how interpretation constitutes its objects. Given cultural codes, hearing sound as music constitutes it as such, just as seeing a blink as a wink constitutes it as such. *Hearing as* and *seeing as* are cultural acts.

Now, what is an interpretation an interpretation of: a score or a work of music? Are these the same? And in relation to what might one urge that a musical interpretation is right (or correct, or valid, or authentic)? One might be tempted to say that rightness (or its cognates) is a function of some match between an interpretation and a score or a work of music. But as several of the present essays make clear, a work of music characteristically underdetermines any unique interpretation of it. That is, a score or a work of music answers to more than one interpretation of it. Further, it is unsettled whether a score or a work of music is determinate, whether its boundary conditions are clearly delineable. Robert Martin and Joseph Margolis, for example, think they are not determinate. On the other hand, Robert Kraut, in disagreeing with W. V. Quine in the parallel linguistic case, holds that works of music are determinate.

Can one reasonably claim that a score should be violated? For example, in the name of faithfulness to a work of music, some interpreters purport to 'improve' upon a score by making cuts, by altering instrumentation, by changing dynamics or tempos, or the like. What constraints are there on such musical licence? What would keep an interpreter from transforming Beethoven's Fifth Symphony into 'Yankee Doodle' (to borrow an example from Nelson Goodman)? If an interpreter may change scores, what guarantee have we that in the end a work of music remains self-identical?

Sometimes there is no one score; there may be several original versions, a version corrected by a noted instrumentalist with or without the composer's approval, or with varying degrees of approval reflecting the composer's own divided or ambiguous attitudes. Yet, if a score is not equivalent to a work of music, or if not all features of a score are defining of a work of music, one would expect that some features of the score might not be respected and still hold that the interpretation could be one of a self-identical work of music.

Robert Martin argues that there is no one thing that is both what composers create and what listeners are familiar with through performances. On his account, what composers clearly do create—instructions to performers for creating performances—is something different from musical works as they exist in the world of listeners. Put otherwise, a work of music is no one thing as between composer, performer, and audience. Martin outlines two distinct areas of social practice in which musical works play a role: the performer's world and the listener's world.

Of course, the very idea of a work of music is not constant in the history of music. Bojan Bujic distinguishes between the idea of music as notated before the moment of sounding, and the idea of music as sounding object in the moment of performance. Bujic shows that as early as the first half of the sixteenth century, works as notated and works as sounding objects were regarded as two separate modes of existence. Notation became a self-contained ideal, the final goal of the process of composition, while the performance followed as a second stage, rather than being a part of a closely linked continuum.

Joseph Margolis notes that much of the recent literature in the philosophy of music shows a strong penchant for the thesis that music is ordered sound, rather along the lines suggested by Eduard Hanslick. But Margolis holds that such a view precludes expressive and representational properties of music. In contrast, he proposes that musical properties should be construed as culturally emergent, these being incarnated in ordered sound but not reducible to ordered sound. He holds that this view allows for the intentional attributes of music.

The logical possibility that a work of music is not to be specifically identified with what a composer created or intended, or with what listeners listen to, raises interesting questions about the identity of musical works at a particular moment and over historical time. It also raises questions about the weight that should be placed on the intentions of a composer in deciding how a performer's work of music should be interpreted. More generally, it raises questions about how a work should be interpreted and performed and how a performance should be assessed.

Clearly various interpretations of the same work (however we understand 'the same') may compete, and they may be mutually incompatible. But in what sense 'incompatible'? Surely they cannot be contradictory in the way that propositions might be; interpretations make no truth claims. They are, as Hermerén suggests, actions. Hermerén and Margolis hold that such incompatibility should be understood in terms of 'incongruence', which assumes no relation holding between contesting interpretations that behave like bivalence among propositions.

Given that there may be a multiplicity of interpretative practices, some of which may oppose each other, it may be a mistake to assume that works of music must answer to a single right interpretation. Where interpretative practices vary historically, and where interpreters have no access to works of music or standards independent of such practices, there may be no single right interpretation. This claim gives rise to the question of the status of standards in music. James Ross, for example, holds that the standards of compositional and performative excellence have no basis outside the historical and hermeneutical circle of the art itself. Music-making makes the standards of musical excellence. One can judge musical innovation only from within the 'musical world'. Standards are outcomes of critical scrutiny of artists and critics only with musical experience. In a Wittgensteinian spirit, Ross rejects any demand for a neutral, disengaged, or independent justification of the performance and compositional standards of leading musicians. Ross holds further that this closed circle of acquaintance and appraisal is not peculiar to music, but is common to all activities that make their own elements on the basis of prior accomplishments. Indeed, this may well be a defining charac- teristic of the cultural world altogether.

Michael Krausz distinguishes between singularism (the view that for a given work there can be only one right interpretation) and multiplism (the view that for a given work more than one right interpretation may be admitted). He argues that multiplism does not entail that there can be no good reasons for rationally preferring one admissible interpretation over another, and that multiplism does not entail an interpretative anarchism. Even if one were to concede that there might be more than one right (or correct, or valid, or authentic) interpretation of a work of music, what sorts of constraints would there be on ideally admissible interpretations? Besides aesthetic ones, J. O. Urmson advances ethical ones. He is concerned with what duties, if any, the performer may have to a composer or to his or her audience. Urmson distinguishes between obligations to composers (dead or alive), to oneself as a player, to a non-paying audience, and to a paying audience.

The suggestion that extra-musical considerations are pertinent to the interpretation of music raises the question whether one can sustain a strict distinction between musical and extra-musical considerations at all. Frank Sibley surveys a considerable extra-musical vocabulary widely used to describe music and our experience of it: he holds that extra-musical descriptions both assist and articulate our experience and understanding of music. Contrary to so-called purists, Sibley urges that such descriptions indicate that our understanding of music is essentially linked to our extra-musical experience and that music is not the mysterious and isolated phenomenon it is often thought to be. In turn, while providing a historical account of the idea of music for its own sake, Lydia Goehr holds that such an idea masks a politics of musical interpretation. And, given the recent resurgence of censorship in the arts in the United States and Western Europe, she uncovers problems latent in musicians' most common 'purist' defence against censors' attacks.

Being intentional, music has meaning in virtue of its place within a culture, where meanings are constituted by that culture's codes. Musical works embody more than physical features; they embody perceptual features as well. To identify perceptual pitch, for example, as opposed to acoustical frequency, is to have entered an intentional context. Diana Raffman emphasizes this point in her critique of Nelson Goodman's discussion of 'supplementary instructions for performance'. Likewise, Hermerén suggests that intentions, conventions, and intertexts give meaning to music. Sometimes, of course, composers follow or violate codes and conventions in their works. In this vein, Francis Sparshott enumerates and discusses the various modes of musical portraiture used by Edward Elgar, bearing in mind that the portraits were not intended to be informative to strangers but to be amusingly recognizable to those who knew the 'sitters'. Sparshott suggests that such musical representation has less in common with pictorial depiction or literary description than it does with oral story-telling, where the artistry lies in the story-teller's versatility and ingenuity.

Numerous contributors resist the idea that music can refer. For example, Rom Harré refutes the idea that musical sounds refer to extra-musical entities. He also resists S. K. Langer's structuralism. Alternatively, he embraces the idea that music is constituted by the listener, somewhat as Kant thought human experience is constituted out of sensory flux by syntheses of various kinds. Joanna Hodge argues that the understanding of music disrupts the picture of picturing as the dominant image through which to develop an understanding of art generally. Correspondingly, she rejects the theory of mimesis or representation in music, as well as both the realist and the idealist conceptions of art. These theories share a mistaken view of art as imitating a domain of entities (real or ideal) outside its own sphere. In turn, Roger Scruton considers and rejects the representation theory, the analogy theory, and the expression theory of musical meaning. Rather, Scruton holds that we should look to the experience of music in order to understand how we understand music. He proposes that dancing provides a paradigm for the experience of music.

The intentionality of music bears on the question of the relation between the analysis and appreciation of music. Kendall Walton and Frances Berenson hold that analysis is continuous with appreciation, and explaining or understanding how one hears is not to be separated from the experience of hearing. Walton says that musical analyses typically specify what one hears in a piece. Although what the analysis tells us does not suffice for understanding, it may assist one in the introspective task of recognizing or acknowledging the content of one's hearing. Some analyses may amount to speculations about what might be included in the as yet unacknowledged content of one's musical experiences. Analyses are sometimes meant to explain and encourage new ways of hearing, rather than to explicate old ones. But the distinction is not sharp. An analysis that specifies what a listener already hears in a piece may alter his hearing just by getting him to acknowledge what he hears. The experience of hearing and noticing certain features of the music, acknowledging one's hearing of them, is different from that of merely hearing them.

Finally, Mark DeBellis explores the idea that the value of theoretical knowledge lies in a greater coherence in the listener's experience. He remarks that recent writing about music theory has tended to polarize its explanatory and interpretative functions: its claim to scientific status and its potential for contributing to the listening experience. But DeBellis argues that the value, for a listener, of hearing music in theoretical terms sometimes derives from the explanatory power of those terms. Music theory is explanatory in the sense of explication: it explicates important musical properties such as closure.

These are among the interconnected concerns of the present essays. The aim of this brief introduction will have been served if it leads its readers to the contributors' own words.

The nineteen contributions to this volume appear in print here for the first time, and I extend grateful thanks to their authors. Also, I should like to acknowledge the encouragement and steady assistance of Angela Blackburn of Oxford University Press, and the help of Jon Newsom of the Music Division of the Library of Congress. He arranged for the facsimile of the opening bars of Brahms's Symphony No. 3 which appears on the cover of this volume.

I

The Full Voic'd Quire: Types of Interpretations of Music

GÖRAN HERMERÉN

1. Introduction

The role and the freedom of the musician or the conductor, if any, is, of course, not always the same; it varies in different kinds of music (jazz, classical music, pop music, raga, folk music, etc.). It is therefore important to specify which music we are dealing with; the problems of interpretation may be very different depending on what sort of music we have in mind.

Moreover, music is not a static phenomenon. It is historical in the sense that the structure and texture of musical compositions have changed over the centuries. This is true also of instruments, forms of production, channels of distribution, and ways of listening, as well as of the expectations and purposes of composers, musicians, and listeners.

Music is sometimes combined with, and closely interrelated with, other art-forms; the relation is sometimes almost symbiotic. There is, of course, pure instrumental (or abstract) music but also opera and film where music plays an important role. Obviously, in these latter mixed cases, the text is important, as well as the movements and gestures of the actors.

The general aim of the discussion will be to focus on attempts to clarify certain conceptual problems, not to study empirically the interrelations between, for example, different kinds of interpretations of illustrated poems (like Blake's illustrations of his own poetry, or various artists' illustrations of Baudelaire's *Les Fleurs du mal*) or cases of mixed art-forms like film and opera.

The differences between, for example, interpretations of aerial photographs in order to get information about enemy activities, allegorical (re)interpretations of classical texts in order to prevent them from being burnt or attacked by censors, interpretations and applications of the Bible to contemporary moral problems, and interpretations of philosophical texts with an interest in systematic reconstruction of a particular discourse should be obvious enough. But how are they—in their turn—related to interpretations of music?

What I will focus on in the present chapter is the relations between

I am indebted to Thomas Anderberg, Jeanette Emt, and Ingmar Persson for various helpful criticisms of an earlier version of this chapter.

different kinds of interpretations of music. The examples chosen will mainly be instrumental (classical and modernist) Western music from the last few centuries. In the course of the discussion a number of more specific problems will be dealt with: the variety of interpreters in music, the requirements of interpretation, types of interpretations, problems of individuation, the role of intentions in interpretations and finally the possibility and tolerability of incompatible interpretations of music.

But first I shall by way of introduction comment on some more or less intuitive and widespread ideas about interpretation, and a way of classifying interpretations.

2. Some Ideas about Interpretations

A study of the conceptual geography of 'interpretation' includes a study of its relations to concepts like 'meaning', 'understanding', 'intention', 'explanation', 'application', 'truth', 'correctness', 'value', and so forth. It is often taken for granted that the concept of interpretation satisfies the following ideas or principles. In this paper I hope to show that this is not true of all types of interpretations of music.

Interpretation has to do with meaning	(P1)
Interpretation facilitates understanding	(P2)

This constitutes part of what may be called the standard view of interpretation. An echo of this view may be found in the writings of Monroe Beardsley,[1] who, however, takes exception to another common idea:

Interpretation has to do with intention (P3)

at least if 'intention' is understood as shorthand for 'authorial intention'. Obviously, 'has to do with' in (P1) and (P3) is vague and ambiguous. By replacing this expression with e.g. 'explains', 'explicates', 'elucidates' more precise versions of (P1) and (P3) can be obtained.

Two other standard pre-analytic intuitions include:

Interpretation implies explanation	(P4)
Interpretation suffers from process–result ambiguity	(P5)

The latter expresses a point once made by Max Black, according to which 'interpretation' in the process sense is not identical with 'interpretation' in the result sense; hence (P5) denies that the process is the result.

Two of Gadamer's favourite ideas about interpretation and understanding can be summarized as follows:

---

[1] Monroe Beardsley, *Aesthetics: Problems in the Philosophy of Criticism* (New York, 1958, repr. Indianapolis, 1981); id., 'The Limits of Critical Interpretation', in Sidney Hook (ed.), *Art and Philosophy: A Symposium* (New York, 1966); id., *The Possibility of Criticism* (Detroit, 1970).

Interpretation always involves application (P6)

Interpretation presupposes the truth (of that which is interpreted) (P7)

Both these ideas are misguided, in my view.

Incidentally, it may be instructive to contrast (P7) with the much more interesting

Interpretation presupposes the truth (of the interpretation) (P8)

This, certainly, does not apply to musical performances and only to some special types of interpretations of texts. And few people have advocated it in the strong form stated above. But if 'truth' is replaced by 'correctness' or (even weaker) 'a tacit claim of correctness', then the situation changes; an echo of this view may be found in at least some of Beardsley's writings on interpretation, and in those of Hirsch and Juhl.[2]

Is this view correct? Does it apply to interpretations of all types? If taken in the strong sense of implying finality, the answer must be *no* to both questions. If, however, taken in the much weaker sense of 'not arbitrary; reasons can be given to support it' the situation is different; then both questions may be answered in the affirmative.

Interpretation presupposes norms (a normative stance) (P9)

An interpretation presupposes a normative stance at least in the sense that it suggests that this is how the work should be understood, that this is a proper (or the proper) way of reading (viewing, playing . . .) the work. This important idea was suggested by Charles Stevenson long ago,[3] and it has been developed, criticized, and clarified by many writers later.[4]

This enumeration makes no claim of completeness. Some people may, for example, be inclined to suggest

Interpretation requires skill and talent (P10)

Interpretation guides action (P11)

But the important thing here is not completeness. Rather, the point is that it is very unlikely that there is a single concept of interpretation which satisfies all these principles. The problem with many of these ideas is that they are vague and ambiguous, and that their range of application has not been made clear. It is assumed that they hold generally, while most of them hold only for certain specific types of interpretations.

For example, I shall suggest that there is a concept of interpretation of music which has little to do with explaining meanings and intentions. This

---

[2] Eric D. Hirsch, *Validity in Interpretation* (London, 1967); Peter D. Juhl, *Interpretation: An Essay in the Philosophy of Literary Criticism* (Princeton, NJ, 1980).

[3] Charles Stevenson, 'Interpretation and Evaluation in Aesthetics', in Max Black (ed.), *Philosophical Analysis* (Ithaca, NY, 1950), 341–83; 'On the Reasons that Can Be Given for the Interpretation of a Poem', in Joseph Margolis (ed.), *Philosophy Looks at the Arts* (New York, 1962), 121–39.

[4] Recently by Jeanette Emt, 'Tolkning: värderingar och normer', *Nordisk Estetisk Tidskrift*, 5 (1990), 24–54.

kind of interpretation is essentially concerned with expression or visualization, with rendering experiences in visual (audible) form, with creating a sound structure (or a pattern of actions) which can serve as something rather like that which Eliot once called 'the objective correlative' in poetry.

This suggests that we should take a look at the possibilities of distinguishing between different types of classifications.

3. Classifications of Interpretations

Interpretations can be classified in different types, using (some of) the following possible bases of division:

1. *The object of interpretation.* What is to be interpreted? Texts, aerial photographs, actions, nature, perceptions, sculptures, motives ... The variety is enormous, and the objects of interpretation can be classified in many ways: physical objects, intentional objects, events, actions, and so forth. This is clearly one possible basis of division, though probably not the most important one.

2. *The problem of interpretation.* What does the interpreter want to know? What the composer intended? The author wanted? How the composition was played by contemporary musicians? How contemporary readers or listeners understood the work? How it ought to be played and understood, given certain overriding normative concerns or interests? ...

3. *The material used in interpretation.* What sort of evidence is used to suggest, corroborate, or criticize proposed interpretations? Diaries, letters, descriptions of performances, textbooks for musicians, dictionaries, information about the subject-matter of the work to be interpreted, facts or conjectures about the pragmatic context of the work, common-sense psychology, psychoanalytical theories, Marxist doctrines ...

4. *The method of interpretation.* What method is used by the interpreter? There are different methods of selection, and different kinds of criticism of the selected passages: internal and external. Anyway, having selected the relevant passages, given the chosen problematics, various more or less synonymous readings of crucial passages can be proposed, and they can be systematized according to principles of rational reconstruction, systematic reconstruction, critical reconstruction, and so on.

This applies to various types of interpretations of literary and philosophical texts. But what about other kinds of interpretations? What method, if any, is used there? Eliot once wrote, '... for there is no method except to be very intelligent'.[5] I disagree with Eliot if this is applied to philosophy, but perhaps

---

[5] Quoted from Jerome Stolnitz, *Aesthetics* (New York, 1965) (motto on page following title-page (no number)).

something similar holds for what below I propose to call P-interpretations in music ('... except to be very musically talented'?).

In philosophical interpretations of a text, the interpreter tries to understand the problem (or problems) discussed in the text; and if it is unclear what the problems are, he or she proposes different possibilities. What answer is given to these problems in the text? Again, if this is unclear, the interpreter proposes different possibilities. The method includes a reconstruction of the chain of arguments, identification of gaps and missing premisses, making hidden assumptions explicit, discussion of different possible ways of dealing with (eliminating) contradictions in the text, and so forth.

But none of this seems applicable to interpretations in the sense of performances. For the actor, coherence, psychological credibility, and emotional depth are important things, and he or she tries to create a pattern (in which movements, facial expressions, ways of speaking fit) which will help to achieve these goals.

But music? For the musical interpreter, aesthetic considerations, including the *Vorverständnis* of the artist (to be discussed below), play a crucial role. I wish I could be more specific on artistic methods, but I am not sure there are any (in the sense in which there are methods in psychology or philosophy). To avoid misunderstanding, let me stress that this is not intended to suggest any value-judgements; to say that X and Y are different in a particular respect, is not to say or suggest that X is better than Y.

Obviously, a concert pianist exercises a great deal before a concert, plays through the pieces he is going to perform, tries different ways of performing them, perhaps listens to the way this composition has been played by others, studies sources about how the composition was played at the time of the composer, and so forth. Clearly, there are considerable variations between the ways in which different performers prepare themselves.

5. *The purpose of the interpretation.* What is the purpose of the interpretation? To discover what the author/composer wanted, to suggest a reading that illuminates a contemporary moral or political problem, to propose the aesthetically most rewarding approach, to rally the masses around common goals, to express feelings of sympathy or agony, to defend the object of interpretation against criticism, to describe the historical, social, psychological conditions for the creation of the work interpreted, to trace its *Wirkungsgeschichte* (history of reception), and so on?

6. *The result of the interpretation.* The idea is here to distinguish between different kinds of interpretation on the basis of the result of the interpretation, such as: a performance, a deeper understanding, a recording of a symphony, a production of a play, a critical article, a book, etc. Perhaps the results can be classified with the help of certain broad categories like actions, texts, and mental events.

There is no need to assume that these possible bases of divisions (and the classifications resulting by using them) are equally interesting in all contexts.

In some contexts, one of them may be more rewarding or illuminating than others, in others the situation may well be different. On the whole, I would think, however, that classifications on the basis of methods and purposes are particularly important.

4. The Variety of Interpreters

But there is more to say about the variety of interpretations, both of music and of the other arts. Here are some further suggestions. Who interprets what, when, and how in music?

> the composer
> the musician(s)
> the conductor/the producer
> the listener
> the critic/researcher

There is no need to assume that these people interpret the same thing in the same sense or for the same purpose. Let us suppose that the composer has experienced something that has made a strong impression on him, or constructs intriguing and exciting sequences of tones, or interprets by such sequences something he or she has experienced. The musicians and the conductor, however, interpret the score (which always leaves a great deal of freedom to the interpreter and hence can be played in several different ways). But the listener tries to understand what he or she hears, tries to relate it to music of other kinds, to experiences he or she has had, making all sorts of more or less free associations, while the critic and researcher tries to put the music in wider (musical, historical, and social) contexts, explaining its meaning and significance.

These are different activities, and their function and point is not necessarily the same. Why bother with these distinctions? For one thing, as I have suggested elsewhere,[6] the criteria of adequacy or success may be different in different types of interpretations. It is not obvious that the relevance of facts about the composer's intentions should have the same weight in all types of interpretations, nor that principles like (P8) are applicable to all types of interpretations.

Similarly, the well-known principle of generosity ('look for the best possible interpretation compatible with the text, score, or script') does not apply generally, to all types of interpretation, though it can be applied to both performances and interpretations of novels as well as philosophical texts.

If the type of interpretations are not specified and distinguished, pseudo-debates and talking at cross-purposes may be facilitated.

---

[6] 'Interpretation: Types and Criteria', *Grazer Philosophische Studien*, 19 (1983), 131–61.

5. Requirements of Interpretation

Let us now look further at the requirements of interpretations. An interpretative effort is made only when it is worth while, e.g. when the text or the script (score, etc.) is considered important or interesting enough. Time is short, and there is much one can spend it on.

This general requirement is clearly vague, and it is difficult to state it in a precise form and to argue that one of these precise versions is a necessary or sufficient requirement of interpretation. But it is, I think, obvious that considerations of this kind do play an important role in interpretative praxis.

What else do interpretations presuppose? In this context, we are not interested in interpretations of aerial photographs (where have the enemies hidden their missiles?) or interpretations of symptoms (what do these red spots in his throat mean?). If it is a necessary condition for anything to be a work of art that it is an intentional object in one or more senses, the first requirement can be stated briefly as follows:

The object of an interpretation is an intentional object   (R1)

This is not intended to deny that one can interpret clouds in the sense that one can see them as different things, or that one can try to read meaning into scribbles or patterns on the walls of caves only to discover later that they were produced by physical or chemical processes. Then one mistakenly believes that x is an intentional object, carries on with the process of interpretation, applying codes and conventions one mistakenly thinks are relevant in the particular case, and so forth.

Here are some further proposals, all of which—with the possible exception of (R5)—should be understood as necessary conditions:

The object of interpretation is open and indeterminate   (R2)

This means that the object of interpretation can be filled in in various ways; it presents the interpreter with choices and possibilities. A score (script) leaves a great deal of freedom to the interpreter; this is something I will return to many times below. Likewise, a philosophical or literary text can be understood in several ways; it can be supplemented in various ways, certain ideas can be connected, others disconnected, the focus of interest can be placed in various areas, behind the literal meanings one may search for different levels of meaning, and so forth.

Some people have objected that it cannot be a logical contradiction to say 'there is only one possible interpretation of x'. I would dispute that an object, action, text, etc., can be produced which admits of only one interpretation. But the point of the objection is perhaps that one must distinguish between empirical and logical claims. It may be granted that as a matter of fact (R2) happens to be true. However, does it follow from the definition of the concept of interpretation? I am somewhat reluctant to take a firm position on this view; I do not think the concept of interpretation is sufficiently well defined.

The important thing, however, is that p can be a necessary condition for q without implying that it is logically true that p is a necessary condition for q. Hence I persist in regarding (R2) as a necessary condition.

The object of interpretation poses problems   (R3)

These problems may concern how the work is to be understood, or explained, what its meaning and significance is, how it is to be elucidated and explicated, and so forth. Obviously, the object of interpretation must be of a kind which logically can be interpreted. But such a logical requirement would be too weak, in my view. The problems of interpretation must be put in a pragmatic context; the object of interpretation is puzzling in some ways, as suggested by (R3).

To say this is to say that this object can be understood in several ways, and it is not clear how it should be interpreted. It is not enough that the object of interpretation is open and indeterminate as required by (R2); we would also want to fill in the gaps. What kinds of problems does it pose? For whom? The musician is puzzled by the score? The reader does not quite understand the text? Feels that there is a 'hidden' message somewhere? Does not quite know how to make sense of the work? Or how to make the most of the work? Is uncertain as to where the emphasis should be put?

By answering these and other similar questions, distinctions can be made between different kinds of interpretations. The main thing is that it should not be possible by direct inspection to settle these problems, otherwise the distinction between description and interpretation would break down. Even if it is an illusion to look for sharp boundaries here, an interpretation has to be an interpretation of something.

To be able to specify what an interpretation is an interpretation of, it is necessary to maintain some sort of distinction between describing and interpreting x, even in a pragmatic context. Similarly, the description of x and x cannot be identified. There has to be some way of identifying that which is described, perhaps ultimately by ostensive definitions.

The object of interpretation is to some extent understandable   (R4)

If the object of interpretation (whether score, script, action, or object) were completely incomprehensible, we would not even know where to begin.

Here, the *Vorverständnis* of the interpreter plays an important role, though in somewhat different ways in different types of interpretation. A text is made up of words, and one has to begin somewhere—usually with a (partial, at least) understanding of the meaning of some of these words, or with a rough idea of what the text is about, or both.

The notes, of course, are well known to the interpreter in the trivial sense that he or she knows what a given note means (C, E, E, F minor, G major, etc.) though the combination of notes may be so complicated that the interpreter has to practise to be able to play the composition without making mistakes. But the problems of interpretation begin only when these technical difficulties have been mastered; and the technical difficulties are, of course, no problem for first-rate musicians.

Thus, the interpreter must understand the options offered by the score, and have the skills required. How should the piece be played? What about tempo? Legato? Emphasis? Emotion? Softness? Distinctness of the tones? Here preconceived aesthetic ideas and ideals play an important role and constitute part of the interpreter's *Vorverständis*. It also includes ideas about the role and the function of music, the relevance of facts about the composer's intentions, the functions of musical criticism, which may influence the choice of interpretative methods and approaches, and so forth. Explicitness concerning these assumptions may help to forestall misunderstandings and pseudo-debates.

> The problems of interpretation cannot be solved by consulting the composer or the author (song-writer)   (R5)

Perhaps, some problems may be solved in this way, at least theoretically , but not the typical or standard ones (though what you get is only information about what the author *now* thinks that he *then* meant). Instead of regarding historical reconstructions and interpretations of the author's or composer's intentions as standard cases, I would rather—when interpretations of the arts are concerned (as opposed to ordinary language conversation)—be inclined to treat them as special or untypical cases (without denying their existence).

Do these assumptions hold for all types of interpretation of music—or just for some? If they hold for all, perhaps they have to be interpreted differently when interpretations of different types are concerned. This is a question that needs to be discussed further.

6. Two Types of Interpretations: P-interpretations and T-interpretations

A performance of a symphony is an interpretation of that work. It is a way of presenting the work to our senses, and thereby also to our cognitive or intellectual abilities. So is a literary critic's interpretation of a poem. A particular performance is a series of events; and performances can be construed as belonging to the ontological category of action types.[7] The literary critic's interpretation. The performance is a series of actions, the latter is a text about a text. Let us, for the sake of brevity, call interpretations in the performance sense for P-interpretations and the others for T-interpretations.

It has sometimes been suggested that there is an analogy between T-interpretations and P-interpretations. 'Like an actor trying out different ways of playing a role we can try reading *The Turn of the Screw* first in a structuralist

---

[7] Gregory Currie has suggested the hypothesis that artworks are action types in his *Ontology of Art* (London, 1989), 7–8, 46–84.

way and then in a Freudian way. On one interpretation one set of features will be important, on another interpretation another set.'[8] I agree with the last observation. But even so, it does not seem possible to identify T-interpretations and P-interpretations.

A producer interprets a drama, an actor interprets a role, and we interpret what we see. In music, P-interpretation is essential; if 'the essence of music is sound in motion' (as Hanslick suggested long ago) or something like that, then: without P-interpretation, music cannot exist. When we read a novel, we T-interpret it. But no P-interpretation is essential for the novel; the work can exist without it.

Let us consider baroque music, from the point of view of both performers and musicologists. The instructions given to P-interpreters of that music, e.g. in various standard works,[9] is different from the kind of methodological instructions given to young musicologists who are about to T-interpret that music. The evidence used to support proposed interpretations are not necessarily the same in the two cases, and this also holds for the criteria of adequacy.

For example, what would the analogy in P-interpretations be to the familiar requirement that one should prefer interpretations that can explain, and hence be backed up by, as many passages as possible in the text, and that one should reject interpretations that are incompatible with passages in the text? If the overall aim is historical, as in the debate about whether one should play Bach with 'inegalité' (and if so, to what extent), sources from the seventeenth and eighteenth century describing contemporary praxis will be consulted in both cases.[10] But what does it mean to say that a certain performance 'explains, and hence is backed up by, the notes of the score'?[11]

The distinction between P-interpretation and T-interpretation crosses several other classifications, for instance, those based on purposes (historical, political, ideological, aesthetic) or methods (of selection, reconstruction, criticism, empathy). Intuitively, the distinction between these two types of interpretations appears to be clear. But it is hard to draw this distinction in an exact way. For example, it may be tempting to base the difference either on the object of interpretation or the result of the interpretation, but none of these will do.

To choose the first option is to say that in one case the object of interpreta-

[8] Anne Sheppard, *Aesthetics: An Introduction to the Philosophy of Art* (Oxford, 1988), 92.

[9] For example, David Boyden, *The History of Violin Playing* (Oxford, 1963); Rolf Dammann, *Der Musikbegriff im deutschen Barock* (Cologne, 1967); Frederick Dorian, *The History of Music in Performance* (New York, 1942); Gotthold Frotscher, *Aufführungspraxis alter Musik* (Locarno, 1963); Jacobus Kloppers, *Die Interpretation und Wiedergabe der Orgelwerke Bachs* (Frankfurt-on-Main, 1965); Betty Bang Mather, *Interpretation of French Music from 1675–1775* (New York, 1973).

[10] E.g. Pietro Aaron, *Thoscanello de la musica* (Venice, 1523); Johann F. Agricola, *Anleitung zur Singkunst* (Berlin, 1757); Bénigne de Bacilly, *Remarques curieuses sur l'art de bien chanter* (Paris, 1668); François Couperin, *L'Art de toucher le Clavecin* (Paris, 1716); Francesco Geminiani, *The Art of Playing on the Violin* (London, 1751); Johann J. Quantz, *Versuch einer Anweisung die Flute Traversiere zu spielen* (Berlin, 1752).

[11] This casts grave doubts on the generality of principle (P4) above.

tion is a score, in the other a text. But what is the precise distinction between the signs making up the text and those making up the score? Or between the sign-functions of a text and the sign-functions of a score? This is not immediately obvious. Moreover, in the case of drama, we speak about productions and performances of a play, just as in music, but here the script is a text.

To opt for the second choice also leads to difficulties. Only a limited class of T-interpretations results in texts. Sometimes the result of the interpretation is presented orally, sometimes it is not presented aloud at all, as when a literary critic reads a poem and interprets it. T-interpretation here fades over into understanding, and understanding, which can be more or less elaborate, more or less qualified, fades over into reading. Besides, even the performer has to read and understand the instructions of the composer; in acting, the difficulties of drawing a clear line is obvious.

Returning to the preliminary ideas about interpretations described in the beginning of this paper, it can be suggested that they might help to draw the line. While T-interpretations—of which there are many kinds—always satisfy principles 1, 2, 4, 5, and sometimes 3 and 6, this is not true of P-interpretations. They always satisfy principles 9, 10, and sometimes 11 but never principle 5. But many of these principles can be interpreted in several ways, and some of them are the subject of lively disputes (8, in particular).

Perhaps the prospects of success are better if the aims of the interpretation are taken as the basis of division. Many artistic aims may be common. The critics are sometimes also artists in their criticism. But the purpose of a P-interpretation is to present the work, or rather a version of the work, to the spectator or listener. This is different from the purpose of explaining the work, of showing what the common, unifying theme or thesis (if any) of the work is, of relating this work to other works, of placing it in a literary, social, and political context, and so forth.

One difference related to this is that the T-interpreter can be much more selective than the P-interpreter. The latter cannot skip certain notes or sections; the performer has to play them all, but he or she can vary tempo, emphasis, legato, vibrato, and many other things. The T-interpreter can be much more selective. The critic does not have to comment on each line in the poem or novel. He or she selects certain passages that in his (or her) view are key passages, comments on them, tries to find a unifying theme or thesis, and so forth.

Another more formal difference is that the process–result ambiguity characterizes T-interpretations in the sense that here it is comparatively easy to distinguish between the process of interpretation and the result, if any: a text. But in the case of a P-interpretation the process is the result in the sense that the result of the interpretation is not a text but a sequence of actions which take time and in that sense is a process.[12]

---

[12] This casts grave doubts on the generality of principle (P5) above.

7. Further Distinctions

If what I have said so far is correct, it is important *not* to identify T-interpretations with interpretations of literature. Drama is also literature, and Ibsen's *Et dukkehjem*, for example, can be both T-interpreted and P-interpreted. Actors and producers read the script, T-interpret it, and understand it; and such T-interpretations form the basis of their performances.

Even if P-interpretations to some extent presuppose T-interpretations, in the sense that it is necessary to understand the instructions of the composer to be able to perform his work, the former kind of interpretation cannot be reduced to the latter. The actions constituting the performance can be separated from both the descriptions of the performance, the reasons given for the performance, and the interpretation required to understand the instructions of the composer, conductor, or producer.

This suggests that we should distinguish between two senses of 'P-interpretations'. In the narrow sense of that word, 'P-interpretation' is used in the restricted sense (performance) indicated in the previous paragraph. In a wider sense, 'P-interpretation' includes both the performance (in this narrow sense) and the T-interpretation required to understand the instructions of the composer, etc., and to be able to carry out the P-interpretation (in the narrow sense).

It is equally important *not* to identify P-interpretations (in the wide or narrow sense) with interpretations of music. Also music can be both T-interpreted and P-interpreted, at least if 'T-interpretations' is used in a somewhat extended sense and 'texts' may include scores and scripts as well. Muzak can be interpreted as a phenomenon significant of our time, and classical music can just as well be put in different kinds of contexts and be interpreted historically, psychologically, sociologically, psychoanalytically, and so forth.

Also, the expression 'T-interpretation' can, however, be used in somewhat different senses. In one sense, a T-interpretation is an interpretation of a text (script or score) which results in another text. But in an extended sense, a T-interpretation is an interpretation of a text (script, etc.) which may, or may not, result in a text, but not in a performance. T-interpretations in both senses are related to explanations.

For example, in one volume three musicologists have provided three different T-interpretations of Carl Maria von Weber's *Der Freischütz*, one historical (H. H. Eggebrecht), one psychological (H.-P. Reinecke), and one semiotic (P. Faltin).[13] It is not necessary to regard music as a system for communication of extra-musical experiences and propositions to affirm the possibility of T-interpretations of music.

---

[13] In Roland Posner and Hans-Peter Reinecke (eds.), *Zeichenprozesse: Semiotische Forschung in der Einzelwissenschaften* (Wiesbaden, 1977), ch. 6.

8. Meaning and Action

T-interpretations have to do with meanings. So: how can statements about the meaning of music be understood? What gives meaning to music? Intentions, conventions, and intertexts.

Music is an intentional object, and these intentions, including those of the composer, can be interpreted. Likewise, a competent and qualified listener makes associations with similar phrases and passages in other works, and with passages from which sequences of tones in the actual work differ in a way that can hardly be a matter of chance. The complex and somewhat dialectical relations to tradition will bestow the 'tönend bewegend Formen' (to use Hanslick's famous phrase again) with meaning and significance.

The underlying idea is simple here. Put in somewhat different words, it amounts to this. Composers sometimes follow codes and conventions, sometimes violate them in their works. To follow a code or a tradition is to perform an action, and so is to violate a code or convention. Actions have a meaning, a point; they can be interpreted. Sometimes they invite or even require interpretations.

T-interpretations of music may include a variety of things, for instance, interpretations of the meaning, significance, and function of deviations from established codes and conventions, also of silence. What do the pauses in a particular work mean? How could or should the silence of John Cage be understood? The codes and conventions constituting a musical tradition serve as a frame of reference for the interpreter. Familiarity with them is a *sine qua non* for the musicologist.

Such interpretations of the meaning of music may be related to the interpretation of the view of life, personality, or (musical) world view of the composer, or be related to types or world views, personalities, and so forth, in the manner suggested by Dilthey, whether, for example, the world view in question was the world view of the composer or not. Looking back on his earlier work, one musicologist (Mikko Heiniö) has described his overall aim as follows: 'I want to study the composer's musical world view'.[14]

To conclude: music is not composed in a vacuum. There are different kinds of contexts, not only personal, but also historical and political. This holds for Bob Dylan as well as for Beethoven. Sometimes music is composed in a nationalistic or patriotic fervour, sometimes in chauvinistic frenzy, sometimes in order to rally people around common goals; sometimes it is used for such purposes whether or not intended by the composer (for example, the opening bars of Beethoven's Fifth Symphony).[15]

---

[14] Mikko Heiniö, 'Composer's Texts as Objects of Musicological Study', in Veikko Rantala, Lewis Rowell, and Eero Tarasti (eds.), *Essays on the Philosophy of Music* (Helsinki, 1988), 293–9.

[15] Winston Churchill was born in 1874. The Morse alphabet was tested for the first time in 1844. Beethoven, as is well known, died in 1827.

9. Problems of Individuation

We may want to distinguish between the following three problems, perhaps using something like Leibniz's principle of identity of indiscernibles as a point of departure:

(a) What are the criteria of identity of a musical composition?

(b) What are the criteria of identity of an interpretation of that work?

(c) Under what conditions is X a P-interpretation of Y?

I will concentrate on the last of these problems. By way of introduction, let us recall that the instructions of the composer are sometimes unclear or incomplete. They may be vague or pull in different directions. Sometimes there are traditions or conventions as to how the work is to be played which are not taken down, perhaps because they are taken for granted; they are too self-evident. Since the script does not say anything about them, some modern performers (perhaps out of ignorance, perhaps for aesthetic or other reasons) choose to disregard them.

Even more difficult examples include cases when musical works consist of pieces which can be combined in different orders, like in some of Karlheinz Stockhausen's works. His *Klavierstück XI* consists of 19 episodes which can be played in whatever order the pianist chooses. What are the criteria of identity of such a work? Suppose the order of the episodes is varied, and each episode is played in a different tempo, with varying legato, timbre, vibrato, and so forth. Then instances of the work may differ in regard to both texture and structure. But it is tempting to say that the work is identical with any combination of the episodes, played according to the instructions of the composer; and to the extent that these instructions are open and unspecified, the work is open and unspecified.

Moreover, the problem is that there may be differences in time, tempo, legato, and so forth, between performances of the same work, and that these variations sometimes are so great that even trained listeners may find it hard to recognize P and P′ as interpretations of the same work. At least they say so. The statement 'But this is not Beethoven's D minor Symphony!' may sometimes be an evaluative statement, said by someone who does not like a particular interpretation of that work, sometimes a rhetorical exaggeration. But we cannot exclude that there sometimes may be genuine difficulties of recognizing P and P′ as interpretations of the same work.

But more precisely, what conditions have to be satisfied for any X to be a performance of Y? Beardsley has suggested a pragmatic definition of performance which differs in several ways from a more strict and objectivistic accounts of the well-known type proposed by Nelson Goodman.[16] According

---

[16] Nelson Goodman, *Languages of Art: An Approach to the Theory of Symbols* (Indianapolis, 1968), ch. 5; id. 'Art and Authenticity' and 'Further Notes', both in his *Problems and Projects* (Indianapolis, 1972), 85–102, 135–7.

to the latter, if an orchestra plays Beethoven's symphony in C minor and makes one mistake, it is no longer playing that symphony.

Beardsley, however, defines 'performance', in the case of a sonata, as follows: 'any rendition of the sonata that is recognizably guided by the composer's instructions in the artifact will be called a performance of that sonata'.[17] Beardsley then goes on to distinguish between two senses of 'performance': productions and performances in a strict sense. A drama, he points out on the following page, 'may have a number of *productions*—the Old Vic's, a college drama club's, the Stratford, Connecticut, Shakespeare Theater's—and each production, if it is fortunate, may have a number of *performances*'. He also suggests that this terminology can be transferred to music.

For example, Toscanini and Furtwängler have both made different productions of the first movement of Beethoven's D minor Symphony, the first of which lasts about 13 minutes, the second of which lasts about 17 minutes. There are different performances of each production (night after night a new concert with the same conductor and musicians), and a recorded performance of a given production can be played many times. Hence we should distinguish, as Beardsley has suggested, not only between productions and performances but also between performances and playings.

There are good theoretical reasons (simplicity, theoretical fruitfulness) for Goodman's proposal. On the other hand it implies a considerable and clear deviation from ordinary language that Beardsley's criterion does not. I am not convinced that the theoretical advantages justify this deviation. The problem with Beardsley's proposal is, of course, that what is 'recognizable' by one person need not be recognizable by another. To avoid some of the difficulties in Beardsley's proposal, the following two criteria might be suggested:

Condition of Similarity. P and P' are performances of the same work X only if there is some minimal degree of resemblance between P and P'.

(C1)

The problem with this requirement is, of course, that it is very difficult, to say the least, to specify the kind of similarities, and the degree of similarity, that are required. It is tempting to define the minimal degree of resemblance in terms of structural similarity. But two performances of Stockhausen's *Klavierstück XI* may differ in both texture and structure, as was mentioned above. But combined with other criteria (C1) may work, even if it does not work alone.

Condition of Causality. P and P' are performances of the same work X only if a causal connection can be established between X and P and between X and P'.

(C2)

The idea is, as in Kripke's well-known theory of reference, that it is possible

---

[17] Beardsley, *Aesthetics*, 55.

in principle to reconstruct the history of a particular interpretation of music. The conductor or the musicians had a particular set of notes in front of them when they played, these notes were copied from notes bought in a music store, these notes in their turn were a reprint of a critical edition of the composer's work, and this critical edition was based on the composer's original manuscript. If such a causal chain connects P and X, then P is an interpretation of X. Thus a genetic or historical aspect is introduced to settle the issue.

Condition (C2) has the advantage that it can handle the problems raised both by vague and incomplete instructions and by modernist works such as those by Stockhausen. Perhaps it could alone be both necessary and sufficient? This would, of course, simplify the exposition. But I think this would be too big a departure from ordinary language. Moreover, and more important, X may be causally connected with several other things (besides P), and P may be causally related to other things (besides X). Irrelevant causal connections can be blocked with the help of (C1).

Many other considerations may be relevant (metaphysical and normative, in particular), but let me for the time being propose that these two conditions are necessary and jointly sufficient.

10. Two Problems

The concept of triangle is open in the sense that a triangle can have many different shapes. If, however, you want to imagine a triangle, you have to imagine a particular triangle of a specific size, with particular angles, etc., as Bishop Berkeley remarked long ago. Similarly, of course, if you want to draw a triangle.

Analogously, if you want to play a composition by Beethoven, you cannot play it in general, you have to play it in a particular way. Historical studies can, of course, be made of how the music was performed in the composer's lifetime, including studies of the distinctness of tones, the extent to which legato was used, of variations in emphasis, tempo, distinctness, vibrato, and so forth.

Similarly, a historian of singing can go to the sources and try to give us a picture of how people sang the works by Mozart during the eighteenth century, including their breathing technique, the extent to which *voce di petto* or *voce di testa* was used, how strong and loud people sang in those days, the extent to which falsetto (*voce finta*) was used, and so forth.

Here it is important to distinguish between contemporary attempts to reconstruct the way classical pieces were in fact played, based on studies of the sources of the time, and modern attempts to provide alternatives to the ways in which 'classical' music has been played. 'Authentic' or 'contemporary' performances receive a great deal of attention these days, and 'authentic performances' sell well.

But 'authentic performances' may mean several things. And it may be well to remember that to reconstruct authentic performances on the basis of available sources is not necessarily to say something about what the composer 'wanted'. Nor is it to say or suggest that this kind of performance is necessarily 'best', 'most exciting', or 'aesthetically most rewarding'.

There is a great deal of difference between the so-called 'specialist praxis' based on the works by N. Harnoncourt, G. Leonhardt, F. Brüggen, A. Biljsma, and others, and what the sources suggest concerning how music by Mozart and other eighteenth-century composers was played at the time.[18] This is, of course, no objection to either praxis; but it shows that there are different kinds of interpretation of music, one of which ('historical reconstruction') is quite legitimate but only one of several possible alternative ways of playing.

The changing ways of performing provide one of the explanations, but certainly not the only one, of the fact that generation after generation can get something new out of music composed long ago. The same goes for theatre, ballet, and other performing arts. But this also raises two very different kinds of problem: how far should one go, in trying to get back to the sources, interpret them, and come closer to the way music was played at the time of its composition? And how far should one go in the attempts to find new ways of performing the music of the classical masters? Is it defensible not only to vary tempo, legato, emphasis, distinctness, vibrato, etc., but also to leave out certain passages (as has been done in plays, when some of the lines in works by Strindberg or Shakespeare did not fit in with the political views of the performing group of actors)?

The extreme liberal view concerning the first historical problem can be summarized in six short words: *Go as far as you please!* The main reason for this is that we will not be able to predict where such attempts will end, and the result may well be a richer, interesting, and more many-faceted musical life. But not necessarily better, of course.

It is tempting to repeat this liberal slogan when the other (musical or aesthetic) problem is concerned. But personally I would hesitate to change the text or the script; a *Hamlet* without certain essential lines is not *Hamlet*, but a *Revised Hamlet* or a *Modernized Hamlet*—though modernized in a different way than a *Hamlet* where the actors drive motorcycles on stage. Thus, new dresses, new settings, new instruments, new emphasis, etc., are not only acceptable but may positively enhance the enjoyment of the work (and the same goes for music), but not leaving out essential parts of the original, nor adding new material.

This idea is easier to suggest than to work out in detail. To clarify 'essential', one way try the various criteria discussed above, e.g. the pragmatic ones proposed by Beardsley. The problems mentioned then will no doubt

---

[18] This is a point made by Gunno Klingfors, *Nytt om gammal sång: tyskt och italienskt sång sätt under 1600– och 1700– talet* (Stockholm, 1990).

reappear here. It could very well be a matter of heated artistic dispute which lines or parts are essential. On the other hand, an application of a Goodmanian view on musical identity (by deleting 'essential') would lead to the rather extreme view that if a word is missing, or is changed, in *Hamlet*, what you watch is not *Hamlet* (but something similar to it).

Anyway, I am not sure this can be rationally defended, if the overriding concern is to maximize the satisfaction of the interests of the beholders, to make the music (poem) as rewarding as possible. Here other considerations come in, having to do with (the value of) authenticity. But why is authenticity valued? This is not quite so easy to answer.

11. Interpretations and Intentions

This raises the further, and more general, questions about the relevance of facts about the composer's intentions in interpretation of music. Is it necessary for the interpreter to trace, or be bound by facts about, the composer's intentions?

Is there a tension in regarding musical works as intentional objects and then refusing to be bound by facts about the composer's intentions? Clearly, we have two problems here. Is it at least a necessary condition that X is an intentional object for X to be a work of art? Is the meaning of X determined by facts about the composer's intentions? But perhaps there is a connection between these problems. Some people would no doubt be inclined to think so.

First of all, it is here necessary to be clear about the many ways in which the composer's intentions can be relevant. The composer can provide instructions (embodying his intentions) of by what—and how many—instruments his composition is to be played ('Composition for flute and guitar'), how it is to be played in a number of respects ('allegretto', 'andante', 'pianissimo', 'crescendo'), and how it is to be understood (what his intentions were, what he hoped to achieve, what he wanted to avoid, etc.); and these intentions can be more or less specific and precise.

Secondly, the difficulties of finding out the intentions of the composer have been discussed over and over again, so there is no need to repeat them here. The composer's intentions are not static; they may very well change over time. But even if we could find out what the composer intended it is not clear why it should be desirable to do so. The view that this is indeed desirable has to be backed up with a communicative view of art, and of interpretation, which is not self-evident, and which I have argued against elsewhere.[19]

Personally, I refuse to restrict interpretations by definitional fiat to interpretations of the intentions of the composer. The intentions are not

---

[19] Göran Hermerén, 'Meaning, Expression and Nonverbal Communication', in J. Emt and G. Hermerén (eds.), *Understanding the Arts* (Lund, 1991).

irrelevant, but they are not the only important things. We are interested in understanding how other people's minds work, but is this the only thing we are interested in, and is the mind of the composer the only mind we are interested in understanding? Besides, is music and its interpretation the only way to get information about this?

We may interpret in order to understand the intentions of the composer, but also to understand his time, the world today, or ourselves, or some combination of all these. There are many kinds of legitimate interpretation, some more or less historical, others not.

12. The Incompatibility of P-interpretations

There are many different interpretations of the same work, different recordings of the same composition, but are they incompatible in any easily intelligible sense? In what sense could Glenn Gould's recordings of Bach be incompatible with those by anyone else? If indeed they are, are incompatibilities intolerable? To be able to answer these questions we need, first of all, to distinguish not only between T-interpretations and P-interpretations but also between several senses of incompatibility. Taken in a strict sense, 'incompatibility' means logical incompatibility. The incompatibility thesis in that strict sense can be stated as follows:

> *Incompatibility Thesis (1).* To say that two interpretations P and P' are incompatible, is to say that they are both interpretations of the same work in the sense indicated by (C1) and (C2) and that P expresses or implies a statement p and P' expresses or implies the contradictory statement not-p.

If we discuss literary interpretations, like the notorious interpretations of the 'Lucy Gray' poem by Wordsworth, a case could be made for saying that they are incompatible in something like this strict sense. But suppose we consider interpretations of music? The question is then whether this thesis can be applied to P-interpretations (by replacing 'interpretations' with 'performances' or perhaps 'productions', but not with 'playings'). For a propositional theorist, i.e. one who believes that music expresses propositions, the answer must be *yes*. But so many good arguments have been levelled over the years against propositional theories of the arts that we should proceed with caution. For one thing, we need to specify how P-interpretations (performances) are related to T-interpretations. This is not too easy, as I tried to show above.

If a clear distinction is maintained between the series of actions, constituting the performance, and the reasons for that particular performance as well as the various descriptions of that performance and the understanding of the composer's instructions necessary to be able to perform these actions, and 'performance' is taken in a strict sense referring only to these actions, I suggest that this thesis is false. Consequently (P8) cannot be maintained.

But the situation changes if a small modification of this thesis is made, for example by replacing '*P*' with '*P* is (correctly) described by the description *D* which' or '*P* is supported by the reason *R* which', and so forth. These descriptions ('is fast', 'is slow', 'is melancholy', etc.) and reasons ('this is the way the piece was played when the composer lived', 'this is the aesthetically most rewarding way of playing the piece') can be incompatible with other descriptions and reasons. Then the following theses can be obtained:

Incompatibility Thesis (2). To say that two interpretations *P* and *P'* are incompatible is to say that they are both interpretations of the same work in the sense indicated by (C1) and (C2) and that *P* is correctly described by the description *D* which implies a statement *p* and *P'* is correctly described by the description *D'* which implies not-*p*.

Incompatibility Thesis (3). To say that two interpretations *P* and *P'* are incompatible is to say that they are both interpretations of the same work in the sense indicated by (C1) and (C2) and that *P* is supported by the reason *R* which implies a statement *p* and *P'* is supported by the reason *R'* which implies not-*p*.

It seems to me that there are good reasons supporting both these theses. But does this mean that (P8) has been estabished? Performances are (series of) actions, and can logical relations obtain between actions? I would be inclined to say *no*; performances do not themselves entail propositions or statements, and logical relations can hold only between propositions (or statements).

But logical relations may hold between descriptions and reasons, so: if there is a connection between certain reasons and a particular performance, and/or the performance and certain descriptions of it, then performances can be incompatible in the extended senses indicated by theses (2) and (3) above.

Let us now return to the first incompatibility thesis. Perhaps it can be made to appear more plausible also in other ways, for instance by using 'incompatible' in weaker senses, defined in terms of violations of certain canons of good taste, for example, of the aesthetic codes and conventions of the artist. Then we get a fourth incompatibility thesis as follows:

Incompatibility Thesis (4). To say that two interpretations *P* and *P'* are incompatible, is to say that they are both interpretations of the same work in the sense indicated by (C1) and (C2) and that *P* is in accordance with the canons of good taste, either of the artist or those prevalent in his society, or those current today) whereas *P'* is not in accordance with these canons.

This seems perfectly acceptable, as long as it is made clear that 'incompatible' is used in an extended and perhaps metaphorical sense. Incompatible interpretations in this sense are perfectly tolerable and may indeed enrich musical life.

Whether incompatible P-interpretations in the sense of Thesis (3) should be tolerated boils down to the question about what kinds of reasons for or against certain performances should be tolerated. If only historical reasons, or reasons which can be supported by historical reasons, are admitted then we have one situation, if other reasons are also admitted the situation is different. If several kinds of reasons are admitted they can be ranked as to their importance. For a strict historical criticism, only historical reasons are admitted; for a moderate historical criticism, aesthetic reasons are allowed, but they are not allowed to override historical reasons etc.

13. The Incompatibility of T-interpretations

In the previous section I focused on the incompatibility of P-interpretations. Can the incompatibility of T-interpretations be dealt with in the same way? An affirmative answer to this question presupposes that (i) T and T' are interpretations of the same work X if and only if (C1) and (C2) are satisfied, *mutatis mutandis*, and (ii) the same normative conclusions can be drawn in both cases.

I am not convinced that any of these two assumptions are fulfilled when it comes to T-interpretations. On the contrary, I believe that, unfortunately, incompatible T-interpretations cannot be dealt with in quite the same way as incompatible P-interpretations. For one thing, the earlier discussed conditions (C1) and (C2) need to be reformulated. The new version of the former can perhaps be stated as

> *Condition of Similarity.* T and T' are interpretations of the same work X only if there is some minimal degree of resemblance between T and T'. (C1)'

The problem with a requirement like (C1)' is, of course, that it is even more difficult in this case to specify the relevant kind of similarities, as well as the degree of similarities that are required. The T-interpreter can allow himself (or herself) to be much more selective than a P-interpreter, as I have already suggested. This makes (C1)' less plausible in the present context.

In view of these problems it may appear more promising to try to elaborate on a modified version of (C2) like

> *Condition of Causality.* T and T' are performances of the same work X only if a causal connection can be established between X and T and between X and T'. (C2)'

I believe that this condition is worth serious consideration; it is a plausible candidate. But these two conditions are not the only alternatives. For example, it can be more tempting to introduce an intentional condition of the following type here than when P-interpretations are discussed:

> *Intentional Condition.* T and T' are interpretations of the same work X only if the authors of T and T' intended them to be interpretations of X. (C3)

The problem with this requirement is, of course, that one cannot intend just about anything to be an interpretation of anything, though it should be observed that (C3) is only a necessary condition for T and T' to be interpretations of X, and not a necessary condition for something to be a *good* or *plausible* interpretation of X. (C3) needs to be supplemented by other conditions, perhaps with some variation of the pragmatic criterion suggested by Beardsley:

> *Pragmatic criterion.* T and T' are interpretations of the same work X only if readers familiar with X, T, and T' recognize T and T' to be an explication or elucidation of the meaning of X. (C4)

But tempting though such a pragmatic criterion might be, it raises the same difficulties as Beardsley's earlier discussed criterion, so it would be an advantage to have others.

So far, the discussion has been rather inconclusive. But let us assume that a set of satisfactory conditions have been found. Then we have to deal with the second assumption (ii) above. And it seems plain to me that this assumption is false. Incompatible T-interpretations of Weber's *Der Freischütz* are harder to find than some people think; usually historical, psychological, and Marxist interpretations emphasize different features and supplement each other rather than contradict each other in the strict sense (i.e. are logically incompatible). Nevertheless, it should be noted that I do not deny that there may be such interpretations. Incompatible T-interpretations may exist in several senses analogous to at least the first three incompatibility theses discussed in the previous section. But if two T-interpretations indeed are logically incompatible I fail to see how this can enrich musical life. Given the strong position in scientific methodology of the requirement of consistency, it would only be natural to look for ways of eliminating the contradition by revising or modifying one or both of the T-interpretations.

However, it may be suggested that such interpretations can be dealt with in the way proposed by Joseph Margolis in his writings about robust relativism.[20] Then the interpretations would not be described as 'true' or 'correct' in the way suggested by (P8) but rather as 'plausible'. But this is a complex and controversial issue that cannot be adequately dealt with in just a few lines or paragraphs; it has to be saved for another occasion.

Finally, to the extent that something analogous to incompatibility thesis (4) is applicable when T-interpretations are concerned, the situation is changed. That would mean that one of these T-interpretations is in accordance with certain normative aesthetic canons, whereas the other is not. In that case I would be inclined to hold that the same normative conclusions can be drawn as above: such incompatibilities are perfectly tolerable and may enrich our understanding and appreciation of the music interpreted.

---

[20] This has been one of the main themes in the writings of Joseph Margolis, from his 'Robust Relativism', *Journal of Aesthetics and Art Criticism*, 35 (1976), 37–46 to his 'Reinterpreting Interpretation', *Journal of Aesthetics and Art Criticism*, 47 (1989), 237–51.

Anyway, if what I have written here is roughly correct, this is an additional reason for insisting on the distinction between P- and T-interpretations, however difficult it is to draw this distinction precisely.

14. Concluding Remarks

From these discussions about the variety of interpretations of music, one may be driven back to certain underlying or overriding (whatever metaphor one prefers) philosophical concerns.

One may, of course, also start with these overriding philosophical concerns and in an a priori fashion derive consequences for the questions discussed here. The principles may shed (illuminating and critical) light on the praxis, and the praxis may suggest revision of the principles. (Personally I would prefer to work with mutual adjustments in the way described by Hilary Putnam.[21]) Which, then, are these deeper philosophical concerns? They include problems concerning:

1. *Individuation and identity*. The distinction between performance, understanding, and interpretation leads inevitably to the question of under what conditions *x* shall be said to be an interpretation or a performance of *y*. If this question can be answered in different ways, as indeed it can, this leads to interesting consequences for problems about the individuation and identity of works of art.

2. *Ontological assumptions*. The idea that to follow a code, as well as to violate a code, is to perform an action; actions can be interpreted; they have a meaning, a point; motives can be provided, explanations can be sought. This explains the sense in which music can be T-interpreted. Moreover, there is a connection here to ontological theories of the kind suggested by Gregory Currie: art as action types.[22]

3. *Semantical distinctions*. The distinction between description, interpretation, analysis, and evaluation is of general philosophical interest. An examination of it in one special area may be interesting and worth while, if related to examinations of these distinctions in other areas. There are not just two senses of 'interpretation', as David Novitz has suggested recently;[23] besides, his particular way of drawing the distinction breaks down, as far as I can see,[24] whether we concentrate on interpretations of music or of literature.

The history of music will have to be rewritten for each generation. Interpretation of music is not just a matter of history in the sense of getting the facts straight, it is an art in itself and it takes a position on many explicit and, not least important, implicit theoretical and normative issues.

[21] Hilary Putnam, *The Many Faces of Realism* (La Salle, 1987), 79: 'Standards and practices . . . must be developed together and constantly revised by a procedure of delicate mutual adjustment.'

[22] Gregory Currie, *An Ontology of Art* (London, 1989).

[23] In his very interesting book *Knowledge, Fiction & Imagination* (Philadelphia, 1987), 91–2.

[24] Cf. my *Art, Reason, and Tradition*, (Stockholm, 1991), ch. 1.

Performative vs. Critical Interpretation in Music

JERROLD LEVINSON

I

This chapter takes as starting-point the curious fact that two activities, on the surface quite different, are called by the same name: interpreting. On the one hand, there is what critics of the arts do with respect to individual artworks, such as Kafka's *Penal Colony*, Picasso's *Demoiselles d'Avignon*, or Mahler's Ninth Symphony—that is, offer interpretations of them. In other words, they try to say, roughly, how such works should be viewed, what they mean, and why they are structured as they are. On the other hand, there is what performers in the performing arts do with respect to individual artworks, e.g. Mozart's Clarinet Concerto, Balanchine's *Four Temperaments*, Shakespeare's *King Lear*—that is, perform them. In other words, they play (dance, enact, recite) them in a particular way. Obviously there is some connection between these activities—it is sometimes suggested, for example, that the performing interpreter is doing implicitly what the critical interpreter is doing explicitly—but the similarities here are perhaps no greater than, and no more interesting than, the dissimilarities. This chapter will devote itself to emphasizing the latter. My particular concern will be to contrast, within the tradition of Western classical music, a musical performer's interpretation of a given piece of music, and a music critic's interpretation of the same. For convenience in what follows I will often abbreviate performative (or performer's) interpretation as PI and critical (or critic's) interpretation as CI.

Since my focus will be on how performative interpretation differs from critical interpretation—i.e. what we tend to understand by 'interpretation' when no qualification in given—I will take for granted a conception of the latter as distinguishable in some way from uncontroversial description of a work of art, as characteristically involving either explanation of a work's manifest features or ascription of features to the work of a more subtle sort, and as centrally concerned with the meaning, significance, or point of a work, taking this to include elucidation of a work's inner workings or internal relations, in so far as this is shown to contribute to what the work is doing or

My thanks to Gregory Currie, Alan Goldman, Susan Haack, Risto Hilpinen, Judy Lichtenberg, and David Luban for their helpful comments.

saying, either in part or in whole.[1] But I will not enter here into any debate as to the exact boundary between description and interpretation, if there is one, or as to the proper limits of a critic's interpretative interest in a work of art.[2] What I have said will be sufficient to make the contrast with performative interpretation plain. Critical interpretation ascribes, explains, and relates, aiming to provide an account of a work's import and functioning, both local and global. As we shall see, performative interpretation essentially consists in something else, though something which is ideally informed by, and informing of, interpretation in that other sense.

II

It is crucial to note at the outset that there are in general two modes or phases of performative interpretation, which we may characterize roughly as follows. The first involves deciding what the score ideally is, i.e. what work was actually written, where there are problems with deciphering the manuscript, or what work was really intended by the composer, when there is reason to doubt whether the score as we have it accurately represents those intentions. The second mode or phase consists in deciding to play a score, taken as unequivocal or uncontroverted, in a particular way, in effect electing particular values of its defining, though never absolutely specific, parameters of tempo, rhythm, dynamics, accent, and phrasing. The first mode of PI, an activity of recovering or reconstructing the text, indeed borders on and invariably intersects with CI, i.e. formulating a view of what a work means or expresses and how it hangs together at various levels. For one could hardly undertake to hypothesize a work's exact shape from an incomplete or doubtful manuscript without adopting some critical stance as to its character or functioning.

An example. Antony Hopkins argues confidently that the notation that has come down to us at one point in Mozart's Piano Concerto in C minor, K. 491 probably does not answer to the piece as conceived, but that what is given as dotted minims in the solo part sixteen bars before the cadenza in the first movement should probably be understood as abbreviation for figuration in the manner just preceding, which Mozart omitted to write out fully owing to lack of space on the manuscript page.[3] Obviously part of Hopkins's reason for his postulation is that the coherence and drive of the passage is reduced if the

---

[1] I accept that on such a broad conception, interpretation of music and analysis of music shade into one another, with no clear dividing line.

[2] Some of the criteria of interpretativeness that have been suggested are: non-obviousness; inferentiality; lack of consensus; concern with meaning or significance; concern with structure or design. For discussion, see Annette Barnes, *On Interpretation* (Oxford, 1988), and Alan Goldman, 'Interpreting Art and Literature', *Journal of Aesthetics and Art Criticism*, 48 (1990), 205–14.

[3] Anthony Hopkins, *Understanding Music* (London, 1979), 111–12. In my observation, however, most pianists play the passage as written.

piano abandons its figuration for notes of long value in the four bars in question.

Nor should one think this problem is confined to music remote from us in time. Here is Paul Jacobs, commenting on the score of a 1908 piano composition of Arnold Schoenberg:

I have taken it upon myself, with the kind help of Elliott Carter, to correct what I believe are mistakes. To enumerate a few: Should not the first beat of the opening piece of Opus 11 be a major third? In the ascending left-hand passage at the end of bar 50 in the same piece, the G-natural should most definitely be a G-sharp. I play a B-sharp on the second beat of bar 55. It makes more musical sense, and I think it sounds better.[4]

Interesting as such issues are, in this chapter my concern is exclusively with PI of the second sort, what we might call *realizational* PI, as opposed to reconstructive (or hypothetical) PI. In giving a realizational PI, a performer is not engaged in postulating *what* a composer has written or intended to write, but at most *how* he would have wanted it played or sounded.

Though I have represented this as a binary opposition, it might be better presented as a continuum of concerns, as in this series of interpretive questions: (*a*) Is the score correct, i.e. is it what the composer wrote or intended it to be? (*b*) What sort of instruments are legitimate as means of execution? (*c*) How should performing indications that are apparently impossible to realize be dealt with?[5] (*d*) How much, if any, ornamentation should be engaged in? (*e*) Should repeats always be taken where indicated? (*f*) Which chords, lines, phrases, sections should be emphasized, if any, when notation does not specify? (*g*) How should various prescriptions of rhythm, tempo, dynamics, and so on be precisely realized within their permissible ranges?

In terms of such a spectrum, then, my interest is largely with the questions towards the end, in particular the last three, and not those more textually speculative ones at the beginning. PI in its realizational mode effectively exhausts itself in considerations such as (*e*), (*f*), and (*g*), and in fact (*g*) could be said, broadly construed, to encompass the other two. In any case, it should be understood from here on that when I speak of PI I have realizational interpretation in mind.

I note also before proceeding that there is a sense of 'interpretative' applied to certain approaches to performing that I will likewise leave to one side. 'Interpreting' in this sense involves a performer's departing blatantly and knowingly from a work as it has been constituted, in an effort to comment on the work in some way, or to show how it might be improved, or to freely express the performer's own flights of feeling. Some writers, in fact, use

---

[4] Liner notes, Arnold Schoenberg, *Piano Music* (Nonesuch 71309, 1975).
[5] Hopkins cites an example from Beethoven's Piano Sonata, Op. 7, where a crescendo is indicated on a held note in bar 39 of the slow movement (*Understanding Music*, 158 –60).

'interpretative' exclusively to refer to this kind of performing activity—Stokowski was a great interpreter by these lights—rhetorical pauses, interpolated bits, sudden improvisations, excisions, reorchestrations, reharmonizations, etc. It can only be in this sense that some performances are described, either approvingly or disapprovingly, as containing no 'interpretative touches'.

III

The main theme of this chapter is that PI and CI are logically distinct sorts of activities, and that a PI and a CI are logically distinct sorts of things. A PI is not equivalent to a CI, nor a CI in disguise, nor necessarily the expression of a CI held by the performer, nor, except in fairly trivial respects, the implicit assertion of a CI.

What a PI is, I claim, is just *a considered way of playing a piece of music, involving highly specific determinations of all the defining features of the piece as given by the score and its associated conventions of reading.* As such a PI is, as has been noted, in effect a type of performance, which, like the work itself, may have numerous instantiations, as when a performer repeats on distinct occasions a PI he has worked out at an earlier time.[6] The performance-type which is the interpretation is obviously a narrower one than the performance-type with which we can identify the work. In any event a PI, unlike a CI, is not as such an explanation of, or view on, a piece of music but a deliberate way of performing it.

What that way of performing is, however, is not to be mechanically read off from a given performance as heard. Mistakes of execution, imperfections of tone, for instance, are not generally accounted part of the PI involved in a performance; we idealize somewhat, bracketing such unintended, unwanted features, so that it is only the performance with those practical blemishes removed that properly represents the performer's PI. For example, we discount the horn burbles in the first and second movements in Horenstein's Stockholm Philharmonic performance of Mahler's Sixth Symphony in registering what his reading of the music is.

One question that naturally presents itself, if the distance between a performative and a critical, i.e. paradigmatic, interpretation is as great as just suggested, is why performing musicians are called *interpreters* at all? Part of the explanation, of course, is that PIs and CIs often occur in close conjunction:

---

[6] See R. A. Sharpe, 'Type, Token, Interpretation and Performance', *Mind*, 88 (1979), 437–40. Sharpe's article was one of the first to draw attention to interpretations as distinct from both performances and works, and stressed that 'a performance must be throughout a performance of a single interpretation' (438). Though his observation is a good one, and we must accordingly recognize 'a tripartite distinction between work, interpretation and performance' (438), Sharpe offers no compelling reason why genuine performances embodying interpretations—as opposed to assemblages from a number of performances—are not thereby also instances or tokens of the piece itself.

CIs can guide the development of PIs, PIs can trigger the formulation of CIs, and PIs and CIs may also originate in tandem. But I think another crucial part of the explanation lies not so much in a performer's resemblance to those whose mission is inherently exegetical and amplificatory, but rather more in his or her resemblance to interpreters of another stripe—those who render foreign languages comprehensible to us. In other words, performers provide us with access to discourse we do not have access to otherwise. Critical interpreters, by contrast, are centrally concerned to explain and construe further works which we can independently access, as with novels and poems, or works once we have accessed them, via performative interpreters, as with symphonies and ballets. A musician, from this point of view, essentially makes perceptually accessible a text or code that a non-musician cannot otherwise grasp, just as an interpreter at the UN makes conceptually accessible to non-speakers of Arabic what the delegate from the Sudan has been saying. The audience cannot 'get' the music from the score unless they can both read standard notation and imagine it aurally at the level of Mozart—a very infrequent occurrence, to say the least—so the performer 'translates' the notes on paper into experienceable sequences of sound. A musical interpreter in this sense is thus primarily a kind of go-between: more a transmitter than an explicator.

Whatever truth there is in this bit of linguistic diagnosis, I do not offer it to suggest that performing interpreters dispense with critical interpreting, or that they, like UN translators, should forbear personalizing in any way what they are charged with transmitting. Far from it. I merely insist that the activities and products of performative and critical interpretation are, strictly speaking, different, and at least in principle, separable. We should not blithely assume that a performative interpretation of a musician, and a critical interpretation—whether that of the musician or not—are basically the same sort of product, only differing in the explicitness of what they in common do.[7]

Though it is sometimes said that a PI incorporates a critical view or conception of a work, reflection shows that this cannot be other than over-statement; the identity criteria for PIs, as we shall see, belie such a assertion. It is also too much to claim that a PI can express the performer's view or conception, in the sense that such a view can be transparently discerned in or

---

[7] The article by Goldman cited above (n. 2), despite containing many illuminating points, is guilty of this: 'strictly speaking, a performance is not in itself explicitly an interpretation of a work, but rather instantiates, exemplifies, or implicitly conveys the performer's interpretation. What it exemplifies or implicitly conveys is an explanation of the work and its elements, one that reflects the performer's view of the values inherent in the piece. Such an explanation, implicit in an interpretive performance, can be made verbally explicit by the critic' (207). I take issue with the idea that a performer's interpreting a piece of music is inherently an explaining of it, and more generally with the idea that there is such a thing as 'implicit explanation'. In addition, I deny that what a critic might make verbally explicit can be identified as *the* content of a performative reading. As my argument in this paper aims to show, Goldman's is too intellectualist a view of the necessary conditions of performative interpreting. The competing analogy with the activity of a language interpreter, if itself imperfect, is at least a useful corrective here.

read off the PI itself, or that it can determinately imply such, in the sense that the view could be reasonably imputed to the profferer of the PI by a musically astute listener.[8] The most we can legitimately say, in general, is that a PI may, on the one hand, reflect a CI in the performer's mind which we have independent confirmation of, or on the other hand, suggest a CI to the mind of a listener, though rarely with uniqueness.[9] Much of what follows will be further elaboration and defence of these claims.

IV

Let us ponder some of the salient differences between CIs and PIs. First, and most obviously, a CI is a conceptual and standardly propositional affair, whereas a PI is neither, but rather a sensuous realization of a work, a particular way of sounding it: a CI is an interrelated set of remarks, a PI is a type of performance. A consequence of this is that there are inevitably aspects of a PI that are irreducibly performative—aspects whose content may be signalled, though not captured, by phrases such as '*this* is how it should go'—and which thus could not be part of a CI, necessarily expressed as it is in articulate terms. We might even allow, in this vein, that there are aspects of what a passage means *to* a performer which are embodied ineffably in his manner of playing, but that would only serve to accentuate the gap between what a PI is and what a CI is.

Second, as already noted, a CI typically aims to explain (or elucidate) a work's meaning or structure—'what is going on in it', in a common phrase—whereas a PI can at most highlight (or effectively display) that meaning or structure. A PI, if successful, may enable one to conceive a work differently in the critical sense—as the performer perhaps conceived it in arriving at the PI—but only a CI actually indicates or details such a conception. A PI without

[8] It should be clear that when I speak of PIs implying or failing to imply CIs I do not mean implication in the *logical* sense—PIs are not, after all, even propositional—but something more akin to 'conversational implicature', in the sense explored by Grice, whereby a certain statement can be said, conversationally (or pragmatically), to imply a proposition it does not strictly entail if it affords, in context, strong or compelling evidence that the speaker or agent believes the proposition and wants to communicate it to an audience. In many cases it will be in virtue of the way the speaker says what he says, as opposed to what he says as such, that he conversationally implies so-and-so, and that is a principal ground of the analogy with what a performer could conceivably convey by a performative reading of a standard work. The analogy of performative implication and conversational implicature, however, is hardly complete. Performative implication might also be thought to operate partly in virtue of what Grice calls *conventional* implicature, which attaches to features of the type (sentence, PI) apart from its tokening in a concrete situation. See 'Logic and Communication', in P. Code and J. L. Morgan (eds.), *Syntax and Semantics* (New York, 1975).

[9] It should be emphasized that when I speak of the failure of PIs generally to imply CIs, or of PIs to express the CIs of performers, I have in mind CIs of some robustness, not ones that are little more than verbal formulations of the musician's actual performing decisions transposed into propositions about the work (see s. VIII).

a CI is relatively mute with regard to the structure or meaning of a musical work; if good the PI allows such structure and meaning to emerge clearly, but does not provide a determinate comment upon them. More concretely, what a particular shading, tempo fluctuation, or phrasing in a performance is pointing up generally remains indefinite without the backing of a specific articulate critical analysis.

A third contrast is this. CI tends to focus on the work, independent of specific performance, whereas PI naturally eventuates in a specific perform-ance, one which in many cases contents itself with bringing out but one side or dimension of a work. In other words, a CI is ideally synthetic, overarching, whereas a PI is typically selective, individualizing. CIs, whether of musical, visual, or literary works, if individually valid on aesthetic and historical grounds, can usually be accommodated to one another, fused, or synthesized into a single defensible comprehensive interpretation, though one that may retain a disjunctive form.[10] PIs of musical works, on the other hand, are inherently insusceptible of such fusion and mutual accommodation.

For example, the oft-noted conflict of possible readings of James's *Turn of the Screw*—as an understated ghost story, or as a tale of repression-induced hallucination—can and should be transcended, I would claim, so as to arrive at an understanding of the novella as constructed precisely in order to be seen equally well in those two ways; in other words, what we have in this, and in many similar cases, is not an irresolvable opposition but a duality that is internal to, and arguably intended in, the work. The situation is different with performative interpretations of musical works, which reside in particular realizations of them, and so entail particular values of all the constitutive musical properties of the work, which obviously cannot coexist with other such choices, either in conception or in sounding. Performative interpretations irreducibly compete for space in a way that individually valid but superficially opposed critical interpretations, when properly understood as partial, do not.[11] The contrast is especially pointed in the case of a musical composition which is equivocal in character. A CI of the piece will correctly identify and analyse that equivocality, giving equal attention to the piece's two faces, whereas an effective PI will typically bring out or accent only one. To aim always in such cases for an encompassing and synthetic PI, parallel to the ideally comprehensive CI just invoked, is a recipe for disaster. What emerges from following it is often just a PI halfway between two opposed but convin-

---

[10] At least something like this is true for works which attain a certain minimum standard of unity or success.

[11] An opposing view is that of Goldman ('Interpreting Art and Literature'), who assimilates critical to performative interpretation and accordingly thinks that the tolerance of multiplicity in performing interpretations indirectly supports tolerance of irreducibly conflicting critical interpretations. Whether musical interpretations of a given piece conflict with one another in the way literary interpretations appear to is also discussed by David Carrier in 'Interpreting Musical Performance', *Monist*, 66 (1983), 202–12.

cing ones—that bland middle of the road where music can expire from indifference.[12]

<h1 style="text-align:center">V</h1>

According to the position I have been endorsing, a PI is in itself a way of playing or presenting; a PI is not inherently a view of or about a work, its meaning and structure, nor, as we shall see, can it be said to include or indicate such. A PI will often reflect, spring from, be guided by a performer's critical conception of a work, to be sure, but it need not do so. A performer's interpretation may give some evidence of his understanding of a sonata's structure or expression, and it may enable a receptive listener to attain the same, where it had previously eluded him, but the PI is not by itself a statement or exposition of that understanding, nor is it even strong testimony to the performer's possession of such in articulate form. In general a PI is not, despite what reviewers of performances often allege, itself capable of saying anything much about the work's structure or expression, in even an extended sense of saying. I now turn to some illustrative cases.

Let's begin with the great dialogue between orchestra and soloist which constitutes the Andante movement of Beethoven's Fourth Piano Concerto. We might find that certain performers, say Fleisher and Szell, play it in such a way that one begins to have a certain conception of the import of that dialogue, perhaps the one sketched by Antony Hopkins in an insightful critical gloss, of which I give some excerpts:

A very special slow movement . . . symbolizing the power of inner contemplation in overcoming aggression . . . The juxtaposition of opposites; starkly aggressive unisons in strings (emphasized by the absence of harmony and the refusal to employ any other orchestral colour), as opposed to contemplative harmony supporting an expressive melodic line in solo piano part. Strings gradually reduced to silence in face of the soft answer that turneth away wrath . . . In the Fourth Concerto [conceived for a fortepiano] it was politic to turn the other cheek in the event of a confrontation . . . That aggressive opening phrase from the orchestra is neither commented upon nor contested. It is quite simply disregarded. In a rapt contemplation that verges towards mysticism the pianist conjures . . . magical chords from the keyboard.[13]

But Fleisher and Szell's PI of this movement does not as such either include or imply the conception—the CI—above, nor could any other imaginable PI, even though, we have allowed, it comports well enough with it,

---

[12] It is worth recalling here a point I have made elsewhere (in 'Evaluating Musical Performance', reprinted in *Music, Art, and Metaphysics* (Ithaca, NY, 1990)) about competing PIs of a given work, which is that even though such PIs cannot be *fused*, given the nature of the beast, in many contexts a given PI is properly *assessed* in light of the possibility or even availability of other, balancing PIs.

[13] *Understanding Music*, 135–40.

and perhaps even gives some reason to believe that the performers, in their guise as critics or analysts, may hold something to that effect. What is truly implicit in Fleisher and Szell's PI—a set of realizational choices—is at most a view as to how the work should be played. And a view as to how a work should be played is not thereby a view *of the work*, in the sense of a critical interpretation, though again, in many cases the performer's view of how to play will indeed issue from and reflect his view of the work, its content and form. Even where a given PI might be said to correspond, in principle, to a particular theoretical understanding of a piece—and I think this is only rarely the case—it does not itself make that understanding available, nor is it good evidence of the possession of such an understanding on the part of the performer who offers it.

Consider next, more abstractly, two conductors whose recorded performances of a given symphony sound virtually identical, allowances made, perhaps, for different orchestral venues—that is to say, they appear to have made all the same performing choices. Would we not hold these conductors to have offered the same PI of the piece, whatever else we might know or learn about the backgrounds of the performances? The answer to this seems clearly *yes*, and shows that a PI, as normally understood, does not include the discursive thoughts or analytical insights which may have occasioned it, or which it may occasion. After all, conductor 1 might have arrived at this PI through extensive structural study, while conductor 2's path to it was largely intuitive, or even fortuitous.[14] A PI may sometimes put into effect, as it were, a performer's conceptual understanding of a piece, but it does not necessarily do so. We thus have reason to refrain, as well, from saying that PIs invariably express performers' CIs: in many cases, there's simply no CI there to express.

Again, if we interview two noted pianists on their effectively identical performances of a sonata, which thus embody a common performative interpretation, we may very well discover that they have different, though defensible, reasons for the same performing choices, rooted in different views about the piece's overall import or the purpose of individual sections or compositional details. But this is just to say they have different CIs of the piece, which in this case happen to lead to the same PI.[15] And the PI can no more justifiably be said to express the CI of the first pianist than that of the second, inference to either being equally unwarranted.

The gap between CI and PI is perhaps particularly evident in the sphere of

[14] Another way to put the point is to note that performance can be more or less *theory-driven* (for example, Gould's vs. Lipatti's), which is to say the PIs they instantiate may be more or less backed by performer's CIs. But they needn't be so backed to be the PIs they are.

[15] I should note that I am taking sounding virtually the same to be a sufficient condition for sameness of PI involved in two performances—assuming they contain PIs at all (see s. VI). But I do not hold this to be quite a necessary condition for sameness of PI. We want to allow a measure of flexibility in judging two performances to embody the same PI even when they are clearly sonically distinguishable, if the differences are few or minor—especially where such differences make no difference in respect to coherence with or support of any possible CI of the work.

Ex. 1 Beethoven, Piano Concerto No. 4, opening, Andante

chamber music, as opposed to symphonies or solo sonatas, where readings can be ascribed to single individuals. Is it plausible to think that, say, the Juilliard Quartet's reading of Beethoven's C sharp minor Quartet automatically embodies a critical conception of the work shared equally by all quartet members? Of course there may be such a group conception, but need we assume there is? No, and it is likely each member has a critical take on the music which differs somewhat from those of his colleagues in either content or depth. What they do of necessity have in common, as a serious performing entity, is a PI they have co-operatively worked out, and which is their statement, so to speak, of how the piece should sound. They agree on a performative reading that does most justice to the piece as they each view it, but this may cover varying conceptions of its meaning and structure, all of which are compatible with the PI jointly endorsed.

Examples such as the foregoing do not represent remote possibilities, but instead remind us of what we could expect to find in many cases were we to excavate the conceptions behind given performative readings—in short, undeniable multiplicity. Thus, not only does a CI held by a performer and reflected in his performance generally fail to be unequivocally expressed by a PI, but it is a mistake to think that such substantial conceptions can be regarded as implicit in readings *per se*, in the sense of being such as one might reasonably ascribe or impute to performers on the basis of their performances alone.[16] There is generally a range of CIs compatible with a given PI, any number of which might make sense of the PI issuing as it does. Thus from a listener's perspective there can be no principled way to choose among them, no way of assigning to a PI a definite correlative CI.[17]

Another, Quinean, way to put the problem with inferring performers' CIs on the basis of PIs offered, or alternatively, of taking CIs to be implicit in PIs, is that critical 'theories' of a work are strongly *underdetermined* by the 'facts' of a performative reading; the latter are generally compatible with a fair multiplicity of the former. Those few critical propositions which might be confidently said to be determined by the data of the performer's concrete choices do not usually go beyond the simplest consequences of how a performance actually goes.

---

[16] Thus, as I am using the terms, the difference between a CI being *expressed by* a PI and a CI being *implicit in* a PI is roughly that the former requires, while the latter does not, that the performer actually hold the CI in question. In both instances, though, inference to the performer's holding a particular CI must be warranted—a condition I claim is not generally fulfilled.

[17] The distinction between CIs and PIs, and the thesis that PIs generally fall short of expressing or implying CIs of any substance, helps to put the difference between recitals and lecture-recitals into relief. In the former, you get a pianist's PIs, full stop. In the latter you get both PIs and CIs, and are instructed in their relationship, at least in this performer's mind; you get to understand why (CI) the pianist made the choices (PI) he did, while remaining aware that other CIs might have led to an identical PI, and that the same CI might have been realized or activated differently by another pianist, resulting in a different PI.

Here, for example, is a representative critical commentary, concerning Karajan's Deutsche Grammophon recording of Mahler's Sixth Symphony:

Karajan's reading of the Sixth is a revelation, above all in the slow movement which here becomes far more than a lyrical interlude. It emerges as one of the greatest of Mahler's slow movements and the whole balance of the symphony is altered.[18]

Although the proposition that Mahler's Andante moderato is more than merely an interlude but is instead a centre of gravity of the symphony as a whole cannot, of course, be accounted a part of the PI itself, it could perhaps just be said to be implicit in the reading alone, since going beyond the datum of tempo choice to such a small extent. In other words, we can hardly understand a broader-than-usual tempo for the movement otherwise than as at least diminishing its tendency to convey the impression of an interlude.

The matter would be quite different, however, with even a moderately robust CI of Mahler's slow movement, such as this by Dika Newlin:

The Andante moderato comes as an interlude of deep, lasting, and unworldly spiritual peace, though not without tragic undertones, certain of its melodic lines showing a kinship with the *Kindertotenlieder*. Mahler 'distances' this movement from the 'A minor world' of struggle and suffering in the other three movements by choosing for it the key of E♭ major, a tritone away—the most remote key-relationship possible within the tonal system.[19]

Or this by Hans Redlich:

The Andante . . . is unashamedly romantic . . . casting a backward glance at a paradise irretrievably lost . . . [its] episodes—pastoral, mysterious and passionate in turn—only tend to underline the rondo-like return to [the movement's chief melody] and its world of wistful retrospect and calm, autumnal beauty. The last lingering look into the swiftly receding past in the final bars of the Andante is one of the supreme moments in music, conceived in Austria by an Austrian a decade before the outbreak of the great war.[20]

No one, I think, could claim to find such implicit in, rather than just concordant with, Karajan's—or any other—performative reading of the symphony.[21]

For another example of a minimal critical view inhering in a PI we may look to Pinchas Zukerman's rendition of Debussy's Violin Sonata.[22] From Zukerman's way of performing Debussy's sonata, it seems a pretty safe conjecture that he thinks of it—in my view, incorrectly—as a late romantic essay, continuous with Franck's or Lalo's efforts in the same medium.

---

[18] *Penguin Guide to Compact Discs* (Harmondsworth, 1990), 583.

[19] Liner notes, Mahler, Symphony No. 6, Abbado/Chicago Symphony Orchestra (DG 2707117, 1980).

[20] Introduction, Mahler, Symphony No. 6, ed. Eulenberg (Mainz, 1968).

[21] It is worth reminding the reader at this point that a CI cannot be *implicit* in a PI, in the relevant sense, unless a listener has good grounds to attribute it to the performer as held, on the basis of the performance offered alone.

[22] With Marc Neikrug, piano (CBS M35179, 1978).

Perhaps there is no other way to construe or account for his generally slow tempos, full tone, and syrupy phrasing. But if this is so, the critical perspective thus implicit in the PI—a simple view of the music's style—is hardly an extensive one. There is no advantage in conflating it with something like this—a not particularly trenchant sample of critical commentary—which concerns the same piece of music:

The first movement, the weakest of the three, is cast in a more or less orthodox form . . . Echoes of the Stravinsky of *Le Sacre du printemps* can be heard in some of the bridge passages. The second movement is again one of those Harlequinesque interludes, the last of Debussy's serenades, less mordant than the slow movement of the cello sonata, but with many touches of a tender, benign melancholy. The finale opens with a reminiscence of the first movement and proceeds with an exuberant rondo on a theme recalling *Iberia*. This theme, the composer explains in a letter . . . 'is subjected to the most curious deformations and ultimately leaves the impression of an idea turning back on itself, like a snake biting its own tail.'[23]

VI

In preceding sections I have defended what might be called a 'lean' notion of performative interpretation, one on which PIs do not include as such the sorts of thoughts or ideas which are unequivocally a matter of critical interpretation, and I have stressed how little, on a critical plane, can be said to be implicit in PIs so understood. It would, on the other hand, be a mistake to go further and embrace what might be labelled a minimalist notion of PI, according to which a PI amounted only to a highly specific type of sound sequence conforming to the score, whatever its provenance or mode of generation. No, a PI, though it need not be backed by a critical analysis or justification, must at least represent a set of choices to play a certain way, with some awareness of, if not active experimentation with, the alternatives available, and not merely a set of realizations of the sonic properties constitutive of the work. If that were all a PI was, then every recognizable performance, however offhand, not to speak of every mere sound occurrence accidentally fitting a score, would necessarily instantiate some PI or other. But matters are otherwise. If we confine our attention only to sound occurrences that actually are performances, the fact is that we do not recognize PIs to be present in all such cases.

The notion of a *performance* of *W*, of course, is already an intentional one. A sound sequence *S* conforming to the instrumentally defined sound structure of *W* is not automatically a performance of *W*; *S* must have been produced with the intent, roughly, to instantiate the sound structure of *W*. But to say a performance involves an interpretation (or reading) of *W* is to make a claim of higher intentionality still. It is to affirm that the way of playing evident in the

---

[23] Edward Lockspeiser, *Debussy* (London, 1936, 3rd edn. 1963), 180–1.

performance has been considered, chosen, espoused by the performer—that he or she has thought about how to play the work, and stands behind the performative result.

Here are some cases, I submit, where performing does not plausibly involve performative interpreting: (*a*) performing by rote, without monitoring, letting the easiest phrasings just fall out of one's fingers, by habit; (*b*) performing an unfamiliar piece in a crunch, hurriedly but adequately; (*c*) performing by slavish or unreflective imitation, as when an awestruck pupil mimics the master's reading. In the first two cases, it seems intuitive to say not only that there is no performative interpreting going on, but that in addition the result fails to embody any PI at all. The third case, in which we might grant that a PI is present, suggests that not every performance embodying an interpretation embodies one attributable to the performer; if the imitation is slavish and unreflective enough, the pupil is not giving his own PI, even via adoption, but simply instantiating that of his teacher.[24]

We see, then, that there are three relations that may obtain between a performance of a work *W* and performative interpretations of *W*. The weakest is that the performance merely *corresponds to* a possible PI; this is true of every performance, which always instantiates some way of playing or other. A second is that the performance actually *embodies* a PI, which may or may not have been generated by the performer. The strongest, and what usually holds, is that the performance in addition *advances* a PI, one the performer has arrived at for himself or at least embraces as his own.

To claim that a performer has a performative interpretation of a work, again, is not to say that the performer necessarily commands a critical interpretation of the work which he can relate to his performative one. Such a requirement could be taken as definitive of a rich conception of performative interpretation, flanking the lean conception I endorse on the left, as the minimalist conception I likewise reject flanks it on the right. But a performer does not need to be able to articulate reasons why his way of playing is right or true to the work's expressiveness or structure in order for us to say he possesses a PI, so long as he feels, upon consideration, that the work should be played in such and such a manner, and is so able to play it. To insist on more is to unjustifiably narrow the gap between a PI and a CI.

To hold that a PI is present in a performance it is not enough, I have suggested, that the performance merely exemplify a way of playing; on the other hand, it is too much to demand that the performance be the direct implementation of a CI in the performer's intellectual possession.

Finally, though, we might note that there is a conception of PIs one could adopt intermediate between those I have labelled *rich* and *lean*, but which in

---

[24] See Sharpe, 'Type, Token': 'Another performer who models his performance upon the initial interpretation [of another] merely repeats it. He does not produce a new interpretation in its own right.' (438).

essence is much closer to the latter than to the former; call this a *semi-lean* conception. According to it, a PI always embodies and inherently reflects a performer's *intuitive, non-verbal* grasp of a piece's structure and expression, where there is no implication that the performer is in possession of any such grasp in an articulate form, which would be tantamount to a CI. However, unless we take having arrived after consideration at a determination that a piece should be played in such and such way as *ipso facto* constitutive or criterial of having an intuitive grasp of the piece's structure and expression, then although PIs will almost always conform with a semi-lean conception of them, it seems they will not invariably or necessarily do so. It is conceivable that a violinist, say, might offer an acceptable reading of a piece, one he was implicitly endorsing, without appearing to have, as judged by other indications—e.g. what he said about the music's emotional import, or the reasons he gave for certain performing decisions, or his response to performances of the piece by others—what we would be justified in calling even an intuitive grasp of the piece's structure or expression; it seems possible that there should be 'idiot joueurs', so to speak, or performers who just happen to 'get it right' by luck, at least some of the time. So I think there is reason to stick with the lean conception of PIs sketched above, though it is clear that a semi-lean conception would not, in practice, cut the cake much differently from a lean one.[25] What is important, once again, is to recognize clearly the inadequacy of the contrasting rich and minimal conceptions of performative interpretation, the latter wrongly requiring performers to possess critical views of what they play, and the latter wrongly requiring almost no intentionality of performers at all.

VII

If PIs neither contain, nor express, nor implicitly convey CIs of any robustness, then what, if anything, is conveyed implicitly by them? What, if any, are the propositions implied in a PI, at least in standard performing contexts?

In short, this. A performance of a musical work by a knowledgeable performer generally carries the implicit claim that the performer believes such a way of playing is an effective projection of the work's expressive character and essential structure, whatever they might be, or more generally, that such a way of playing does justice to a work or makes it come off well. But two points

[25] One writer who defends what I have labelled a semi-lean conception of performative interpretation is Peter Kivy, in his recent and excellent *Music Alone* (Ithaca, NY, 1990), 120–3. But I have suggested that we have cause to be sceptical of the claim that all performative interpretation *necessarily* embodies and conveys a performer's 'understanding' of the music performed, if this means any more than how it can be, or is to be, played. Nor do I find this scepticism dissolved when I am told that a performance is always a 'nonverbal description' (122) of a work, as well as a sounding of it; 'nonverbal description' strikes me as a contradiction in terms.

must immediately be stressed. First, the performance may, in the performer's mind, represent only one such way of optimizing the work; performers may, without inconsistency, favour and even advocate in practice two or more different ways of playing a work. Second, the implication that the way of playing exhibited is one approved by the performer is only clearly carried by the performance in the standard performing context, i.e. that of concert halls and recording studios. The implication will be absent in other circumstances, for example, if the performance occurs as part of a nightclub comedy routine, or as an illustration during a master class, and can in any case always be cancelled by the performer's explicit disavowal.

The statement implicit in a PI of a work in the standard context of public performance[26] is roughly *invariant*, being more or less just 'this is the (or a) way to perform W'. In other words, we take public performance standardly to involve tacit endorsement of the way of playing exhibited. On the other hand, the statements constitutive of a CI are naturally *work-specific*, ascribing expressiveness, allusiveness, formal coherence, thematic interrelatedness, originality, historical significance, and so on to the work in question.

VIII

Is it, then, never implied in a PI, which consists of a considered way of rendering a score, that such-and-such passage expresses so-and-so, or that the piece is structured in this or that fashion—to go no further? We need to examine some more cases before drawing final conclusions. Can PIs have implicit critical content beyond their fairly constant one of self-endorsement (s. VII), or the sort of minimal extrapolation from the literal progress or shape of a performance which we acknowledged earlier (s. V)?

Take the simplest kind of case. Does the fact that X plays a piece jauntily (PI) show, or warrant one in concluding, that he views it as basically jaunty (CI)? I think not. He might regard the piece as essentially grave, but hope to hint at its repressed levity. Similarly, when we read in a review that X takes a sombre (cheerful, expansive, etc.) view of the opening of Y's symphony in his performance of it, we should not understand this as a report or inference regarding X's *critical* view of the expressiveness of that opening. The content of the remark should rather be understood as no more than that X conducts (i.e. has the orchestra play) Y's symphony in such a way that the opening appears sombre (cheerful, expansive), or so that the sombre (cheerful, expansive) potential of the opening is to the fore. On the basis of X's PI we can say, if we like, that X 'sees' the symphony's opening as sombre, but we go too far if we attribute to X or his PI the critical proposition that the opening of the symphony *is* sombre. What we are licensed to infer, it seems, is little

---

[26] Or perhaps in the *offering* of the PI in such context.

more than that X believes the symphony's opening benefits, and perhaps not exclusively, from a sombre approach.[27]

A common occurrence in music is for a passage in the middle of a composition to be a variant of and allude to an earlier passage. An example is the transition from the slow movement to the rondo in Schumann's Piano Concerto, where Schumann recalls his first movement theme before transforming it, before our ears, into the tune of the finale. Suppose A's performance makes this very plain, while B's performance simply allows it to be discerned. Can we say that A's performance entails the critical claim that the resemblance of the two passages is aesthetically important, while B's does not? Hardly. For one, the piece may work best when such resemblances are detectable but backgrounded, and this could very well have been a guiding idea behind B's reading. Nothing on a critical level regarding the importance of the thematic reference involved is clearly implied by either PI. Of course, it remains true that given analytical observations about a piece will fit with some PIs more than others, if only for the fact that some performances are so lacklustre or misconceived that they will cohere with no valid critical insights; but the match-up will hardly ever be one-to-one.

If certain performances of the Scherzo from Mahler's Sixth Symphony, e.g. Horenstein's rather than Abbado's, are more suggestive of the clumsiness of children's games—which Alma Mahler claimed was her husband's inspiration for the movement's heavy rhythms and metrical shifts—the possibly defensible proposition that the movement contains echoes of such games cannot yet be held to be implicit in the former performance. It belongs, instead, to a critical reading of the symphony, one which, admittedly, would more likely engender Horenstein's PI than Abbado's, but which is not, given underdetermination of critical explanation by performative choice, reasonably attributed to Horenstein merely in virtue of the PI arrived at. Recall next the famous inspiration in the symphony's first movement where a trumpet chord of A major melts diminuendo into one of A minor over a fateful kettledrum tattoo (bars 57–60). As numerous commentators have noted, this musical gesture is an almost perfect expression of the final expiration of hope. But could that insight be said to be *implicit* in any performance of the passage? Not that I can imagine—which is not to say that there do not exist performances, for example Horenstein's, which do more justice to, or seem more cognizant of, that insight than others.

If the Adagietto from Mahler's Fifth Symphony is played in such a fashion as to give the impression of glimpsing a far-off land which slowly approaches, gloriously arrives, and then gradually recedes—as does, to my ears, Sinopoli's 1985 reading for Deutsche Grammophon—this propositionally expressed

---

[27] Similarly, we can if we like say that X's PI shows how he 'feels' the music, but we are on safer ground if we take this to mean primarily that the PI indicates how he feels the music should *go*, rather than what he feels the music *expresses*. For inference to the latter is just more likely to go astray.

idea cannot (of course) belong to the PI (a reflectively considered way of playing) that the performance involves. Rather, it represents a CI of the piece, or of the piece *under* that PI, or perhaps just a CI *of* that PI—this last construction being apt for much of what one finds in reviews of recorded performances. Grant that this CI captures part of the metaphorical content of Mahler's wonderful tone structure. It is yet scarcely credible that such an image is implicit in Sinopoli's PI, something we could expect to be communicated to any sensitive and attentive listener. What is instead the case is that the PI is well suited to foster a critical notion of that sort, and for all we know may have sprung from the like in the conductor's mind, but is simply not implied by it.

According to Leonard Bernstein, the dreamy quality of the Adagietto's opening is crucially dependent on the ambiguity of key and metre in the bars in question, which are given to rhythmically vague arpeggios on the harp over sustained As and Cs in the lower strings, with no tonic Fs.[28] If this is so, then that quality can probably be augmented or diminished according to the exact tempo adopted, since a quicker tempo will tend to clarify, or more quickly resolve, the double ambiguity just mentioned. But should a performance in line with Bernstein's observation, i.e. one broad in tempo within the limits of 'adagietto', be understood as implicitly advancing the proposition that the dreamy quality of the opening is mainly owing to the ambiguities of key and metre resident in Mahler's initial bars? This seems to be more content than one is reasonably entitled to attribute to the choice itself of playing those bars in a particular way. Naturally CIs have implications for performance, and to be sure, Bernstein's own 1988 reading of the Adagietto[29] arguably follows and implements the critical insight expressed above. But his PI by itself does not seem clearly to require support from any CI for its validity, or to imply any CI univocally, or to constrain very narrowly the possible CIs it might be called on to confirm.

Sticking with the performance just mentioned, when Bernstein adopts a notably slow and flexible tempo at rehearsal 12 in the first movement, this strikes me as a way of underlining the suggestion of village marching band music in those bars. But this is *my* CI of Bernstein's PI at that point. The PI itself does not clearly convey that content, does not implicitly affirm that the passage is a sophisticated allusion to such music, even though it *is* such, Bernstein surely knew that it was, and the PI is well adapted to bring that out. Notice that if we insist that Bernstein's PI implicitly affirms the allusion, because the resemblance in question (which exists anyway) is emphasized, it seems we would have to attribute the denial of the allusion to PIs which underplayed, without completely obscuring, the resemblance. Neither seems warranted. Affirming the existence of allusions in a piece of music, as opposed to

---

[28] *The Unanswered Question* (Cambridge, Mass., 1977), 196–9.
[29] With the Vienna Philharmonic (DG 423608-2).

Ex. 2 Mahler, Symphony No. 5, opening, Adagietto

facilitating their appreciation if present, is irreducibly a matter of critical, not performative, interpretation.

IX

It will be instructive to consider one more musical example. A standard issue of interpretation in regard to performance of Schubert's Piano Sonata in B flat, Op. posth. is whether to observe the repeat of the exposition in the first movement, a movement which, however one comes down, is of considerable length. Assuming the choice of repeat or no repeat to be within the sphere of realizational performative interpretation, that is, assuming that whether to repeat or not is truly an option in the work as Schubert envisaged it, a matter for the performer's discretion, then what critical view of the movement might be said to be implicit in, say, the decision not to repeat? That the movement is too long for optimal appreciation with the repeat taken? That the balance between exposition and development sections is upset by reprising such a long exposition? That the repeat is only appropriate when most concerned listeners were coming to the sonata for the first time, as was the case for Schubert's contemporaries? That the balance between the opening movement and the three succeeding ones is then inapt? That the exposition is so heart-breakingly sublime that it would wear out a listener to have to go through it twice in quick succession? That the music of the transition back to the opening, omitted when the repeat is declined, is not of particular interest or structural importance?[30]

None of these, which represent critical perspectives on the music and its performance with at least some prima-facie validity, can really be implicit in the PI itself, unless we are prepared to say they were all so implicit, which makes little sense. The truth is that a PI and the plausible reasons one might have for advancing it, or views of a work one might hold that cohere with it, are logically separable. Granted, in loose parlance we say that a performer's PI indicates how he or she conceives the work in question. But again I would insist that as such it only strictly indicates—or rather just is—the way he or

---

[30] This opinion, by the way, is firmly opposed by a number of commentators, who cite the interest of this transition as a major reason for observing the repeat. First, Philip Radcliffe: 'In view of the length of the movement it is not surprising that the repeat of the first movement is seldom played, but the passage that leads back to it is remarkably powerful; here, for the only time in the movement, the mysterious trill that punctuates the phrases of the first theme appears fortissimo.' (*Schubert Piano Sonatas*, BBC Music Guides (London, 1967), 51.) Antony Hopkins's judgement is remarkably similar: 'to have started once more after so quiet a conclusion would hardly have been effective; some change of mood was needed. [Schubert] introduces a new, restless little figure, toys mysteriously with the last three chords of [a previous phrase], then suddenly startles his audience out of their wits with a great thunderclap, the only time that that distant rumble [a bass trill] which had lent such an individual colour to the first theme is allowed to reveal its latent power.' (*Talking About Music* (London, 1977), 412.) For the record, I side with those who maintain that the repeat should be observed.

she plays the work in question, which though it might conduce to certain analytical conceptions of the work rather than others, is compatible with a number of them, or with no conception at all.

Consider next the following critical disagreement regarding the sonata's third movement, particularly its middle section. First, here is Philip Radcliffe:

[Schubert writes] a scherzo of fairy-like delicacy, full of delightful melodic phrases... The main part of the scherzo ends almost in mid-air and the change to the much more sombre atmosphere of the trio, in Bb minor, is electrifying. The lively quaver movement ceases, and there is a curious sense of foreboding due largely to the cross-rhythms and the ominous-sounding detached notes in the bass.[31]

In strong contrast, the view of Antony Hopkins:

The Scherzo is a delight of a different kind, quicksilver and delicate, imbued with the wit that Schubert may have learned from Beethoven... The central Trio is a subtle example of the village-band joke. All the lads are playing quietly except for old Joe on the tuba, whose isolated notes stand out like farts at the vicarage.[32]

Clearly one performance, say that of Maria-João Pires, might be more congenial to Radcliffe's CI, and another, say that of Richard Goode, to Hopkins's CI, but no PI can be said to unequivocally express either Radcliffe's or Hopkins's characterizations of the music. The most one can affirm is that if the trio is played Pires's way, it suggests something akin to Radcliffe's CI, and if played Goode's way, something akin to Hopkins's. And this is more content than we are usually in a position to project, even hypothetically, onto contrasting PIs.

To sum up, performers most often do harbour critical interpretations of the pieces of music they play, to be sure, and they may reasonably hope that such critical conceptions will be fostered by the modes of performance chosen. But that such conceptions are inherent in those modes themselves is simply not borne out. From a performer's CI we may be able to infer something about the PI he will elect, or at least rule out certain PIs as ones he would eschew. But from a performer's PI alone we cannot safely infer anything as to what CI, if any, he subscribes to, and thus we must regard the idea that PIs themselves are tantamount to CIs, only implicit ones, as just one more rhetorical exaggeration. Once we learn, if we do, how a musician sees a work in the articulate sense (CI), we can often put this together with how he sees the work in the realizational sense, the specific shape and shading he gives it in performance (PI), and so partly account for the latter in terms of the former, but we cannot in general safely move inferentially in the opposite direction.[33]

---

[31] Radcliffe, *Schubert Piano Sonatas*, 54.
[32] Hopkins, *Talking About Music*, 415–16.
[33] Can we rest with the modest claim that PIs, even if they neither incorporate, express, nor imply robust CIs, often at least suggest them to the minds of competent listeners? Possibly. But note that a PI may very well suggest, broadly speaking, just about anything to a listener—especially a suggestible one. It seems we only arrive at a suitably restrictive notion of suggestion

Ex. 3 Schubert, Piano Sonata in B flat, Op. Posth., Trio of Scherzo

When we hear a striking PI of a familiar piece, the question we put to ourselves as interpreters of such interpretations should be not, 'What CI does that PI embody or convey?', for that question, we now know, has no answer, or only rather thin ones, but instead 'What CIs might such a PI support or reflect?' An insightful PI might prompt one to arrive at a new CI, or allow one to confirm the validity of a CI already proposed, or induce one to question a CI regarded as authoritative, and so on, but it cannot itself unambiguously communicate a CI. We have seen how a given PI of a work can be reasonably judged to have different conceptions behind it or to have sprung from different objectives, and how different PIs of a work may coexist with identical articulable views of its content. Though ideally there should be, and often is, substantial interaction between critical-analytic and performative-practical notions about a piece of music, the former are not equivalent to the latter, nor are they strictly implicit in them to any extent. Performative interpretations stand almost as much in need of critical interpretation as the works they render audible in specific fashion. That, of course, is part of what we have reviewers of performances for.

X

Having stressed throughout this chapter the logical distance between performative and critical interpretation, I try in this last section to shed some light on the relations that typically exist nevertheless between PIs and CIs in a musician's experience, by focusing on the interpretive task with respect to one small piece of music. What goes on could be fairly described as a species of dialectical development, or mutual modification in stages.

The piece in question is the third movement (Andante) from Bach's Sonata No. 2 for solo violin. On a first run-through, I may well carry away an impression of the piece, with its constant quavers in the bottom voice and gently moving melody above, as basically song-like, a simple diversion from the heavier business of the preceding Grave and Fuga movements. My initial playing might then have a light and carefree tone, with a fairly brisk construal of the tempo indication. Soon, however, I am struck by the drama inherent in the first half of the second section of this two-part form; C major and G major give way to A minor and E minor, and there are curious discontinuities in the melodic line and grinding dissonances, at two points in particular, the first beats of bars 15 and 17. Now I start to reconceive the piece as more plaintive and soulful than before, one whose untroubled first half conceals the seeds of

by restoring an elision in the foregoing: PIs suggest CIs to competent listeners in the sense of striking them as the sorts of PIs one would offer if one held the CIs in question. Thus, the relevant notion of suggestion of CIs by PIs is roughly equivalent to the one we have been discussing under the rubric of implication of CIs by PIs, and inherits the same problems of either underdetermination or else minimality of CIs involved.

Ex. 4 Bach, Sonata No. 2 for solo violin in A minor, Andante

distress which are to flower later. I try out a slower, more deliberate tempo, and perhaps a less legato phrasing throughout.

Next my attention fixes on those points of highest harmonic tension, at bars 15 and 17. I may now decide, in light of my darker critical view of the music, to make the most of these moments, and to maximize their expressive potential. I do this, for example, by emphasizing the octave leap (A' to A") in the top line at the juncture of 14 and 15 and digging in on the Bs in the middle voice played in usual broken fashion as grace notes to the motion above (A" to G♯"), while doing similarly with the leap of a fourth and middle voice D♯s at the beginning of 17. I also adopt an increased dynamic for these bars, in comparison with the rest of the piece, and lean on the appoggiatura F♯ in bar 19.

Now, though, I reflect that I have perhaps gone too far. This slender Andante, as I am now playing it, seems to me as highly charged as the St Matthew Passion, at least at the opening of the second half. And that is part of the problem, for it is now difficult to come down from the emotional extremes of bars 14–18 and resume the unruffled air of the piece's first half, which is back in place by bar 22 and continues as such to the end, four bars later. I seem now to have two choices. One is to tone down my exploitation of the tensions in bars 14–19; the other is to inject more tension or seriousness into my rendition of the remainder of the piece as well, perhaps slowing the tempo further, perhaps shaping the phrase bridging bars 19 and 20, with its unexpected hint of D minor, as a third point of climax, thus achieving a more continuous emotional transition from peak (17) to valley (27) in the piece's second half.

Electing the latter, I am now pretty satisfied with my performing reading.[34] As a result, I now reconceive the piece as indeed a song after all, but one whose lyric persona harbours, beneath an outwardly calm exterior, a hidden distress, and which finds consolation in confronting this distress openly and working through it. On such a critical perspective, the peace reflected in the closing bars of the two halves of the movement is not really the same state in both cases—any more than the identity of mountains as mountains grasped before and after the study of Zen, so we are told, is one and the same proposition.

If the above is a recognizable illustration of how performative and critical ideas about a piece of music may interact, what I would emphasize, in conclusion, is just the contingency of most of these connections, and thus the implausibility of thinking that any sort of one-to-one correspondence can be demonstrated between given sets of performing choices and given critical conceptions in regard to a musical work. The performative reading of Bach's Andante that I imagined opting for in my little narrative reflects, I believe,

---

[34] The PI I have described here takes its inspiration, as it turns out, from a remarkable peformance by Anner Bylsma on violoncello piccolo (Deutsche Harmonia Mundi 7998-2).

the critical conception of its structure and expressiveness I there end up embracing, but the latter is neither equivalent to, nor inferable from, nor expressed by, the former. Ideally, though, the former will facilitate a listener's coming to the latter. That is enough of a responsibility, I think, to charge a performative interpretation with.

Interpreting the Emotional Content of Music

F. M. BERENSON

The Concise Oxford Dictionary renders 'interpretation' and 'interpret' as follows: 'expound the meaning of (abstruse or foreign words, writings, dreams, etc.); make out the meaning of; bring out the meaning of, render, by artistic representation or performance; explain, understand, in specific manner (*we interpret this as a threat*)'.

Interpretation, in the context of music, is almost invariably taken as referring to performers and critical writings are, therefore, primarily concerned with judgements of the quality of performances in terms of whose or which interpretation comes nearest to the spirit of the music, etc. Interpretation focuses on bringing out what there is in the music, on what is perceived, on what there is to be discovered, rendered audible and to offer what has been understood about the music to the audiences; all this is in keeping with the above definition. The audience, in turn, try to capture this understanding in some way. In this important sense the audience are also engaged in interpretation of what it is they are listening to (as opposed to merely hearing music passively). The activity of listening to music is inextricably bound up with interpreting what one is listening to and with experiencing the richness of the music in all its aspects. Yet, in most writings on this subject the emphasis is on the performer's interpretation; very little is said about the listener's interpretation.

The above definition emphasizes meaning but the problem of meaning in music is an extremely complex one. Given the complexity, it is nevertheless clear that any kind of meaning is directly related to understanding. I wish to concentrate on one particular aspect of the *listener*'s interpretation, on what he or she can legitimately discover and interpret and thus understand of a given composition. The very fact that members of the audience, which includes critics, take up a critical stance towards any given performance implies logically that they are also engaged in interpretation; in understanding and responding to what that particular composition contains that is of importance. The significant difference between performers and the audience is that while the former normally interpret for the listener, the latter primarily interpret for themselves.

The question to which I specifically address myself is whether it is legitimate to engage in interpreting and attempting to understand the emotional content of music and, if so, what this interpretation/understanding is centrally concerned with and how it is to be rendered in performance, in explanation, and what kind of response is to count as an emotional response to what has been understood.

It is necessary to stress that any kind of valuable aesthetic appreciation and response is dependent on how a listener interprets the object of appreciation. Because of this, we need to look carefully at what belongs properly to aesthetic appreciation and what does not belong precisely because it is not a part of genuine interpretation. This point raises the controversy which still rages between the so-called 'purists' and 'emotivists'. In a nutshell, most purists wish to lay down rigid boundaries to what can legitimately be appreciated and offered in explanation about music: structure and form; anything over and above these is irrelevant and unimportant. The emotivists want no such boundaries but, in the course of their various theories, many come close to giving accounts of emotive qualities of music on analogy with contagious diseases in claiming that sad music makes one feel sad—the listener catches the sadness from the music and is 'infected' by it. The purists are really concerned with factual analysis which has little to do with interpretation as such. The significant question here is whether we can legitimately insist on a priori strictures of this kind without losing something of paramount importance in our enjoyment of music. In the course of discussing this controversy I shall indicate what I take to be a fruitful direction for explanation of the area of audience interpretation and understanding of the emotional content of music which avoids the pitfalls of both these extreme factions.

I start with a story attributed to Robert Schumann. It is about a young German intellectual who is attending a performance of an opera by Donizetti. He listens with a superior smile on his face; he judges the orchestration crude, the harmonies trite, the melodies vulgar. He is enjoying his minute dissections and decides that the opera is just vulgar stuff altogether. Suddenly panic grips him. In the middle of an aria he feels a tear running down his cheek. The symptoms seem unmistakable, he is about to weep! Instantly he leaves the theatre and rushes home. Sitting at the piano, he pounds out the aria he has just heard, grotesquely distorting the melody. After continuing in this fashion for an hour, he leans back with a sigh of relief. *Reason* has returned. The tear was only sweat after all. Here we have an example of a deliberate refusal to interpret the affective experience that the music forced on him.

There are a number of very recent and no less dramatic statements of similar sentiments. R. A. Sharpe writes:

I do not think that emotion qualities are of any great significance in the appreciation of music. 'The gifted listener', as Copland felicitously called him, appreciates music without being very interested in emotion qualities or in his own emotional reactions ... expressionism is obviously the most influential ... theory about music even if its advocates have been less articulate and *less intelligent than their critics*.[1]

[1] R. A. Sharpe, review of M. Budd, *Music and the Emotions*, *British Journal of Aesthetics*, 26, No. 4 (Autumn 1986), 398 (my italics).

He argues that the problem of musical expression, i.e. the problem of accounting for the ascription of 'mental' predicates, is of no importance to aesthetic appreciation, that there is nothing calling for an interpretation, that the superior judgement of the connoisseur should be used to guide the beginner's listening and that the scientific terms used in legitimate explanation form the totality of musical discourse. But are we engaged in interpretation here or in mere technical analysis? He goes on to say that those who cannot talk about music in acceptably scientific terms must rid themselves of the emotive vocabulary and the pursuit of trivia and replace them with technical predicates or, as he puts it: 'Let them learn.'[2] I take the injunction 'Let them learn' to be on par with that of Marie Antoinette's 'Let them eat cake.' It arises from an analogous ignorance and dismissal of any aesthetic life different from that which is advocated. The problem then is one of priorities: do we go for bread followed by cake or are we prepared to live with the substitute?

There are, of course, many others who hold such views. M. Budd in a recent paper on Hanslick[3] says that his views are particularly impressive in their opposition to theories (which Budd calls vague and full of unrigorous arguments) that seek to explain the value of music by reference to some relation in which it is thought that music can stand to the emotions. Budd, in common with Hanslick, argues that music is an end in itself and not merely a means for the achievement of something to do with the emotions, that it pleases for its own sake, that its beauty/value is 'specifically musical'. On the face of it, his sentiments are unexceptional but just how rigorous are his own arguments as compared to what he calls the vague and unrigorous arguments of the opposition? Surely, the first issue to be settled is what is 'specifically musical'. He argues that music involves pure contemplation of beautiful forms and sounds and that the beauty of these musical forms is entirely a matter of the content and internal structure of the work. Certainly, but it is precisely the question of content of a work which is at issue. He says that 'A certain melody is anguished' simply means that it has extreme melodic leaps to dissonant intervals. One could easily produce several counter-examples to this. What sort of meaning are we concerned with here? All these so-called rigorous arguments just seem to sweep the main problems under the carpet.

Preference for detached intellectualism implies logically a rejection of any kind of personal involvement. My aim is to provide some grounds for showing that those of us who take involvement to be an essential part of an aesthetic experience and of a true interpretation of content, may cease to be embarrassed and refuse to submit to being relegated to the silent majority. The indisputable fact remains—in spite of enormous efforts of the purists, the problem about the role of emotions in music just does not disappear. Whether we like it or not, we constantly discover that sounds are suffused with feeling.

[2] R. A. Sharpe, review of P. Kivy, *The Corded Shell*, *British Journal of Aesthetics*, 22, No. 1 (Winter 1982), 82.

[3] M. Budd, 'The Repudiation of Emotion: Hanslick on Music', *British Journal of Aesthetics*, 20, No. 1 (Winter 1980), 29–43.

Another point which should give us serious pause is that the logical consequence of what the purists advocate as the only true, possible talk or explanation in terms of technical descriptions could go on as it does at present without anyone *ever having to listen* to a single note of music. All the structures, combinations, cadences, and the like, are there in the score. Why then do people want to listen to music? What is it that is added beyond the stuff that purists talk about and urge us to learn about? Whatever it is, it demands identification and interpretation.

If music alone among the arts is regarded as in some way hermetic by virtue of the discontinuity of music with the rest of experience, as is argued, why then does it play such an extremely important part in so many people's lives, to the point that we would consider it an intolerable and horrifying punishment to be condemned to live without it? Michael Tanner[4] makes the point that pitches, timbres, intervals, chords, etc., are the ingredients like various edibles are ingredients in cooking but what goes on in the kitchen has no bearing on how one finds the meal. Here we have an illuminating example, which needs a small modification because what goes on in the kitchen *has* a direct relationship to the quality of the meal but my enjoying the meal is not dependent on what *I know* about what went on in the kitchen.

In common with chefs, whose skills are the means to producing a meal to be savoured, composers have not, as a rule, written music for the benefit of professional analysts and academics; the primary aim was that their music should be listened to and enjoyed in various ways. As for performers, we only have to observe their facial expressions to see that their deepest engagement is with feelings during the performance. Janáček, in his autobiography, writes that when he listens to human speech, he listens to the tone, how something is said, much more than what is said in words. His notebooks, he tells us, are full on *tone* of speech which he tries to capture in music. Analogously, mere sounds are not music, the tones of the sounds are; music is the art of sound.

While talk about the emotional content of music is indisputably very difficult, could it not also be the case that our purists merely indulge in preserving their unsullied existence of non-involvement with the emotions and denigrating any work simply on the grounds that it has strong emotional content? We need only to look at music examples used to support their theories, in recent work, to find abundant evidence of such dismissal. Such an attitude is on par with the sort of remarks that we have all grown up with: 'He is incapable of thinking objectively, he gets emotional.' We still cling to the deeply rooted belief in our culture that emotions interfere with reason and intelligibility, or to use R. S. Peters's telling phrase: 'Emotions are mists on our mental windscreen',[5] in spite of the wealth of recent work in philosophy

---

[4] M. Tanner, 'Understanding Music', *Aristotelian Society Supplementary Volume* 59 (1985), 219.

[5] R. S. Peters, 'Emotions and the Category of Passivity', *Proceedings of the Aristotelian Society*, 62 (1961–2), 119.

which shows that no such dichotomy or opposition makes sense. Is it not the case that a moving passage provokes us into finding out more about it, how it was achieved rather than vice versa? Just as when we feel an emotional reaction to another person which provokes questioning about why we feel this way and leads us to an understanding of what is going on, so the music provokes questioning about its emotional content responded to in our aesthetic experience which may lead to a deeper understanding of the work. Understanding here amounts to interpreting what it is that we are responding to in our aesthetic experience.

If, as is generally accepted, there are expressive conventions in music, through which expressive functions of music can be explained, then it follows logically that they are *devices* used to achieving the primary ends of expressiveness; they are means to a further end. We may speak of Bach's meticulous contrapuntal calculations or Wagner's carefully premeditated placement of leitmotifs; fascinating as these are, they are only a part of the story of interpretation. This version of aesthetic experience adapted to our intellectual preferences is not an acceptable substitute for the lived experience of music. It is time we rejected such antiseptic indulgences and continued with serious attempts to come to grips with what makes music so important for so many people.

How then should we tackle any alternative account? The most obvious way is by examining what is to count as an aesthetic experience of listening to music and just what is involved in this. Surely, its essence is to experience music in all its richness—to understand and interpret particulars as particulars and, in so doing, perhaps, to grasp them as universals. Mahler's music is the most brilliant example of this. We concentrate here on the acknowledgment of the *qualitative* richness of a true experience.

Lawrence Gilman, the well-known New York Philharmonic annotator, writes of the middle section of the first movement of Mahler's Fifth Symphony:

It is that passage in B flat minor in which the music, grown suddenly and passionately vehement, breaks upon the measured tread of the Funeral March like an uncontrollable outburst of shattering, maniacal, wild-visaged grief. . . . The plangent, tumultuous despair of this passage is like nothing else in music that one can recall. Tchaikowsky's is restrained . . . beside it. Mahler has here imagined an elemental and *universal* human condition with sensibility and with justice. The artist is in no need of personal verification of universal themes; but it is easy to believe that this music is an intimate declaration, a personal souvenir of exceptional authenticity.

Reading this passage makes one aware of the power and grandeur of Mahler's music, it brings his music alive for the reader, it makes him/her want to hear it for him/herself. To ignore the overwhelming emotional content of Mahler's music as something of no importance is to completely fail to understand it, completely to misinterpret it. A friend of Mahler's once asked him about the Sixth Symphony: 'How could a man, as kind-hearted as you, have written a symphony so full of bitterness?' Mahler replied: 'It is the sum of all the suffering I have been compelled to endure at the hands of life.' It is the universality of the human condition which Mahler's music so brilliantly conveys; that has brought him disciples all over the world. Audiences respond to his music with an astonishing degree of personal involvement.

Here then the talk is of content of music described in emotive terms. The understanding of and response to that content is what constitutes primary aesthetic experience; we are constantly engaged in interpreting what it is that has the power to affect us. The analysis of a work in terms of how the given content was achieved is, and has to be, logically secondary. Those who limit themselves to the pursuit of secondary features of music perform a valuable service but aestheticians have a much richer field of endeavour to occupy them—the music itself. While structures are related to explanation, emotional responses are related to the interpretation of the experience of music. The former play a role in explaining the latter, in part only.

In any attempts to elucidate the aesthetic experience of music we come up with the necessity of confronting and accounting for emotions. I cannot attempt to produce a general or comprehensive theory of music and the emotions here, that would require a book. I shall, therefore, take as read the widely accepted analysis of emotions in terms of their cognitive content, of their having objects, and of the objective judgements which are tied to our conceptual understanding of the appropriateness and inappropriateness of emotional responses to given objects of emotions. In other words, I start by accepting that emotions are rational except in cases where emotional reactions become over-emotional to the point of losing contact with situations which gave rise to them. I have discussed these issues in detail elsewhere.[6]

My enquiry is part analytic and part phenomenological. It is concerned with the experience of opening out to whatever the music will offer and responding to it in an appropriate manner. We need to ask what our experience involves, how it is to be interpreted, not how it is stage-managed. Music has its own phenomenal content which needs interpretation and explanation. Ideas and structures are objectively in the music and can be unambiguously and adequately specified. Emotional responses and explorations are subjective, and I include in this the recognition of a given emotion in the work, and as such they are said to be necessarily ambiguous, irrelevant, and somehow not in the work, in spite of the fact that there is a remarkable consensus in our emotive judgements. My main aim is to show that the subjective responses are not exclusive of objectivity and to draw attention to some important distinctions between various kinds of responses, some of which are legitimately aesthetic responses to what is objectively in the music and some of which are not legitimate in the relevant sense. The legitimacy of the response is entirely

---

[6] F. M. Berenson, *Understanding Persons* (London, 1980; 2nd edn. San Francisco, Calif., 1992).

dependent on the appropriateness of one's interpretation of what is there in the music.

The crux of the matter is the question: 'What does it mean to claim that music has the power to arouse emotions?' It has been accepted since Plato that music has such power; disagreements arise at the point where we try to offer explanations of what this arousal consists in, what is its importance, if any, for our aesthetic appreciation and whether or not this subject is a legitimate subject of aesthetic discourse.

I wish to concentrate on one particular aspect of this controversy—to focus on those theories which claim that emotions like grief, despair, etc., are not evoked by the music expressive of it because there is *no object* at which the grief or despair is aimed. The argument goes something like this: one of the necessary conditions for *x* to count as an emotion is that it is directed towards an object, in contrast with moods, feelings, and the like, which have no such necessary objects. (Hence the claim that music conveys moods rather than emotions.) Objects of emotions enable us to distinguish emotions one from another. It follows that the artistic medium of music, which can neither represent objects nor convey specific thoughts about them is conceptually debarred from expressing an emotion. It is the inability of music to describe and represent the world that makes talk of expression of emotions in music empty, empty because objectless.[7] Such arguments may apply if we were to claim, as many do, that the despair in the music makes me feel desperate. It is precisely these sorts of claims (what I call 'the contagion theory') which lead to vague and fuzzy theories of the emotional content of music. One alternative is to accept the view that music is essentially abstract. Just in what sense is it abstract? Obviously, in the sense, that it is not material. This leads us to the distinction between the material world and a world of experience or Husserl's *Lebenswelt*.

All art, including music, has been created in order to be experienced. As Sartre[8] says: 'There is no art except for and by others.' The creator of art experiences its creation at every point and so does the spectator or the audience. The objective world provides us with concepts that classify the world in terms of the appropriate action and the appropriate response. A rational person has need of such concepts because to understand the objective world involves, far from creating a separation between subject and object, understanding the world in terms of what it is like to experience it and to act within it. Thus the distinction between scientific, provable, unambiguously objective aesthetics of music and that which involves *Lebenswelt* is that the former confines itself to explanations of structures, etc., while the latter includes the nature of the world's experience by the subject; it consists of a certain experience of that thing. Our emotions, which are a part of that

[7] R. Scruton, *The Aesthetic Understanding* (London, 1983), 58.
[8] J.-P. Sartre, *What is Literature?*, trans. B. Frechtman (London, 1950), 29–30.

experience, are based on our perception and understanding of the world. Our emotions no more consist of mere sensations, internal disruptions, or blind, thoughtless, mindless indulgences than do our beliefs, intentions, desires, and purposes.

Now, if the despair in the music does not make me feel desperate and so on, then what is it that I experience? Whatever it is, I wish to make it as clear as possible that it cannot be a *transference* of the emotion in the music to the emotion in me. The emotions we feel while listening to music are radically transformed versions of the emotional quality of the music itself and hardly ever identical with it. That is one reason why the argument about objects of emotions has no force here. However we finally attempt to describe the listener's emotions in aesthetic experience it will not be in terms of some kind of transference by listening and passively receiving the given emotion. Aesthetic experience is not passive; it requires a response and a recognition, both of which are activities of interpretation.

The main source of confusion in this area stems from the fact that no one, to my knowledge, has attempted to stress the fact that the emotional content of music is received in several different ways and belongs to *different categories*. The main distinction is that between emotive explanations of music which refer to the music but based on my experience of it and response to it and those which refer exclusively to the self. This is a very important distinction and difficult to describe precisely but it is essential to the kind of objectivity which I am arguing for, objectivity which is applicable both to understanding music and to talking about it. We could, perhaps, first look at a seemingly similar distinction made by Roger Scruton[9] between meaning and association. He asks us to suppose that someone is asked to give an account of what *The Prelude* (Wordsworth) means to him. The distinction enters in terms of whether he is prepared to refer to *The Prelude* as descriptions of its meaning and those that refer only to himself, as *the particular reader he is*. Scruton writes that the first he offers as part of understanding the work, the second may be important in understanding *him*. A reader who is not prepared to make this distinction between meaning and association does not have a conception of the objective meaning of the work. Now, in as far as Scruton talks about points of reference in explanation, the distinction is a valid one but he overlooks the crux of the matter. His notion of 'the particular reader that he is', is inseparable from what he is able to understand about the work. He may or may not refer to his experience of it yet his personality is present implicitly in his interpretation and discussion of the work. That is precisely what enables us to say things like: 'His depth and sensitivity of understanding *The Prelude* opened my eyes to all the things I have missed.' The further important point here is that Scruton takes an odd view of 'association'. The two points are vital for what follows.

Personal involvement in a composition is not to be understood in terms of

---

[9] Scruton, *The Aesthetic Understanding*, 19.

having private mental events. Nobody would wish to deny that emotions are necessarily related to thoughts but they are not reducible to thoughts or words, they are a part of experience. Experience is always experience of a subject in relation to the object; its power stems not only from my relationship with the object but also from my feelings and emotions about it. There are two kinds of personal involvement at stake:

(a) responding to something which is within my experience;
(b) association with something specific in my past.

The latter is indeed arbitrary and irrelevant while the former kind of involvement enables us to recognize a kind of identity between our own life experiences and the work, which enhances the understanding and the depth with which we experience the work. Thus my first category embraces cases of complete involvement with the music, in the second category we use the music as a backcloth for extra-musical experiences. In the first category the reference to the self focuses on explaining how I came to understand some emotion in the music. Where emotions are concerned we need, unavoidably, reference to the self at every level of understanding of the work; it is a reference which is inextricably bound up with what is objectively in the music. It is the receiving and responding personally to what the music offers. That sort of reference is different in kind from reference to the self where the music is used merely as a means to some further end which can only be linked to some specific episode in my past which I then proceed to dwell on.

Each of my main categories has several subdivisions. Under the heading of *Reference to music* fall the following:

1. Characterization of the work as overwhelming, powerful, sad, happy, amusing, etc. This mainly consists of a statement of observed characteristics or of a translation of my reactions to the music, in general terms. In other words, it may be a report of an observation or a report of the sum of the feelings which I responded to. Statements describing music as powerful or sad are not very informative because they leave out of consideration what is of utmost importance in a given work—its uniqueness.

2. My experience of the music, my personal reactions, like learning something new, receiving a revelation to which I respond emotionally; my discovery that music can sound the way emotions feel.

3. My life experiences which enable me to hear and recognize specific emotions in the music.

Reference exclusively to the self concerns one's personal preferences, personal associations, and personal indulgences.

This list is by no means exhaustive, my aim is to give some indication of the complexities involved. For the remainder of this chapter I shall discuss mainly 2 and 3 of the first category as these are the most important. Broadly they involve our understanding of music through the emotional experience which the music provokes.

In listening to music we do not just perceive sounds or patterns for the

music has a power which is in the 'object' to invade our experience, provide
new experiences, and connect with our past experiences. Objectivity is assured
in that experiencing a work amounts to an inspired exploration, it is the art of
interrogating the music according to its wishes. That is, surely, the essence of
interpretation. Understanding music involves a relationship which is set up
between the listener and the music and this is akin to what is involved in
understanding a situation, as something complex is going on. It is never
simply a question of noting any feature or features of the music by observation. What experiences the music evokes is to a large extent dependent on
the particular experiences of the listener, although we are open to the music
itself, which has an objective existence, we are open to it by what Merleau-
Ponty calls 'intertwining', through what might be termed a creative process in
which both the listener and the object co-operate. In reflection we try to
objectify the process and can to some extent talk about it with constant
reference to the music, in objectively acceptable ways. I say 'to some extent'
because this will vary with different persons and relationships which are set
up. However personally involved one becomes, one's response has to be one
which the music does not reject but which is completely adapted to it. One's
work of interpretation has to be basically objective but it stems from our
personal possibilities.

R. K. Elliott[10] writes that personal knowledge of a work is an important
aspect of one's engagement with it, an engagement which has the character of
a relationship which is akin to friendship. The hearer does not clearly distinguish the work from the composer in so far as he is present in it as its
creator. A shared experience is a profoundly important part of the value of
music, just as it is in friendship. This may have little or nothing to do with the
historical person of the composer but he created things for the listener and
that is by no means the extravagant notion some claim it to be. Music
becomes an intimate friend, a confidante—'I know how it feels and I am with
you.' Music has essentially human characteristics. Elliott goes on to say that,
at the conscious level, even if the relationship is only with the work as such, it
is still like a relationship with a person because there is a reciprocity between
the listener and the work. Any limitation set upon aesthetic response devalues
some range of qualities which a work may have and depreciates some other
range of experience which may be greatly cherished by individuals. This is a
great price to pay for aesthetic judgements to be objective in the sense which
enables them to be assessed as right and wrong rather than in terms of
objectivity which judges interpretation to be appropriate and inappropriate to a
given work. Can one really appreciate works of art aesthetically with cool
detachment? Such a demand is an unjustifiable imposition which curtails
severely one's freedom and sincerity in what one may 'dare' to say about it.
One's freedom to experience music and learn what one can from it is neither

[10] R. K. Elliott, 'The Critic and the Lover of Art', in S. C. Brown and W. Mays (eds.),
Linguistic Analysis and Phenomenology (London, 1971), 117–27.

irrational nor is it inappropriate. Through our subjective involvement with the work our knowledge may be enriched in a way which only the experience of music can provide. Music conveys the feel of an emotion which is not reducible to mere words; it is not so much a matter of what one says but what one points to in the music and how one says it. The understanding comes in experience not merely in thought.

Finally, I wish to stress that the above is quite different from any kind of association of ideas or feelings. Let us take as a contrast the well-known example from Proust's *Remembrance of Things Past*,[11] the '*petites madeleines*' episode, which *is* a case of pure association, a recollection of a unique subjective childhood experience:

. . . in that moment all the flowers in our garden . . . and the water-lilies . . . and the good folk of the village . . . and the whole of Combray and of its surroundings taking their proper shapes and growing solid, sprang into being, . . . from my cup of tea.

The *madeleines* bring about recollections and memories which return with the taste, that particular past episode becomes the object of the narrator's emotions which he then proceeds to dwell on, whereas the understanding and the experiences we were discussing are concerned with new understanding, new discovery and a recognition of a familiar emotion which the music conveys in some unique way. Those are elements which form the necessary basis for our undestanding of anything at all, the progress from the known to the unknown. In pure association there is nothing new to be discovered, it is a calling forth of a specific past experience which we get emotionally involved with, forgetting the object which gave rise to it. It is for these reasons that I think that Scruton's dichotomy between meaning and association is mistaken; it does not differentiate between *personal* understanding which inevitably focuses on the music and association which focuses on a private episode in our past.

Just as we analyse musical structural forms in order to give objective explanations so do we analyse the emotional content in order to understand and offer objective explanations of our interpretations. We interrogate the music according to its wishes. The point of difference is that in the latter the procedure has to be dialectical; we cannot demand direct proof or anything like it in this context. Anyone can learn to analyse music in the scientific way. The understanding, explanation, and interpretation of the emotional content of music requires much more subtle learning. As Wittgenstein writes (in a similar context):

Can one learn this knowledge? Yes; some can. Not, however, by taking a course in it, but through '*experience*'.—Can someone else be a man's teacher in this? Certainly. From time to time he gives him the right *tip*.—This is what 'learning' and 'teaching' are like here. . . . There are *also rules*, but they do not form a system, and only experienced people can apply them right. Unlike calculating-rules.[12]

[11] M. Proust, *Swann's Way*, trans. C. K. Scott-Moncrieff (Harmondsworth, 1971), i. 62.
[12] L. Wittgenstein, *Philosophical Investigations*, trans. G. E. M. Anscombe (Oxford, 1963), 227e.

I have concentrated throughout on the acknowledgment of the qualitative richness of a true emotional experience of music and on ways in which we can talk about its unique character. The insistence on reducing talk of music to a scientific vocabulary has no power here. Just like the qualities of a loved one cannot be substituted for another so one piece of music and the way it conveys an emotion cannot be substituted by another. The emotional content of music has to do with qualities of the feel of an emotion to which we respond emotionally in some manner and which can only be explained in reference to the relevant passages in the music itself, never in terms of some identity of a transferred emotion. The feel of an emotion does not require an object, hence arguments about the inability of music to express emotions, because of their not fulfilling the necessary condition of having objects, just will not do here.

The musically uneducated often respond to bad music but the response is sincere. The intellectuals or the purists are deficient not in what they judge to be good music but in *how* they respond to it; they are incapable of feeling the intimacy. As a result, their ability to interpret the music in all its richness, in its depths, remains forever out of bounds to them.

II

Rightness and Reasons in Musical Interpretation

MICHAEL KRAUSZ

I

In this chapter I shall argue that works of music characteristically admit of a multiplicity of ideally admissible interpretations and that he who requires that there must be a single right interpretation of musical scores as classically construed will do violence to musical interpretative practice.

No work of music can be understood as such, nor can it be evaluated as one of its kind, independently of the practices in which it is found and fostered. Such practices shape the idea of a work of music as a kind of cultural entity, and they provide the terms in which works of music can be made intelligible and appreciated. Indeed, in order to formulate the category of works of music, we need to fix upon good cases, and fixing upon good cases depends upon considerations of historically variable practices.

Such contextualism is made apparent when considering musical performances based upon written scores. Now, a musical score is a notation of instructions for performances, but it is characteristically incomplete in that it cannot fully specify all pertinent aspects of an interpretation. This incompleteness is a feature of the presently entrenched genre of musical interpretation.

We should note that while there are differences between interpretations and performances, they do not bear on the general argument developed here. Still, we may observe that different performances may be of a given interpretation. In general, scores underdetermine interpretations and interpretations underdetermine performances.[1] Interpretations are more complete than scores, and performances are more complete than interpretations. For example, one may speak of interpretation as bearing upon a musician's conception of a work as opposed to an actual performance of it. So, the difference between, say,

---

[1] I have in mind typical cases of Western notated music. The point is complicated in jazz improvisation. It is also complicated where a composer intentionally specifies instructions which cannot be performed, or where a faithful performance cannot be heard. For example, the second movement of Charles Ives's Symphony No. 4 contains scored tunes which, given other simultaneous elements, cannot be heard in a performance. And, in his 'No. 53, In the Alley' (part of his '114 Songs') Ives instructs the pianist to turn the page of a newspaper with his right hand while playing the piano. This instruction appears to have nothing to do with how the hearer should hear the piece. (I am indebted to Jon Newsom for these examples.)

Nathan Milstein's and David Oistrakh's interpretations of Bach's Partita No. 1 concerns their conceptions of the work and does not depend upon their actually performing it. Further, either may perform his interpretation more than once. Whatever idiosyncracies there might be between different actual performances, if conceptions of the work are appreciably unchanged, they may perform the same interpretation on different occasions. Put still otherwise, numerous performances may embody a single interpretation. Yet there is a close connection between one's interpretation of a work and a performance of it. For example, the timbre or volume of an instrument's actual tone may bear upon the interpretation of the work, and vice versa. The actual instruments used or the hall in which they are played may prompt adjustments that bear directly upon one's interpretation. This is especially true of ensemble playing where performance adjustments inevitably give rise to interpretation adjustments. For example, on 27 April 1986 the Philadelphia Chamber Orchestra performed Mozart's Sinfonia Concertante under guest conductor Lawrence Leighton-Smith. In rehearsal with violin soloist David Arben and viola soloist Michael Tree, it became apparent that the natural volume of Tree's viola was too great in relation to the natural volume of Arben's violin. The solution to this balance problem was found in physically repositioning Tree so that the F holes of his instrument were turned further away from the audience. Exactly where he was repositioned was a matter of judgement concerning the interpretation of the work. It might appear that this is a case in which the interpretation affects the performance. This is so to a large but limited degree, for the precise level of volume finally established as acceptable was as much a function of the natural volume of the instruments as of interpretative considerations. In this way, interpretation practice is symbiotically related to performance practice. But, again, this distinction between interpretation and performance will not bear directly upon the major line of the argument advanced here. Let us return, then, to the question of the relation between scores and interpretations.

One might argue that the incompleteness of scores in relation to interpretations is a contingent matter, that given sufficient subtlety of notation and completeness of description one could, in principle, specify all pertinent aspects of the interpretation. Just as one could, in principle, provide a complete physical description of the molecules of pigment on a canvas, the argument might go, so one could give a complete physical description of the sound patterns and frequencies of an interpretation in a fully specified chamber. This description would presumably include all physical aspects of the sound-producing instruments as well as all aspects of the sound-producing persons, and so on. Then, according to the proposal, if one took this complete description as a set of instructions for a future interpretation, one would have a 'complete' score. This complete score would mandate what the single ideally admissible interpretation would contain. (I have, of course, been speaking of interpretation in its performance sense, and not in its critical sense.[2])

Now, on such a 'complete score' construal, all in-principle specifiable aspects of the interpretation would be defining of the work. So, for any two interpretations, if there were any discrepancies between them, at least one could not be of the given work of music. And further, since not all fully specified aspects of the completed score could be reproducible, we could not even have two interpretations of the same work. Given this 'complete score' construal, Milstein's and Oistrakh's interpretations could not be both of the same work; nor, for that matter, could either of their interpretations on two different occasions be of the same work.

Further, a typical score may comply with a range of interpretation practices. Specifically, on stringed instruments, the multiplicity of interpretation practices may arise in the face of unspecified bowings, fingerings, positionings, phrasings, or the like. When executing a three-note figure, violinists who favour the Paganini Stroke play one downbow and two upbows. When executing a four-note figure, those who favour the Viotti Stroke play two downbows and two upbows, and so on. But these strokes are by no means mandated by most scores, and appropriate passages may be admissibly performed otherwise.

Also, while fingerings and bowings may be indicated, precise finger locations and precise stresses within slurs cannot be. While positions may be indicated, the manner of sliding into and out of particular positions cannot be. While broad indications of vibrato speed may be indicated, precise speeds of vibrato cannot be. This is also true of the position of the bow on a string, and with what pressure it should be applied. While a general pitch is notatable, the precise pitch is not, as for example where C sharp is played slightly (but not indicated by how much) higher than D flat. Such non-notatability holds as well for balance and pacing. Pauses and fermatas admit of variation. Accents and stresses may be broadly notated, but not with full precision. There is no precise volume to 'forte' or 'piano'. Phrasing, the grouping of musical elements into coherent wholes, is not fully notatable. And tempo is not the simple beating of time but the phenomenal experience of time. A performance whose elements are distinct and crisp will seem faster than one whose elements are less distinct and crisp—despite the latter taking the same or less time than the former. In this respect it is interesting to note that Beecham's

---

[2] Following Jerrold Levinson, I shall assume the distinction between performance interpretations and critical interpretations, the latter—with which critics are characteristically concerned—being philosophically distinct from the former. See Levinson's 'Performative vs. Critical Interpretation in Music', elsewhere in this volume.

Wagner actually took longer than Richter's.[3] As Riccardo Muti has said, 'Tempo is not a number.'[4]

That these things are not fully notatable, however, does not mean that they are not learnable, perhaps through apprenticeship. Indeed, most of what violin pedagogue Josef Gingold teaches master students is non-notatable, such as the length of bow to be used, the rendering of gracenotes, the execution of certain fingerings, the sliding into certain positions, the execution of accelerandos, marcattos, staccatos, rubatos, and the like. At another level Gingold instils general musical approaches or attitudes, such as when he exhorts students to 'live with' the instrument; to play 'what the music demands'; to 'make something' of the music; to 'play the unobvious'; to be mindful of the construction of the piece as a whole; not to be 'taken away by the beauty of the sound'; to 'avoid doing too much'; to 'cry at every shift'; to play 'in a modulated rather than a mechanical way'; to play 'with taste'; to 'not keep it in'; etc.[5]

Perhaps the complete score construal is appropriate in computer music performance, where the computer program is the score and the performance is what the computer audibly produces as a mechanical function of the program. But such is not an interpretation as classically construed. Yet it might be urged still that even here the score is incomplete, for the music will sound quite differently in different rooms, depending whether they are empty or full of people or furniture, whether the sound-making devices are affected by humidity, elevation, or the like.

Now, if (as is urged here) we do not accept the consequences of the idea of a complete score for an interpretation as classically construed, then we must allow that there is a certain latitude between a characteristically incomplete score and an interpretation of it. While a score underdetermines an interpretation of it, a score indicates the 'essentialities' of the work which an interpretation must—within limits—embody if it is to be an interpretation of that work. On the rejected 'complete' score construal, all in-principle specifiable aspects of the interpretation would be defining of the work.

Some interpretation practices may involve violating what is mandated by the score. For example, according to a literalist reading of waltzes, each of the three-beat figures are to be equally spaced. But according to the so-called 'Viennese style', the second beat is to be played slightly before its notated time, thus leaving an extra gap between the second and third beats. It is noteworthy, therefore, that Johann Strauss performed his own waltzes in the Viennese style (perhaps assuming others would too), having himself composed the waltzes without special indication to do so. Here one might hold

[3] Brian Magee, *Aspects of Wagner* (London, 1968), 92–4.
[4] Riccardo Muti, in conversation with the author, Mar. 1987.
[5] Josef Gingold in a master class at the Curtis Institute of Music, 7 Nov. 1986, and in violin lessons of the author in years past.

Ex. 1 Beethoven, Symphony No. 1, first movement

that no conflict need result, since Strauss's interpretation practice might simply be assumed, if not notated.

But consider another sort of case of interpretation practice where the performer is supposed to violate the score, and it is almost universally agreed that doing so is favoured for good reasons. The first movement of Beethoven's Symphony No. 1 opens with an introductory Adagio of twelve bars. There follows the Allegro con brio which constitutes the rest of the movement. Now, the upbeat to the Allegro con brio (a descending scale from G to D)—printed still in the Adagio tempo—resolves itself on the tonic C, which is the first note of the Allegro con brio. The G to C descending figure is repeated and varied often within the Allegro con brio. So, for the sake of aesthetic consistency the upbeat to the Allegro is almost always performed as if the Allegro actually begins with the upbeat rather than with the downbeat as notated. Sergiu Comissiona and Christopher Hogwood are among a very few number of conductors who actually perform the Allegro con brio as literally indicated in the score. No one suggests that Beethoven did not mean to notate the score as he did, or that there has been an editorial error, or anything of the kind. Yet most conductors hold the view expressed by Riccardo Muti that it is a 'mistake' to perform the work as written.[6]

Good reasons can be given for performing the passage either way, that is, according to the principle of faithfulness to the score, or according to the principle of aesthetic consistency. Despite the fact that the overwhelming tendency is to favour the principle of aesthetic consistency, neither is conclusively right. Even if Muti is right to say that it is a 'mistake' to interpret the upbeat as printed because doing so violates aesthetic consistency, it cannot be

---

[6] Riccardo Muti, in conversation with the author, Mar. 1987, and in an interview conducted by the author at the American Society for Aesthetics, Eastern Division, Philadelphia, 21 Apr. 1989.

simply wrong to do so. Here there is no meta-standard in virtue of which literalism or aesthetic consistency can be conclusively ranked. Conceding that interpreting the upbeat in the Allegro tempo is better than interpreting it in the Adagio tempo is not to discount the literalist reading as ideally inadmissible.

The general point, then, is that the difference between what is notated and what is admissibly interpreted is 'the score in the context of interpretation practices'. Here extra-score considerations enter which are required for an adequate interpretation of the work. In this way, as an entrenched classical genre, scores as such are in the relevant sense incomplete.

Now, given that extra-score interpretation practices vary historically, and given that there may be no univocal or uncontentious overarching standards in virtue of which one may conclusively adjudicate between interpretation practices, it follows that for pertinent cases there can be no singular ideally admissible interpretation. To insist that the range of ideally admissible interpretations must in all cases be singular is to violate an entrenched feature of classical scores, namely their incompleteness in relation to a multiplicity of admissible interpretation practices. Since the ideally admissible interpretation is not fully notatable in the characteristically incomplete score, and since extra-score considerations are needed for the completing interpretation, we must allow that there can be more than one ideally admissible interpretation of a given work, one whose 'score in the context of interpretation practices' may vary. Thus, it is a mistake to assume that there must be a singular ideally admissible interpretation.

We may dub the rejected 'one right interpretation' view as 'singularist' and the embraced 'more than one right interpretation' view as 'multiplist'. Let us then consider more fully the singularist and multiplist ideals. The singularist holds that the range of ideally admissible interpretations should be singular, that the range of contending interpretations should be conclusively narrowed to a limit of one. He or she construes rightness in an exclusivist way, and takes the rightness of a given interpretation to be logically incompatible with the rightness of alternative interpretations. He or she requires that the single right interpretation should conclusively unseat alternative interpretations. The singularist holds that this condition is inherently more rational in that the most satisfactory result of informed considerations about competing interpretations is one in which there is full convergence or consensus according to a single set of agreed-upon standards. Even if there seems to be no reasonable expectation that the singularist's ideal could obtain in real-time terms, he or she contends that one should still hold out the singularist conditions as an ideal.

In contrast, multiplism holds that singularist conditions may obtain in some but not all cases. The multiplist holds that nothing mandates that an interpretation must answer to a singularist ideal. Rather, such ideals are shaped by historically variable circumstances. The multiplist allows that the range of ideally admissible interpretations may be multiple, that the range of competing interpretations need not be conclusively narrowed to a limit of one. The multiplist does not construe rightness in an exclusivist way. While he or she allows that ideally there may be tension between competing interpretations, it should, on the other hand, be logically weaker than contradiction or exclusivity.[7] The multiplist further allows for non-conclusive grounds for comparing and rationally preferring contending interpretations. The multiplist holds that the standards appropriate for the evaluation of one interpretation might not be fully commensurable with the standards appropriate for the evaluation of another. And importing some overarching standard *in order to* conclusively eliminate all contenders but one might violate the nature of the practice in question. Here evaluative demands should not be strengthened. Further, the multiplist holds that this condition reflects no defect. Rather, it is characteristic of an enduring feature of interpretative practice. Multiplism is no second-best ideal. Correspondingly, the grounds one might give for preferring one interpretation over another should not be question-beggingly defined in terms of singularism.

A singularist might counter that the single right interpretation is always to be found in the intentions of the composer. But this is problematic. A composer may be self-deceived as regards his or her own work. For example, Alberto Ginastera's 'Concerto per Corde' contains a lengthy and exceedingly difficult solo passage of some two full pages for the concertmaster. Given pressures of rehearsal time while on tour (on his own account) former Philadelphia Orchestra Concertmaster Anshel Brusilow virtually improvised the entire passage with only the remotest relationship to the score.[8] By coincidence, Ginastera was present at the performance in Mexico City. After the concert, Ginastera eagerly sought out Brusilow to embrace him and to exclaim with delight, 'I never imagined that my work could sound like *that*!'

Further, works are emergent in the sense that their finished character often embodies properties that are unanticipated. A work may embody features that the creator never intended. This means that, at least with respect to pertinent emergent properties, the creator carries no special status as one to assign salience or significance or meaning. So, the intentions of a given composer need not locate or exhaust ideally admissible interpretations of a work. For these sorts of reasons, the original intentions of a creator need not fulfil the singularist's requirement.

In light of these sorts of considerations, a singularist might propose that one should then *postulate* a composer—perhaps not to coincide with the historical

---

[7] See Göran Hermerén, 'The Full Voic'd Quire: Types of Interpretations of Music', elsewhere in this volume.

[8] Anshel Brusilow, in conversation with the author, 12 Apr. 1987.

composer—in relation to which ideally admissible interpretations should be determined.[9] The postulated composer would be an idealized creator whose counterfactual 'gaze' would be constructed based upon the work as received in the context of appropriately designated interpretative practices. He or she would be a rational reconstruction of a creator whose postulated intentions could conclusively adjudicate between competing interpretations. But consider what would be involved in postulating such a composer. What one might *take* as salient or significant in the background information on the basis of which to postulate a composer (that is, the work and its surrounding interpretative practices) is already multiply interpretable. Such background information is characteristically such that no one composer can be plausibly postulated.

Now, a singularist might suggest that we should imagine a conversation with a postulated composer in which we engage him or her about a contested interpretation. We might ask a postulated Beethoven, for example, whether Muti's interpretation of the passage considered above is admissible or not, whether Muti's interpretation and Comissiona's interpretations are both admissible, or, if both admissible, whether they are equally desirable or preferable.

The singularist might suggest that we could be justified in overriding the score only on the condition that a postulated Beethoven could be convinced that the alteration was an improvement, given Beethoven's overall intentions. Without that we would not be justified in departing from the received score. That is, the changes would be justifiable of the condition that a Beethoven who reflected upon the options would have endorsed them. Without that the revised interpretation could no longer present itself as an interpretation of Beethoven's symphony. According to such a view, we need the imprimatur of the composer in order to preserve a claim to validity.[10]

But, first, it is unclear why such an exercise should issue in one rather than a number of postulated Beethovens. And, on its own account, the postulation advocate must concede that the historical Beethoven is impotent to settle the matter. So, if not one postulation, why not several? Correspondingly, it is altogether unclear why any of the plausible postulations should be put in Beethoven's historical name. Should we not say, rather, that given what we do know about the historical Beethoven—limited as it must be—we, as unhurried interpreters, think it better to interpret the work this way rather than that? Ours is a present postulation, and other postulations may be plausibly offered at other times under perhaps different circumstances. Those postulations may take different, perhaps incongruent, forms. Since a number of interpretations may be issued from a number of reasonably postulated Beethovens, it will not help to identify one single interpretation as the single valid Beethoven interpretation.

[9] See Alexander Nehamas, 'The Postulated Author: Critical Monism as a Regulative Ideal', *Critical Inquiry* 8, No. 1 (Autumn, 1981), 133–49.

[10] I am grateful to Jerrold Levinson for suggestions in this regard.

This does not mean that all changes that produce aesthetic improvements could be the basis for valid interpretation. While one might be tempted to 'improve' upon a score, if such improvement is not in the name of the composer at all—that is, if no plausible story can be told in which the postulation takes no account of the composer's project as we do know it—it is indeed no longer an improvement on his or her score. But, again, this does not mean that there is a single right interpretation *within* the range that is attributable to a reasonably postulated composer, one who has a plausible relation to the historical composer. In sum, to disallow the historical composer as the final arbiter of ideal admissibility, and to recognize that the postulated composer may be multiple, does not accede to the view that any postulation will do, nor that any interpretation will do.

A singularist might rejoin by conceding that scores in the context of interpretative practices may underdetermine interpretations. But it does not follow from this that there can be no singularly ideal interpretation. For such a concession does not rule out the possibility that with a sufficiently full accounting of competing interpretative practices—and with more—it will become clear that finally there can be only one ideally admissible interpretation. That is, a sufficiently full accounting of the 'score in the context of interpretive practice *and more*' will show that the range of ideally admissible interpretations is singular. Put otherwise, conceding the multiplicity of interpretative practices, one might appeal to yet further conditions to ensure that there always is a single right interpretation. Such an argument might proceed along the lines suggested by pianist and music theorist Charles Rosen. It holds that the singularly ideal interpretation is to be found above and beyond composers' intentions and interpretative practices. It holds that the singularly ideal interpretation is *found* via faithfulness to the score in conjunction with informed interpretative practices, and something that is quite illusive but altogether critical for an authentic interpretation, namely a sense of rightness in execution. On this view, the singular ideal interpretation is an emergent product of the score, of reconstructable composer's intentions, of interpretative practices, of a musical sense or the like, each adjusted in light of the other as the interpretation emerges. One 'finds' the right interpretation by adjusting such considerations taken jointly.[11]

But here one faces the question on what basis one can adjust such considerations in a singularly right way. While one's emergent interpretation might seem to a performer to be necessitated given his weighing pertinent considerations, there seems no reason why one could not plausibly weigh those considerations in a different way, such that they would in turn issue in another interpretation that would also have the appearance of necessity.

[11] This view is reconstructed on the basis of numerous exchanges with Charles Rosen in May 1988. Rosen himself does not embrace this argument, however. See his 'The Shock of the New', New York Review of Books, 19 July 1990: 46, 48.

Under these conditions it would still seem that more than one interpretation could appear to be 'necessitated'. There is nothing in this emergentist view that mandates that there is a single overarching standard in virtue of which a multiplicity of postulated composers is ruled out.

II

Let us now consider further refinements in the multiplist's programme. First, the distinction between admissible and inadmissible interpretations may be sharp or gradual. For example, where one holds that admissible interpretations require strict adherence to all instructions of a score, the distinction between admissible and inadmissible is sharp. But where one holds that the score may be arguably overridden for good reasons, then the distinction between admissible and inadmissible interpretations becomes as gradual as the nature of pertinent reasons will allow. Put otherwise, one could, but need not, take strict adherence to the score as a criterion for separating admissible from inadmissible interpretations. If one does so, though, one should not take such adherence as the grounds for rationally preferring one admissible interpretation over another admissible interpretation. Such judgements would need to be grounded in other sorts of considerations, such as musicianship or the like. In any event, as already indicated, we should not commit the multiplist to the view that, specifically, strict adherence to the score should separate admissible from inadmissible interpretations. The particular grounds for doing so remain open and contestable. Correspondingly, Riccardo Muti's remark that sometimes it is a mistake to interpret a work of music as strictly notated could mean either that an interpretation which strictly adheres to the score is inadmissible, or that it might be admissible but is not rationally preferable. I take Muti to be affirming the latter view.

Second, for the singularist, grounds for rational preference just are the grounds that separate admissible from inadmissible interpretations. Accordingly, he or she would understand Muti's remark as suggesting that whatever grounds separate admissible from inadmissible interpretations, they do not include strict adherence to the score. Yet there are other grounds that do. Here the putative 'mistake' would be judging as admissible an interpretation which strictly adheres to the score.

On the other hand, the multiplist would hold that the grounds for separating admissible from inadmissible interpretations cannot be the same as the grounds for preferability between admissible interpretations. He or she would understand Muti's remark as suggesting either that strict non-adherence to the score is necessary for the interpretation to be admissible, and further that the preferability of remaining admissible interpretations would have to be assessed along other lines; or that Muti is not addressing himself to the criterion for separating admissible from inadmissible interpretations at all; he is not laying down that either strict adherence or non-adherence to the score is a necessary condition for admissibility. Rather, as a ground for rational preferability, Muti would be disvaluing strict adherence to the score. Either way, it would be most implausible to think that Muti would hold that those interpretations which strictly adhere to the score are on that account in-admissible. The general point is that, for the multiplist the grounds for admissibility should not be the same as those that distinguish between preferred admissible interpretations.

Third, I have suggested that, while what is specified in a score may be sufficient—but perhaps not fully necessary—for the identification of a work, it is not sufficient for an interpretation of it. Extra-score practices are required for the completing interpretation. Since these practices may vary, and no one of them can be established as the singularly right one, the view that there is a singularly right interpretation must yield to the view that there may be a multiplicity of ideally admissible interpretations of a given work.

Now, along multiplist lines, an interpreter might allow that both his and yet another's incongruent interpretation might each be allowable as ideally admissible, and still for good reasons prefer his interpretation. He could allow that the alternative interpreter might have standards independent of his own standards that would license such a judgement. And there might be available no further overarching meta-standards in virtue of which these standards could be conclusively ranked.

Yet one might urge further that this would not do to capture the idea of an interpretation's 'fidelity' to a work of music. That is, without some account of works of music which is fully independent of interpretations, one could not hold that an interpretation was or was not 'faithful' to the work. The work, according to this argument, should be the touchstone for admissibility. But the admissibility of interpretations *is* constrained by such sufficiently deter-minate limits as the score in the context of interpretation practices, and no more is required. It is not required that there be a work as such that is fully autonomous of interpretation, if that is a coherent thought at all.

Fourth, multiplism holds that competing interpretations may be simul-taneously admissible and that the standards pertinent to each are incommen-surable. Conceding that competing interpretations may be multiply admissible does not rule out that there may be good reasons for preferring any one of the interpretations in question. Without a commensurating standard between competing interpretations it does not follow that there is no room for critical comparison. Incommensurability does not entail arbitrariness.

That competing interpretations may incongruously coexist in the absence of commensurating standards should not be taken as an imperfection, or the result of critical consideration cut short, or anything of the sort. In pertinent cases this should be taken as fulfilling an ideal condition. Such incommen-surability, resulting in *inconclusivity*, arises from no epistemic lack. It is not the case that in the long run, with more information, a singularist condition must obtain. Such is the case in the Beethoven example. There the standards of 'faithfulness to the score' and 'aesthetic consistency' are incongruent, and there is no available overarching standard which could conclusively rank those standards in turn. Yet, proponents of each interpretation may urge the appropriateness of their interpretation. Each may provide good, though inconclusive, reasons for their interpretation. With respect to each standard, in turn, one interpretation may be thought to be preferable over the other.

Fifth, highly personalized interpretations, such as those of conductors Wilhelm Mengelberg or Leopold Stokowski, might prompt the singularist to pursue a 'pluralizing' strategy to reinstate a singularist condition. The singularist might argue along the following lines: concede the multiplicity of interpretative practices, but bifurcate the object of interpretation. That is, construe each admissible interpretation as ideal *for a given occasion*. The interpretative practices then in place would mandate one and only one ideally admissible interpretation. That other practices on other occasions mandate other singular ideal interpretations would be allowable too. Put otherwise, a full description of the interpretative practices on a given occasion would mandate the singularly right interpretation for that occasion. On another occasion another full description of interpretative practices would mandate another singularly right interpretation. But it would not be allowed that these interpretations on different occasions would be interpretations of the same work of music.

As a general strategy this manœuvre will not go through, since the very idea of a range of ideally admissible interpretations—whether singularist or multiplist—is predicated on 'practice' construed as a social rather than individual phenomenon. Being a function of a practice, the range of ideally admissible interpretations is socially constituted over historical time. A practice is consensually sanctioned by appropriate practitioners. A practice is not comprised of any particular persons at an instant. And while there must always be a collection of persons in a social group, the rules, guide-lines, and values of a practice are not embodied in any one or number of particular individuals in the group. So, there can be no such thing as a single-person, single-occasion practice. This is an important constraint on singularists who seek to dismantle putatively multiplist cases by distributing admissible interpretations over bifurcated works of music. So seen, the idea of a single-person, single-occasion practice would be an oxymoron; it undercuts the essentially social and historical character of practices as such.

III

In sum, an ideally admissible interpretation is not fully notatable in a characteristically incomplete score. Extra-score considerations are required for the completing interpretation. While what is specified in a score is not sufficient for an interpretation of it, what is specified in a score may be sufficient—but perhaps not fully necessary—for the identification of the work of music. So, if there is a multiplicity of ideally admissible interpretative practices, it is a mistake to assume that there must be a single ideally admissible interpretation. There is a certain latitude between what is interpreted and what is notated as instruction in a score. The difference between what is interpreted and what is notated is 'the score in the context of its interpretation practices'. Within this latitude is the room for interpretation. Here extra-score considerations enter which are required for an admissible interpretation of the work. In this way, as an entrenched classical genre, scores as such are in the relevant sense incomplete. Now, where extra-score interpretative practices vary historically, and where there are no univocal and overarching standards in virtue of which a number of competing interpretation practices may be conclusively ranked, there can be no singularly ideal interpretation. To insist that the range of ideally admissible interpretations must always be singular is to violate an entrenched feature of classical interpretations, namely the incompleteness of scores in relation to the multiplicity of interpretation practices.

Musical Standards as Function of Musical Accomplishment

JAMES ROSS

1. Introduction

Typically, human practices that are aimed at excellence[1] have regulations, principles, procedures, customs, rules, and other routines for 'how to do it'—some with very great force and others that belong to beginners or intermediate stages but give way in maturity—that, with other factors, make a framework against which competence and excellence can be discerned. Thus, fingering, bowing, intonation, metre, rhythm, accent, breathing, phrasing, drive, intensity, stance, and indeterminately many other physical conditions with which musicians deliberately, or with practised elections, make perceptually discriminable features of the sound, are elements of objective competence and of measurable objective excellence. Excellence is understood here as competence developed to certainty, ease, sensitivity, and musicality.[2]

I explain somewhat how the making of music gives rise to the standards by which it is judged in four steps. First, for music, the basic elements both performers and composers work with, as well as the final products to be judged, are made by musical art. The elements and the works are ontologically musical creations. They have their being, as well as their identities, from musical practice. Therefore, although performative and compositional excellence are objective, interpersonally assessable, and perceptually accessible, the basis for justification and appraisal has to be vantaged within the historical (and hermeneutical) circle of refined composition/refined performance that is the development of the art itself. That is because excellence is a kind of fulfilment of potentiality, and the potentiality, to be fulfilled (at any stage) in music, what 'can be done', is dependent causally upon what *is* done already, musically, with elements whose very being is a product of the art.

Music supervenes on sound; its elements are musical entities; themes, notes, inversions, cadences, triplets, variations, sonatas, songs, even ragas—the very things that a dog, who can hear every sound, cannot hear at all. What

---

[1] Excellence provides a pleasure of its own, dependent on fulfilment of one's will in one's making (say a composition, a theme, a performance, or an Olympic dive), with a further enjoyment from the ease, and from the appetite for the doing.
[2] Excellence, qualified, as above stated, is perhaps limited, in an individual, to one instrument, to one period, or otherwise.

'can be done' gets its content from what 'has been done' that has survived
critical scrutiny of the ways 'things are to be done', not only at the broad scale
or 'how Bach is to be read' but at the particular level of how breathing is to
be done in oboe playing of a Mahler song. Even though the medium of
expression is sound and the normal medium of comprehension is hearing,[3]
the compositional elements, especially harmonically and polyphonically, are
musical elements, not just sounds. Yet the relevant experiential content, both
perceptually and emotionally, for warranted judgements on such matters, is
musical; it is unattainable without participation (as composer, performer, or
trained hearer) in the art or craft to be judged.

The second main element, in section 2 below, is that the development of
conditions of excellence is *successive* in the quite definite sense that what 'has'
to be done, in the way of phrasing, articulation, fingering, breathing, tempo,
bowing, melodic drive, and every other particular of playing, is dependent
upon the critical reflection and critical success, among performers and
composers, of what 'has' been done (e.g. the lifting of a bow at the end of a
bar to attack the first note of the next, with a resultant 'cheating' of how long
the final note was sounded).

Thirdly, to the great extent that *possibility*, both physically and perceptually,
depends upon prior actuality and upon discriminations previously achieved
(for instance, as to pitch constancy, tempos and regularity of beats, up-bowing
vs. down-bowing, or the permissibility of transposition into keys with different
'personalities', and as to what counts as unison of tone or legato or vivace, or
attack 'together', or unified phrasing or dynamic change), one can judge
musical innovation, both in composing and performing, only from within the
musical 'world', from within the actualities of music itself. 'What can be done
next' depends upon the practicality of bridging to it from what is being done,
as the dynamic problems in Babbitt's *Transfigured Notes* will illustrate nega-
tively (see below), and the appropriation of the Stravinsky *Rite of Spring*
from only the most skilled orchestras to fine performances by good college
orchestras[4] illustrates positively.

Fourthly, I have adapted a general line of argument I call 'Wittgensteinian',
to undermine general scepticism and mere relativism, based on our 'failure'
to provide an independent 'justification' for our cognitive and evaluative
practices about music. I also argue that global scepticism (about science, law,
music, or religion) is self-refuting because it supposes access to the content of

---

[3] There is a distinction between the medium of expression and that of comprehension, as well
as between the elements of composition and performance, because properly scored music can be
understood through reading as well as hearing (and need not involve imaginary hearing), and
composition can be done with musical elements and without one's either playing or imagining the
sounds.

[4] It does take a skilled conductor. I heard a controlled but moving performance by the
Princeton University Orchestra a few years ago. Fifty years ago the student players would have
been unable to read the score, much less produce the sounds properly.

what might have been, that would be unavailable if we did not know what is actually so.

My overall line of argument applies to any of what I call 'the craft-bound human excellences', even excellences with practical outcomes, like cabinet-making, architecture, or surgery, provided (*a*) new possibility is the outcome of accomplishment, (*b*) human capacity, physical capacity, has to reach new levels of agility and ease in order to meet the demands arising from prior accomplishments, and (*c*) the novice/apprentice/journeyman/master/ structure of initiation is required. Moreover, I concentrate here on the craft-bound excellences that produce the very elements and objects that are appraised, objects which are not tools or techniques for another craft, and thus present ontological barriers to 'externalists'.

My thinking, as applied to the *whole* of 'how-to-act lore', is expressed in Aristotle's *Nicomachean Ethics* where *what* is humanly excellent, while in broad outline determined by the nature of humans and by what they are 'for', in detail and in particular develops by our refining our reactions by mimesis of good men.[5] A mimetic paradigm displays both what it is we are to do, and how to do it, and does so, attractively enough, so that we want to do likewise, for an activity that can only by learned successfully by 'doing the same thing', the way we learn to talk and to reason. Just as in a life of virtue you know it is 'going right' from the special enjoyment of 'doing it right' (that you learn by mimesis), so music too has a rightness perceptible only to those who are doing it right. In music, 'what doing it right' is develops in content more rapidly, it seems, than does the content of moral virtue.

2. The Progression of Excellence

The *practice* of a craft objectively determines its conditions of excellence. There is no access to the 'right' way of playing arpeggios or chromatic fourths, or lip position for trumpet or trombone, apart from the ways that have survived criticism and been incorporated into 'how to do it' and draw admiration from those who understand. Most basically that is, as I said, because everything from singing a tune to playing triplets, scales, viola intonations and bowing, rhythm, and phrasing, is made to be by musical art itself. Secondly, 'better than' is comparative *among* such products of the art. Natural rhythms of waves and natural melodies of birds and scales the wind plays through cracks, and natural rumbling and roaring and humming, and all

[5] In 1989 John McDowell read a paper on Aristotle's Ethics at the University of Pennsylvania that I took to imply that for Aristotle there is no knowing what the life of virtue leading to happiness consists of, in its particulars, from outside the community of good persons leading such lives. Perhaps McDowell was, in fact, making that point about Aristotle. I confidently think that is why Aristotle emphasized *mimesis* as the sure path to goodness. Moreover, in what follows, mimesis is the key into the hermeneutical circle of musical ontology and appraisal.

the animal cries, are just 'there', none, as music, any better than any other, even *understood* by us as musical. But music, as I mentioned, in all of its features, is exactly what a dog cannot hear, though it hears all the sounds with acuity far surpassing our own. Music is a reality detectable to an intelligent being alone. The elements detectable by understanding alone are, as it were, made to be made out of sound, but are not mere sounds, because it is their musical identities that we appraise and use as elements in other musical entities. The first note of a Bach Partita is no particular sound; it can be played on transposing instruments; it can be played or sung beginning with any pitch at all, provided the rest are properly related.

Further, musical accomplishment has to be teachable, not idiopathic (like a four-octave vocal range), or the marks of individual style.[6] Otherwise, it cannot be the basis of objective capacity. So, piano playing with equal strength and agility in all fingers could not be made a standard of accomplishment until teachers determined how to teach such agility, just as the use of the thumb had to be developed for keyboard instruments earlier. Teachable potentiality is exploited by new excellence, performatively and compositionally.

Excellence requires possibility, as I said. Now I do not mean to rule out all externalist advice, especially as to musical technology, and especially based upon physiology, acoustics, or medicine. Certain musicians do hurt themselves, sometimes being disabled by doing things in physiologically unsound ways. But apart from avoiding what physically defeats continued performance, or compositionally demanding what is physiologically damaging, and apart from a technological standpoint to be mentioned next, there is no external standpoint from which to judge how things ought to be performed, or ought to sound, or ought to be musically constructed. It would be like attempting to say of some material thing, apart from any economic system, how much it is worth.

The relevant technological standpoints or judging potentialities include such things as the recognition, in the seventeenth century, that there might be a way of tuning keyboard instruments so that compositions in different keys could equally well be performed ('equal temperament'), which, of course, immediately opened the new possibility for compositions that made key progressions that were previously beyond the capacity of the instruments and for performance skills that were previously undemanded. The change also made a basis for purists to argue that everything now played on a keyboard instrument is 'out of tune' as is, in a sense, deomonstrable from the 'shortening' of the fifths and 'lengthening' of the fourths, as well as the progressive 'lengthening' or 'flattening' of octaves downward from middle C or A and the progressive 'sharpening' of octaves upward from the middle.

---

[6] Many of the remarks about excellences' being accessible to objective evaluation only from within the hermeneutical circle of accomplishment will, of course, apply to the incommunicable excellences too. That fact that they cannot be taught does not make them less objective, just inappropriate for being conditions of general excellence.

Similarly, with the progression from the harpsichord to the pianoforte, skills at dynamic modulations were required that previously lay beyond instrumental capability. The synthesizer and other electronic devices have changed what can be done, and of course, out of those new capabilities of both instruments and performers come new conditions for excellence, compositionally and performatively—for instance, compositional figures in eighth-tones and, by using digital-audio sampling, successions of real instrument sounds that cannot be produced in such sequence by a performer.

Recent possibilities are dizzying, especially because potentialities for form clash with communicability to a new hearer. Glass, Crumb, even Penderecki seem to be mere dots, specks among the new, barely manageable possibilities. Does a composer now write something, using all the syntactical resources he can master and all the sonorities he can control, hoping it will survive, like Shostakovich's 9th Symphony (1945), and be listened to for fifty years until it is understood? Or, like Korngold, does he write for more immediate consumption? Is Penderecki's Concerto for Five-Stringed Violin (1967–8) a genuine compositional innovation (as is his *Dies Irae*, 1967), or just a novelty? Rapid changes in material resources throw evaluations temporarily out of stability: whether a composition is too conservative in its resources (William Schuman?), too lavish in its displays (Del Tredeci?), too cerebral (Wernick?), without development enough of the ideas, and so forth. Worthwhile composition has to progress, has to transform established capacities, as Prokofiev did in the 'Classical' Symphony. But what at the cutting edge of the new will last is uncertain, not because of (inevitable) defects of evaluation, but because the internal rationality of the art requires time for comparisons and articulation of principles.

We do not, however, have to reach a stable agreement about what compositional and performative resources have to be employed for the music to be 'worthwhile', because the very question presupposes my key premiss: that musical possibility develops[7] with musical accomplishment and, incidentally, with technological advance.[8] Thus, yesterday's accomplishment makes for tomorrow's possibility and new possibility makes for new excellence. For, in the arts that make their own elements, if there is any way to do something, there is a way to do it right.

---

[7] Where 'develops' means that the historically 'new' uses the historically earlier, transforming or supplementing it, or deliberately supplanting it. One can alter a violin with a mute, replace diatonicism with serialism, or one can mute horns, and with moving mutes make them wail, or one can invent a saxophone or an electronic piano or a synthesizer. Compositionally one can alter harmony by writing with consecutive fourths or fifths, dissonances, or with voicing like Bartók's; or one can replace harmony by atonal systems with mathematical or even random voice-leading.

[8] Such advances include equal temperament and the invention of valve horns, and synthesizers or adapted birdsongs, washboards in water, sheet-metal rattling, clips on piano strings, sirens, cannon, bells, and breaking glass; and, most importantly, conceptual innovations, from atonality, serialism, chromaticism, quarter-tone systems, microtonal densities, and tonal clusters, to mathematical (or even topological) formulae for tones, rhythms, pulses, and cadences.

But excellence also makes possibility. When Liszt played in his own way, what was previously undreamed to be within the capacity of a pianist became something that was to be, eventually, part of the training required for pianistic mastery. Similarly with the violin wizardry of Paganini. Performative greatness that employs an advance of instrumental technique creates a hunt for the way to teach it, and to employ and surpass the idea musically. Until the Karl Czerny (1791–1857) and Hannon piano exercises were rigorously mastered and the Chopin *Études* and Bartók *Microcosmos* were teaching pieces, there were many sequences of notes (e.g. in Boulez's *Structures*, 1952, for two pianos) that no ordinary pianist could play, and hence, that few composers would employ. Now we expect an advanced student to have so mastered sequences of notational figures that the four thousand notes of the first movement of a Schubert Sonata (without the repetitions) will take about four and a half minutes to play, all accurately and expressively, even though each note requires some two hundred or more fine muscle movements, some with great force (and imagine how many neural messages) to produce.

A performer learns many more component skills, and all their sequences, than existed a century ago. A page of composition is a sequence of 'figures', something like pictures but more like sentences, that are comprehended as wholes and, without further thought, rendered as physical actions causing sounds, just as sentences read aloud are ordinarily transferred from sight to speech without an intermediate consciousness except of their meaning (and not always of that). Once the general *physical* level of skill was more or less standardized by common progressions of tasks, études, repertoire, strength and accuracy exercises, and facility at sight reading, new capacities came within the reach of practice. One could read Satie, Bartók, and Stockhausen, *Kontakte* (1960). Repetition of figures, like crossing hands or interlacing fingers, develops neurological sequencing and muscle stability, so that incredible velocities can be attained.[9] Such skills, widely attained, give composers material to work with and from which to demand new skills, rhythmic and tonal, from the players, so that Webern, Boulez, and Stockhausen could experiment with tone, dynamics, rhythm, tempos, metres, etc., *all* controlled by serialist principles, and in Boulez's Third Piano Sonata (1957) tempo, loudness, and even ordering of segments are left to the performer.

Olympic gymnastic routines that were winning routines a decade ago have become opening (more or less qualifying) routines now. Such leaps of technical ability cannot, of course, go on indefinitely, any more than the Olympic record for 1,500 metres can keep dropping as it has since 4 minutes, 33.20 seconds in 1896 to 3 minutes, 35.96 seconds in 1988, almost one minute per century. Yet the range of new musical potentiality, within

---

[9] There is, of course, a reciprocal dependence of technology and skill in instrumental performance. The piano velocities common today would be impossible without the repetition mechanisms new at the turn of the century. So too with valve horns, clarinets, and tympani tuning.

broad outer auditory limits, seems nowhere nearly exhausted, and new instruments and resources appear regularly: for instance, under Boulez's direction of Institut de Recherche et Coordination Acoustique/Musique. Similarly, the velocity, accuracy, articulation, dynamic control, physical strength, and neurological alertness of instrumental soloists nowadays, playing music of incredible technical difficulty, is truly amazing. The same goes for dancers, gymnasts, fighter pilots, rock climbers, runners, racers and baseball pitchers. We know now that once we achieve excellence, in a way we understand and can teach, new performative possibilities arise, by refinement or by sequencing, that make us able to do things previously out of reach and, usually, unimagined.

3. Limitations of Access to Abilities and Limitations

There really are limitations both to a grasp of what 'can be' and of what 'has to be' in the way of performative or compositional excellence. There are limits even to specialists at new music. That should not be surprising because there are limits of perceptual discrimination attached to every highly developed skill, and with new music in score one often does not know how to produce the sounds or how it is 'supposed' to sound, especially when it looks as if the conductor should have eight hands that move independently. Ian Hacking remarks on similar evolution of visual discrimination and detection by the use of microscopes, sonograms, and electro-magnetic resonance imaging.[10] Experience with paradigms is needed in all areas of music. It is like the ward rounds in medical school that turn book definitions of 'ascites' into what the hardened abdomen feels like, as opposed, say, to peritonitis. How fast 'adagio ma non troppo' is takes experience. With some newer methods of scoring there is neither the scoring of definite relative intervals[11] nor of discrete frequencies, and it is obvious that one has to be familiar with paradigms of the sounds (tonal clusters), or to do experiments to make paradigms, even to read the notation, just as to read the *puncta* and *neumes* of Gregorian chant, one needs to hear examples of (what musical scholars take to be) adequate paradigms.

Do we just have a *reference* problem for what the musical notation refers to? That is not (the heart of) what is at issue. Rather, it is lack of acquaintance

---

[10] See Ian Hacking, *Representing and Intervening* (Cambridge, 1983).

[11] I reject N. Goodman's view (*Languages of Art*, Indianapolis, 1968) that notes in a diatonic score denote frequencies or narrow frequency bands (to cover the A-440 and A-444 difference between the Boston and Philadelphia Orchestras, and the raising of concert pitch by a whole tone since 1685, so that Bach's B Minor Mass would now sound in a different key to Bach). The idea that notes in a diatonic or early serial score denote frequencies was just a mistake. Nowadays some scores, e.g. for electronic devices, do designate frequencies. You might even find a 'wavering sweep' from below one note to above another for a violin, marked by what looks like a blurry pencil-dash.

with paradigms that determine the *kind* of sound or quality referred to, e.g. triplets, syncopation, quarter-tones, glissando, and various velocities. Only insiders know how much wind it takes to fill the trombone before any sound emits, and how long one breath can sustain a certain volume and pitch, and what clarinet and oboe fortissimos alone sound like. Without practising membership, one lacks a cognitive basis for informed judgement; one is an outsider to the circle of informed evaluation.

Judgement, say about the playability of a new composition, requires a very high degree of insider's knowledge and skill. In the case of Milton Babbitt's *Transfigured Notes* there was a disagreement among experts. The work was commissioned for the Philadelphia Orchestra in 1985 by Erich Leinsdorf, who then decided not to programme it; Dennis Russell Davies, a specialist in new music,[12] scheduled it for 1987, rehearsed it for 'about an hour and said the piece could not be played as written'. In 1989, Hans Vonk 'assured of 18 hours of rehearsal time, settled in to make it work'. He prepared it with small groups of players, but when it came time to put the whole orchestra together, 'the work was cancelled again' with the orchestra calling it 'unplayable', and Babbitt saying the conductors did not know how to rehearse. Then, in 1991, Gunther Schuller of the New England Conservatory of Music performed it at Boston's Jordan Hall, with an orchestra of freelance players, after nine rehearsals. Schuller told critic Daniel Webster, 'I think the dynamics Milton wrote are not playable yet. It may be 10 or 15 years before an orchestra can do that part of the music as Milton imagines it.' Webster, the critic, goes on to say the first $3\frac{1}{2}$ minutes was 'music of almost unearthly beauty' providing 'justification to the tenth power for the work', but then 'unease' and 'growing desperation settled into the playing. What had been right and expansive became tense and uneven'. Webster apparently knew the tension, desperation, and disintegration of organization did not belong to the piece:

In preparing the score, Schuller had found that the music proceeded with a regular beat and pulse—a discovery not made in the Philadelphia approaches. But in performance, the intricacy of the joining of notes, the dynamic scheme and the metrical detail obscured the music making, and the last 15 minutes of the work could not have been the music that Babbitt had envisioned.[13]

...Whatever dialogue and development propel the work could not be heard in this performance. In a sense, the music remains unperformed, for the beauty of the opening minutes vanished in the tension and search for notes that followed.

This is certainly a case where 'insider knowledge' is required for both conductor and critic. Moreover, Schuller's reported judgement aptly illustrates

---

[12] I am virtually tracking the review 'Babbitt Work Finally Performed' by critic Daniel Webster in the *Philadelphia Inquirer*, 12 Feb. 1991, p. A1, col. 1; the quotations are from that article.

[13] There is always the possibility that Vonk and Davies, and composer Richard Wernick (who, Webster says, was 'in essence giving Babbitt advice on how to write his music' because he said it might be performable if scored for nine players) will turn out to be right; perhaps Babbitt could not write his vision out playably.

my main claim that musical potentiality is the product of musical accomplishment, namely, that Babbitt's daunting metric, tonal, rhythmic, beat and pulse challenges will be assimilated into orchestral competence in ten or fifteen years as the demands of other compositions make the orchestras ready for the challenges Babbitt presented.

A virtuous circle

The knowledge bound up with distinctive human practices makes a hermeneutical circle, especially when the very elements of the practice are the product of the practice itself. Such a circle looks vicious, like a cognitive swamp; you seem to have to know what is meant (or good) in order to find out what is meant (or good). But it is not. It is a virtuous circle that allows entry by a series of trials and tests: initiation. Novices learn the paradigms, learn discriminations and evaluations, by mimesis of the members acknowledged as seers and masters, and compete for their own positions of acceptance and authority against the insight and perceptiveness (and performance skills) of the other initiates, and eventually compete even to surpass the teachers, according to the very criteria all acknowledge for telling what is best, knowing the teachers will with joy, and sadness, welcome their new peers and, even, betters. One learns the content of right judgements and right actions from 'doing what they do', the masters and seers, and 'making it one's own'.

4. The Central Argument

If what 'can be done' as accessible potentiality—even though not discernible to everyone who is skilled—is a function of 'what has been done that is excellent' and has been made part of what is needed for competence/excellence, then there is no *external* cognitive access (unless parasitic) to 'what ought to be done' and 'how it ought to be done' without acquaintance with what has been done and is taught, and with the *process* of appraising and revising 'what is to be done' within the circle of those who recognize one another's accomplishment and recognize varying figures as outstanding and great. All the more so, when the entities to be appraised are products of the art itself.

We avoid a vicious hermeneutical circle by initiation: novice, probation, audition, and competition, evaluated by group-acknowledgment of accomplishment (e.g. by customs ranging from applause, graduation, prizes and laurels, to respect and deference, even awe).

Morality and music, medicine and law, and crafts far less exalted, many of them essential for survival (like farming and fishing), have all these features analogously. Without training, one lacks requisite acquaintance with the *sorts* of things the craft concerns and modulates and evaluates. The craft invents sorts of things to do its business: diatonic scales, tone series, inversions, minor modes, dissonances, cadences, expositions, orchestrated instrumental choirs, sonorities, keys, scoring techniques, reading practices, instrumental practices, tempos, and rhythmic contrasts. Only by apprenticeship can aspiring practitioners learn what to do and how to do it, and, by *trust* in their teachers, attain component skills (e.g. finger movements, muscle control, and sequencing), whose purposes they cannot fully appreciate until they become able to use them in sequences unimaginable at the outset. Eventually performers and composers enter the competitions that select the standard-bearers, the masters and teachers, and acquire a ranking they have to maintain competitively in the group of appraisers of excellences that maintain the art.[14]

The new Byzantine clerks

Conservatories, like graduate schools or the professional schools, turn out journeymen, not masters. John Delancy had many good oboists as students, but few competed with him; and Zabaleta, too, with harp students; so too, with Casals, Serkin, Bernstein (though Koussevitzky and Charles Munch had Bernstein to boast about). A few great teachers are not even competitors for their best students: Mozart's father; the many musicians in J. S. Bach's family; Karl Czerny, the teacher of Franz Liszt, and in our time Nadia Boulanger, with whom many of the major performers and composers studied. Like the clerks of Byzantium, teachers are the custodians and transmitters of accomplishment and of the internal rationality of the arts. Knowledgeable critical appreciation, especially among journeymen, can exceed ability to create or perform, while being based in considerable technical skill and comprehension; that tends to stabilize and objectify the judgements of excellence and the recognition of new achievement; what teachers hand on is what tradition accepts. Orchestral auditions, with conductor, manager, concertmaster, and first desk of the section, apply performance tests competitively.

The liveliness of a craft requires a sufficiency of masters, journeymen, apprentices, novices, initiates, and a supportive following to keep the refinements progressing and maintain an outlet for its products (where there are products). The clerks also preserve disused arts, e.g. medieval instrumentation, whaling songs, and carving, and keep alive Gregorian chant and early polyphony.

Arts under two measures

Sometimes mimetic arts are 'externalized' by claims to truth. Astrologers, necromancers, card readers, fortune tellers, medicine men, shamans, and

---

[14] Some naturally gifted individuals, like Mozart and Picasso, need only see the process to master it and to maintain their leadership once it is displayed. Those are so prodigious in talent as to progress to mastery in a fluid passage from initiation. In some orchestras there can be an 'internal desk' audition challenge, any time.

voodooists mimic science and art. But the mimics either lack the internal rationality and creativity that make art, or, despite a strong and objective internal discipline, they, like the practice of medicine, fall under another criterion than the internal criteria of 'how to do it', namely the criterion of truth.

Medicine hit a low point when King Charles II's fourteen royal physicians responded to what appears now to have been a stroke with several days of bloodletting (16 ounces at a time) and enemas and oral purgatives (all dehydrating), intensifying the treatments every time the king showed any sign of alertness, until several days later, he finally died.[15] Medicine is under the eye of chemistry, biology, gas pressure theory, gas chromatography, and hundreds of other enquiries. Truth is an additional test for a discipline that purports to tell the truth, provided there is, or will be, some independent access to reality, like pathology and chemistry.

Music does not, however, purport to tell the truth. But what about an analogue of the 'double measure' question,[16] namely, is music, like any other art, under assessment for its spiritual depth and moral worth? Certainly. But that kind of merit, or lack, gradually 'becomes public', accessible to the sensitive and educated in general. American spirituals, made with a simplicity purified by great pain, touch us deeply and over and over, with inexhaustible depths of the spirit. Musical value becomes public with familiarity; it can be elevating or merely diverting. Nevertheless, music does not have two faces, an inner one of excellence and order, and another outward one of reading the world right.[17]

5. The Wittgensteinian Version

There has, of course, been wide recognition that Wittgenstein in his later philosophy emphasized the inextricability of meaning from the practices that talk modulates, and more generally, considered it a disorder of the understanding[18] to expect someone to step outside the activity of using words in our

[15] See Charles Panati, *Panati's Extraordinary Endings of Practically Everything and Everybody* (New York, 1989), 266–7. Scarburgh's record reads more like de Sade than annals of medicine. Similarly, 'radical mastectomies' were practised from the 1940s for breast cancer, long after it was known that in early stages minor surgery was more effective and less damaging.

[16] Some arts and crafts have a double dimension, as Plato saw, not just in terms of truth, but also in terms of moral elevation, as opposed to coarsening (physical violence to women), or outright corruption (cultivating greed and compassionlessness).

[17] In analogue of Plato's considering some music virtuous, a Canadian shopping centre, plagued by lounging teenagers, drove them away like starlings by switching the broadcast music to classical.

[18] The phrase 'disorder of the understanding' is my invention. See David Pears, *Wittgenstein* (Cambridge, Mass., 1986). Also the two entries on Wittgenstein in *The Oxford Companion to the Mind*, ed. R. L. Gregory (New York, 1987). I think Pears reads Wittgenstein as I do on this general idea: that sceptical argument directed to meaning, cognition in general, or mathematical knowledge can be deflected and confounded by a systematic exposure of the deformity of any kind of claim that there has to be a standpoint outside the practices, from which one should be

'forms of life' (like prayer, giving direction, telling stories), to provide some account of 'what meaning is' in terms of something else, whether it be images, ideas in the mind, things referred to, or even following a rule; for, of course, meaning does not consist of something else, and there is no epistemic problem of knowing what we mean when we mean what we say.[19] More generally, we cannot step out of the circle of judgements and evaluations in science as a practice, or in mathematics or in religion or in aesthetics, to justify those practices because there is no place to stand apart from the practices engaged in life to make such an evaluation, and no place to look for justifications of our convictions in any *other* sort of belief or cognition. Thus to demand that we make and survive such an 'unbiased, independent' evaluation of our claims to mathematical, logical, religious, or musical knowledge, is to demand that we do what is transparently futile.

Even more generally, there has to be something wrong with the intent of a critical enterprise that demands global justification of our cognitive practices, because no design could carry it out. So, musical evaluation, and the nature of its entities, cannot require some extrinsic justification, any more than meaning or knowing can. Attempts to separate something that has *what*-it-is determined by its role in some activity involving judgement and evaluation (say, music), so that it can be evaluated and, perhaps, justified, while disengaged from the practice, music, that gives it content and life (and its peculiar limitations), is pathological thinking.

Evading scepticism

Sceptical challenges are typically based on 'but what if . . . not' suppositions, proposed counter-possibilities, like 'Maybe you were asleep', 'Maybe you miscounted', 'Maybe you forgot'. One can reply, 'Maybe; but that's not what happened. Besides, logical consistency is a poor guide to real possibility, and imaginability is worse; so your hypotheses as to what might have happened have to be based on some additional *knowledge*. Therefore, a general sceptical attack fails. For you can only know what might have happened if you know to a considerable extent what does happen.'

The sceptics' trick is to get you to admit that, given how things seem to you, they might still have been otherwise, and get you to attempt to show that what

---

able to 'justify' one's claims and the whole practice, by thinking that in no way depends on the success or rightness of the outcomes of the practices themselves, or, otherwise, the practices cannot be justified.

[19] This reading of the *Investigations* and of the posthumous collections of remarks on religion, aesthetics, psychology, and the foundations of mathematics does conflict with Saul Kripke's reading of the *Investigations* in *Wittgenstein on Rules and Private Language* (Cambridge, Mass., 1982). However, I agree with Warren Goldfarb's criticisms, see his 'Kripke on Wittgenstein on Rules' in *Journal of Philosophy* (Sept. 1985), 471–88, and I go further to say Kripke's reading misses the point of what Wittgenstein was doing: undercutting the lines of thinking, the rationales used, to demand externalized or neutralized justification where none is appropriate.

might have happened instead did not happen at all, but without your using your knowledge of what did happen as part of your reasoning. Thus, the game is fixed.

So, take the questioner on a tour of his twisted thinking. How does he *know* such a thing, or anything else, might have happened? It is possible because it is imaginable? It is possible because it is semantically consistent? Or it is possible because I *know* it sometimes happens? Imaginability does not assure possibility; neither does consistency. The third option defeats the global attack because it grants that we sometimes know what is the case. So it is with our musical knowledge. Because possibility with content is not prior to what is, but is consequent on it, scepticism, by counter-possibilities, is cognitively parasitic on knowlege of what is, and is, thus, self-refuting.

Practices with interior rationality

The interior rationality of our practices is the basis of evaluation and judgement, for instance, in legal interpretation and adjudication, as well as in the arts. For it is the interior rationality of practices that is their justification (except in so far as they depend upon truths for which there is cognitively independent access to reality, or serve as instruments in other practices). Just as in law there is no authoritative access to the meaning of the Constitution or a statute apart from the practice of adjudicating real cases,[20] so there is no stable cognitive access to musical meaning, or how to perform a work or how to interpret it, or even to what the musical elements are, such as what a C clef is, or what a 'key' is, what a diatonic scale is or chromaticism, or what counts as 'together' on an attack (notice the slight separation in sound for a piano duet, a separation evidently not repeated for each pair of choirs in a symphony orchestra), apart from musical practice.

It is not only that 'what is done' is the ground for 'what can be done' and for 'what is to be done' in music; even more, 'what there is' to be known and evaluated is the product of the activities of music making and music performing.

6. Conclusion

The closed circle of appraisal is not peculiar to music, but common to every human activity whose potentialities develop from prior accomplishments. The phenomena, especially fulfilment of new potentialities, to be understood and appraised are in the relevant respects to be understood and evaluated, products of the art being practised. They are cognitively inaccessible from

[20] See Douglas Lind, 'Constitutional Interpretation and Adjudication', 1991 University Microfilms. Ph.D. Thesis, University of Pennsylvania.

outside, because they have no being at all outside the practice. There is sound without music, but not notes, tunes, songs, operas, concertos, or even codas, voice-leading, or melodic line. There is then no critical standpoint, apart from an insider's knowledge, or parasitic on it, to assess the potentialities of voice-leading or polyphony, or serialism, or twelve-tone systems, or of using the full range of audible frequencies with synthesizers, or various mathematical patterns, etc. Therefore, there is no authoritative access to what constitutes performative musical excellence from any standpoint disengaged from the critical practices of musicians, teachers, performers, conductors, and even audiences.[21]

The relativity of what is new and a possibility to be exploited in no way supports scepticism or 'judgemental relativism' or 'cultural nescience'. It only has the consequence that cognitivity challenges and justification challenges that would demand an independent access to the subject-matter (e.g. to mathematical objects) or to the 'right answer', e.g. as to what the law is, or how to play Scarlatti, or what is the best polyphonic system, are misconceived, self-refuting, and maintained only by contortions of thought and denials of what is plainly before our experience that amount to a disorder of the understanding, which is usually intellectually fatal.

---

[21] Even audiences have a limited role. Probably audience satiation wore out the trying tempos of Toscanini, themselves a response to the 'romantic' latitude of his predecessors. More importantly, audience incomprehension has become a distinct barrier to musical development, as well as creating great economic obstacles to new music. On one estimate, less than 1% of all the compositions by America's ten thousand composers are performed even once. Yet the intellectual density of the new music is simply not penetrable at a single or a few hearings. It is not the fault of the audiences (in general) or of the composers, but a limitation in communicability from *within* the art.

Perceiving the Music Correctly

ROBERT KRAUT

I am interested in a certain dispute. It concerns the metaphysics of musical meaning; more specifically, it involves a certain confrontation between a variety of pluralism and a variety of monism. At different times I have taken different sides in the dispute. More recently I have begun to worry about what kind of dispute it is, and about what sorts of considerations—psychological, music-theoretic, or philosophical—could possibly resolve it one way or the other.

I

We are prone to talk of meaning, or content, or significance, or semantics, in connection with music. Theorists of various persuasions are led to talk this way for various reasons. For example, given the prevalence of 'syntactic' considerations about music, one might ask whether a 'semantic' dimension is somehow presupposed. My focus here is different: I am led to countenance musical semantics because of a concern with the phenomenon of *understanding music*. I want to know what it is to understand a musical event, and how musical understanding relates to other varieties of understanding—for example, to the varieties of understanding at work when a native speaker (or a translator) understands a grammatical sentence, or when a scientist understands the data, or when a person understands another person's actions or mental states. What must I be able to do, or say, or feel, or what must I believe, in order to qualify as understanding—for example—Stravinsky's music? The question matters to those interested in architectural and computational aspects of the human mind. It also matters within the art world. After all, some of us understand John Coltrane's music and some of us do not; New Wave aficionados view traditional critics as not understanding their music, and thus as ill-equipped to provide legitimate criticism. Jazz enthusiasts of the 1960s regarded Sonny Stitt's rejection of Eric Dolphy's music as based, in part, upon a failure to understand it. Many of us are willing to talk this way,

I am grateful to Daniel Farrell, Mari Riess Jones, Stewart Shapiro, George Schumm, and Robin Vachon-Kraut for helpful comments on earlier versions; and especially to Diana Raffman for ongoing discussions concerning these topics. Portions of earlier versions were presented to the American Psychological Association, the American Philosophical Association, and the Philosophy Departments at Purdue University and the University of Texas at Austin; I am grateful to those who participated in discussion.

but it is not clear what such talk amounts to, or the conditions under which ascriptions of musical understanding are true. We need to know what it *is* to understand a musical event.

We should be careful with analogies and borrowed paradigms. Musical genres are not, in any straightforward way, natural languages: understanding music might or might not involve the processes and achievements involved in attaining linguistic competence. Enquiries into the semantics of music are usually puzzling: after all, musical phrases do not have truth conditions; no matter how you twist the logician's concepts of reference, extension, and satisfaction, music simply is not a phenomenon for which one wants to seek a Tarski-style recursive theory of truth. 'Expressivist' semantics, according to which music is somehow a vehicle for the expression of emotion, is implausible in connection with a wide range of music. Here the issue is perhaps terminological (what precisely is an emotion?); but caution is nevertheless required. Seasoned listeners rarely experience joy, jealousy, indignation, envy, love, fear, or other stereotypical emotions in response to uptempo Ornette Coleman performances. Not every phenomenological episode corresponds to an emotion; there is more to emotion than feeling. The complex experiences and intricate sensory-perceptual states associated with such music cannot be assumed, pending further discussion, to constitute emotions.

But there are additional options: there is more to semantic content than truth conditions or the expression of emotion. Words are artefacts. They serve complex social-institutional functions; they play roles in the games of gathering evidence, theorizing, communicating, deliberating, and countless other activities. Semantical roles are thus many-dimensional, involving relations between word-use and parameters such as perceptual evidence, appropriate behaviour, and inferential transformations. The analogy between music and natural language appears irresistible; for, though natural language and music might subserve quite different roles, musical phenomena are none the less located in a complex system involving many of the parameters relevant to linguistic meaning. Musical event-types (i.e. repeatable, reidentifiable musical events) are implicated in 'inference-like' practices (for example, certain temporal orderings of pitches imply specific tonal centres); moreover, musical events are often thought to warrant certain affective and/or behavioural reactions rather than others (one can, after all, dance incorrectly). Facts of this kind provide the resources for characterizing a dimension of musical significance, and thus provide help in understanding musical understanding.

Having gone this far, a certain question appears tantalizing. One of the more hotly disputed issues in metaphysics and the philosophy of language concerns W. V. Quine's claim that natural language meaning is indeterminate.[1] The claim, enshrined in Quine's Indeterminacy of Translation thesis

---

[1] See W. V. Quine, *Word and Object* (Cambridge, Mass., 1960), ch. 2.

(hereafter IT) is this: for any given language L, it is possible in principle to construct incompatible translations of L, all of which are equally correct. As Quine puts it, 'manuals for translating one language into another can be set up in divergent ways, all compatible with the totality of speech dispositions, yet incompatible with one another'.[2] The envisaged manuals are 'incompatible' or 'rival' in so far as they assign distinct and non-equivalent interpretations to the same expressions. Given the existence of such manuals, Quine urges that there is no 'fact of the matter' as to which translation scheme provides the correct translation; in an absolute sense, there is no such thing as correct translation. The claim is not epistemological: Quine is not insisting that, in light of underdetermination of theory by data, there is no way to be certain which translation scheme is correct. The claim is rather ontological: within certain constraints, there simply is no fact of the matter as to what an expression means.

It takes time and work to formulate IT properly, and to provide the kinds of examples that render the thesis even remotely plausible. For the present, note that IT bears upon varieties of understanding which involve *interpretation*: in claiming the existence of rival translation manuals, IT entails that two agents could lay equal claim to understanding the same linguistic phenomenon despite serious disagreements with one another (assume for the present that achieving a translation is sufficient for achieving understanding). Thus IT underwrites a kind of *pluralism* about semantic meaning: over and above what is captured in stimulus meaning (and that is not very much), there is no such thing as the unique meaning of a word (because of the availability of alternative global translation schemes). Moreover, there need be no consensus, beyond a point, between those who understand a native utterance.

There is little agreement in the industry about the correctness of IT, the cogency of the arguments for it, or its precise consequences; one can hold IT to be importantly true, or importantly false, or a trivial consequence of too minimal a set of constraints on proper translation, or self-refuting, or even unintelligible. It takes a few months to sort out the options and even longer to make up one's mind. Prima facie, IT is profound: it tells us that if there is one way to correctly translate a linguistic item, there are many ways. But the thesis is also bizarre, and flies in the face of deep-seated intuitions about linguistic meaning;[3] thus philosophers motivated by common sense, as well as those unimpressed by behaviouristic arguments against the possibility of a 'science of intention', join forces in rejecting it.

[2] Ibid. 27.
[3] The bizarreness may be merely apparent, or it may be insignificant. Davidson, for example, urges that IT is 'neither mysterious nor threatening', and represents no failure to 'capture significant distinctions'. See Donald Davidson, 'A Coherence Theory of Truth and Knowledge', in E. LePore (ed.), *Truth and Interpretation* (Oxford, 1986), and 'Belief and the Basis of Meaning', in Davidson's *Inquiries into Truth and Interpretation* (Oxford, 1984). For present purposes, what matters is the prevalence of the intuition among ordinary speakers that semantic meaning is determinate whereas musical significance is not.

Generative-transformational theories of natural language suggest an account of musical understanding, one which provides a foothold for raising questions about indeterminacy concerning music. Jackendoff and Lerdahl, for example, urge that 'the understanding of a piece of music by the idealized listener consists in his finding the maximally coherent structural description or descriptions which can be associated with the piece's sequence of pitch-time events'.[4] According to this account, understanding music is a matter of having appropriate representations stored and/or played somewhere in the head. Such representations derive in part from musical grammars unconsciously mobilized by the listener, and involve computational operations performed on mental representations of the musical kind: the representations code information about relative beat strength, metrical structure, melodic tension, stability among pitch-time events, parsing into rhythmic groups, and so on. In light of the above discussion about indeterminacy, it is natural to ask whether for each given musical event there exists a *unique* 'maximally coherent structural-descriptive representation' corresponding to it.

But this is not the only way to think about musical understanding. Indeed, it is doubtful that ordinary attributions of musical understanding are best illuminated in terms of these theoretical constructions of computational psychology. Another approach—not incompatible, but prima facie distinct— depends on the premiss that not all understanding involves translation or even interpretation (we must be careful here, since 'interpretation' means quite different things to different theorists). A deep-seated intuition is that under- standing music is primarily a *phenomenological* matter: to understand a musical event is to hear it in certain ways—the correct ways. One understands a musical event if and only if one experiences appropriate qualitative states in response to it. As Roger Scruton puts it, 'musical understanding is a form of hearing. The content of music is a heard content, and it is heard *in* the tones.' Moreover, 'if a work of music means something . . . this is a fact about the way it sounds.'[5] In what follows, I want to reflect upon whether 'those who hear with understanding' do so only by virtue of having precisely the same per- ceptual experiences, or whether, owing to some musical correlate of trans- lational indeterminacy, musical understanding tolerates distinct (and in some sense 'incompatible') perceptual experiences of the same musical event.

II

By *musical significance* I mean whatever is grasped in musical understanding; it is best thought of as a syndrome of experiences correlated with the musical

[4] Fred Lerdahl and Ray Jackendoff, 'Toward a Formal Theory of Tonal Music', *Journal of Music Theory*, 21 (1977), 118.
[5] Roger Scruton, 'Analytical Philosophy and the Meaning of Music', *Journal of Aesthetics and Art Criticism* (1987), 169–76

stimulus—experiences of stability and tension, of metrical groupings, of tonal centres, of variations on harmonic, melodic, or rhythmic structures, and the like. Question: is it the case that, to each musical phenomenon, there corresponds a unique *correct* syndrome of experiential responses to it? Or are there many ways of hearing the piece, each as 'legitimate' as any of the others? Is there even any basis for distinguishing proper from improper experiences of the music? This is, I think, a close correlate of questions about the indeterminacy of linguistic meaning. Let us say that we are enquiring into the *indeterminacy of musical significance.*

Having discussed these matters with both lovers of music and lovers of language, my impression is this: IT flies in the face of common sense and seems wrong; but its musical counterpart, once articulated in the terms I recommend here, tends not to offend. There are, I am told, facts about the meaning of a natural language sentence, but there are no facts about the significance of a musical event (and thus no unique syndrome of perceptual-phenomenal experiences of the musical event which is, to the exclusion of others, 'correct'). This is an interesting set of intuitions: either it signals a profound difference between music and natural language; or we should side with Quine (and the 'semantic pluralists') and insist that semantic content is indeterminate; or we should insist, against the musical pluralist, that musical significance is determinate.

Quine offered various considerations in favour of IT. I can think of several possible arguments for the indeterminacy of musical significance (hereafter IMS)—that is, for the thesis that the nature of musical understanding leaves latitude for incompatible but equally correct perceptual experiences of a musical event. Here I consider three such arguments and find that none of them succeeds. My conclusion is not that IMS is likely mistaken, but rather that it is best construed as the expression of a commitment rather than the conclusion of an argument.

One argument for IMS might be inspired by a certain semantic theory about attributions of understanding. Rosenberg, for example, suggests that such attributions do not serve to *describe* any particular state or achievement; they rather serve to *appraise* a person's achievements as having earned them the right to be taken seriously. As he puts it,

The person whom we acknowledge as understanding a proof, a poem, a painting, or another person is one to whom we grant the right to be listened to. We undertake the obligation to take her opinions seriously. Our acknowledgement of her understanding *just is* this granting of rights and undertaking of duties.[6]

This 'ascriptivist' notion of understanding is not intended to be equivalent to any indeterminacy thesis; but perhaps it underwrites such a thesis via the following line of reasoning: if we grant that understanding consists in

---

[6] Jay Rosenberg, 'On Understanding the Difficulty in Understanding Understanding', in H. Parret and J. Bouveresse (eds.), *Meaning and Understanding* (Berlin, 1981), 41.

'achievement grounded rights and responsibilities', we wonder whether there is any single achievement that corresponds to 'understanding a symphony'. What counts as understanding a symphony depends upon who is allocating the alleged rights and responsibilities. Musicians, critics, uneducated listeners, historians, are likely to mobilize different standards in granting the dialectical authority in question. Rosenberg urges that there is no particular achievement common to all instances of understanding; by parity of reasoning, there is no particular achievement—even an 'experiential' achievement—common even to all instances of understanding a given symphony.

If this is right, then any theory of interest-transcendent 'objective significance' is misguided. 'The real significance of the piece', like 'the one who really understands', emerges as a vacuous notion pending relativization to a social, cultural, or communal context. But this is relativism, not indeterminacy; pending a demonstration that the achievements demanded by one set of communal standards are in any sense 'incompatible with' the achievements demanded by another, ascriptivism of Rosenberg's sort provides no basis for IMS.

Thus the problem remains. When Scruton speaks of 'the perceptual experience of those who hear [music] with understanding', we wish to know whether such experiences are type-identical among all those who 'hear with understanding'. IMS dictates that they need not be.

Earlier we noted an interesting asymmetry in ordinary intuitions concerning natural language meaning and musical significance. The intuitions are these: IT is false (words have determinate semantic meanings); whereas IMS is true (there is no single syndrome of experiential responses to a given musical event which is, to the exclusion of others, correct.) The next argument for IMS purports to be compatible with these intuitions:

A person understands a musical event M if and only if that person has appropriate (i.e. proper) qualitative experiences of that event; moreover, a syndrome of qualitative states is an *appropriate* response to M if and only if it is a response provided by enough members of the relevant community. But such criteria provide no foothold for the uniqueness of musical significance, because there are no facts of the matter as to which people constitute the relevant community.

That is: attributions of musical significance and musical understanding depend upon the specification of a relevant community. To understand a musical event just is to *experience it the way members of the relevant community experience it*. But which is the relevant community? Whose typical reactions to the music are paradigmatically correct? The objection urges that there is no principled procedure for specifying the relevant community; thus the notions of musical significance and musical understanding are contaminated with arbitrariness. And this marks an important difference between linguistic meaning and musical significance.

The problem is that this form of argument applies to natural language as well as to music; if the argument establishes IMS, then a parallel argument establishes IT. This is because word meaning, like musical significance, is determined by social practice, and any attempt to specify the relevant social practices often seems contaminated with arbitrariness. The norms that govern linguistic activity are sustained in patterns of communal behaviour. But which communal behaviour? Which is the relevant linguistic population, and thus the relevant set of semantical norms? Suppose Emily is *en rapport* with several populations; which of those populations bear upon the semantic interpretation of her utterances? All of them? Different ones on different occasions? Is there, for each utterance event, a non-arbitrary procedure for identifying the semantically relevant community?

The point is that natural language translation must reflect the relevant linguistic norms, those upheld in the speaker's community; we say 'it is the word's usage in *this* population that constitutes its meaning', thereby signalling the relevance of *this* collection of communal practices rather than some other. Admittedly, circumscribing the relevant linguistic practices involves assumptions and idealizations (one must, for example, distinguish semantical differences from differences in collateral information). But these methodological necessities do not undermine the determinacy of semantic content; so why should their musical counterparts undermine the determinacy of musical significance?

Here is another way to put the same point. The communal factors that contribute to linguistic meaning are importantly similar to those that contribute to musical significance; if the presence of these factors in linguistic cases is no source of indeterminacy then it should be no source of indeterminacy in the musical cases either. Speakers belong to linguistic communities—communities which are often difficult to circumscribe, but which none the less control the semantical values of the speakers' utterances. Similarly, musicians *qua* musicians belong to communities: those with whom they work, those by whom they have been influenced, those to whom they defer. Why not take the experiences prevalent among *that* community as constitutive of the significance of a musical event?

Analogies of this sort suggest that a musical event, like an utterance episode, is an artefact; it must therefore be treated as occupying a position in a social-institutional framework, within which are upheld the norms that constitute the significance of that artefact. But which is the relevant framework? The appearance of indeterminacy was fostered by the pluralistic idea that no single population enjoys special status in this connection: different listeners perceive the music differently (depending upon background, training, expertise, and interest); and all such perceptions are equally correct. But this pluralistic idea fails for natural language: given an utterance event, the interpreter usually manages to identify a unique relevant linguistic population.[7]

---

[7] The interpreter's latitude in selecting a relevant linguistic population is often ignored. Putnam, for example, in discussing the meaning of our ancestors' natural kind terms, treats speakers in 1750 as members of our own linguistic community, responsible to the norms—

Whatever procedure he uses can be applied to musical events, thereby eliminating the appearance of pluralism and indeterminacy of musical significance.

No compelling argument has yet been found for IMS which does not
simultaneously vindicate IT.

Here is another way to think about this language–music analogy, and
why the present argument for IMS does not give us what we want. The
interpretation of an individual speaker's words often rests upon the interpreter's choice of a 'relevant linguistic community' to which that speaker
belongs. Because word meaning is partially determined by the canons of
linguistic propriety which constrain a speaker, the meaning of an expression in
an individual speaker's mouth is a function of the community to which that
speaker belongs. The interpreter asks, 'To what language does this individual
utterance belong?', and assumes that there is a determinate answer. Perhaps
this assumption is misguided: perhaps there is no 'fact of the matter' as to
which communally upheld linguistic norms constrain a speaker; this might
give rise to semantic indeterminacy. But pending arguments to this conclusion, the intuition persists that a quite specific linguistic community is
relevant to the correct translation of an individual speaker's words; part of the
interpreter's job is to identify that community. We thus defuse the argument
from the communal character of meaning to the indeterminacy of meaning
by eliminating the pluralism: an individual speaker is regarded as tied, via
determinate patterns of linguistic deference and shared linguistic norms, to
one group rather than another. A plurality of 'equally acceptable' interpretations—those which rest upon viewing the speaker as belonging to a plurality
of different linguistic communities—is thereby eliminated, thus allowing us to
sustain our pre-Quinean faith in determinate linguistic meaning.

Precisely this strategy is applicable to musical phenomena, thereby eliminating the spectre of pluralism and any indeterminacy that might be thought
to follow from it. We only require the premiss that corresponding to every
musician is a determinate deference class—those people whom the musician
recognizes as having the right to judge him. He recognizes the relevance of
their criticisms and suggestions: they matter, and they affect his artistic
behaviour. They are the listeners, critics, and other players to whom the artist
has undertaken a commitment. It is no more difficult to identify this class than
it is to identify, for a given natural language speaker, the class of persons by
whose semantical norms the speaker is constrained.

The striking analogy, then, is this: just as linguistic communities play an

especially the standards of similarity—which constrain us. (See, for example, Hilary Putnam,
'Meaning and Reference', *Journal of Philosophy*, 70 (Nov. 1973), 702.) But even if we
acknowledge the 'division of linguistic labor', and grant that the semantical interpretation of a
speaker's words is constrained by social facts—facts about the verbal dispositions of those to
whom the speaker defers—Putnam's suggested interpretive schemes (e.g. ' "water" in 1750
referred to all and only H_2O aggregates') are not forced upon us. The connection between this
semantic problem and that of invoking relevant stylistic norms when interpreting artworks is
discussed in my 'On Pluralism and Indeterminacy', *Midwest Studies in Philosophy*, 16 (1991).

essential role in the constitution of semantic content—it is the word's use in *this* group which constitutes its meaning—music communities play a corresponding role in the determination of musical significance. The music world is constituted by a vast network of partially disjoint communal structures; each such structure is defined in terms of recognition and deference relations among its members. Each such structure, moreover, sustains norms and conventions definitive of a given genre and style.

But analogies are not arguments; the present analogies strain at the intuitions that prompted our enquiry. Granted, understanding a neighbour's utterances rests in part upon properly identifying the linguistic community to which he belongs. But do we wish to say that understanding the neighbour's musical output rests upon properly identifying the musical community to which he belongs? Music is not natural language; the touted similarity between linguistic meaning and musical significance seems implausible.

This is fascinating. Despite all the striking analogies between the social-institutional dimensions of linguistic meaning and those of musical significance, there remains a difference between our concepts of natural language and our concepts of artistic phenomena like symphonies. For we balk about designating any particular population as the one in which 'property rights' for a piece of music (and thus its significance) reside. We may be willing to insist that native discourse belongs to the natives—or, more broadly, to those with whom the natives would be willing to converse. But Beethoven's Fifth belongs to the world. *No* population enjoys privilege over any other in fixing the musical-perceptual facts constitutive of the 'real significance' of a musical piece. And this spells doom for strict analogies between semantic content and musical significance. Prevalent lore about music, in contrast to that about linguistic meaning, endorses a thoroughgoing pluralism: immerse yourself in the musical event and enjoy the resulting rhythmic and harmonic tingles. Do not worry whether the tingles are correct, or appropriate to the musical event, or sufficiently similar to those of a maximally hip listener. One set of tingles is as good as another.[8]

That, at any rate, is a prevalent view. It is interesting that most musicians with whom I have discussed these matters find such pluralism objectionable. They usually urge that Beethoven's sophisticated peers constitute the background population relevant to attributions of 'proper experience' of his work (it is McCoy Tyner, and not Lawrence Welk, whose perceptions of Coltrane's 'sheets of sound' are the standard of correctness). There might occasionally

---

[8] This view is fostered by the dogma that qualitative experiences, unlike propositional representations, cannot be assessed for appropriateness; they are not the *kinds* of states susceptible to appraisal in a context. Cf. Collingwood's claim that 'There is nothing in the case of feeling to correspond with what, in the case of thinking, may be called misthinking or thinking wrong.' (R. G. Collingwood, *The Principles of Art* (Oxford, 1938), 159.) I discuss the origins and plausibility of this cognitivist prejudice in my 'Feelings in Context', *Journal of Philosophy*, 83, No. 11 (Nov. 1986), 642–52.

be serious disagreements—interesting disagreements—about which listeners qualify as the paradigms of correct experiential response to the music; and there will, consequently, be disagreements about who does or does not understand the music. But there is a way to get it right, and many ways to get it wrong. Thus speaks the monist, thereby sustaining the dispute.

The dialectically clever pluralist, in contrast, insists that his musical reactions are as legitimate as any others. Natural language analogies which suggest that musical events, like well-formed sentences, can be misunderstood, strike him as bizarre. The 'expert's' remarks about designated populations and proper musical experience strike the novice as parochial: manifestations of a mere prejudice in favour of a specific population. The novice sees no reason to dignify that particular population as a tribunal against which to measure the correctness of musical experiences.

For the present, the advocate and the opponent of IMS are at a stand-off.

III

I shall sketch a final argument for musical indeterminacy; the argument fails, but it points toward a way of understanding the dispute at hand.

Kendall Walton stresses the distinction between correct and incorrect perception of an artwork. He argues that the kinds of experiences requisite for a proper understanding of a work are determined by the *category* to which the work belongs, and he tries to specify a set of conditions which determine, for any given work, the artistic category to which it belongs. But sometimes it happens that one cannot specify the rules for deciding how works are correctly perceived, because the stated conditions determine *no unique category*. In discussing situations of this kind, Walton considers a possible critical dispute concerning Giacometti's thin metal sculptures. He says,

To a critic who sees them simply as sculptures, or sculptures of people, they look frail, emaciated, wispy, or wiry. But that is not how they would strike a critic who sees them in the category of thin metal sculptures of that sort (just as stick figures do not strike us as wispy or emaciated). He would be impressed not by the thinness of the sculptures, but by the expressive nature of the positions of their limbs, and so forth, and so no doubt would attribute very different aesthetic properties to them. Which of the two ways of seeing these works is correct is, I suspect, undecidable . . . So perhaps the dispute between the two critics is essentially unresolvable. The most that we can do is to point out just what sort of a difference of perception underlies the dispute, and why it is unresolvable.[9]

If there is any foothold for the indeterminacy of musical significance, it surely involves cases such as this. But there exists a simple strategy for restoring determinacy, a strategy actually employed in attributions of artistic under-

---

[9] Kendall L. Walton, 'Categories of Art', *Philosophical Review*, 79 (1970), 362.

standing. Suppose that a diagram can be seen either as a duck or as a rabbit, and that Walton's conditions point to neither experience as more correct than the other; in such a case, we say that the person who 'genuinely understands' the diagram is the one who alternately sees it as both. A viewer incapable of—or unaware of the possibility of—both sorts of perceptual experience has fallen short of the mark: he has merely partial understanding. So it is with musical experiences. It is, for example, extremely important to hear Led Zeppelin's 'The Crunge' (from *Houses of the Holy*) not only as a more-sophisticated-than-usual instance of Heavy Metal, but also as a sarcastic commentary on James Brown's more involuted performances. This is not simply collateral knowledge about the piece: it involves hearing certain modulations and syncopations in special ways. One who does not hear this has yet to understand the piece totally.

There is, then, no reason to believe that musical significance is any less determinate than word meaning. Ambiguous words do not *ipso facto* lack determinate meaning: *ambiguity is not indeterminacy*. When confronted with an alleged case of indeterminacy, it is easy enough to invoke duck-rabbit analogies, claim that each of the touted rivals is merely *part* of the total syndrome of appropriate responses, and that both responses are requisite for proper understanding. Determinacy restored.

As restorations go, this one is suspicious and disappointing because it is too easy. Recall that we were seeking a basis for the possibility of genuinely rival though equally appropriate perceptual responses to a musical event. The rejoinder is that the touted rivals are not really rivals at all, but are rather parts of the single correct syndrome of experiential responses. It is no longer clear, then, how anyone who advocates IMS can win; whenever he provides an example of indeterminacy his opponent argues that it is not really an instance of indeterminacy. It is no longer clear what the excitement is about.

There is excitement because indeterminacy and pluralism were born twins: IMS underwrites the legitimacy of distinct syndromes of experiential response to musical events. Those who find such pluralism uncongenial seek a basis for judgements of objective correctness. (Walton, for example, eschews accounts of aesthetic perception which 'do not allow aesthetic judgments to be mistaken often enough.') The dispute, though unresolved, seems genuine.

A review of the dispute is helpful here. The advocate of determinate musical significance regards a musical event as an artefact. Like any artefact, its features cannot be properly explained except in relation to the social/institutional forces that shaped it. Just as linguistic utterances have determinate semantic content by virtue of location in a complex causal/inferential network, musical events have determinate significance by virtue of location in a complex network of perceptual/phenomenological reactions. In each case there is a tribunal of hard facts which serve as a ground for attributions of understanding: for meaning and translation, the facts concern socially upheld causal/inferential roles (thus the importance of identifying the linguistic community to which a speaker belongs). In the case of musical significance, the facts concern the experiential roles of musical event-types in the relevant communities (hence the importance of identifying the artistic community to which a composer or performer belongs). Thus speaks the monist, intent upon rejecting IMS.

The pluralist opposition, advocating IMS, grants that artefacts are shaped by social/institutional forces, and thus possess certain features that cannot be understood apart from those forces. Therefore, corresponding to each musical event—considered as an artefact—there exists some population which enjoys *explanatory primacy* regarding those features. But the relevance of that explanatory primacy, and thus of that population, is controversial. Musical events are *not* linguistic utterances; no serious music listener need regard his musical experiences as answerable to a tribunal of explanatory adequacy. The advocate of IMS is content to immerse himself in the music and tingle with aesthetic rapture. The suggestion that the 'meaning' of the music renders certain modes of rapture more appropriate than others seems inimical to the very spirit of music. Consequently, the population which the advocate of determinate musical significance elevates to privileged status has, for the advocate of IMS, no privileged status at all: it is simply one community among many, one interest group among many, one set of norms among many. There seems little reason, given the nature and purpose of music, to dignify that population as the tribunal against which to measure the correctness of one's musical experiences. Thus speaks the pluralist, intent upon vindicating IMS.

It is interesting, and perhaps profound, that we still do not know how to settle the dispute. Perhaps there are further constraints, as yet unspecified, that would resolve the matter. Or perhaps the entire dialectic—between 'pluralism' and 'monism' generally—is less a disagreement about a matter of fact and more an instance of disparate commitments concerning music and musical understanding. We tried to determine whether pluralism about musical understanding—as codified in a doctrine of indeterminacy of musical significance—is true. But it might have been a mistake to proceed this way. Perhaps it is not the truth of the indeterminacy thesis that matters, if indeed the thesis has a determinate truth value. What matters, perhaps, is the kinds of commitments incurred, or the kinds of stances manifest, when one endorses (or rejects) IMS. That is: having sought arguments for and against IMS, and having repeatedly reached a stand-off, perhaps we should ask about the purposes served by advocating–or denying—the thesis.

The recommendation that follows exploits the controversial but venerable distinction between 'descriptive' and 'projective' (or 'expressive') uses of language.[10] The suggestion is that the discourse in which IMS and IT are formulated is best understood as playing a non-fact-stating role.

[10] A helpful general discussion of projectivist methodology is Simon Blackburn's *Spreading the Word* (Oxford, 1984), esp. chs. 5–7; irrealist conceptions of the descriptive/expressive distinction are further explored in my 'Varieties of Pragmatism', *Mind*, 99 (Apr. 1990), 157–83.

We imagined a monist who insisted that Beethoven's peers—his know-ledgeable peers—constitute the 'reference population' for attributions of appropriate experience of Beethoven's work, thereby providing a ground for the 'objectivity' of musical significance. I suggest that we view the insistence upon determinate musical significance as the expression of a commitment: to the explanatory importance of the musical perceptions and standards of taste upheld in the particular population which he believes to be *responsible for* the musical event in question. This monist believes that only in terms of such perceptions and standards can various aspects of the piece be adequately explained. His attributions of determinate musical significance manifest his commitment to the norms upheld in a particular population: a commitment to seeing himself as 'one of them'. The significance of a symphony, he argues, is as much an artefact of social/institutional forces as the meaning of an utterance. In insisting upon the determinacy of that significance, he manifests his unwillingness to divorce the musical artefact from the very population that constitutes it.

The pluralist opponent is no fool: he may agree that the designated population occupies a distinguished position *vis-à-vis* the kinds of explanations which concern the monist. But lacking any urgent drive to provide such explanations, the pluralist is willing to cut the piece loose from its causal-historical ancestry and let a thousand equally legitimate audiences bloom. He insists that music is just the sort of thing from which people should derive whatever experiences they can, none being any more or less correct than any other. The monist, annoyed by this sentiment, is thereby annoyed by IMS. What we have, I think, is a clash of sentiments concerning the proper role of music, a clash manifest in arguments about the correctness of IMS. I do not see that any further discovery or argument can resolve the issue. The monist regards population relativity as no threat to the determinacy of musical significance because he, like the translator of natural language, has selected a specific population as maximally relevant to explaining the structure of the musical event, and thus as the reference frame for attributions of musical significance and musical understanding. In this he may have been injudicious, but it seems misguided to accuse him of error concerning some matter of fact.

So it is with arguments about IT: Quine's denial that there are objectively real meanings in addition to dispositions to verbal behaviour is not itself a description of the way things are. IT is the expression of a commitment to a physicalist explanatory strategy. In making this commitment Quine might have been injudicious: he may be unable to carry out the programme, or he may be overlooking data that we believe worthy of explanation. But it seems misguided to accuse him of factual error.

If this is right, then we should not have asked whether musical significance is, like semantic content, objectively determinate; there is room to manœuvre in either direction. We should instead have asked about the purposes served by insisting upon objective determinacy, and whether those purposes are worth achieving.

Musical understanding, like natural language understanding, is attributed against a backdrop of several parameters, foremost among which are relevant community and standards of normalcy within that community. Every attempt to specify a procedure for determining unique values for these parameters invites charges of arbitrariness. Musical significance, like semantic content, *can* be made to appear indeterminate if we dwell upon this; alternatively, we can specify enough constraints as to rule out all but one community and one coherent class of musical experiences within that community as relevant. This, joined with additional constraints, might restore the appearance of determinacy. I opt for the latter strategy; the deeper question is whether anything can be said in its defence.

III

Musical Works in the Worlds of Performers and Listeners

ROBERT L. MARTIN

Familiar problems arise when we ask what sort of an object a musical work is (for example, Beethoven's String Quartet in C, Op. 59 No. 3).[1] The work itself is not any particular score of it (the autograph score, or the plates of the first edition, or any other score or set of parts), or the type of which any actual scores are tokens; this is clear because a person can be familiar with the work without being familiar with the score. The work itself is not any performance or set of performances; this is clear because there can be works that are never performed; it is possible for a person to admire the work without admiring any particular performance or set of performances of it. A musical work is none of the relevant physical objects or acoustical events.

Most of the views I know of characterize musical work as a type (sound structure).[2] They disagree about its nature and about its relation to various particulars—instances, performances, etc. Most accept the challenge of characterizing an object that is both what the composer created[3] and what we as listeners are familiar with through the performances we hear. I want to explore the possibility that the motivating question—what is this object that Beethoven created and with which I am familiar?—may be based on a

I have benefited from discussions with Tyler Burge, Kit Fine, Lydia Goehr, Andrew Gould, Peter Heinrich, Warren Quinn, Robert Winter, and Arnulf Zweig.

[1] I restrict my attention to central cases within the Western art music tradition of the past several hundred years. I doubt whether the concept *musical work* is usefully applied to all kinds of music making (for example, to jazz improvisation), though its useful application probably extends beyond the narrow range of cases I am considering here.

[2] For example, Nelson Goodman, in *Languages of Art: An Approach to the Theory of Symbols* (Indianapolis, 1968), holds that a musical work is a type of which performances are instances. He holds that a work is defined by a score, which, given the notational system in which it is written, uniquely determines the class of performances that belong to the work; further, the score is itself uniquely determined, given a performance and the notational system. Goodman points out a counter-intuitive consequence of his position: 'since complete compliance with the score is the only requirement for a genuine instance of a work, the most miserable performance without actual mistakes does count as an instance, while the most brilliant performance with a single wrong note does not' (186). Goodman considers modifying his position to allow 'some limited degree of deviation in performances admitted as instances of a work'. However, given transitivity of identity and a principle of limited deviation ('performances differing by just one note [omission, addition, modification] are instances of the same work'), it would follow that all performances whatsoever are of the same work! Therefore, within 'technical discourse' (as opposed to everyday speech) Goodman retains his strong view concerning instances of musical works. Other views are presented in K. Walton, 'The Presentation and Portrayal of Sound Patterns', *In Theory Only* (Feb. 1977), 3–16, in N. Wolterstorff, *Works and Worlds of Art* (Oxford, 1980), and in J. Levinson, 'What a Musical Work Is', *Journal of Philosophy*, 77 (1980), 5–28.

mistake. That question assumes that there is such an object. I think there is no such object: that what Beethoven created (namely, instructions to performers) is not the same thing as the musical work that plays a role in the musical practice of knowledgeable listeners. Put most provocatively, musical works, as they are known to listeners, are not created by composers.

Musical works play roles in at least two very different arenas of social practice.[4] The first I will call the performers' world. Here the experts are the master performers. Novices begin study at a very young age, often in one-to-one contact with the experts, in conservatories, schools of music, seminars, and institutes. The novices listen to recordings and attend concerts; they read books and study scores. A major part of what they learn, after acquiring a certain degree of skill on their instruments, is a process of interpreting a musical score. Since musical notation vastly underdetermines the details of performance, performers learn an extremely complex mode of interpreting notation and going beyond it. The performers learn about, or in many cases unconsciously adopt, performance conventions from a variety of historical periods, some that existed at the time the work was first performed, and others that have developed subsequently. They use these conventions to interpret musical notation and to guide musical decisions in matters left unspecified by the notation. The experts in this practice can be seen as collaborators with the composer in the final product—a performance.[5] There is a moral dimension to the players' effort (though it is only one of many dimensions): performers recognize that it is the composer who is the primary creator associated with the work, and the performer has the responsibility to honour his intentions; the performer honours his intentions by studying the score. The score is at the heart of the performer's practice.

A rather different area of musical practice is that of the audience—the world of the informed listener.[6] Viewed from the inside, this seems a very loosely defined group, consisting of whoever wanders into a concert hall, or tunes in to classical music on a car radio. But from a broader perspective this is a rather small and specialized group, with its own experts and novices, with rules and values accepted by those who seek entry into the practice. The experts are familiar with large segments of the classical repertoire, are likely to have large collections of recordings, are knowledgeable about composers and artists, and know the social conventions of concert attendance.

---

[3] Wolterstorff (*Works and Worlds of Art*, 89) holds that composers do not, strictly speaking, *create* works of music; rather they select properties that constitute the work.

[4] For discussion of the concept of social practice, see Alasdair MacIntyre, *After Virtue* (Notre Dame, Ind., 1981). The notion is applied to music by Nicholas Wolterstorff in his 'The Work of Making a Work of Music', in Philip A. Alperson, *What is Music?: An Introduction to the Philosophy of Music* (New York, 1990), 101–30.

[5] I have argued for this picture of the relationship between performer and composer in 'The Quartets in Performance: A Player's Perspective', in R. Winter and R. Martin (eds.), *The Beethoven Quartet Companion*, (Berkeley, Calif., forthcoming).

[6] I do not suggest that the worlds of performers and listeners are wholly distinct—clearly they are not.

Performances of musical works, rather than scores, are at the heart of the listener's world. The listener's mode of connection with a performance is straightforward; however, his mode of connection with musical works, whatever they are, is subtle. I have heard of musical works that I have not heard. Of the works I have heard, I have surely forgotten most parts of most of them, even if remembering a part only requires that I be able to identify it, not to sing or play it. My relationships with musical works are rather like my relationships with people: ranging from cases in which I think that I may have met a person, but remember nothing more than that we met, to cases of familiarity and intimacy. Performances I have heard are in some ways like the stretches of time I have spent with a person; each performance allows me to become more thoroughly acquainted with a work, and sometimes with different facets of a work. But there are strong differences: the musical work does not develop and change, independent of the performances, as a person develops and changes, independent, for the most part, of the time I have spent with the person; performances are not windows on the developing work. Rather, performances are realizations (even if partial) of the entire work. Most importantly, musical works are not physical objects that underlie interrupted stretches of acquaintance with parts of the history of the object.

What then, within the world of the informed listener, are musical works? We may list some of their most important properties:

1. Musical works are capable of being performed an unlimited number of times. It is the need to account for this fact that in part supports the view that musical works are abstract objects.

2. The conditions under which a performance counts as a performance of a particular work, as opposed to a performance of an arrangement or an adaptation of that work, are adjustable. We may speak of a performance of Franck's A major Violin Sonata on the cello, whereas we would speak of a performance of an arrangement of the work for string orchestra (since Franck seems to have given his approval for the former, and the changes in the former case are very minimal compared with those in the latter case). There is no difficulty with the idea of performances on different groups of instruments of a baroque trio sonata, though there would be serious difficulties with allowing that a quartet of wind instruments had actually performed Beethoven's Op. 18 No. 1, as opposed to an arrangement of it. The point is that the relevant information for deciding on the identity of performances includes information about the composer's intentions and the practices of the time of composition.[7]

[7] J. Levinson's treatment of this issue ('What a Musical Work Is', 14 ff.) seems to me too rigid. He offers as a criterion for a correct definition of 'musical work': 'Musical works must be such that specific means of performance or sound production are integral to them' (p. 19). This has the consequence, of course, that a transcription of a musical work (e.g. as above, the version—apparently authorized by Franck—of the Violin Sonata for cello) is a distinct musical work. It appears, from my perspective, that Levinson is led to this extreme position by the nature of the conceptual machinery he works with: if he wants to take performance-means seriously (as he

3. Musical works are generally not susceptible of ideal or definitive performances. Musical works are understood as being interpretable in a variety of valid though substantially different ways. This is accepted, in fact treasured, as part of the richness of musical works. One explanation is that it is understood that performers collaborate with composers in the creation of performances, so that the contribution of new performers will produce new interpretations.

4. Performances of musical works are governed by rules of correctness. Listeners realize that performances can contain mistakes; they assume that such rules are known by the experts in the performer's world, and that these rules have to do with compliance with the composer's instructions.

5. Musical works have value, both as causes of valuable experiences and in themselves, and have some kind of significance or meaning—i.e. some kind of connection with the extra-musical world. It is believed that works do not simply cause certain states in us, but rather that they have related qualities themselves (a section of the work may be sad, as opposed to causing sadness in the listener or reflecting the putative sadness of the composer). Works can have personal significance of a programmatic or emotional kind, and also social and political significance of a certain kind.[8] It is understood that a work has significance relative to a particular audience at a particular time, and that the significance of the work therefore changes over time.

We come now to the crux of the matter. Is it a property of a musical work, within the world of the listener, that it was created by a particular composer at a particular time? There is certainly a strong inclination to say yes—that, for example, the musical work, Quartet in C, Op. 59 No. 3, was created by Beethoven in Vienna in 1805. Three comments, each requiring explanation, are in order:

(a) There are serious difficulties with accepting this view, and there is an alternative account that escapes those difficulties.

(b) There is a plausible explanation for our strong inclination to hold that Beethoven created the work, even assuming that the view is mistaken.

(c) There are insights to be gained by accepting the alternative account.

With regard to point (a): the difficulty emerges by asking (1) what is the ontological status of a musical work within the world of the listener? (2) Is it (a musical work) the sort of thing that could have been created by a particular composer at a particular time? I see two plausible answers to question (1), and

should), then he is constrained to make them part of the sound structure that he regards as the work. I prefer to look to the composer's instructions, and inferred intentions, as the basis for determining the identity conditions for performances.

[8] This is not to endorse what I regard as trivializing accounts of musical works as, for example, expressive of the uprising of the servant class (the harpsichord solo in Bach's Fifth 'Brandenburg' Concerto) against the forces of conventional society (orchestra tutti). See S. McClary, 'The Blasphemy of Talking Politics during the Bach Year', in R. Leppert and S. McClary (eds.), *Music and Society: The Politics of Composition, Performance and Reception* (Cambridge, 1987).

with either the answer to (2) is *no*. The first answer to (1) is that a musical work is a type, of which performances are tokens. Actual performances are created through the collaborative efforts of composer (via his or her instructions to performers) and performers. These performances may vary as widely as is permitted by the constraints imposed by the instructions and the rules and conventions of the then-current performance practices. The source of the similarity of the performances is no mystery—the similarity derives from the fact that each performance can be traced through a historical chain to the composer's instructions. In saying, on this view, that the musical work is a type,[9] I want to emphasize that it is an abstract object that exists because of, and reflects the characteristics of, a series of performances, many of which will be very far removed from what the composer may have imagined. It is because of this that musical works may be said to grow and change, as they are performed by successive generations of performers.

The second answer to question (1) is to say that musical works, in the listener's world, simply do not exist. I find it plausible that there are only performances (exactly as above, created collaboratively by composer and performer), more or less similar to one another. On this view, all statements purportedly about musical works are really about past, present, or future performances, and the composer's instructions at the root of those performances. For example, 'I am familiar with the work' goes into: 'I have heard or imagined some performance.' 'I admire the work but not any performance I have ever heard of it' goes into either: 'On the basis of past performances I have heard but not admired, I can imagine an admirable one'; or, perhaps: 'On the basis of my study of the instructions, I can imagine an admirable performance.' 'That work was never, and will never be, performed' goes into: 'The relevant instructions never were, and never will be, carried out.' 'That work has taken on new and enriched meaning over the years' goes into something like: 'Performances (following the given instructions) have changed over the years.' On this answer to question (1), musical works are fictions that allow us to speak more conveniently about performances.

The point about the second answer to (1), of course, is that the alleged work is nothing that a composer could have created, because it is nothing. The point about the first answer is that types are abstract objects—pure structures of sound—and therefore, prima facie, not the sorts of things that are created by composers.[10]

---

[9] Cf. Richard Wollheim: 'Where we can correlate a class of particulars with a piece of human invention: these particulars may then be regarded as tokens of a certain type. This characterization is vague, and deliberately so: for it is intended to comprehend a considerable spectrum of cases. At one end we have the case where a particular is produced, and then is copied: at the other end, we have the case where a set of instructions is drawn up which, if followed, give rise to an indefinite number of particulars ... an example of the latter would be the Minuet.' (*Art and Its Objects: An Introduction to Aesthetics* (New York, 1968), 67, 68.)

[10] For the remainder of this chapter I shall accept the first answer to question (1)—that musical works in the world of the listener are types of which performances are tokens.

The fundamental difficulty with the view that composers create musical works as known by listeners is not, however, that it is impossible that types—abstract objects—be created by humans at particular moments of time.[11] The fundamental difficulty is that what a composer clearly does create is entirely different from objects of this kind. More simply: the problem is not that musical works, as described, could not have been created by composers, but rather that they are not what composers actually create.

What Beethoven, for example, created was a set of instructions[12] on the basis of which, with the collaboration of performers, new performances are generated. Beethoven created directions to each of the players in the quartet as to pitches, durations, metre, inflection, expression, etc. It was this that he finished at midnight, for which his publishers paid him, etc. I believe it is clear that these instructions are not at all what we have in mind when we characterize musical works as they enter in the world of music listeners.

Point (b) above was that there is a plausible explanation for our strong inclination to hold that Beethoven created the work, even assuming that the view is mistaken. Why, then, are we so inclined to say that, for example,

---

[11] J. Levinson (in 'What a Musical Work Is') seeks to show precisely that works can be treated as types and still created by composers. To do this he distinguishes between two kinds of types: implicit types ('all purely abstract structures that are not inconsistent') and initiated types (those that 'begin to exist only when they are initiated by an intentional human act of some kind'). One of Levinson's examples of an initiated type is the Ford Thunderbird: 'not simply a pure structure of metal, glass and plastic. The pure structure that is embodied in the Thunderbird has existed *at least* since the invention of plastic (1870) . . . But the Ford Thunderbird was created in 1957 . . . It begins to exist as a result of an act of human indication or determination . . . Musical works are indicated structures too, and thus types that do not already exist but must be initiated.' The doctrine of initiated types seems to me unnecessary for musical works or for Ford Thunderbirds. Why not say that what was created in 1957 were the directions for producing cars called Thunderbirds, and that the car itself is the type ('pure' type) of which the vehicles coming off the production line are tokens?

[12] I speak somewhat guardedly here of instructions rather than scores. One has only to consider a few actual cases to see why this is necessary. A number of scores are sometimes available for a single work—in a fairly typical case there is an autograph of a work (a manuscript in the composer's hand); there is a fair copy, produced by the composer or someone else for the engraver; there may be differences between the two, and it may be difficult to decide whether the alterations are corrections or slips of the pen. Then there may be a first edition, different in various ways from the autograph or fair copy. There may be a series of letters between the composer and the publisher correcting misprints or making changes. There may be a subsequent version produced by the composer, again with significant changes, involving sketches, fair copies, and first and subsequent editions. There may be multiple performer's editions, full of the suggestions of celebrated practitioners. There may be a 'critical edition' prepared by a team of scholars, based on all available sources, and incorporating the musical and scholarly judgement of the editors. Where in all this is *the* score of the musical work? In fact the performer must often play the role of detective, trying to determine what was the intention of the composer on which to select the operative instructions. Even here we are on thin ice—it is an idealization to speak of *the intention* of the composer. What we find are a variety of ideas, changes in judgement, accommodation to the limitations or desires of particular performers, and downright inconsistencies. To a greater or lesser degree, the performer fulfils part of his role as collaborator by settling, whether consciously or not, on a particular set of instructions that is typically a composite of the available instructions.

Beethoven created the Op. 59 No. 3 String Quartet? I can see three closely related reasons. The first is that, within the world of the performer, it is generally quite correct to equate the work with the set of instructions, which is exactly what Beethoven did create. When a performer studies a work, it is the score that he or she studies. When we speak of the Guarneri Quartet's interpretation of Schubert's G major Quartet, it is their interpretation of Schubert's instructions that we mean. There are apparent exceptions: when a performer says, 'I don't understand the Finale of the F major Brahms Cello Sonata,' he probably does not mean that he fails to understand the score; I suspect he speaks in this case as a knowledgeable but puzzled listener. His problem is not how to interpret the score, but is rather that he does not find coherence or appropriateness in the work itself, in any of the performances he has heard or can imagine. Such apparent exceptions actually support my point: the central objects of attention when performers speak of studying, interpreting, and performing musical works are the instructions that they must bring to life. So the first reason we are inclined to regard composers as creators of musical works is because, within the social practice of performers, musical works *are* instructions, composers create instructions, so composers are indeed creators of musical works.

The second reason is that, even within the listener's world, one can easily be misled by the very close connection between what the composer does create and the musical work. The connection is that the composer's instructions result in performances, and performances are the tokens of the abstract type that is the musical work.

The third reason is that we want to credit the composer with features of the work that are not properties of the instructions. For example, we credit Beethoven with the wonderful idea, indeed every detail, of the slow-motion 2nd violin passage towards the end of the fugue movement, set against the 'perpetual motion' semi-quaver notes of the other three instruments. This passage is not among the properties of the instructions, but it does belong to every correct performance. So we can credit the composer with having produced instructions that will in turn produce performances with these properties.

Point (c) above is that there are insights to be gained by accepting the alternative account I have offered. This account can be helpful in resolving at least one difficulty in recent discussions of the early music movement. In a *New York Times* piece ('Why Mozart Has Become an Icon for Today', Sunday, 9 September 1990), Richard Taruskin criticizes the view that he sees as supporting the quest for historically accurate performances: (1) 'that the meaning of an artwork is complete at the time of creation, and that the passage of time entails nothing but loss of meaning. (Tradition, in this view, is only noise and distortion, a cosmic game of "telephone.")' He proposes the counter-view: (2) '[an artwork's] meaning for us is mediated by all that has been thought and said about it since opening night, and is therefore incomparably richer than it was'.[13] The opposition between (1) and (2) strikes me as unwelcome and unnecessary. It is unwelcome because, though one surely sees that there is truth in (2), it seems to follow that our inclination to take seriously the original performance context of early works is based on a false assumption. It is unnecessary, I shall argue, if one makes distinctions suggested by our discussion of musical works and composer's instructions.

There should be initial scepticism about the opposition proposed by Taruskin because the expression 'an artwork's meaning' is modified by 'for us' in (2); one would not think of adding 'for us' to 'the meaning of an artwork' as it occurs in (1). This suggests, rightly I think, that 'meaning' is playing a different role in (1) than in (2).

We need to distinguish the following: (a) the composer's intentions with respect to performances, expressed partly through instructions; (b) the musical work as it functions in the listener's world. The composer's intentions are of undeniable importance, quite aside from aesthetic reasons, because of the composer's role as primary creator. The performer undertakes to represent the composer to the public, and is therefore morally obliged to do so as faithfully as possible.

We get at a composer's intentions in a variety of ways—via the score, remarks to performers recorded in other places, the composer's common predilections and practices, other performances that the composer seemed to approve of (or at least tolerate), the then-current conventions that probably lay behind the composer's decisions as to what required marking or emphasis in the score, etc. It is a detective job of great complexity, the more difficult the further we are in time or culture from the composer.

Once the importance of the composer's intentions is understood and granted, Taruskin's polemical thrust is disarmed. One need not accept the contentious view (1) to be justified in one's interest in historically informed performances. Something important about a muscial work *is* complete at the time of creation—the instructions to performers. It will help us understand those instructions today—to know what the composer intended by what he wrote—if we learn as much as possible about what he would have expected from those who performed his works.

With respect to (2), I have already stressed that musical works within the world of the listener change over time, and have importance and value for particular people. In our account, musical works in the listener's world have been unhooked, so to speak, from direct connection with the activity of the composer, and linked to the experience of the listener. Since musical

[13] The reader will recognize that Taruskin is engaged in criticism of what he takes to be the mission of the early music movement—to restore a sense of the original context to performances of early works. He regards (1) above as the implicit assumption, 'still regnant in the musical academy', of, for example, N. Zaslaw's *Mozart's Symphonies: Context, Performance Practice, Reception* (Oxford, 1990).

works are the types of which performances are instances, and since the performances change in interesting ways over the years, musical works can be seen as being altered accordingly. Therefore, of this object, Taruskin's (2) is clearly true.

In summary, let me try to clarify the exact character of the claims I have made. I claim that the expression 'musical work' is used in at least two ways. It is sometimes used to refer to a composer's instructions, and sometimes used to refer to the type of which performances are tokens—to refer, that is, to an abstract object that is not, I claim, created by a composer (or anyone else). I claim that people engaged in the social practice of music performance typically use the expression in the former way, and that people engaged in the social practice of music listening typically use the term in the latter way.

Notation and Realization: Musical Performance in Historical Perspective

BOJAN BUJIC

Music has played an important, sometimes an essential part in systematic and speculative aesthetic theories from the late eighteenth century onwards. The main intention of the philosophers was not to pronounce an opinion on the music of their time, but rather to formulate general principles which determine the position of music within the system of the arts, or the universal nature of its meaning and expressiveness.[1] Very often their whole view of what music was appeared condensed in brief maxims: 'Music is the universal imageless language of the heart' (Schopenhauer); or 'Music is the abstract inner life of feeling' (Hegel); or 'The content of music consists of forms set in motion by sounding' (Hanslick). In all these cases 'music' was taken to be a sounding object, music at the moment of performance, without any consideration of whether the performance was a spontaneous act or whether it followed a notated score. It is probably fair to assume that the question of relationship between performance and score did not even arise as a significant one, although some general cultural assumptions of their time stood behind their view of music. These, not unreasonably, would have assigned the position of primacy to the sounding object which revealed music in an actual mode of existence whereas the notation, as a preparatory state, represented only the potential mode, a set of signs in a score. Even extemporizing, since it tended to adhere to the salient features of style, could easily be imagined in notated form—the processes of notation and performance would appear to be reversed—without bringing any new dimensions into play.

It is likely that in the background of the understanding of music as a sounding object there was an acceptance of a previous existence of a score which occupied an intermediate position in the threefold division linking the composer's imagination to a performer's action. It was, after all, particularly apt to see the second and third stages as a continuum in an age of composer-performers, even if in various genres or stylistic periods the continuum appeared differently structured (in baroque music the written score was extended in the act of performance by the realization of the figured bass).

The apparent certainty of the knowledge of what a musical work of art is may in fact easily lull us into believing that, historically speaking, Western

[1] In this Chapter the term 'music' will be taken to mean 'Western art music'.

tradition of art music in the age of literacy depended on a well-attested relationship: a continuum that flows from the notated to the performed piece of music, or, in the case of extemporization, that one component of the pair completely overshadowed and, indeed, excluded the other, though without qualifying or changing any of the basic notions. However, as the standard notions relate predominantly to the music of the last 350 or so years any attempt to stretch the enquiry further back into the past confronts us with the need to re-examine the categories of notation and performance. It may be fairer to say that in fact the long history of Western civilization shows a changing attitude to the status of the components of the pair. Although dealing here with modes of existence, suggesting an ontological and hence a-historical approach, the relationship discloses its own interesting history.

Towards the very end of *Poetics* Aristotle states that:

tragedy has everything that the epic has (even the epic metre being admissible), together with a not inconsiderable addition in the shape of the music which very clearly gives pleasure. Next, the reality of presentation is felt in the play as read, as well as in the play as acted (*Poet.* 1462^{a}15).[2]

The passage follows a discussion of the relative merits of the two genres of poetry, epic and tragic. It could be said, Aristotle admits, that epic poetry appeals to cultivated readers, those whose imagination could be stirred by the act of reading alone, and that it is a sign of an inadequately developed mind if external stimuli, such as gestures of actors, are needed in order to engage our attention. But then, 'the censure does not touch the art of the dramatic poet, but only that of the actor' (*Poet.* 1462^{a}5). Tragedy, commonly understood to be indissolubly linked with the theatre and acting can, on the other hand, fulfil 'its effect even without movement or action in just the same way as epic poetry; for from the mere reading of a play its quality may be seen' (*Poet.* 1462^{a}10). This is an important qualification for it introduces the notion of differing aspects of existence of a tragedy: as a text and a work of art it exists in another form before it is enacted and it is in that form too that we can absorb it and its meanings. Indeed, its existence as a written text may by implication be understood to be in some way 'better' or 'purer' than the acted version, since in the progress of performance various imperfections, exaggerations, and deviations may be introduced into it.

Is it legitimate to ask whether the tragedy, before its text has been put down in written form, exists elsewhere, say, in the imagination of the playwright? Aristotle provides part of the answer in *Poetics* 1449^{a}10, where he introduces a historical dimension into his argument and points out that both tragedy and comedy 'certainly began in improvisations'. Plato, though his overall intention is different, and the full sense of his argument develops in a

---

[2] Trans. I. Bywater, in *The Complete Works of Aristotle: The Revised Oxford Translation*, ed. J. Barnes (2 vols.; Princeton, NJ, 1984), vol. ii. All quotations from the *Poetics* are taken from this edition.

different direction, offers us a glimpse: the moment of creation is in fact a moment of a particular sort of madness, the poets are inspired and possessed (*Ion*, 533e–534a), they form a chain which connects them to the Muses. Both Aristotle's improvisation, and Plato's inspiration essentially point in the same direction: the literary work of art may be created in a state of immediateness, literally without any intervening stages of writing down and reading. In the process of laying out the arguments Plato can be seen as recognizing the full force of poetry as an essentially oral form of art, connected also with a religious role of the poet as seer and prophet, while Aristotle, a mere generation later, acknowledges the importance of fixing that originally oral art in written form.

If we were to try and look how music fits into all this, Aristotle again seems to offer a view which introduces a clear distinction between the six constituent parts of the tragedy: plot, characters, diction, thought, spectacle, and melody (*Poet.* 1450^{a}10). Aristotle groups the first four as belonging together and they all reside in that aspect of the tragedy's existence which we may call text. The remaining two are mere additions though music is the more important. Language is only enriched by having rhythm, music, and song added to it. Yet, the Greek term *mousikē* is customarily interpreted as a close and indeed indivisible union of music and text. There seems to be some uncertainty in Plato about the nature in which this union is perceived. In *Republic* II 376e he indicates that while speaking of literature he also intends to include music in his argument, though he may mean nothing more than that he intends to treat them in the same manner. The theme is developed slightly further in *Republic* III 398d: a song or ode has three parts: the words, the melody and the rhythm, and the latter two are, not unlike in Aristotle, later additions. Yet they too exist as a pattern of pitches fixed in their relationship through use and tradition. This much may be concluded from Plato's description of the established musical pattern which is enshrined in the concept of *nomos*. The notes of the *nomos* have their existence outside and independently of the words, and at least a theoretical possibility exists that words could be set to a number of different patterns:

To another class of song they assigned the name '*nomoi*' itself, adding the title 'kitharodic'. With these types and various others properly distinguished, it was not permitted to use one type of melody for the purposes of another. (*Laws* 700c)[3]

That only certain tunes are right for a particular text has, of course, to do with the ethical aspect of music. Of particular interest to us is that there exists a physical possibility of putting together different texts and different tunes— and although the result may not be 'right' we are at least able to conclude that a 'tune' has an existence of its own, and may be imagined outside its

---

[3] Quoted after A. Barker (ed.), *Greek Musical Writings*, i: *The Musician and his Art* (Cambridge, 1984), 156.

customarily recognized indissoluble union with poetry. The implications both of Aristotle's *Poetics* and Plato's *Laws* are that music may be thought to have such a separate existence although it is by no means clear what conditions must be met for the two separate existences—of music and of poetry—to be united. This is important for it has been a long-established custom to claim that the Greek term *mousikē* stands for an indivisible union of words and music, whereas it is by no means clear how this union comes to be established in technical terms.

Although in Greek thought primacy was given to the union of words with music, instrumental music was acknowledged as having its own existence. Yet there too, Plato seems to have been troubled by the difficulty of defining the nature of that existence within the terms of music as a sounding object. In *Phaedo* 86a–e he offers us a glimpse of what faces him in an attempt to relate music as a sound to music as a potential which exists within a musical instrument by stressing the incorporeal nature of harmony. The image of the lyre as an instrument and harmony as a reflection of the perfect harmony stand really for the soul and its immortality in relation to the mortal body, for this is the real topic which is at this stage being debated. The full understanding of music, therefore, cannot according to Plato or Aristotle be accomplished on the level of the discussion of it as a physical datum, or indeed as a written text, but must move towards such concepts as harmony and appropriateness of a particular combination of words and music in a system of ethics. This, though the predominant theme of Greek aesthetics, leads outside the boundaries of this chapter.

Although we now know that notational signs were in use in ancient Greece, the writing down of musical pitches and durations must have been regarded as a specialized activity, well beyond the interest of the philosophers. Indeed, they may have regarded the art of notation as an inessential activity and therefore there could not have been an easy comparison of poetry in a written form with music which came into full focus only when the words appeared in the comparable, actual mode of existence in which music was customarily held to appear. Aristotle could, therefore, imagine a tragedy as a written text, whereas music, unless taken in the sense of ideal harmony, was primarily thought of in the moment of performance. Yet even there an awareness of the quantifiable aspects of music must have been the starting-point: music exists in durations and the melody comes into existence when through juxtaposition of unequal pitches the voice appears to 'move' from one pitch to another. The concept of 'movement' therefore becomes the common denominator between music as an actual sounding object and the moral and symbolic aspects that transcend the moment of sounding. Pseudo-Aristotle (*Problems* 919^{b}26, Bk. xix. 27) offers a useful illustration of how the concept of motion may be used to connect the sounding of music and its moral character:

Why is it that of all things which are perceived by the senses that which is heard alone possesses character? For music, even if it is unaccompanied with words, yet has character; whereas a colour and an odour and a savour have not. Is it because that which is heard alone has movement, not, however, the movement in us to which the sound gives rise ... but we perceive the movement which follows such and such a sound?[4]

'Motion' easily assumes several separate, yet not disconnected, meanings since through the link established in antiquity it covers not only the 'motion' of sounds in a melody, but also motion as an astronomical concept, invariably represented in discussions of the harmony of the spheres. In scholastic literature the concept surfaces in the Latin term *modulatio*, where apart from a symbolic meaning it serves to underline the skill of the *musicus* in manipulating and moving musical sounds. The humanists tend to refer either to *modulatio* or *motus*, usually in the process of presenting their credentials as scholars who have perused and understood the ancient authorities. Thus, to take but one example, Nicolaus Burtius in *Musices opusculum* (or *Florum libellus*, Bologna, 1487) talks of music as 'motion':

Just as arithmetic is the ratio of numbers, and geometry of sizes, and astrology of the movements, sizes and distances of heavenly bodies, so music is the movement of sounds.[5]

It is interesting to note that as late as the middle of the nineteenth century Eduard Hanslick, pursuing his intensely autonomist aesthetics, invokes the term again, though probably without any conscious reference to its older usage: 'The content of music consists of forms set in motion by sounding.'[6] This wording may have been Hanslick's conscious attempt to establish that the 'motion' belongs to the very structure of the artistic object, rather than suggesting the existence of a separate content, reminiscent of the ancient ethos, as seems to be implied in Hegel's claim that 'music ... has to do with the inner movement of the soul'.[7]

Separate, yet connected, appearances of music in notated form and as a sounding object were for Hanslick and, indeed, for all his contemporaries a matter of established fact. His discussion of music's identity assumes this duality though stressing the importance of the sounding object:

Only the person who retains not just the general aftereffects of feeling, but also the unforgettable, specific image of just this particular piece of music, has heard it and enjoyed it.[8]

---

[4] Trans. E. S. Foster, in *The Complete Works of Aristotle*, ed. Barnes.

[5] N. Burtius, *Musices opusculum*, 1.1; trans C. A. Miller (Musicological Studies and Documents 37; Neuhausen-Stuttgart, 1983), 29.

[6] 'Der Inhalt der Musik sind tönend bewegte Formen.' E. Hanslick, *Vom Musikalisch-Schönen*, 3.6, ed. D. Strauss (Maniz, 1990), 75. Translation mine.

[7] G. W. F. Hegel, *Aesthetics: Lectures on Fine Art*, trans. T. M. Knox, 2 vols. (Oxford, 1974), ii. 855.

[8] Hanslick, *Vom Musikalisch-Schönen*, 3.27; quoted after *On the Musically Beautiful*, trans. G. Payzant (Indianapolis, 1986), 66.

The reference to memory enabling the hearer to form a full impression of a piece of music is a significant indicator of the central importance of a piece of music as heard. Although the notation and the existence of a score as a prerequisite for performance were in his time taken for granted he did not particularly question the details of the score's relationship to performance. Yet the mention of memory, albeit implictly, initiates a whole set of questions: what is the mode of existence of music? Does it reside in memory? Is it only manifested in the moment of sounding? What is the status of notated music as a written document?

For a late classical or a scholastic author an answer to such questions would have been an easy one. Isidore of Seville (c.559–636), altering and varying St Augustine's words (from *De ordine*, II. xiv) is responsible for the definition of music later widely disseminated:

Music is an art of modulation consisting of tone and song, called music by derivation from the Muses. The Muses were so named ... because, as the ancients would have it, they inquired into the power of songs and the modulation of the voice.... Hence it was fabled by the poets that the Muses were the daughters of Jove and Memory. Unless sounds are remembered by man, they perish, for they cannot be written down.[9]

Some two and a half centuries later Aurelianus Reomensis is able to repeat this:

It was said that the Muses ... were the daughters of Jupiter, and were said to aid the memory, since this art, unless committed to memory is not retained.[10]

It is perhaps unimportant in a larger historical context whether these statements are to be taken as proofs that musical notation was not known to the cited authorities. Even if it existed in a rudimentary form, it was essentially an aid to memory: non-diastemmatic neumes can serve as memory aids to those who know the melodies but can scarcely benefit the uninformed. The whole subsequent course of Western notation represents a move away from memory towards the state in which a written document can stand on its own, as it were, representing the work as such and offering to the performer clear indications how to recreate it in musical sounds. In the early fourteenth century Johannes de Muris referred to musical notes as being 'arbitrarily representative of numbered sound measured in time', but then went on to praise the notational possibilities that existed in his time.[11] Some earlier attempts, like the one to be found in the treatise *Musica enchiriadis* (c.900) solve the problem by offering what amounts to a visual equivalent of rising and falling melodic lines, strikingly reminiscent of lines in a scientific graph. A

---

[9] Isidore of Seville, *Etymologiarum sive originum libri XX*, 3.15; Eng. trans. in O. Strunk (ed.), *Source Readings in Music History* (New York, 1950), 93.
[10] Aurelianus Reomensis, *Musica Disciplina*, ed. L. Gushee (Corpus Scriptorum de Musica 21; n.p. 1975), 61. Translation mine.
[11] Strunk, *Source Readings in Music History*, 175.

polyphonic, or at least a two-part, composition is represented as if exemplifying motion and thus giving to the term an empirical rather than a metaphysical significance. In this case the visual presentation clearly shows the simultaneity of lines but it is precisely this visual simultaneity that disappears from most notated music within a very large time-span stretching from the thirteenth to the early seventeenth centuries. Whether presented (rarely) in score or predominantly in separate parts or part-books, the notation throughout this long period shows an intense preoccupation with the minutiae of precise rhythmic detail. Examples such as the intricate 'mannered' notation of the late fourteenth century indicate that the written text had to be pondered rather than recreated in performance with ease, thus diminishing the sense of immediacy or spontaneity.

The independent status of notation as a written document may be seen by inference from the way in which Nicolaus Burtius, fully aware that as a humanist he should show his knowledge of ancient sources, returns to the old description of Isidore and Aurelianus, but mentions the impossibility of writing the sounds down as a thing of the past.[12] In Burtius's terms, giving life to music through performance is not an act of creation in an absolute sense, not a spontaneous release of some hidden emotional energy, as the evolutionists in the nineteenth century tried to argue. Rather than recreating the music from memory the process presupposes a potential existence of the material of music beyond and before individual memory: the performance is a method of actualizing something that exists as a precondition, as a given quality, to be comprehended through the process of learning. Not just a simple 'learning to sing' or 'learning to play', but an approach which specifies 'learning to sing (or to play) correctly', by recognizing objective values contained in the material of music. The paths of approach and the ways of recognition may differ, but they ultimately lead to one and the same given set of qualities:

Dearest friends, even if the practices of singing are varied, as has been said, and the manner of teaching varied, yet however anyone may sing, he cannot raise or lower a tone unless following the diatonic genus he sings a whole tone or small semitone, a ditone or semiditone, and similar intervals, for the entire study of music revolves about them.[13]

And if Burtius states his case in a somewhat circumlocutory manner, then Stephano Vanneo in *Recanetum de musica aurea* (Rome, 1533) sharpens his focus to direct the attention not simply to the objective existence of the material of music, but to a definite set of relationships that govern a composition:

Measured music consists of various quantities of notes, or indeed, this is said of whichever song consisting of measured time, of which the notes, in name or form, in

---

[12] Burtius, *Musices opusculum*, 29.   [13] Ibid. 51.

essence and in quality, are determined, whose quantity can be neither augmented nor diminished.[14]

In the precision with which the components are marked as fixed in the particular aspect given to them in a composition, it contrasts sharply against the vagueness of those general definitions which abound in musical treatises stretching from the late antiquity throughout scholastic literature, and still persist in the sources of the fifteenth and the early sixteenth centuries. Compared with such universalist scholastic assertions one may appreciate all the more Vanneo's desire to point to the condition governing the existence and the uniqueness of a composition as an embodiment of relations arising from the material of music.

In a complete contrast to Vanneo's stand Leonardo da Vinci's comparison between the arts of painting and music is firmly dependent on the Augustinian revision of Aristotle's classification of the senses. As the sense of hearing, though in a higher group of two, comes nevertheless second to sight, music loses out in the comparison and is in Leonardo's opinion particularly disadvantaged by its transience:

Music may be called the sister of painting, for she is dependent upon hearing, the sense which comes second, and her harmony is composed of the union of its proportional parts sounded simultaneously, rising and falling in one or more harmonic rhythms. . . . But painting excels and ranks higher than music, because it does not fade away as soon as it is born, as is the fate of unhappy music . . .[15]

It is clear that Vanneo and Leonardo do not speak of the same aspect of a musical work of art. Vanneo, however, starting from the viewpoint of a composer is intensely aware of the existence of a definite set of relationships which determine the work 'as it is' even before it sounds forth, while Leonardo, in spite of his lip-service to the notions of proportion and harmony fails to appreciate the complexity of the relationship of notated and performed music. The parallel existence of such diverse views is a strongly persistent feature of Western thought and is often conditioned by the position of the speaker in relation to the tripartite division between composition, notation, and performance. Leonardo is unequivocally placing himself at the receiving end of the third stage, minimizing the importance of the preceding two.

Vanneo's contemporary Nicolaus Listenius in his *Musica* of 1537 is even more concise in directing the reader to appreciate the uniqueness of a musical work of art:

---

[14] S. Vanneo, *Recanetum de musica aurea*, 1.5; (photographic reprint, Documenta musicologica 28), ed. Susanne Clercx (Kassel, 1969) 7. Translation mine.

[15] *Selections from the Notebooks of Leonardo da Vinci*, ed. Irma A. Richter (Oxford, 1977), 197. Hegel likewise holds that the notes 'with their fleeting passage . . . vanish again and therefore the musical composition needs a continually repeated reproduction, just because of this purely momentary existence of its notes.' Hegel, *Aesthetics*, ii. 909.

[*Musica poetica*] consists, indeed, in creating or making, that is, in an effort of an especial kind, which even after it is accomplished, and author having died, leaves behind a perfect and complete work.[16]

Listenius's definition achieves a fine balance between the work as an entity in itself and its ultimate cause, the exercise of craft coming from the composer. It seems to suggest that by the sixteenth century a view was well established that the primary mode of existence of a composition is its notated form, the one that survives its author and remains as a document. The objection may be raised that at best such reasoning is appropriate for Listenius's time, or at worst for Listenius himself, and may be of little relevance for the music of other periods. A possible answer to this should again be sought in the notation and the relationship of the notated to performed music.

It may be suggested that as a possible counterbalance to the notion of a modern, i.e. nineteenth- or twentieth-century, score as a faithful embodiment of a composer's intentions stretching beyond the notes themselves and encompassing diverse expression marks or verbal descriptions of a desired effect, musicologists at one stage resorted to extolling the virtues of the past ages where notation, it was claimed, was only a hint to the performer, who was allowed a degree of freedom, becoming as it were a co-author of a composition under the guidance of good taste and generally accepted style. The starting point in this argument was the music of the baroque, but the principle was allowed to extend beyond the early seventeenth century. In itself this may not have been an erroneous attempt at reconstructing historical or 'authentic' performance practice, but in their search for the sound of music, musicologists allowed themselves to fall into a methodological trap confusing the identity of music as performed with music as conceived by a composer.

If we accept the undeniable existence of two separate phenomena—the intricacy of the score and the circumstantial evidence provided by historical musicology that music in performance was altered and embellished—then we must conclude that there existed a strong separation of the categories of music as notated and as performed/heard. This suggests that our modern notion of performance as a logical continuation of the process of composition should not be uncritically projected into a historical period in which composition and notation on the one hand, and performance on the other, seem to be conceived of as two separate modes of existence of a composition. This does not render a performance of an ornamented version of, say, a fifteenth-century chanson or an Italian madrigal invalid, but the failure to recognize the different 'degrees of objectivation' denies us a chance to understand the aesthetic conditions under which a composition first came into being. The task of music history is, surely, to recognize the existence of both the 'pragmatic' and the 'ontological' dimensions, for without such under-

---

[16] N. Listenius, *Musica* (Wittenberg, 1537), ch.1; quoted from the 22nd edn. (Nuremberg, 1549, repr. Berlin 1927). Translation mine.

standing artefacts and documents remain dangerously dissociated from the
intellectual climate in which they came into existence.

Earlier it was mentioned that the baroque score appears to be in a sense
incomplete since the realization of the figured bass was supplied only in the
moment of performance. But it ought to be stressed that it may only appear to
be the case since the pieces as notated exhibit an implicit recognition that the
work exists in differentiated levels and only those which are an essential part
of the work are notated. The substance of the work is enshrined in the
forward flow determined by the melodic parts and the bass line and it is these
elements that are given priority in the act of notation. It transpires that no
such differentiation existed in the polyphonic music of the preceding centuries
when the totality of individual, yet mutually dependent, lines of greater
structural equality provided a closer identity between the conception in a
composer's imagination and the notated form. Subsequent embellishment,
together with chromatic changes occasioned by the practice of *musica ficta*,
appear in this case as optional addenda to the originally well-balanced structure. It is this structural aspect of the work that informs Vanneo's and
Listenius's attitude.

Figured bass as a separate stratum of a work ceases to be a structurally
important aspect of music in the second half of the eighteenth century, yet
the period inherited some important features of the baroque taste: dynamic
differentiation and expressive nuances of phrasing. While some new graphic
signs were introduced in order to record such features, essentially additional
to the standard notational picture, a great deal of responsibility in the process
of interpretation rested with the composers, who in a large number of cases
were also performers of their own music, thus helping to establish and
disseminate their individual style within the boundaries of current taste. We
only need to remind ouselves of the fame of Domenico Scarlatti, C. P. E.
Bach, or W. A. Mozart as performers.

The romantic insistence on the uniqueness of individual creativity
diminishes the importance of checks and balances so strongly manifested in
various eighteenth-century styles. E. T. A. Hoffmann, the standard-bearer of
the romantic aesthetics of music offers a fascinating parable in one of his
novellas. A ghost dressed as an eighteenth-century courtier leads the author
through the dark Berlin alleys into a room and shows him bound scores of
Gluck's operas. The ghost places a score on the piano and, having asked
Hoffmann to turn pages for him, begins to play. Hoffmann is astonished to
see that the score contains only blank pages. Yet, he recognizes the music his
ghostly companion plays, it is *Armida*, sometimes faithful to the original but
mostly better and improved, and invested with an intensity and power that
outshines the work as known to Hoffmann. At the end the ghost introduces
himself as 'Ritter Gluck'.[17] In the form of a vibrant fantastic story Hoffmann

[17] See E. T. A. Hoffmann, *Ritter Gluck*, in *Werke* (5 vols.; Zurich, 1946), i. 289–301.

expounds his view of the ontology of a work of music: it exists, complete and perfect, in the imagination of the composer; its notated form, though perfect in its own right is not up to the ideal appearance that resides in the mind of the creator. Enthusiastically praising Beethoven's instrumental music through another of his literary creations, Kapellmeister Kreisler, Hoffmann makes a profession of faith in the power of the piano claiming that a 'full score, that true musical book of charms preserving in its symbols all the miracles and mysteries of the most heterogeneous choir of instruments, comes to life at the piano under the hands of a master'.[18] The thought is developed further as if to qualify not only the earlier of Kreisler's statements but also the point made in *Ritter Gluck*: 'The true artist lives only in the work that he conceives and then performs as the composer intended it. He disdains to let his own personality intervene in any way...'.[19] The work must, therefore, in some significant way reside in notated form as a complete and significant picture. We have here a return to Vanneo's position with an important new element—the recognition of the continuum between the written and performed piece, albeit with a caveat about the limit of the performer's right to interfere with the substance of the work.

It is not too far-fetched to propose that Hoffmann throws an interesting prophetic light on Beethoven's attitude to notated text. Traditionally Beethoven is seen as a composer using to his full advantage the new expressive potential of the piano. We have, however, to take into consideration Beethoven's diminishing ability to provide a reliable continuum between notation and performance: as he gets progressively more isolated from the physical datum of sound, he has to rely more and more on the verbal and graphic additions to the score instead of providing through his own performance the model of how music is to sound. It is instructive to compare the relatively sparse expressive markings in the early sonatas with the profusion that can be observed in late works (Op. 106, the 'Hammerklavier', and Op. 111 are particularly telling examples). The notation becomes more and more invested with details which are designed to ensure that the image of the notation, its visual appearance, contains within itself the determinants of 'the Work'.

Subsequent generations of composers, critics, and performers alike take this kind of image for granted, yet perpetuating the while a Hoffmannesque duality in which on the one hand 'music' exists in a state of immediacy and on the other hand cannot be properly thought of without the status of significant importance being accorded to the work's visual image in the score. It is therefore regrettable that nineteenth-century philosophers have left us without any account of their attitude to the issues that this duality may generate.

Twentieth-century analysts have shown some considerable faith in the

---

[18] E. T. A. Hoffmann, 'Beethoven's Instrumental Music', in *Kreisleriana*, quoted after *E. T. A. Hoffmann's Musical Writings*, ed. D. Charlton, trans. M. Clarke (Cambridge, 1989), 101.
[19] Ibid. 103.

visual presentation of musical processes since critical accounts of the purely structural musical meaning of a work cannot now be conceived of without the aid of graphic presentation. In their act of analysis which re-presents the significant inner structure of a work Heinrich Schenker in particular and the modern analytical practice in general are in an elaborate way trying to add weight to and interpret the substance of Listenius's statement. At the opposite end of the spectrum, John Cage's *4'33″* is an attempt to remove the allegedly obtrusive presence and dictate of the composer and the score, allowing 'the work' to grow beyond mere notes on paper, or sounds that they generate, and to encompass the whole of a hearer's mental and auditive experience. But there is a paradox here, for under the pretext that he wishes to remove the dictate of the author, Cage has in fact given significance to an otherwise 'empty' stretch of time only by imposing his authority on the potential hearers, instructing them to regard that stretch as 'the work'. Far from removing himself he has in fact intervened with an act of dictatorial arbitrariness. Presumably his answer would be that a paradox is all that he is interested in. May it not be that he is trying to tell us that after many centuries we do not still know where and how a musical work of art exists? Has he, perhaps, only extended the meaning of the concept of sound, and raised the ontological status of the last of Aristotle's six constituent parts of the tragedy above the level of all the others?

Music as Ordered Sound: Some Complications Affecting Description and Interpretation

JOSEPH MARGOLIS

I

Ever since its appearance in 1854 Eduard Hanslick's *On the Musically Beautiful* has exerted a remarkable influence on the discussion of what music is, or is capable of arousing or expressing or representing; in fact, on Hanslick's view, the latter (three) options are already suspect since 'the content of music is tonally moving forms'.[1]

Hanslick's classic essay surely deserves the enormous respect it commands—but not for the reasons one might insouciantly suppose. It is not because it actually captured the 'essential' nature of music (or, paradoxically, missed it in a corrigible way). It is, rather, remarkably sensible about the nature of human mental states, the complexity of emotions in particular, their dependence on physiology and thought: it is in this sense that it is perceptive about the utter difference between music and mental states.[2] It certainly announces what it takes the 'specifically musically beautiful' to be and to exclude: for instance, 'The representation of a specific feeling or emotional state is not at all among the characteristic powers of music.'[3] But it never says why it must be so, or how we should ever demonstrate that it is indeed so. In making its claim, moreover, it obliges us, by its own indirection, to consider a neglected constraint on all theorizing about musical expression and representation (as well as about expression and representation in the other arts): namely, that we must be prepared to support a conceptual 'adequation' between whatever we impute as the *nature* of music and what, congruent with that 'nature', we concede or insist is possible or impossible regarding expression and representation and similar functions. Hanslick is particularly instructive in this regard.

In short, Hanslick shows, though this is not what he sets out to do, that if we mean to assign music the variety of properties we are tempted to—that

---

[1] Eduard Hanslick, *On the Musically Beautiful; A Contribution Toward the Revision of the Aesthetics of Music*, trans. and ed. from 5th edn. Geoffrey Payzant (Indianapolis; 1980), 29.

[2] Ibid., chs. 2, 4.

[3] Ibid. 30, 9; cf. 15. Hanslick actually says: 'The autonomous beauty of tone forms in music and the absolute supremacy of thought over sound as merely a means of expression in spoken language are so exclusively opposed that a combination of the two is a logical impossibility' (42).

'expression' and 'representation' signify in only the largest way—then we must also be prepared to argue that the nature of music is quite other than Hanslick says it is. Otherwise, music's properties should not be 'adequated' to its putative 'nature'. Once we see this, then good sense requires that we should wonder why, *if* it is deliberately produced, made, invented, altered intentionally through its own history in order to find what (as the artefact it is) we cannot make it do, music could not be more than mere 'sound and motion'. That is, we should wonder why music could not be construed—by those alone who make and appreciate it: human beings, after all—as genuinely possessing a 'nature' congruent with what *they* take themselves to make and then discern, interpret, judge, and savour ('in it') in a reasonably disciplined way.

Read thus, Hanslick's essay certainly affords a sustained account of what follows from restricting the essence of music in the way Hanslick does; but it is even more interesting as an implicit 'meta'-reflection on the nature of dispute about the essence of music. After all, there is no single, self-evident, direct inspection of music's 'essence' that we could ever claim to have completed: the 'analysis' of music's essence is really a proposal of what, theoretically, best fits (for the time being at least) the historical achievement actual musical communities convincingly take themselves to be focused on.

To press the point rather lightly here, the 'adequation' between music's nature and its imputed functional properties is, quite simply, the upshot of a first-order *analysis* of *some* music: an analysis that is itself equilibrated, conceptually, with a certain second-order *proposal* (reciprocally equilibrated, on its side) regarding what we *should* construe as its nature—suitably, for that analysis. Regularized as a distinctive form of enquiry, such second-order proposals may be dubbed 'legitimative', 'pragmatic', even 'transcendental', although elevating them thus hardly vouchsafes that they will capture any greater musical necessities or deeper essential invariances than the first-order 'analyses' they are fitted to. The distinction between 'first-order' and 'second-order', here, is itself 'second-order', in the deflationary sense (the epistemic sense) that the distinction of levels of discourse is not a distinction of increasing cognitive power or privilege. Both spring from precisely the same cognitive sources.[4] (That is just what 'equilibration' is meant to suggest.)

We need to be clear that the quarrel we have set ourselves is likely to appear a fussy one: whether, that is, music can, or ought, to be restricted or not to mere 'ordered sound'? The issue lends itself, it seems, to a simple choice. But a great deal hangs on the matter, and there is no simple test by which to settle it. Briefly put, the question before us is this: whether music can, or ought, to be restricted or not to how mere physical sound is ordered; whether the (apparent) intentional (*and* intensional) complexities of

---

[4] See Joseph Margolis, *Pragmatism without Foundations: Reconciling Realism and Relativism* (Oxford, 1986), ch. 11.

musical representation and expression and rhetoric and the like *are* musically admissible and not reducible to mere 'ordered sound'; whether musical notation, the interpretation and appreciation of music, the aesthetically pertinent properties of music, and similar concerns exceed the resources of any physicalism or extensionalism? Our own answer is that physicalism and extensionalism are indeed inadequate, and that therefore many well-known theories of music cannot but be adversely affected. What follows, then, may seem excessively quarrelsome—and in a way it is. But, given the long, distinctly favourable innings accorded Hanslick's thesis and others that move only a few steps beyond it, it offers a compendious sense of just how much is at stake in the quarrel posed. Needless to say, to make the case is to bring the theory of music into closer accord with the obvious complexities of literature and painting.

Now, the usual rebuttal to Hanslick's sort of argument favours the empirical availability of an informed consensus regarding the expressive or representational in music. This is, for example, the point of Peter Kivy's well-known effort to confirm 'musical expressiveness'.[5] But even if such a consensus held, it would not, as such, resolve the adequation question. (We shall return to the issue.)

There is, actually, some question as to whether Kivy rightly construes his examples uniformly as examples of expression rather than of representation, though Kivy himself is quite explicit about his own preference.[6] There is, also, an odd qualification in Kivy's account: first, because the distinction between expression and representation is a fair one, one that needs to be appraised with respect to music's capabilities, one that is hardly exhausted by limiting representation to representation *of* expression or 'expressive behavior'; and second, because Kivy's own intuition is grounded in a passage taken from Dryden's 'A Song for St. Cecilia's Day 1687', though, as Paul Thom, confronting Kivy's account, shows, referring chiefly to Handel's 'Ode for St. Cecilia's Day' (which Kivy does not actually discuss) as well as the rhetoricians of the period who claim that music is capable of imitating rhetorical figures, a more than fair case may be made to show that the baroque music Kivy had in mind (initially) *is* representational of expression (whether or not it is also intrinsically expressive).

Thom manages to show just how straightforwardly the detailed figures in baroque views of music may be recognizably illustrated in the music of the period. The baroque theorists, he says (Caccini and Mattheson, for instance), 'recommend that musical execution be modelled on oratorial delivery and that music "be composed in Imitation of a Discourse". The comparison between

---

[5] Peter Kivy, *Sound Sentiment: An Essay on the Musical Emotions, including the complete text of The Corded Shell* (Philadelphia, 1989). The pagination of the material from *The Corded Shell* remains the same in *Sound Sentiment*. Kivy adds four additional essays in *Sound Sentiment*.

[6] Ibid. 64.

music and rhetoric, not just in terms of their effects, but in the most specific details of form and technique, pervades the baroque age.'[7]

Thom makes good his charge in abundant detail. 'What Passion cannot Music raise and quell!' the Dryden poem affirms. So Thom proceeds to identify a series of representational (rather than expressive) parallels between the rhetorician's figures and musical details taken from Handel's text. Mattheson, for instance, 'says of a musical Exordium that it should reveal the "purpose and intention" of the piece "in order to prepare the listener and arouse his attention".' Quintilian's advice, followed in the eighteenth century, suggests that 'we shall derive some silent support from representing that we are weak, unprepared, and no match for the powerful talents arrayed against us'. So, the figure of Aporia or doubt is sometimes invoked, where, that is, we 'pretend to be at a loss where to begin'. Handel begins his 'Ode' with a musical aporia, in which 'the main subject is ... stated in a hesitant and incomplete form by the solo cello'. He then 'closes this ... Exordium [Thom notes] with a striking Epiphenomena', which, as he explains, is 'an exclamation attached to the end of some section of a speech by way of climax', and which (following Quintilian) was common in the eighteenth-century school texts. Handel uses a variant of this epiphenomena 'at or near the end of each section of the aria'.[8]

Thom offers a considerable number of such illustrations. But what is more important about his account is that the examples *are* examples of specifically rhetorical devices that are not expressive (in Kivy's sense) and not grammatical or semantic (in any ordinary sense): for instance, they instantiate figures of 'pause, accent, emphasis, articulation' that encompass expression but are not restricted to expressiveness (or, not initially governed by it); and, on the thesis, 'Rhetorical analysis can uncover the ways in which the music is structured'.[9] Thom finds in Handel further illustrations of anaphora, climax, narrative structures such as hypotyposis (vivid description) and ecphonesis (a characteristic intonation and timing of voice), epizeuxis (an immediate or strong repetition)—Dryden's line, for instance, 'When Jubal struck the corded shell' is actually repeated—enantiosis (antithesis), and (beyond the 'narrative' elements) even a proof (a structural analogue of a syllogism), which links the early solo cello motif with the main subject.[10] Such examples clearly challenge the thesis that music is mere ordered sound, though the matter is not so easily settled.

Kivy's theory favours the expressiveness of music because it is based primarily on a perceived 'resemblance' (a 'congruence') between 'musical "contour" with the structure of [human] expressive features and behavior'— or, by way of extension, with certain further conventional linkages.[11] But,

---

[7] Paul Thom, 'The Corded Shell Strikes Back', in Joseph Margolis (ed.), *The Worlds of Art and the World* (Amsterdam, 1984), 95.

[8] Ibid. 96–8.   [9] Ibid. 108.   [10] Ibid. 106–7.

[11] Kivy, *Sound Sentiment*, 77, 83. See, also, Stephen Davies's review of *Sound Sentiment*, in *Journal of Aesthetics and Art Criticism*, 49 (1991).

although he does not specify music's 'essence', it is clear that Kivy's thesis is largely restricted to certain systematic relations between music and 'expressive [human] features and behavior'. So two limitations suggest themselves: first, the relational account is just as convincing for a representational function as for an expressive one (as per Thom); and second, it might well be possible to attribute both expressive and representational (as well as the sort of rhetorical and similar properties Thom considers) as intrinsic properties *of* the music, *if* music's 'nature' were construed in a way rather different from that of Kivy's model. Kivy's own attraction to eighteenth-century empiricism suggests that, although he reaches a different conclusion, he is not altogether opposed to the sort of model that attracted Hanslick, that is, a model of music as 'ordered sound'.

II

In a curious way, a limitation related to Kivy's and Hanslick's (and Thom's, so far at least as it is developed in the paper cited) appears in Susanne Langer's view of musical expressiveness. For Langer is persuaded that music is inherently restricted (as a 'presentational' rather than a 'discursive' symbolism): it is not, 'logically speaking, a language, for it has no vocabulary'. Musical tones 'lack the very thing that distinguishes a mere vocable: fixed connotation or "dictionary meaning"'. They possess only 'the purely structural requirements for a symbolism'—structures that bear only 'a close logical similarity to the forms of human feelings': 'music is a tonal analogue of emotive life'.[12] Here, again theory tends to favour a model of musical 'tones' moving in the direction of something like mere 'sound and movement'—even if semiotically much enlarged beyond Hanslick's vision.

Much of the impetus in favour of the restrictive thesis comes from an impression of the minima of musical notation. Hanslick had already urged the point. Hanslick offers an analysis, for instance, of some of the features 'of melody, rhythm, and harmony' that he finds in the theme of Beethoven's Overture to *Prometheus*; he flatly declares, confining the 'music' to the 'sounds' *designated in the score*, that: 'Beyond this we cannot by any means discern any further content in the theme or, at any rate, anything we might call a feeling which it represents or must arouse in the hearer.'[13] Even the alternative relational accounts of expressiveness and representation (as in Langer, Kivy, Thom) tend to converge toward the notational limit. But what if we rejected that model, even where we conceded the instructive and individuative function of a score (a matter also obviously open to dispute)?

It is very curious that Nelson Goodman's account of notationality (not

---

[12] Susanne K. Langer, *Philosophy in a New Key: A Study in the Symbolism of Reason, Rite, and Art* (Cambridge, Mass., 1963), 228–9, 232, 238; *Feeling and Form* (New York, 1953), 27.
[13] Hanslick, *On the Musically Beautiful*, 14.

restricted to music but paradigmatically illustrated there) should have come to dominate the recent analytic aesthetics of music. For, as Jerrold Levinson neatly observes, *contra* Goodman, 'a [musical] work's aesthetic meaning is too fine-grained to inhere in an extensionally defined sound structure'.[14] There can be no question that, on Goodman's view, the invariant structure of a musical composition is adequately identified in terms of an extensionally defined system of ordered sounds (disjoint 'compliance-classes' of 'sound-events' answering to a given notation[15]). Still, disappointingly, Levinson's objection goes only a short distance beyond Goodman's formula (contestably: its complaint may actually be recoverable by Goodman, given Levinson's intentions). For Levinson maintains:

the standard musical work [Levinson means to restrict his account here to 'the fully notated "classical" compositions of Western culture'[16]] is not a *pure* structure at all [that is, mere sound as such], but an *indicated* structure—a pure structure of sounds and performance means-as-indicated-by-a-person-at-a-particular time. Thus, Brahms's Piano Trio in C, Op. 101, is not simply a sequence of sounds performed on a piano, violin, and cello, but rather that sequence-as-indicated-by-Brahms-in-the-summer-of-1880. . . . the aesthetic and artistic attributes of a work are not fixed solely by the relevant sound/performance means structure. This precludes identifying such works with the pure structures comprised in them.[17]

Now, Goodman might reasonably claim: first, that *he* means by 'compliants' of notated 'characters' (or, that he is prepared to accommodate, in speaking of '*compliants*') sounds *produced* on 'indicated' musical instruments (more or less in Levinson's sense); and, second, that such compliants, though admittedly 'compos[ed] in different musico-historical contexts', as Levinson rightly insists,[18] *are* still recoverable *in extensional terms suited to or congruent with the extensional treatment of ordered sounds*. Levinson thinks 'musico-historical contexts' are intensional—*a fortiori*, 'musical works' are 'intensionally individuated by their more fine-grained aesthetic meanings and artistic significances', beyond 'pure sound (or tonal) structures', because he accounts for that intensionality 'via the occasion-bound intentionality of the composer who creates them'.[19] But Levinson never disproves—and, of course, Goodman could claim, as far as the objection given is concerned—that *non*-auditory criteria (that do behave extensionally) could pick out time, occasion, instrument, even 'history' extensionally, in a way that would suitably qualify or

[14] Jerrold Levinson, 'What a Musical Work Is, Again,' *Music, Art, and Metaphysics; Essays in Philosophical Aesthetics* (Ithaca, NY, 1990), 257. See, also, David Pearce, 'Musical Expression: Some Remarks on Goodman's Theory', in Veikko Rantala, Lewis Rowell, and Eero Tarasti (eds.), *Essays on the Philosophy of Music*, Acta Philosophica Fennica, 43 (Helsinki, 1988).
[15] See Nelson Goodman, *Languages of Art: An Approach to the Theory of Symbols* (Indianapolis, 1968), 177–92.
[16] Cf. Levinson, 'What a Musical Work Is', in *Music, Art, and Metaphysics*, 64–5.
[17] Levinson, 'Autographic and Allographic Art', ibid. 97.
[18] Levinson, 'What a Musical Work Is', 72 (in the context of § ii).
[19] Levinson, 'What a Musical Work Is, Again', 249; cf. the rest of § x.

restrict, without disturbing, our reliance on ordered sound. Nothing that Levinson brings to the discussion precludes such a move. And, indeed, Levinson's principal objective in advancing his own account is *not* so much to attack the extensional treatment of musical sound—*once suitably contexted*—as to oppose Peter Kivy's musical Platonism.[20]

III

Perhaps a final specimen theory will help us here, one that is defective in quite a different way from those we have already examined—one that, by default, nevertheless still points to the sort of complication we are featuring.

Kendall Walton has recently offered a comprehensive theory of the arts, including music, that, first of all, recognizes the functional nature of the arts in so far as they are representational—also, in so far as they are (however marginally) expressive, or in so far as they involve rhetorical or quasi-linguistic features. Walton's strategy is completely opposed to that of the options we have been considering.

We must step back a bit to prepare the ground for Walton's manœuvre. Here is one line of entry into it:

When it is 'true in a game of make-believe,' as we say, that Jules goes on a buffalo hunt, the proposition that he goes on a buffalo hunt is *fictional*, and the fact that it is fictional is a *fictional truth*. . . . To call a proposition fictional amounts to saying only that it is 'true in some fictional world or other.'[21]

It is quite remarkable that, in his pursuit of this thesis applied to all the arts (including music), Walton never pauses to consider the representational *properties of* music or of works in the other arts. He restricts himself entirely to the 'fictional' or 'make-believe' world (or, better, 'world') we imagine, or that 'obtains' when we imagine (when we play the game of 'make-believe' regarding) what a given artwork putatively licenses us to imagine. It may be entirely fair to say (with Walton) that 'a couple strolling in a park' *in* Seurat's *Grande Jatte* (Walton's own illustration) is only 'fictionally-strolling' (or that, *of* 'that couple', it is only 'fictionally-true' that they are strolling). But that says nothing of what *is true of* Seurat's *Grande Jatte*; or, in fact, of what *is* 'rightly' licensed (for imagining) *by* what is true of the *Grand Jatte's properties*— including its *actual* representational properties. Preposterous as it may seem, Walton does not draw attention to the fact that the painting, *Grande Jatte*, *presents a visual image of* a couple strolling (if that is what they are doing). Discerning that is certainly not imagining (fictively) a couple strolling and, presumably, *is* what, 'in' the painting, rightly licenses our imagining a couple

---

[20] This *is* the entire point of 'What a Musical Work Is'.

[21] Kendall L. Walton, *Mimesis as Make-Believe: On the Foundations of the Representational Arts* (Cambridge, Mass., 1990), 35.

strolling—as an active counterpart of what we might more quietly directly describe or interpret among the parts of the painting.

To put the objection in a slightly unfriendly way: Walton declares at the outset of his study that 'only fiction will qualify as "representational" in my special sense,' and that 'an integrated theory [of the arts, or of the representational in the arts] in which both aesthetic and metaphysical matters are treated in a unified fashion is much to be desired';[22] but he then proceeds to examine, carefully and by his own lights, the metaphysics of fiction, not the metaphysics of artworks that, as representational, license certain fictional worlds. In short, he conflates the function (or a function) of representational works with their functional properties (or, with whatever may be their more complex properties, from which the functional feature of representation may be provisionally abstracted). Clearly, without such a conceptual linkage, it would be quite impossible to discern ('metaphysically' as well as 'aesthetically'—speaking with Walton) just what is descriptively and/or interpretively licensed by the discernible properties of a particular artwork.

We can now see—at least as far as our charge is concerned—what the benefit is of opposing Walton's theory to the ones we have been considering: the earlier theories failed to identify (suitably) the properties of music in terms of which we could be said, convincingly, to understand precisely what are the representational, expressive, rhetorical, quasi-linguistic, semiotic, stylistic, and similar features *of* music: mere ordered sound seems inadequate for the job; Walton's theory and others like it, that is, purely functional accounts, accounts that identify how, *in general*, *we* are to act in responding to what is functionally licensed by representational artworks, simply fail to analyse, 'metaphysically' as well as 'aesthetically', the properties *of* musical and other artworks. Both what is postulated by the theory of ordered sound and whatever, in music, might replace mere ordered sound simply threaten to vanish altogether from Walton's conceptual net.[23]

This is the looming consequence of Walton's claim that 'representational works of art are props'; for *props*, on Walton's view, 'are generators of fictional truths, things which, by virtue of their nature or existence, make propositions fictional'.[24] The term suggests that artworks ('props') are hardly interesting in their own right; and, in fact, Walton does say at the very outset of his lengthy account that 'I will not take the concept of art very seriously, for the most part'.[25]

In any case, there is an inexplicit prejudice in Walton's account regarding

[22] Ibid. 6.
[23] A related difficulty appears in Nicholas Wolterstorff's *Works and Worlds of Art* (Oxford, 1980), Part Two, particularly §§ 7–8, and Part Three, particularly §§ 4–6. For a brief overview of the implausibility and difficulties of Wolterstorff's 'Platonism', see Joseph Margolis, *Art and Philosophy* (Atlantic Highlands, NJ, 1980), ch. 4. For an alternative Platonism, cf. Peter Kivy, 'Platonism in Music: A Kind of Defense', in Margolis, *The Worlds of Art and the World*.
[24] Walton, *Mimesis as Make-Believe*, 37–8. See, also, nn. 24–5 (p. 36) and Part Four.
[25] Ibid. 2.

what, about the properties or 'nature' of the painting (*Grande Jatte*), 'makes it fictional . . . that a couple is strolling in a park'. It 'is the painting itself', he says: 'the pattern of paint splotches on the surface of the canvas'.[26] (The musical parallel begins to dawn.) Of course, it is no such thing: 'the pattern of paint splotches on the surface of the canvas' is *not* a description *of the painting* (even if it is a description of the canvas); the painting includes, in the appropriate sense, an *image* of a couple, when rightly seen in accord with a historically developed practice and manner of painting.

Turn, now, to Walton's remarks about music. Here is very nearly all that he says that is pertinent:

Representational music is depictive, typically, when it represents auditory phenomena. But as often as not—more often than not, I think—what it represents is not auditory. . . . Cross-modal representation in music, as in painting, is unlikely to be depiction, and certainly representations of nonperceptual things or events is not. It is not fictional of the listener that he hears or otherwise perceives someone's ascending into heaven, or at least it is not fictional of his hearing an ascending passage of music that it is such a perceiving. . . . So depiction would seem to be far less important and far less central in music than in painting, even insofar as music is representation. The apparent affinity . . . between music and painting is partly illusory. Music is less perceptual, less an aural art than painting is a visual one. . . . The listener imagines experiencing excitement, passion, fervor, despair, conflict. . . . In place of fictional perception of external objects we have fictional introspection or self-awareness.[27]

There can hardly be any doubt that Walton, too, tends to think of music as strongly centred in ordered sound, even if he also thinks the representational and depictive powers of music are less developed than they are in the seemingly cousin art of painting. But how does he know? And how would he defend this view? The theory of representation he favours does not directly provide an answer; nor does he supply his own theory of the intrinsic properties or medium of music that would settle the matter. (The mere contingencies of Western music are hardly decisive.) For instance, why should we not say that Handel musically depicts aporia, exordium, epiphenomena, even proof—along the lines Thom has illustrated: but now more forcefully (than Thom maintains), by claiming that the *medium* of music is not mere ordered sound but (rather) complexly and indissolubly such that it is *incarnate in* ordered sound? Then, granting literary depiction and depiction by painting (or, more generally, granting representation), we could easily admit musical depiction in the strongest sense, without introducing fictional functions at all. We could for instance directly admit reference and representational predication. The conceptual oddity of Walton's account becomes suddenly clear, regardless of the final outcome.

[26] Ibid. 38.
[27] Ibid. 335–6; see also id., 'What Is Abstract about the Art of Music?', *Journal of Aesthetics and Art Criticism*, 46 (1988), 351–64.

IV

We may proceed, now, to collect our options a little more pointedly. One intuition that nearly everyone concedes in speaking of music (here, we may draw on Levinson again) is that what composers compose and what performers perform is, at the very least, *performable (in) sound, not* sound *tout court*. What is composed and performed is music, after all, not mere sound; and what music is is a matter that may be determined and decided quite differently by the practices of historically distinct societies. There are, in fact, no obvious antecedent constraints that could not be overcome by one ingenious invention or another. Here, Arthur Danto's well-known formulation about the arts in general is most helpful: 'To see something as art [he says] requires something the eye cannot decry—an atmosphere of artistic theory, a knowledge of the history of art: an artworld.'[28] Just so. But we can also go Danto one better: *artworks* (not merely the 'artworld') possess properties 'the eye [or ear] cannot descry', even though whatever properties are most distinctive of this or that art (painting and music, say), are incarnate *in* what is sensorily perceptible. Danto is not prepared to go that far.

There is a great deal that is rather glibly neglected in moving through these two adjustments: first, the lesson that what is produced and performed is music, not ordered sound; and second, the lesson that the historically, intentionally, significatively complex aspects of the cultural world of the arts (what, we may say, is semiotically incarnate) is not merely holistically assignable to that world but also distributively predicable of particular artworks in it. Music *possesses historied properties*—not merely properties (that is, ordered sound) that are the precipitates of creative efforts that have their own history and intentional energy. Joseph Straus makes the point very sensibly and matter-of-factly:

Music composed in the first half of the twentieth century [he says] is permeated by the music of the past. . . . Sonorities like the triad, forms like the sonata, and structural motions like the descending perfect fifth are too profoundly emblematic of traditional tonal practices to meld quietly into a new musical context. Traditional elements inevitably retain their traditional associations. As a result, they become the focus of a productive musical tension. They evoke the traditional musical world in which they originated, even as they are subsumed within a new musical context.[29]

Straus draws here on the rather florid theory of the paradigm, in poetry, that Harold Bloom has so notoriously expounded (which Straus freely acknowledges).[30]

This is not to attack Bloom—or at least not to attack him here—but only

---

[28] Danto, 'The Artworld', *Journal of Philosophy*, 61 (1964), 580.

[29] Joseph N. Straus, *Remaking the Past: Musical Modernism and the Influence of the Tonal Tradition* (Cambridge, Mass., 1990), 1.

[30] Ibid., ch. 1; cf. also Harold Bloom, *The Anxiety of Influence: A Theory of Poetry* (New York, 1973); *A Map of Misreading* (New York, 1975).

to say that, in supporting Bloom's emphasis on the *presence of attributes* that cannot rightly be described except as the presence of the historically influenc*ed* and intensionally respons*ive*, we are not obliged to endorse Bloom's entire theory. We need only acknowledge the presence of attributes actually thus structured. That alone breathes an entirely fresh life into the theory and practice of the description and interpretation of music (as well as of literature). Merely take that step: you supersede at once the grudging concessions of Goodman, Kivy, Levinson, Walton, and many others.

Certainly, for instance, in (our) admitting the point in favour of Bloom and Straus, Goodman's fundamental distinction between the autographic and the allographic utterly founders: what is usually not noticed by those who press the distinction (Levinson, for instance) is that, for Goodman, autographic art, though not 'notational' in the strict sense of allographic art, remains 'extensional' nevertheless (the sly meaning of 'projectible' in the passage cited just above).[31] The essential point really concerns the analysis of the historied, the intentional, the significative or semiotic, the stylistic, the 'influenced' and 'responsive'—the culturally significant—*in* actual artworks.

We can afford to lay out only a few central distinctions here. The full argument would require an enormous undertaking. First of all, there is the general distinction between 'ordered sound' and 'music' to consider. If music or musical sound possesses historied properties, properties that are at once inten*t*ional ('about' discernible elements in the musical tradition), and inten*s*ional (as bearing the significance of their historical and intentional relationship to such elements, or in the representational, expressive, and rhetorical respects already sketched, or in similar respects),[32] then we are obliged to give a suitable ('adequational') account of just what sort of properties musical properties are. It comes as a surprise to be able to say that there are still several options that are initially eligible: (*a*) the reduction of all musical properties to the properties of mere ordered sound (or the elements of some such stratum suitably augmented in an extensionally manageable way—including even history and intention); (*b*) the treatment of such musical properties as are not reducible in the manner of (*a*) in terms of an extrinsic relationship to such properties as are reducible per (*a*) (as in invoking our emotional responsiveness, or as involving our aptitude for make-believe, or for inducing associated images and feelings); and (*c*) the admission of emergent, indissolubly complex, properties incarnate in, but not reducible to, ordered sound (or some suitably augmented stratum in accord with (*a*)), *sui generis* to music, not characterizable relationally (in accord with (*b*)), and distinguished by historied, intentional, and intensional features (say, style, tradition,

---

[31] See Nelson Goodman, *Languages of Art*, chs. 3–5; also, Leonard B. Meyer, *Style and Music: Theory, History, and Ideology* (Philadelphia, 1989), ch. 1.

[32] Properties that are intensionally qualified intentional properties I call 'Intentional'. See Joseph Margolis, *Culture and Cutural Entities: Toward a New Unity of Science* (Dordrecht, 1984), ch. 1; and *Science without Unity: Toward a New Unity of Science* (Dordrecht, 1987), ch. 9.

composer's and performer's intentions, rhetoric, language, and analogues of language, semiosis, cultural context and atmosphere, representational and expressive function, and the like).

We have been sketching reasons why (*a*) and (*b*) are inadequate; and we may, fairly, take Levinson's and Walton's accounts to converge toward (if not to instantiate) (*a*) and (*b*), respectively. Hanslick clearly subscribes to (*a*); Kivy seems inclined to split the difference between (*a*) and (*b*), though his Platonism makes for further difficulties (as does Wolterstorff's); Danto favours (*b*); and Goodman seems clearly to incline toward a functionally augmented version of (*a*).

Our own proposal favours (*c*): musical properties are culturally emergent *incarnate* properties.[33] The important things about their being incarnate are that: they are not merely abstractly functional (hence, they are unsuitable for option (*b*)); they are not divisible in a dualistic way but are indissolubly complex (as the properties they are); and they betray profound intensional complexities that cannot be managed extensionally (hence, they are unsuitable for option (*a*)).

Now, the important generic feature of musical properties rests with their being, or including, historied properties, properties that are distinctively what they are because they are (as incarnate) not characterizable apart from their being 'historied'. What does that mean? Two sets of considerations prove decisive. For one, pertinent properties are, or may be, fully predicable as intrinsic, *historically contexted* properties—they will then be (in some intensionally determinable intentional sense) 'about' some part of a pertinent history; for another, pertinent properties are, or may be, *historically referential* properties, or properties of a sort that entail or depend on such properties. For example, when Béla Bartók accounts for the motivic structure of his Suite No. 2 for Orchestra, Op. 4 by reference to the structure of folk melodies, he may not be referring (in the music) to those original Romanian and Slovak folk songs, he may not be alluding to them; but they are still part of the historically contexted structure of the music, they are intentionally implicated in the music—quite apart from Bartók's own intentions regarding their further use in resisting the pull of the Western classical tradition.[34] In Charles Ives's music, on the contrary, it sometimes happens that Ives actually 'quotes' American pop music in his own compositions (in addition to venturing some very bold representational efforts).[35] That would not be possible unless (*contra* Langer) music could possess a structure that was strongly analogous with the

---

[33] The logical distinction of 'incarnate' properties is provided in Margolis, *Culture and Cultural Entities*, ch. 1; and *Science without Unity*, ch. 9.

[34] See Straus, *Remaking the Past*, 40–1; also, Béla Bartók, 'The Folk Songs of Hungary', *Béla Bartók Essays*, sel. and ed. Benjamin Suchoff, trans. Richard Tószeghy *et al.* (London, 1976), No. 42 (particularly p. 335); cited by Straus. Cf. also Nos. 43, 45.

[35] See e.g. Charles Ives, *Memos*, ed. John Kirkpatrick (New York, 1972): for instance, No. 28 (on the First Piano Sonata), No. 3 (on the *Second Orchestra Set*), No. 37 (on *The Fourth of July*).

referential and predicative powers of language. The important point is that, in possessing historied properties, music does possess (acquire) just such referential and predicative powers; and, it must be said, both reference and history cannot (have never been effectively shown to) be entirely extensional.[36]

History either *refers to* some historical past or context or it *pervades* (in a predicatively relevant sense) whatever is 'historied'—or both. So the mere admission of the historical dimension of music undercuts the tenability of any version of option (*a*)—*a fortiori*, any version of option (*b*). Prokofiev's 'Classical' Symphony (Symphony No. 1), for instance, invokes or alludes to classical forms, though it may not refer to any one of them, as in the very selection of the orchestral ensemble and in the use of forms 'reminiscent' of classical forms. Here we begin to see a whole armoury of possibilities that cannot be suitably captured by any version of (*a*) or (*b*). We must leave the account at that.

It remains only to be said, once again, that the nature of musical description and interpretation cannot fail to match the nature of music itself. So our argument begins to set constraints on the scope and logic of what is interpretatively admissible in the criticism of music. We need only be bound by the practice: for music is not a 'natural kind'.

---

[36] I develop the supporting argument in *Texts without Referents: Reconciling Science and Narrative* (Oxford, 1989), chs. 7–8.

IV

The Ethics of Musical Performance

J. O. URMSON

In this chapter I propose to consider what ethical constraints, if any, may be thought to limit the freedom of a performer in playing a piece of music by a composer other than himself. While doing so I shall from time to time consider what seem to me to be closely analogous problems concerning the culinary arts. It has long seemed to me that there are certain formal analogies between music and cookery. For example, the Dundee cake seems to be an abstract entity rather like the 'Unfinished' Symphony, and a Dundee cake seems to be related to the Dundee cake rather as a performance of the 'Unfinished' Symphony is related to the 'Unfinished' Symphony. Similarly the recipe for the Dundee cake and copies thereof seem to play a formally analogous role to that of the score of the 'Unfinished' Symphony and copies thereof. There are also formal disanalogies; a performance of the 'Unfinished' Symphony takes time, whereas a Dundee cake does not, even though it takes time to bake it. I do not propose to defend this view in this chapter; rather I intend to suggest that the ethical considerations involved are also interestingly similar. Readers who find this proposed comparison derogatory to the art of music can, of course, abandon this paper at once or skip the relevant portions.

Before embarking on these questions I may be permitted to utter a word of caution. It may appear that, at the other extreme to those who dissociate art and morality, I regard the performer as predominately faced with ethical decisions when determining questions of interpretation. Nothing is further from the truth. The performer, most of the time, will rightly be concerned with purely musical considerations. But in regard to general policies of performance, particularly professional performance, ethical considerations do, I think, arise. Let us consider one concrete example. Bach's second 'Brandenburg' Concerto is scored for concertante trumpet, recorder, oboe, and violin, with string ripieno and continuo. For a long period in the nine-teenth and earlier twentieth centuries a transverse flute was always, and inevitably, substituted for the recorder, since recorders and recorder players were not available. Often, also, a ripieno of a size certainly not contemplated by Bach was used. Is it legitimate nowadays to represent a performance with transverse flute substituted for recorder, or with such a large ripieno, as being a performance of Bach's work? Some performers will say that the balance between trumpet, recorder, and violin is impossibly bad, and a stronger instrument should replace the recorder. Should they not, then, say that this is a badly composed work that should not be performed and represent themselves as playing a new work, based on, and an improvement on, Bach's work? Or is opposition to such a substitution mere pedantry? Personally, I feel defrauded and cheated by such a substitution ethically, and, aesthetically, that such performers should conclude that if they cannot achieve a balance with Bach's scoring then either their technique or their performing practices are at fault. But on this I do not now ask for agreement. I only point out that questions like this do have an ethical as well as an artistic dimension. But the fact that the ethical dimension is almost exclusively considered in this paper should not be taken to imply that it is of exclusive, or even predominant, importance. Even I prefer a well-played transverse flute in that 'Brandenburg' to a badly played recorder.

In considering these questions it would be as well to distinguish three different situations in which a performer or a performing group might play a piece of music. In the first situation the performer plays for himself alone, and not to an audience, whether or not he is overheard by others as he does so. In the second situation the performer plays to an audience, but without any commercial transaction being involved; the audience is not a paying audience but, perhaps, a group of friends. In the third situation the performer plays professionally to a paying audience. Analogously one may bake a cake for oneself, for one's family, or as a professional baker. Perhaps ethical questions also will arise in an analogous way.

Now let us ask what ethical constraints might reasonably be thought to apply in any or all of these three situations. Most obviously, it might be suggested that one has a duty or obligation to the composer, to the audience, if any, or, perhaps, to oneself. It might also be suggested that one is constrained by certain abstract principles of morality akin to truthfulness or justice. Beyond these I cannot, myself, think of any other moral constraints which could plausibly be considered to be relevant.

If we consider the first situation, in which the performer plays for himself alone, we can manifestly eliminate at once any duty to an audience. Has one, then, any duty to oneself? I am inclined to answer that the whole notion of duties or obligations to oneself is, unless interpreted very loosely, incoherent. We can, and do, speak of such things as promising oneself a day off tomorrow, if one completes a piece of work today; but since, as promisee, I can forgive myself performance of any promise I make to myself, any such promise has no constraining force. Advertisers tell us that we owe ourselves various luxuries, but we can always forgive any debt that we owe to ourselves; there is no constraint. It is, no doubt, usually foolish and self-stultifying not to try one's best; one may have a duty to try one's best, if, for example, one's musical education is being paid for by someone else. But neither of these considerations involves a duty to oneself, though the latter case involves a duty to one's benefactor. So let us exclude the notion of a duty to oneself as being in principle incoherent, and one that need not be considered further, whatever the situation.

It remains to ask whether the lone performer has a duty to the composer.

There are those who hold that one can have no duties to the dead. If that be so, we have the curious situation that whether the performer has a duty to the composer may depend on whether the composer is still alive. For myself, I find it hard to understand why one cannot have duties or obligations to the dead. Certainly there are those who hold that a promise made to a dying person has no weight after his death. If this is claimed as an intuitive certainty, philosophical argument is, obviously, irrelevant; if the claim is made on the ground that the dead cannot benefit from the performance of the promise, or that they cannot know if it is not performed, then the basic moral claim is that promises which do not benefit the promisee are null and void, or that promises the non-performance of which cannot be discovered by the promisee are null and void. Such claims seem to be inherently unacceptable; if made, they render the case of death simply a circumstance which makes the more general principle applicable, not morally significant in itself.

The true reason for denying that the solitary player has a duty to the composer seems to be quite different, and to make the question whether the composer is dead or alive simply irrelevant. If one has, when playing to oneself, a duty to the composer, it will presumably be one of some sort of fidelity to the instructions in his score—I do not now enquire what such fidelity involves in detail since that important question is at present irrelevant. Now let us suppose that the score specifies that the instrument intended is the organ and the piece is in the major mode. Let us suppose that the solitary player decides to play it on the piano and to transform it into the minor. How now do we answer the question whether this is a performance failing in a duty of fidelity to the composer or whether it is a variation, improvisation, or what you will on a theme by the composer, a perfectly respectable activity? Surely in these circumstances the question of fidelity to the intentions of the composer cannot arise. The questions whether it is, or is intended to be, an accurate performance of the written score certainly do arise, as do such questions as whether the player has produced a worthwhile improvisation based on the score. But that is all. The suggestion that the only legitimate use of a score by the solitary performer is to play it as accurately as one can is surely one that no reasonable person would make and one which, I believe, no composer has ever made. A composer might well complain if a performance that departs in some way from the directions in the score be represented as faithful. But if one intentionally departs from the score in solitary playing, that misrepresentation cannot arise.

If the solitary player has no duty of fidelity to the composer for the reason just given, it would seem to be hard to imagine what general abstract principles might be relevant. No general considerations of truthfulness, honesty, fidelity, and the like seem capable of being relevant. The solitary performer seems to have no relevant duties at all as such. The situation seems to be exactly the same as when one cooks for oneself. Thus, if one decides to make for oneself a loaf of bread and puts before oneself the recipe for what is known as the Grant loaf, as contained in Mrs Grant's *Your Daily Bread*, one reads that one is to include one ounce of salt and one ounce of sugar. What, then, are one's duties? Is one failing in them if one prefers a little more (or less) salt, and uses a yeast that requires no sugar? Or if one decides to add a few raisins or a little grated cheese not specified in the recipe, as an experiment, what then? Why should Doris Grant, or anyone else, complain? It is clear that once again the distinction between a variation on the recipe and lack of fidelity to it is empty in the envisaged situation.

Let us now turn to the case of a performance to a paying audience, leaving aside for the moment the intermediate case of an amateur performance to a non-paying audience. It seems clear, now, that the performer has duties and obligations. If, as is customary, the performer, or his agent, has published a proposed programme, the performer seems to be in a quasi-contractual situation in relation to the audience of a commercial kind to deliver, for a consideration, the programme promised. I say 'quasi-contractual' since, no doubt, the legal obligation of the performer is tenuously connected to the rights of the audience through a series of agents, concert-promoters, concert-hall owners, and the like, but this complication seems morally irrelevant, and I shall ignore it. Morally, no performer is likely to deny that he has a duty to his paying audience; the problem is to decide just what that duty is.

Let us take it that the performer's duty is to play the advertised programme, unless unforeseen circumstances prevent him from so doing. But how is he to play it? To raise still unclear questions, should he play it in the way that he believes the majority of his paying customers would choose, since the customer is always right? Or should he play it in the way that the composer would have wished (or intended, or liked), since so to do seems to be a near equivalent to obedience to a Trade Descriptions Act in the commercial sphere? Or should he play the programme in the way that he thinks sounds best, since so to do is to give the best value for money? These possibilities are unclear, for it would be naïve to suppose that the audience has definite and unanimous desires or that the wishes of the composer are usually known to the performer. But, in any case, they are not necessarily mutually exclusive. The audience is unlikely to be unanimous, but some members, at least, are likely to wish the performer to play it as he thinks it sounds best, others to play it authentically (whatever that may involve), others to play it in the way that they have always heard it before. None of these wishes, not even the last, is altogether unreasonable. For, to a member of the audience, the works in the programme must be such works as he expects them to sound; if some anachronistic conductor who held views on Handelian performance like those held in scholarly circles today had presented such a performance to a late Victorian audience, at least a majority of that audience would surely have been outraged and have thought of themselves as defrauded; that was not what they had paid for. Perhaps a performance in nineteenth-century style, not advertised as such, would cause outrage today.

The condition of the audience is, no doubt, more complicated than so far represented. They wish the performer to perform the work in the way familiar to them, not in preference to correct performance but because they believe that the familiar way is the correct way. They probably also wish the performer to play it in the way he thinks best, in the expectation, or at least the hope, that it will conform to their own view. All their hopes and expectations cannot always be fulfilled.

But, it may be said, we surely cannot expect, or wish, the performer to play the work in any way other than that which he considers to be, aesthetically, best. If we cannot, then are not the wishes and expectations of the audience irrelevant? It is at this point that we can no longer avoid the questions of the identity of a musical work and of authenticity. We must, for example, ask what the name *Messiah* designated to a late nineteenth-century audience: did it designate a certain sound pattern very familiar to them?; did it designate the sound pattern that Handel intended to be designated by that name?; or, since they no doubt took for granted at least a rough identity between the two, does the question perhaps not arise? They might certainly have said 'That's not what I call the *Messiah*'. We must also raise the question how far, mistakes apart, two sound patterns may diverge, and for what reasons, if they are to be accounted as performances of the same work. Is there some norm of authenticity, approximation to which is decisive in determining the identity of a work?

We must raise these questions, though manifestly it would be absurd to try to answer them merely in passing in the present chapter. What is at least clear is that every performer must recognize some bounds of authenticity beyond which he should not go in representing to the audience that it is a performance of a certain work, though we know that not all performers will agree on where those bounds lie. There are some changes which are mere corrections to slips of the pen, which all would agree to be legitimate; some would also agree with, for example, Tovey's opinion (*Essays in Musical Analysis* (London, 1935), i.41) that at one point in Beethoven's Fifth Symphony horns should be substituted for bassoons since, in Tovey's opinion, Beethoven used bassoons at that point only because he 'had not time to change the horns from E flat'; some have even thought it legitimate to add all kinds of instruments to Handel's scores; in the early nineteenth century it was thought legitimate to insert songs by other composers into a Mozart opera—Haydn and Mozart themselves both wrote a number of insertion arias to be used in other people's operas. Where limits of legitimate interpretation lie will, no doubt, never be agreed. They vary from time to time and from performer to performer. But there are limits, and the performer surely has a duty of honesty to the audience not to overstep them, as he understands them. If his views on interpretation differ very widely from those of his intended audience, perhaps he should warn them. I certainly wish that opera houses whose views on the legitimate limits of departure from the composer's directions for staging vary widely from those traditionally held would warn me in advance.

In the end, the performer's duties to his audience seem not to differ widely from those of any purveyor of goods to his customer. There may be other and more important reasons for faithfulness of performance, but one reason is akin to that for obeying the Trade Descriptions Act; people should know what they are buying. To revert once again to the analogy with cookery, while I may legitimately, for my own consumption, introduce any changes I wish to the recipe for the Grant loaf, there are limits to what one may do in producing Grant loaves to be sold to the public; perhaps a little extra or less salt is legitimate, perhaps not; but the introduction of, say, 20 per cent white flour obviously is not; it is cheating, as is unfaithfulness in musical performance. I do not even try now to determine where the bounds of legitimacy or authenticity lie. I merely say that the performer has a duty to his audience not to overstep them, as he understands them.

Thus the professional performer may well be thought to be faced with a number of different and possibly, but not necessarily, competing considerations in determining how he ought to play his programme; no doubt these considerations will include others beyond those that I have mentioned. No doubt compromise will sometimes be thought to be appropriate. If this be so, then the performer's situation will be typical of all departments of life. Doing one's best in the face of possibly competing considerations is the common lot.

But the situation is yet more complicated, for so far we have considered only the performer's relations with the audience; we have not considered other possibly relevant factors. Has the performer not a duty to the composer? It seems reasonable to suppose that the performer has a duty to the composer not to misrepresent him. To avoid the difficulty some feel about duties to the dead, we may for the present limit ourselves to the case where the composer is still alive. It seems hard to deny that avoidance of misrepresentation is a relevant consideration, and it might seem to override others. If this be so, then authenticity as a duty to the audience may seem to be at least reinforced in relation to other duties to the audience. But once again, one's duty to the composer is no more clear than one's duty to the audience without a standard of authenticity. There is no objective, and no intersubjectively agreed standard of authenticity. The performer can only be honest in these matters as he conceives them.

If we ask what the duty of the performer to the composer is, here are some possible answers: it is his duty to interpret it in the way in which he believes the score sounds best in accordance with the understanding of musical notation current at the time of composition; it is his duty to interpret it in the way in which he believes it sounds best, even if this involves some departures from the instructions contained in the score: it is his duty to interpret it according to the known views of the composer on interpretation at the time of composition; it is his duty to perform it in a way that would, to his best belief, be approved by the composer if he heard the performance, however surprising to him. These are some of the possible views; and they themselves must be further complicated if we allow for some uncertainty about the conventions of musical notation at the time of composition and some uncertainty about the views of the composer on interpretation at the relevant time, and total uncertainty about what novelties the composer might approve of if he heard them. Probably, once again, we should say that all such considerations are relevant, but none overriding and exclusive of others. Thus, if there is a recorded performance by the composer himself, it would be cavalier to disregard such wishes on interpretation as clearly emerge from that performance; but, equally, few would hold that subsequent performers should aim merely to duplicate that performance as closely as possible. It is also clear that composers themselves hold different views about the status of their scores in relation to the interpreter. Thus Handel, who included very few indications of dynamics, phrasing, and the like, and occasionally was satisfied to write 'ad libitum', obviously allowed more freedom to the interpreter than, say, Stravinsky, who plastered his scores with such indications. There can be no universally valid answer to the question how much freedom the interpreter may use without misrepresenting the composer; nor is there a universally valid answer to the question what sorts of departure from the written score count as misrepresentation. Some sorts of departure from the written score have at some times been taken for granted as legitimate and even desirable. The question remains just what departures are legitimate; even the Venetian Ganassi, who wrote 175 different decorated versions of a single five-note cadence, regarded himself as obliged to begin and end on the same notes as the original, a restriction presumably generally accepted at that distant time. There is no universally valid set of rules by which one can answer that question, insufficiently determinate in formulation as it is, for our needs. Perhaps it is not clear what idiom we should adopt in raising it: if Mozart could come back and hear one of his operas played on modern instruments, we do not know whether he would, perhaps, ask why it had been transposed up a semitone or comment that pitch had gone up since his day. Whether he would have liked it is yet another question, and it is not clear how relevant it is, if at all, to the questions under consideration. If a reborn Handel had enjoyed a late nineteenth-century performance of *Messiah*, would that make such an interpretation legitimate? These are questions to which there is no definitive answer. But it does not follow that they need not be raised and considered.

What seems to emerge most clearly from these discussions is that there is a very large number of relevant considerations regarding the legitimacy of an interpretation, unclear in themselves and, in so far as they are clear, often difficult to weigh from lack of information. Myself, I do not think this to be a deplorable situation. I think it is deplorable if the performer does not face these questions, unclear as they are, to the best of his ability and give an honest answer; I think it deplorable that there should be arrogant performers who believe that the satisfaction of their individualities, their artistic visions, or what you will, are of such central importance that all other considerations can be legitimately ignored by them. But we should, perhaps, be glad that we have the opportunity to hear performances of old works in which the performers strive to the best of their knowledge and ability to reproduce the sounds that contemporaries of the composer would have heard, and also performances in which the performers think themselves entitled to make use of the technical resources of modern instruments. We should, perhaps, be glad that we can hear performances of Mozart's Clarinet Quintet both as in the published score and as scholars believe that Mozart originally wrote it.

The issues involved are, as we have seen, too complex for anyone sensibly to be dogmatic on these matters, whatever his personal preferences may be. We may also be glad that, on the whole, we live in a time when performers, unlike operatic and theatrical directors, and far more than composers in other days, do in general take their responsibilities seriously.

The intermediate case of performance by amateurs seems not to raise any serious new issues. They would seem to have the same obligations as professionals, particularly to a paying audience, but somewhat relaxed. They have not the resources that professionals ought to have, and so more licence is justified. In particular, replacement of rare and costly instruments by ones more easily available is easily tolerated. But in general, though amateurs have less knowledge and fewer resources, the same general duties as face professional performers surely remain to be obeyed by them as best they can.

If the general lines of thought expressed in this paper are acceptable, what is clearly missing, and what no effort has been made to supply, is clarification of such notions as authenticity and legitimacy that have been freely used in it. Such clarification is needed, and the problems involved are of great interest and great complexity. They are not the less important because no simple rules are likely to emerge from their discussion. But while such discussions as are contained in this paper are incomplete without such clarification, they are I believe, only incomplete and not useless.

Making Music Our Own

FRANK SIBLEY

This chapter is about interpretation of music in the broadest sense, about how and why it interests us. And since examination of practices should precede theorizing about any topic, I shall consider the role played by certain common descriptions of music. For this, I shall ignore the much discussed descriptions that employ the language of feelings and emotions, e.g. the familiar 'sad music', and the problems these supposedly raise. Musicians and critics draw equally upon all manner of other non-musical phenomena both mental and physical. If when writing on music they feel the need of so many kinds of descriptions in order to say what is important to them, to neglect so much of the language of criticism might be to risk impoverished theory. Besides omitting feeling and emotion vocabulary for the moment, I omit much else, e.g. 'aesthetic' terms like *beautiful* and *graceful*, the technical vocabulary of music, and so on.

The samples that follow are all drawn from writings by musicians and critics; they are all, I think, intelligible to anyone familiar with music, though what they say could not obviously be expressed as well, if at all, in other, particularly technical, language: 'It has querulous energy and lean writing'; 'The work is coarse-grained'; 'In his symphony he is, as always, a tough plain speaker'; 'Shostakovich's Seventh Symphony has some of his loneliest music'; 'Sibelius's Fourth Symphony is brooding, dark, spare and bleak'; 'superfine richness, with deep-pile carpets of sustained wind sound'; 'those imposing and sombre pyramids of sound of the old Italian and Dutch schools, and the finely chased salt cellars and silver candlesticks, so to speak, of venerable Sebastian Bach' (Hanslick); 'The playing is sensual yet refined, with the slight edginess of the strings preventing the textures becoming languorously sumptuous'; 'Its playing of the wonderful water music prelude suggested that the Rhine must be a river of treacle—and rather lumpy treacle at that' (G. B. Shaw). Such descriptions are given both of works, and, as in the last two, of performances. In addition, I list some adjectives, extracted from typical descriptions, to exhibit their variety: from light—*sparkling, shimmering, bright, luminous, glowing*; from weight—*light, ponderous*; from movement—*sinuous, abrupt, soaring, turbulent, placid*; from sound and speech—*thundering, murmuring, sobbing, conversing, arguing*; from smell and taste—*bitter, sour, sweet*; from atmosphere—*sinister, threatening, spooky*; from feel, touch, and textures—*soft, supple, gritty, thick, melting, liquid, brittle, sinewy, icy, silky*; from physiognomy—*smiling, laughing*; from gait—*ambling, strutting, striding, plodding*; from character—*gentle, bombastic, aggressive, plaintive, tender, wistful, bold, good-*

humoured, solemn, animated. The list could go on indefinitely. These sorts of examples are not more important than feeling and emotion descriptions, but, besides being neglected, they offer little temptation towards certain kinds of theories that beckon with the others: it is implausible to think that, where music is so described, a composer or listener was, or felt, icy or brittle or shimmering, or that music expresses grittiness or sinuousness.

One might propose that descriptions of all kinds, those I exemplified and those I omitted, help us 'interpret', 'understand', or grasp the 'meaning' of music. I shall not quibble with this though these locutions are not always the happiest. We may indeed come to understand how parts of a work connect or interact, or why a composer uses certain devices; we may not understand music from innovative composers or non-Western traditions; it feels alien and excludes us. But they are not always appropriate locutions with familiar music. For me, 'Do you understand the "Appassionata"?', 'Have you grasped the meaning of Scarlatti K. 115?', and 'What's your interpretation of Bach's Third Violin Partita?' are odd questions. But we can use other locutions. Descriptions may help us grasp, realize, pin down, the character and qualities of works, appreciate them for what they are. They may 'give a face' to music—or, less narrowly, a gait, sound, feel, or physical texture as well as a physiognomy. Similarly with people, animals, or scenery. We understand or interpret their gestures or facial expressions. But we recognize, grasp, or realize, not understand, that a figure, posture, or gait is solid, haughty, or shambling, that gestures are brusque or speeches florid. We see, not interpret, scenery as stark or smiling, streams as skipping or leaping. Chaplin's walk, a bloodhound's face, the Matterhorn, each has a distinctive character, not meaning; similarly with music which we characterize as jaunty or murmuring.

Describing music in such diverse extra-musical terms is a practice that almost everyone who discusses music falls into naturally. Such descriptions, if neither strictly true nor false, can be good or poor, apt or inappropriate. Bringing music under non-musical concepts often seems to help us, musicians included, to connect with it, articulate our experience of it, humanize it, make it our own. It is worth asking therefore what music and our experience of it must be like for such descriptions to perform these roles.

But despite the facts I have cited, there are familiar objections against the possibility of verbal descriptions playing so central a role. It is sometimes said, for example, that music is not really describable, that words cannot capture something so non-verbal and unique. Sometimes such objections seem to rest on misunderstandings about the nature of description. If the demand is for a description to provide a substitute for music, the demand is absurd; descriptions are never substitutes, or intended to be. Some suppose that *music*, which can only be *heard*, must be indescribable in words. Another absurdity: the *Mona Lisa*'s smile can only be seen, not heard or felt; that does not prevent its being described. Nor does the fact that music does not depict, portray, describe, or narrate prohibit description; nor do some paintings, or any natural objects. Again, no description, some assume, given the complexities of music, could be *adequate*. But this flirts with a spurious notion of adequacy that no description could meet, in two respects. (*a*) 'Exactness'. Performed music is determinate in every detail—timbres, pitches, duration, etc. But no description is exact in this way; any description will fit many similar but distinguishable things, whether music, paintings, or faces. (*b*) 'Completeness'. Any piece of music is complex, much is going on; to describe everything at once—rhythms, harmonies, melodies, whole movements—is impossible. But the same is true with pictures—their colours, brushwork, lines, subjects— or anything else, say, street riots or horse-races. Such 'exactness' and 'completeness' are unattainable limits, and not uniquely with music. For given purposes, descriptions, being always selective, can be exact or complete enough. Skimpy descriptions are still descriptions, and often adequate; calling the opening of the 'Moonlight' Sonata serene or the sea angry is to describe, and excludes contrary descriptions. Finally, perhaps the main objection: music should be described, if at all, in purely musical terms; extra-musical descriptions are improper.

Before I consider this, some further points about descriptions. Besides the question of *what* is described—rhythms, timbres, melodies, phrases, movements—there are *kinds* of descriptions. These range from literal and technical to those I shall loosely group as 'figurative'—various non-univocal uses, 'secondary senses', and obvious metaphors; certainly it is sometimes unclear whether some well-established descriptions should be regarded as 'figurative' or not. Figurative descriptions again are roughly separable into *levels*. There are (*a*) what I shall call 'scenarios', more or less extended pictures, programmes, or narratives: e.g. 'A Ländler danced by ogres', 'A conversation between a cheerful man and a melancholy man, who . . . argue with each other, each trying to win the other over to his point of view; until at the end of the second movement . . . the melancholy man at last gives in, taking over the main theme of the other . . .', etc.; (*b*) descriptions in terms of substances and processes: *steely, silken, shimmering, murmuring*; (*c*) those in terms of qualities: *heavy, cold, grey, smooth*. These three types constitute different levels because, roughly, scenario descriptions imply substance/process descriptions, which in turn imply quality descriptions.

One kind of 'purist' objection to figurative description can be seen as insisting that genuine descriptions should be literal, in 'purely musical', not borrowed terms. But it is not obvious what counts as literal here: presumably most technical terms, both purely auditory and structural (*C major, 6/8 time, pentatonic, sonata-form*); non-technical auditory terms (*loud, silent*); and some shared with non-auditory phenomena (*augmented, slow, repeat*). Many other pure or borrowed auditory terms (*ring, gallop, murmur*) would not generally figure in technical descriptions, and many are arguably figurative. Some musical terms are hardly technical for speakers of some languages (*pianissimo, martellato*), and many true technical terms are, however clumsily, dispensable by paraphrase. 'Literal' descriptions would therefore employ whichever of the above musico-auditory types could be regarded as non-figurative.

But now it must be asked what these literal descriptions can achieve. Certainly they can serve to analyse the construction of a work and explain by what devices its character is achieved. Attention to them can change our view of a work or reveal qualities we might otherwise have missed. But despite their importance, they fail to articulate what, following others, I have been calling the 'character' and 'qualities' of music, and do little to explain why music may engage us as appreciative listeners—which is why non-musicians and musicians alike employ figurative characterizations. Without such appreciation, they are little more than nuts-and-bolts descriptions. But music is only exceptionally composed to interest analysts. One might even risk putting it more forcibly. Consider a typical 'dry' description (totally 'dry' ones are rare):

It is based on three ideas: the tone-row, Ex. 1a; the Carinthian folktune, Ex. 5; and the Bach chorale, Ex. 8; the last comes into full prominence not until the finale. Yet looking at the tone-row more closely you will find that the chorale's opening motif, which consists of four notes in whole-tone progression, is already contained in the last four notes of the row . . . As for the first nine notes of the row, they form an arpeggio—an unusual arrangement as most rows go.[1]

It seems possible that, suitably trained, someone who had never appreciated music could give a purely musico-auditory description of a performed piece, and even someone deaf from birth who had seen music only in score might learn, however profitlessly, to give such descriptions, just as someone ignorant of the aims of chess might learn to describe games in the approved manner. By contrast, listeners incapable of technical description who felt impelled to describe music in the figurative ways illustrated might convince us of their genuine grasp and appreciation.

If literal musico-auditory vocabulary truly is ineffectual for describing much of what appeals to us in music, and if some hitherto non-existent language developed specifically for the purpose is, as many agree, necessarily unavailable, two alternatives remain. Either much that matters to us in music is genuinely indescribable; or we must, without qualms, employ the extra-musical language that comes so naturally, recognizing that to eschew it here would be as much a self-inflicted impoverishment as denying ourselves figurative language elsewhere, both within and outside the arts, where it occurs equally naturally, and unavoidably. Smiles are sweet, remarks sour, sleep is deep, scenery mournful, clouds race, streams leap. In the arts, colours glow, designs are exuberant, buildings severe or serene. It is less the literal comments, that there is a haywain on the right or a cathedral in the distance, but the others that are significant—Constable describing a picture as 'pearly, deep, and mellow', Roger Fry describing Matisse's line as 'rhythmic' and 'elastic'; Ruskinesque descriptions of paintings parallel 'scenario' descriptions

[1] Mosco Carner, 'Alban Berg', in Ralph Hill (ed.), *The Concerto* (Harmondsworth, 1952), 371.

of music. There is no more reason to cavil at extra-musical descriptions of music than at extra-visual descriptions of paintings; they are not resorted to because of the special nature of music. Figurative criticism is alive where, appreciatively, literal comment is inert.

If these considerations can allay some of the misgivings about extra-musical descriptions, though most of us who find music important often feel them, we can return to the question, given the pervasiveness of such descriptions, of the role they play. To recapitulate the facts. People conversant with music unreflectively describe it in figurative ways. It is widely accepted that such descriptions (*a*) can illuminate and aid appreciation (otherwise why programme notes or the comments of professional critics?); (*b*) can modify our grasp of music we previously supposed we appreciated; (*c*) can articulate explicitly, in ways listeners find apposite, those qualities they have experienced a piece as having. If these successes can often be achieved by bringing music under extra-musical rather than musico-auditory concepts, the question arises how and why such concepts can be aids to musical experience, and what light is thrown thereby on the understanding of music.

So far my remarks touch only cases where descriptions are actually offered or accepted. But much music is heard and appreciated without any verbal intervention. So even if extra-musical concepts are sometimes implicated in achieving or articulating understanding, usually words play no role. Could there be reason to think that, even when we listen wordlessly (and non-pictorially), when no one offers or seeks descriptions, we nevertheless make sense of music by, without realizing it, bringing it under verbalizable concepts, and without thinking of the words that might verbalize them? Equally, failing to understand it and misunderstanding it would be either failing to bring it under such concepts or bringing it under inappropriate ones. That might explain why, when descriptions *are* offered, we can often say, and confidently, that they do, or do not, fit the music. This view, that grasping the character of a piece involves hearing it in such a way that some possible extra-musical description(s) would be appropriate to our experience, would stand sharply opposed to the belief that extra-musical description is always improper. Much that is centrally appealing about music would be, paradoxically, essentially extra-musical.

For any musical purist—including most of us sometimes—the supposition is one to invite ridicule. To entertain it opens one to the charge of musical unsophistication, not knowing how to listen. But were it true, anyone obviously devoted to music who refuses, unlike many musicians, to countenance extra-musical descriptions must presumably be subject to some purist dogma. The supposition I am considering, however, if defensible, would lessen the 'mystery' of musical understanding by questioning the supposed 'isolation' or 'purity' of music and the 'discontinuity' between it and the rest of experience. To attempt that might be worth some effort. So since my intention is not speculative theorizing, I shall enquire how the supposition might be rendered plausible, not as speculation, but as an implication of familiar facts and practices, and whether opposition to it might rest on beliefs either dogmatic or incoherent.

One clear implication of the supposition is that *all* music must be describable (within the limitations of description itself) in aptly figurative language. Consider the evidence for this. I have stressed that critics, programme writers, and analysts constantly employ 'quality', 'process', and 'scenario' descriptions; even, in off-guard moments, those ascetic analysts who on principle would eschew them. Conductors rehearsing orchestras often do likewise. Composers not only mark their work *légèrement, maestoso, martellato,* etc., but may offer scenario-like programmes or titles (*Poissons d'or, La Poule, Peasants Merrymaking,* and *Storm*).[2] Composers' and critics' descriptions operate in contrary directions: roughly, composers' descriptions turn 'absolute' into 'programme' music, critics' descriptions do not. But they must still fit; Beethoven could not plausibly have described the opening of his sonata, dubbed 'Moonlight' by Rellstab, as furious, leaping, or strutting.

Obviously, the supposition that music is always describable does not imply that the listener could always provide a description, or even that anyone could in fact hit on a suitable one for a particular piece, though that is only a remote possibility; critics are seldom completely tongue-tied. Nor need description be easy; it demands a combination of appreciation, verbal expertise, and imagination. But these are not difficulties unique to music. Many people could not easily give more than scrappy descriptions of, say, a horse-race, a friend's face, or Chaplin's walk, particularly if figurative descriptions are called for as they often are for artworks. Fortunately, for most purposes, as I said, descriptions need not be highly detailed. As 'ragged' may suffice to describe an ice-hockey match, or 'angry' to describe a torrent, so 'fugal' may often suffice to describe a piece literally, and 'gently rocking' or 'gritty' to characterize it figuratively.

All these facts suggest that most music could be described figuratively. And if most can, why not all? I add two further considerations. Possibility of description entails possibility of misdescription. Most, I suspect, would find the description of the 'Moonlight' I gave wholly incongruous, not because such description is automatically disallowed but because it absurdly mischaracterizes the music. But anyone denying the legitimacy of figurative description must hold all such descriptions equally improper. To say the piece is or is not serene would be as inadmissible as saying it is or is not furious or that the number 4 is or is not green. That would be an extreme departure from common practice. Secondly, there is a game few are genuinely unable to play. Given a piece of music we know, and offered some pair of contrary descriptions, most would agree that one fits better than the other. For the

---

[2] The 'conversation' example of a scenario description quoted above was modelled on a programme C. P. E. Bach provided for one of his trios.

opening of Stravinsky's *Symphony in Three Movements* most would favour spiky, spare, or athletic, rather than melting, languorous, or gentle. It is sometimes said that pre-Romantic music is not open to these figurative descriptions; that might be true with 'scenario' descriptions.[3] But I doubt that there is any music for which no one could find some suitable 'quality' descriptions; and anyone who can play the alternatives game at all is already allowing description. If anyone who patently appreciates music cannot play this game, which I doubt (Hanslick and Tovey certainly could have)—though some might refuse on principle—they are certainly uncommon. One would wonder whether they are equally baffled by figurative description elsewhere. Are they uncomprehending with 'heavy sleep', 'pearly pictures', etc., or does their inability occur only, and suspiciously, with music? Too many undeniable facts and practices make it difficult to understand how anyone could hold extra-musical description of music improper unless the conviction rests on some general theory about music.

Suppose now that all music is open to appropriate extra-musical description. What bearing has that on our understanding of it, given that we mostly listen wordlessly? What happens to the suggestion that some extra-musical descriptions or other would always fit our experience of music even though those words do not cross our minds, and that that is, at least in part, why music means something to us? Certainly, unless we are critics we rarely attempt to articulate in words the qualities we hear in a piece. The more common case is where someone else gives a description and we feel that it is exactly right, or hits off the music rather well, or must be rejected as unsuitable. When this happens, it is, I suggest, a criterion of our having previously heard it in such and such a way that we sincerely assent to the proffered description.

But here one may encounter the objection that, if one can sincerely say, 'That describes the way I heard it', one must previously have had those words (or equivalent pictures) in mind. Yet this is surely a version of the philosophical theory that thinking—and, I shall add, perceiving, recognizing, realizing, experiencing, and hearing—must occur in words, pictures, images, or other 'vehicles'; that to have heard something as silky or exuberant one must have entertained those words, though subvocally. Against this, we may retort that to think, and equally to realize, understand, or hear that something is Φ, and to experience, see, or hear it as Φ, need not involve the saying or thinking of any words.[4] This is linked also to another general philosophical question. Music, it is sometimes urged, is not properly describable in words because it should be heard, understood, appreciated 'in purely musical terms'. The genuine musician, unlike the unsophisticated or philistine amateur, enjoys a purely musical experience appreciating music 'in its own terms'. If

---

[3] But see n. 2 above.
[4] Cf. Gilbert Ryle, *On Thinking*, ed. Konstantin Kolenda (Oxford, 1979), 33–4: 'some thinking does, but most thinking does not, require the saying or sub-saying of anything'.

verbal and other extra-musical notions obtrude, tacitly at the time or sub-sequently, there has not been a pure, but a tainted, experience, merely literary, narrative, or pictorial. Hence, to be willing to give or assent to extra-musical descriptions raises doubts about, even impugns or discredits, one's musicality. The charge is familiar and has analogies elsewhere.[5]

But this purist charge, I suggest, rests on an incoherence, and, if so, it must fail. Recall Ryle's attack on 'the obsessive philosophical notion of "thinking *in*", such as thinking *in* words or pictures . . .'. In some cases, he says, it makes no sense to say that the thinker 'is thinking *in* . . . words or phrases—or anything else instead'.[6] To suppose so is to enter an infinite regress. Thinkers choose words to express what they are thinking or have thought. They sometimes have to think what words they want, but they do not do this in words either. I suggest that, just as we do not think in anything, we do not experience or listen in anything, either words, pictures, music, or musical terms. We do not grasp, realize, or perceive the character of music—or of faces, paintings, or scenery—in words or in anything else. If this is so, there are no terms in which we hear or understand music; our hearing, grasping, or understanding of it is therefore not in musical or extra-musical terms, for to say either is nonsense.[7] *A fortiori* we do not have to experience or grasp it in musical rather than figurative terms. *Having* grasped its character, however, or while trying to, we may try to describe it in either terms. The argument for describing it only in musico-technical language—or for not describing it in words at all—was that we should experience and appreciate music only 'in its own (purely musical) terms', in a way so distinct from anything extra-musical that no language, unless technical, can properly fit that experience. But if it cannot be said that we experience it in *any* terms, there is no question of language, technical or extra-musical, fitting or failing to fit, or of one fitting better than the other. The argument evaporates.

Music is not special in this respect. When I notice the colour of something or see it as having a certain colour ('a purely visual experience'), I do not notice or experience it in colour, in visual terms, in colour words, or in anything. I may, however, seek words to describe it as experienced; and as I may describe music literally as loud or fugal, or figuratively as chattering, so I may describe the thing's colour as orange, or as warm and cheerful. Anything capable of description may be described either literally or figuratively; that it is heard, or music, no more prohibits this than that it is seen, or a painting. If this disposes of objections to the legitimacy of describing a 'purely musical experience', and if with music, paintings, and many other things the figurative

[5] Cf. Clive Bell, *Art* (London, 1947), 25: 'to appreciate a work of art we need bring with us nothing from life, no knowledge of its ideas and affairs, no familiarity with its emotions'.

[6] Ryle, *On Thinking*, 41.

[7] If, however, experiencing music 'in purely musical terms' means no more than experiencing it as music, i.e. as an art, not as natural sounds, this no more prohibits description than experiencing paintings as paintings, not as natural objects, prohibits describing them.

can capture what the literal cannot, figurative description, far from being disallowed, is justified.

If experiencing is not *in* anything, the earlier alleged difficulty, that you could not have grasped the character of music (or anything) without the words that might subsequently describe your experience of it occurring to you, evaporates too. Hearing, listening, looking, watching, or experiencing in any way, like most thinking, requires no saying or sub-saying of anything. The fact that music is complex, and that much that is going on is unmentioned in most descriptions we actually give, makes no difference. Grasping music more than superficially certainly means noticing a good deal of what goes on, not just, say, the melody. But we would hardly try to articulate or describe to ourselves everything we hear as it goes along. The same is true, however, in our dealings with other complex things. If we are attentive as we walk through a building or watch the passing countryside, we notice many things and their features: warmth or coolness of colours, calm or turmoil of rivers. If we watched a horse-race or surveyed a painting, we could, immediately after, describe much of what we had seen; but unless alerted to do so, we probably formulated few or no words at the time. We experience most things, in varying detail, without words, aloud or subvocal. Many, like music, are complex passing sequences. Commentators, travel-writers, or critics may attempt fuller descriptions and probably draw on figurative language. But mostly we do not; full descriptions would usually be difficult and to little purpose. Brief impressions usually suffice: here the water thunders, there the river is peaceful, the room has warm colours, the Mondrian is flat. Likewise with music; having taken in its character, we describe it, if at all, sketchily, say, as harsh, anguished, or exuberant. Were there need, and had we verbal skill, we might describe more than such salient characteristics. But description of music, in any complexity and detail one wishes, is not proved less possible or legitimate than description of anything else.

If experiencing needs no words, my emphasis throughout on possible *description* needs explaining. To perceive something as having this character rather than that is to acquire various abilities; to misperceive is to acquire liabilities. To perceive something correctly as red is to be equipped, say, to use it as a danger signal; someone who misperceives something as a shadow when it is a dog is liable to get bitten. Exercise of such abilities may be limited by lack of other abilities. One cannot use red to signal danger without knowing red is used for danger, or perceive the dog as a shadow without knowing what a shadow is. Nor could one perceive music as silken or aggressive if one lacked these notions. Grasping something as having a certain character is not ordinarily one-track. To have grasped the character of a piece of music might involve any of many abilities: to recognize it again, to recall in your head roughly how it went, to know if it is wrongly played next time (but not necessarily these; you might have poor musical memory); to whistle parts of it (but not if you cannot whistle); to know, when whistling it, when you have got it wrong, without necessarily being able to correct it; to realize what harmonies are lost in whistling; to know, when it is being played, that an oboe or a new motif will shortly enter. Grasp can be partial, e.g. ability to vamp a melody correctly but with wrong harmonies. With these may go ability to describe aptly, but not if, being too inarticulate, one cannot command appropriate words; and ability to assent to proffered descriptions, provided one's literacy extends to the words used. So to take the.music in a certain way may include, but does not require, ability to give or assent to descriptions that would fit your experience of it. Lack of these verbal abilities need not count against one's understanding the music in the way they describe it. But if acquisition of abilities other than verbal might constitute understanding a piece, why the emphasis on possible descriptions, even ones the listener might be unable to give or assent to? Why, in effect, stress that, in the ways indicated and contrary to purism, extra-musical notions may play a significant part in understanding music?

The reason is that acquiring and exercising abilities like the others I mentioned would not guarantee that one had grasped the character of the music—any more than ability to describe it in technical terms would. Someone might be able to whistle a piece perfectly, remember exactly where the oboe enters, tell when one performance differs from another, even conceivably play or conduct in exact imitation of a recorded Schnabel or Toscanini performance; none of this need conclusively show such a person to be more than an ear-and-memory-perfect mimic. It need have no tendency to establish the mimic's understanding of what, following others, I have called the musical character or qualities that we draw on figurative language to describe. Without that person's offering or genuinely assenting to some such description we could remain sceptical of there being understanding rather than reproductive mimicking. Similarly, a skilful copyist could conceivably copy the lines and colours of a painting, an actor read poetry with stresses and intonations modelled on the author's, and have no grasp of the work; analogously, a draughtsman might copy an engineer's drawings understanding nothing of their function. It is true that other indications may be convincing. That people spend time listening may rightly convince us that they find it rewarding, but we take their interpretation of the music largely on trust. Gestures and other bodily movements in listeners or performers may count for something. Stresses, emphases, ways of playing, if someone is performing or conducting, not copying, may be decisive. But descriptions sincerely given or accepted would be among the primary, most conclusive, and most explicit indications of understanding the music's character.

One further note about figurative descriptions. Since they are apt rather than true, equally apt alternatives drawn from other pictures, narratives, or sense-modalities may always be possible. Except with programme music there is no *right* description. Offered several, one could sometimes say only, 'something of that sort will do'. An 'intermingling streams' instead of a 'conversation' description might have suited C. P. E. Bach's trio equally well. 'Aggressive, hard, and energetic' might suit the Stravinsky as well as 'spiky, spare, and athletic'. Nor need there be any general answer to why rival descriptions may be equally apt, any more than to why some music is describable as 'bright' rather than 'dark' or 'icy' rather than 'warm'. Possibility of alternatives does, however, encourage charges of 'subjectivity': true in that I may not employ the same descriptions as you; false in that 'sighing, sobbing, and liquid', say, would incongruously misdescribe the Stravinsky. It is here too that the 'abstractness' of music and its *sui generis* character show, not in any supposed impropriety of extra-musical interpretation. Imposing one rather than an alternative description is somewhat like pinning a play down in a particular staging and performance. Hamlet's voice must have some timbre, his face some features, his stance and walk some peculiarities. But neither Gielgud's nor Olivier's are the *right* ones, for there are no right ones. Such matters are unspecific in the play or a silent reading of it. Yet Hamlet with no legs or a Donald Duck voice would be wrong if not absurd. Music is different again: whereas Hamlet must have a voice and legs, but not specifically Olivier's, music is abstract, in this respect, as it were, specifying nothing.

A corollary to the fact that descriptions constrain experience of music, rather as performed plays inject specificities absent from silent readings, is that listeners, like readers, may want to avoid them. Descriptions, whether of music, buildings, or mountains can be hard to shake off and can come to dominate one's experience. Inability to read *Hamlet* without hearing or seeing Olivier may become as infuriating as inability to hear the 'Pastoral' without seeing the cavortings of Disney's *Fantasia*. Even without this, one may want to hear music—or see paintings or scenery—without the necessarily selective intrusion of any words. Listening, looking, and enjoying are compatible with desiring to avoid all attempts at verbal articulation.

This chapter has been wholly about descriptions, particularly figurative ones, and their relevance to, in a certain sense, the understanding or interpretation of music. I have deliberately avoided mention of feelings and emotions, important as they are; but my discussion is intended to apply equally to them. I have said nothing about the 'meaning', the 'language', or the effects of music, or about listeners' responses (in so far as these differ from understanding its character). I have not questioned the importance of technical description and analysis in enhancing understanding, only its ability to do certain things. I have not denied that there are 'purely musical experiences'—something we do not get from worded song or opera—or 'purely musical qualities'—the warmth or chill of music is only audible; it is not the warmth or chill felt in bath-water or seen in smiles. I have said nothing about the question pursued by many theories: why or in virtue of what—resemblances, analogies, shared features—we supposedly can employ figurative language; I simply accept that we do. Nothing I have said implies that listening with understanding requires or ordinarily involves having words or pictures in mind; it can be, and usually is, wordless, as is looking at pictures. If it is an assumption that any connection between music and extra-musical phenomena must imply this, I have challenged it. I have questioned the coherence of certain 'purist' positions and of the notion of understanding or experiencing 'in purely musical terms'. I have explored the possibility that an important element in the proper interpretation of music is covertly extra-musical, and questioned the supposition that extra-musical phenomena are merely peripheral except to programme music. Obviously there is vastly more to say about music. Much of what I have said applies to extra-musical sounds and noises as well as to music. It largely ignores the part played in our interpretation of music by the fact that it is an art working within structures, conventions, and a history, familiarity with all of which affects crucially the characteristics we hear in it. But we do, after all, characterize natural and extra-musical sounds in similar ways, as mournful, sighing, chattering, cheerful, murmuring, harsh, sweet, and so on. This at least suggests some continuity between music and other sounds, and so questions the alleged hermetic and isolated nature of music.

'Music Has No Meaning to Speak of': On the Politics of Musical Interpretation

LYDIA GOEHR

'Silence, the walls have ears'
Beethoven, 1815

I

'The most profound truths, the most blasphemous things, ... may be incorporated within the walls of a symphony.'[1] So James Gibbons Huneker remarked in 1898—to which Robert Schumann, had he still been alive, might have responded: 'I am more interested in judging whether the symphony is beautiful than in determining whether it has an extra-musical programme.'[2] Schumann believed that the musical (audible) content of a symphony is the primary determinant of its meaning. He may even have believed that it is its sole determinant and that music has no extra-musical meaning to speak of at all. 'The best way to talk about music', he once wrote, 'is to be quiet about it.'[3] But if silence has satisfied those, like Schumann, of 'purist' tendencies, it has worried others who suspect that there is more to music than meets the ear—especially those who have held, as Huneker did, that a symphony can sometimes be blasphemous.

Historically, the tension between purists and those that oppose them has reflected a worry over the claim that the institution of Western art-music is autonomous. What does this claim involve? Recall, first, the belief that this institution functions and acquires significance independently of the dictate of extra-musical institutions—religious, political, and moral—and then the kind of priorities musicians have shown to sustain this belief. Such priorities have

---

The title of my chapter refers to words of Ned Rorem, 'Random Notes from a Diary', *Music from the Inside Out* (New York, 1967), 128. Thanks to Mary Devereaux and Brian Fay for their useful comments.

[1] Quoted in I. Crofton and D. Fraser, *A Dictionary of Musical Quotations* (New York, 1985), 113.

[2] Cf. *Schumann on Music*, trans. and ed. H. Pleasants (New York, 1965), 184: 'If a composer shows me his composition along with ... a programme, I say: "First show me that you can make beautiful music; after that I may well like your programme."'

[3] Ibid. 112.

been articulated as purely aesthetic ones: beautiful music is produced only for the sake of beautiful music. Here, musical autonomy amounts to no more than musical purism.

But this reading of autonomy is overly restrictive. While it is agreed that music has a purely musical meaning, it is also believed that music can be used to comment upon extra-musical matters. Thus, that music is autonomous has not always prevented its being connected to the world outside itself. Rather, musical autonomy has involved two kinds of freedom, *freedom to* and *freedom from*: freedom for music to speak about the extra-musical 'Other' as well as music's freedom from the dictate of this 'Other'.[4]

This double-sided reading of musical autonomy has prompted theorists to consider the ways music connects itself to society. Obviously, music so connects itself when it explicitly comments upon society. But it also finds itself connected in less obvious ways even when it claims not to be so. When George Orwell remarked that 'the opinion that art should have nothing to do with politics is itself a political attitude', he showed how denying a certain connection can sometimes be a way also of asserting it.[5] The purist's opinion that music has nothing to do with society exemplifies this paradox well.

In this chapter, I shall investigate the double-sidedness of musical interpretation, specifically, the way that it can be political and apolitical simultaneously. I have three aims: to unravel the complexities involved in claims about musical autonomy; to demonstrate that traditional debates over musical interpretation, usually treated apolitically, are better understood when one recognizes that interpretation has a political dimension. Finally, given the recent resurgence of censorship in the arts in the United States and Western Europe, my aim is to reveal the assumptions latent in the composer's most common defence against the censor's attack.

II

What is a politics of interpretation? Many theorists define the constituent terms of the phrase broadly, and I shall do likewise.[6] 'Politics' refers to ideologies that incorporate references to private and public moral systems and principles, to bodies of values 'affirmed by a community', as well as to the 'social conventions, rules, and relations' of given institutions. What makes the ideologies political is that they sustain 'the structures of power' that 'organize human life'.

Interpretations themselves are social acts that express or enforce values and power relations favouring personal and communal interests. Such expression

---

[4] Cf. Wayne Booth, 'Freedom of Interpretation: Bakhtin and the Challenge of Feminist Criticism', in W. J. T. Mitchell (ed.), *The Politics of Interpretation* (Chicago, 1982), 52.

[5] 'Why I Write', *A Collection of Essays* (San Diego, Calif., 1981), 313.

[6] I have borrowed here from essays in Mitchell (ed.), *The Politics of Interpretation*. I shall only provide references to direct and full quotations.

and enforcement function on various levels in various ways. Sometimes, interpretations support, or as Hayden White suggests, lend themselves to use by particular ideologies. Other times, entire interpretative strategies, rather than particular interpretations, endorse given ideological systems. Wayne Booth has described 'how various forms of power, open or covert, enforce various kinds of interpretation' and how given interpretations serve different established powers.[7] Generally, interpretation involves strategies of criticism, explanation, and meaning-disclosure that reinforce the power of particular discourses that, in turn, empower or sustain the existing power of human individuals and groups.

More or less consciously, interpreters make commitments to political stances. In existentialist terms, human acts reveal the way actors are in the world. Ways of being in the world involve endorsements of the structures of power which enable or sustain these particular ways of being in the world. Acts of creation, reading, writing, and performance are such acts motivated by politics and/or are of political consequence. As Sartre famously concluded, the question now is not whether we should be politically committed; it is how we should be so.[8] Interpretations can revolutionize existing political systems by articulating alternatives to them. They can also reinforce existing systems by preserving the relevant traditions, canons, prejudices, and myths. Finally, to interpret presupposes that something gets interpreted and that someone does the interpreting. And from everything said so far, it follows that the 'what', the 'how', and the 'who' of interpretation all have a political dimension.

This is true no matter what strategy of interpretation one adopts. In the art world, essentialists maintain that interpretations disclose the fixed and essential meanings of artworks. This interpretative strategy is allied to a so-called *autocratic* (author-based) view of artistic meaning. Other theorists consider interpretations to be constitutive acts of 'writing' meanings for works. Meanings do not exist as fixed or stable in works, but emerge from relational acts of interpretation that enjoin interpreters to those works. This approach, based in 'reader-response', is *allocratic* by contrast. Though both strategies have political character and consequence, it has been the allocrats more than the autocrats who have acknowledged this fact. Allocrats have maintained that the works, interpreters, and the interpretative strategies they adopt are deeply embedded within political networks. Autocrats have presented their interpretations and strategies for interpretation as apolitical.[9]

That the autocrat's stance has met with more favour among scholars is not surprising. Autocrats comprise only one among many academic groups that have urged the sublimation of the political. Hayden White describes this sublimation by distinguishing between two sorts of 'politics of interpretation'.

[7] Hayden White, 'The Politics of Historical Interpretation: Discipline and De-Sublimation', Wayne Booth, 'Freedom of Interpretation', in Mitchell, *The Politics of Interpretation*, 142 and 51.
[8] Cf. Edward Said, 'Opponents, Audiences, Constituencies and Communities', ibid. 7–32.
[9] Cf. Eli Hirsch, 'The Politics of the Theories of Interpretation', ibid. 321–33.

The denial of the political is hardly possible in the politics *of* interpretation, he writes, in those interpretative practices such as political theory and commentary 'that have politics itself as a specific object of interest'. But it is possible in the *politics* of interpretation, 'in those interpretative practices which are ostensibly most remote from overtly political claims', or in those 'practices which are carried out under the aegis of a purely disinterested search for the truth or inquiry into the nature of things which appear to have no political relevance at all'.[10] In the same spirit, Edward Said maintains that the sublimation of the political is encouraged by our culture at large. 'Culture', he writes, 'works very effectively to make invisible and even "impossible" the actual *affiliations* that exist between the world of ideas and scholarship . . . and the world of brute politics, corporate and state power, and military force'.[11]

It is no coincidence that what is said here of the Academy of Scholars can also be said of the Academy of Fine Art; the histories and internal workings of each are inextricably connected. The rationale of fine art derived in large part from the romantic aesthetics of autonomy as developed at the end of the eighteenth century. But it derived also—because romantic aesthetics did itself—from Enlightenment theories of moral, political, and scientific autonomy and from theories of cultured or cultivated disinterestedness more generally. The result was an inordinately complicated conception of artistic and aesthetic autonomy. Musical autonomy was no exception.

III

Classical music, especially of the purely instrumental sort, has always presented extreme difficulties for those interested in deciphering the meaning of things. Just what do those bunches of sounds mean? 'In no other field of criticism is it so difficult to offer proof as in music', Schumann wrote: 'Science can argue with mathematics and logic', and 'to poetry belongs the golden, decisive word'. But 'music is the orphan whose father and mother no one can determine'.[12]

Before the late eighteenth century, theorists—philosophers, clerics, scientists—attributed to music specific 'extra-musical' meanings that rendered it a worthy contribution to a moral, rational, and religiously upright society.[13] Music's meaning came from 'outside' itself. It derived either from music's cathartic ability to influence and sustain a person's religious, moral, and

---

[10] 'The Politics of Historical Sublimation', ibid. 119.
[11] 'Opponents, Audiences', 8.
[12] *Schumann on Music*, 36.
[13] The musical/extra-musical distinction is anachronistically employed when used to speak of theories of musical meaning offered before the late 1700s. I have discussed this point in detail, as I have other claims in this section, in *The Imaginary Museum of Musical Works: An Essay in the Philosophy of Music* (Oxford, 1992).

political convictions, or from its mimetic ability to imitate the nature of persons and the world.

This attribution of meaning had an important consequence—the near-complete rejection of purely instrumental music. Music could achieve referential significance only if it used words. Words rather than pure melodies were intelligible. They had concrete, semantic content and produced effects of similar concreteness. For complicated reasons, composers of the period generally agreed that instrumental music was neither completely meaningful on its own, nor reliable in conveying moral and religious truth.

In the late eighteenth century, attitudes began to change. Theorists, alongside increasingly powerful composers, insisted that music no longer be awarded significance according to an extra-musical principle. Their motive was in part defensive, reflecting a desire to counter the extremely low esteem in which instrumental music had for so long been held. A related motive was to protect music from the judgement of those whose 'moralizing tendencies' hindered their ability to listen to music with an open ear.

Theorists found protection in romanticism. They found here that they could use the idea of instrumental music's lacking concrete and specific content to find for music a supreme meaning as well as a protection against the censors. Their argument rested on an interplay between two claims which nowadays we separate more sharply than theorists did earlier. One claim concerned the *transcendent* move from the worldly and particular to the spiritual and universal; the other concerned the *formalist* move which brought meaning from music's outside into its inside.

First, music was allied more closely than ever before to the other fine arts, then it came to be regarded as paradigmatic of fine art. Of fine art, theorists wrote that its significance lies not in its ability to inspire particular feelings or to imitate worldly phenomena, but in its ability to probe and reveal the higher world of universal, eternal truth. This ability originated, according to Gustav Schilling, in 'man's attempt to transcend the sphere of cognition, to experience higher, more spiritual things, and to sense the presence of the ineffable'. Then theorists argued that instrumental music, lacking particularized content, was the most plausible candidate for being the 'universal language of art'. Unable fully or directly to transcend semantic specificity or cognitive content, poetry and painting failed in this regard. 'No aesthetic material is better suited to the expression of the ineffable than is sound', Schilling thus concluded.[14]

The shift from imitation of particulars to immediate expression of the transcendent helped give instrumental music its new meaning. Indeterminate on a concrete level, such music was utterly meaningful on a transcendent one. This shift also helped music achieve a two-pronged emancipation: first from its *service* to extra-musical goals, second from its *dependence* on words. 'Music

---

[14] 'Romantik und Romantisch', *Encyclopädie der gesammten musikalischen Wissenschaften, oder universal Lexicon der Tonkunst*, trans. in P. Le Huray and J. Day (eds.), *Music and Aesthetics in the Eighteenth and Early-Nineteenth Centuries* (Cambridge, 1981), 470.

has developed into a self-sufficient art, *sui-generis*, dispensing with words', Johann Gottfried Herder proclaimed in 1800.[15]

Whereas emancipation from the word was relatively unproblematic, music's emancipation from the extra-musical was not. The move towards transcendence was insufficient to give music a musical meaning. Though freed of the constraints of specific social functions determined by church and court, the transcendent move had not freed music of its obligation to be meaningful in spiritual and metaphysical ways. Formalists provided the necessary next step. Music is intelligible, they said, not because it refers to something outside itself, but because it has an internal, structural coherence. It consists of an internal and dynamic stream of purely musical elements—in Hegel's terms, in an 'abstract interiority of pure sound'.

Was there a contradiction in romantic theory? How could the formalist demand that music 'mean itself' be reconciled with the demand that music have spiritual and metaphysical meaning? Friedrich von Schelling provided the answer:

Music brings before us in rhythm and harmony, the (platonic) form of the motions of physical bodies. It is . . . pure form, liberated from any object or from matter. To this extent, music is the art that is least limited by physical considerations in that it represents *pure* motion as such, abstracted from any other object and borne on invisible, almost spiritual wings.[16]

Schelling achieved reconciliation by using the notion of pure form in two ways: to show how music could be a universal, spiritual language and to show how music could have purely musical meaning. His reconciliation took place, however, against the background of a complex theoretical transition in aesthetic theory.

The transition had four dimensions. First, there was a shift away from seeing music as having value and meaning solely by virtue of its service to another thing. In place of this view, music was now seen as having value and meaning in itself. Second, the 'extra-musical' obligation of music to resonate with our spiritual lives became a musical obligation. The purely musical was treated as synonymous with the moral, the spiritual, and the infinite. Third, matters considered extra-musical in some circumstances could now be regarded as purely musical in others. Here, it was a case of musical theorists appropriating notions and values from 'the outside' to fill out their new concept of the purely musical. Fourth, the distinction between the musical and the extra-musical was deemed meaningful only in worldly but not in transcendent terms. At the level of the transcendent all the usual principles of individuation and difference were suspended. In Schopenhauer's terms, music could now mean its purely musical self at the same time that it meant everything else.

This entire transition helped make sense of music's double-sided autonomy.

---

[15] *Kalligone*, ibid. 257.   [16] *Philosophie der Kunst*, ibid. 280.

IV

As music achieved theoretical autonomy, composers increasingly demanded that they be treated as autonomous in practice. In part they achieved this by moving away from the court and church to the 'free', urban metropolis. They ascended also into the ivory tower, with all its 'divine' associations. But if transcendent and formalist emancipation gave composers the theoretical means to dissociate themselves from the world altogether, social emancipation demanded that they position themselves in the world according to their new independent and individual consciences. This presented problems.

Some took the purist route, luxuriating as best they could in their liberation from 'worldly' constraints and devoting themselves to the composing of a purer, higher, and finer sort of music. Beethoven felt and wrote of such desires, though not without conflict. He found he was unable to cut himself off entirely from the ordinary, extra-musical world. While purist ideals prompted him to seek detachment in his music, democratic ideals prompted him also to seek through music political freedom for himself and others. He had, he recognized, a concern for 'needy humanity'.

Beethoven was not alone. In the early nineteenth century, artists generally felt allegiance to two ideals: 'art for art's sake' and 'art for the people'. Surely conflict would arise in anyone who tried to meet both at the same time. Apparently it did not. When Goethe wrote that one 'cannot escape the world more certainly than through art and [one] cannot bind [oneself] to it more certainly than through art', he showed how in art one meets both ideals, for art has a double-sided autonomy.[17]

Conflicts emerging in the musical world were resolved as well. Writing on Gottfried Weber's *Te Deum*, Carl Maria von Weber pointed out that no critic could ignore the dedication of the piece to 'Germany's victorious army'. But then he worried: had the composer produced a work 'remarkable more for its suitability to the occasion than for absolute artistic value'? Weber simply asserted that it was a great achievement for a composer to succeed in pro-ducing either sort of work.[18] If Weber did not meet the conflict head on, Liszt did. Asking himself whether a composer should 'be reproached with having given way to his genius rather than to the requirements of the worship', he answered that, in his music, the religious had become the purely musical.[19]

Composers found further resolution when they began to describe their music either as absolute or as programmatic. Such descriptions rested heavily on the romantic terms that had given music her autonomy. In neither sort of music did meaning derive from service to an extra-musical occasion. In both, meaning was achieved through the unique qualities of *instrumental* sound,

[17] *Elective Affinities*, trans. R. J. Hollingdale (Harmondsworth, 1971), 196.
[18] *Carl Maria von Weber: Writings on Music*, ed. J. Warrack, trans. M. Cooper (Cambridge, 1981), 127.
[19] P. Merrick, *Revolution and Religion in The Music of Liszt* (Cambridge, 1987), 100 and 156.

though whether the music embodied 'transcendent' content of a spiritual, religious, or political sort was believed to indicate a significant difference between them.

That no one ever agreed on what exactly this difference was complicates the story considerably. Many believed that music should be distinguished according to whether the music had musical content only or extra-musical content in addition. 'Absolute music' would refer to *purely* instrumental music that was expressive of nothing but a musical idea; 'programme music', by contrast, to instrumental music whose formal development is guided by, or implicitly refers to, an extra-musical idea, whether political, religious, or poetic. But with the distinction understood in this way a problem kept arising.

How could one tell what belongs, in general or even in particular cases, to the musical and what to the extra-musical? Is Beethoven's 'Pastoral' Symphony a work of absolute or programme music? Were his sentiments about the countryside, embodied in his symphony, transformed at some point in the creative process from extra-musical sentiments into musical ones, or did they remain extra-musical? Beethoven provided notes at the symphony's first performance in which he contrasted modern musical expression with traditional notions of imitation. The symphony is 'not a painting in sounds' but 'a record of sentiments' evoked by the composer's 'reminiscence of country life'.[20] Unfortunately, he left it ambiguous (supposing that he was even thinking in these terms) whether his mention of pastoral sentiments described the music's content literally or even metaphorically, or whether, perhaps, it was intended just to serve as an aid but not really as a description to help listeners comprehend his music.

That composers did not conceive of the difference between absolute and programme music only in terms of the musical/extra-musical distinction is the critical point. For it means that the problems of the latter distinction cannot automatically be transferred to the former. In fact, the concepts of absolute and programme music seem to have emerged less because composers wanted to classify their works as one or the other, and more because they wanted their music to be at once both purely musical and politically, poetically, or religiously meaningful. Some believed this could be achieved through absolute music, others through programme music. Composers were functioning less with a distinction between two sorts of music than with competing concepts that seemed ultimately to have the same function.

Whether composers called their music absolute or programmatic, they believed that being faithful to the musical medium was crucial. Despite the presence of a programme, therefore, the music still consisted only of sounds and thus retained a purely musical meaning. That it also had a programmatic meaning was a fact learned not by listening to the music, but by reading the

---

[20] *Beethoven: Letters, Journals, and Conversations*, trans. and ed. M. Hamburger (New York, 1951), 68.

title, the preface, or the programme notes. Announcing and recognizing a work as programmatic did not, however, render its musical meaning impure. That a work could have both purely musical and 'programmatic' meaning was explained by reference to the 'transcendent move'. Describing their music as programmatic, in other words, composers could still claim that its meaning was transcendent and, on this level, reconcilable with the demands of formalism. Liszt once claimed that his 'Revolutionary' Symphony represented not just 'a particular battle', but the 'glorious feelings aroused by revolution in general'.[21] Other composers found they could achieve the same reconciliation through absolute music. Beethoven's Ninth Symphony quickly became paradigmatic of a work whose absolute status is not affected by the presence of its 'Ode to Joy'.

Thus, music could serve its purely musical and political or religious roles simultaneously whether described as absolute or programmatic. This fact might have stopped composers from looking for differences between the two descriptions, but it did not. Composers chose to take sides. That both descriptions could capture the same compositional aims complicated the choice. Mahler constantly wavered between the two descriptions. Inspired by Nietzsche's *Die fröhliche Wissenschaft* when composing his Third Symphony, he could have claimed the result to be a work either of absolute or programme music. He chose the former, suggesting on this occasion that, once created, the work broke free from its inspirational source, as a house loses its scaffolding once built. On other occasions, he saw the advantages of calling his music programmatic.[22]

The debate between composers of absolute and those of programme music helps to demonstrate how important it had become in the nineteenth century for composers to produce music that could say something about the world without that admission compromising the independence and purity of the musical medium.

V

Composers found that romantic solutions to the conflict between the musical and the political did not always work in practice. That, of course, did not prevent them from asserting that they should. When Schumann remarked that we should first hear whether the music is beautiful before looking for a programme, he was identifying the continuing difficulties of a composer's admitting any inspiration from the outside world. All too often, he realized, such an admission still resulted in the music's being assigned a trivial and

[21] A. Walker, *Franz Liszt: The Virtuoso Years* (Ithaca, NY, 1983), 144.
[22] H.-L. de la Grange, *Mahler*, 2 vols. (New York, 1973), i. 357.

'ludicrous' meaning.[23] To avoid this, he said, one should concentrate on the work's musical content, asserting, if need be, its utter purity.

But it was not 'ludicrous' meanings of a trivial sort that composers had to fear, but meanings that could get them into trouble with the censors. Amidst political upheaval, composers increasingly found their music subject to the dictates of the censors, and themselves unable to take advantage of the autonomy awarded them by romantic theory. It was under these circumstances that they began to stress the purist side of autonomy. Indeed, it was much safer to claim that music had nothing to do with politics than the reverse. Unfortunately, avoiding politics was not easy. 'To seek the beautiful in art' amidst this turmoil, Berlioz remarked, 'is like trying to play billiards on a storm tossed ship.'[24] Attempts to escape often had to be accompanied by demonstrations of loyalty.

The purist retreat was not the only route composers found to defend themselves; in romantic theory they found another. This route placed music in a highly advantageous position. Musical works had no intelligible reference or concrete effect. They had taken on the status of an *opus metaphysicum* losing in the process any 'ordinary' or 'worldly' aspect. Any apparent 'ordinary' connection or reference suggested by a work, every concrete effect and connotation, could be suspended and ignored. Now, if musical sounds were thought to incite fury in the masses, or if a style suggested approval of something 'foreign' to the society, composers had only to claim that such associations and effects did not capture the music's 'real' meaning.

Though this argument found favour with artists of many sorts, it most clearly suited composers. It was much harder for those who used visual images or words to convince the censors that the content of their artworks was really something other than the 'worldly' content it appeared to be. Many noticed the composer's advantage. When Huneker said that a symphony could contain blasphemous content, he also pointed out that the censors would be 'none the wiser'. Grillparzer went so far as to conclude that composers did not even 'have to bother about the censors'. 'But', he added wryly, 'if only the censors knew what [they were] thinking as they compose.'[25]

Romantic theory imposed an essential epistemological barrier between music and the censors. Even when biographical comments, programme notes, and titles were attached to the music, it was well-nigh impossible to tell whether the music really had the extra-musical message it appeared to have. Even when composers used familiar 'folk' tunes with obvious extra-musical associations, one could not always hear as such whether the tune was being quoted with approval. A change of title often helped composers avoid trouble:

[23] *Schumann on Music*, 52.
[24] J. Barzun, *Berlioz and His Century: An Introduction to the Age of Romanticism* (Chicago, 1982), 266. For details of the censorship policies, see R. J. Goldstein, *Political Censorship of the Arts and the Press in Nineteenth-Century Europe* (New York, 1989), 155–74.
[25] Quoted in H. Raynor, *Music and Society Since 1815* (London, 1976), 6.

a revolutionary symphony could have its appearance transformed to make it look like a work of purely musical significance. Such a change was usually unnecessary, however. With the epistemological barrier in place, it sufficed for composers simply to assert that their music did not mean what the censors thought it meant. Of course, this barrier also gave composers the opportunity to use music as an 'Aesopian language'—a language that makes 'critical political remarks without using language direct enough to run foul' of the censors.[26]

With the epistemological barrier in place, some composers bore the consequences of engaged political activity; some celebrated such engagement. Those who looked also found. A credo was emerging which said that if composers showed a concern for politics it should not compromise their right to free expression. The conflict and rhetoric in this century regarding the threat of censorship policies to the First Amendment and equivalent protections in other countries is well known. Also well known are the Enlightenment origins of liberal notions of autonomy. Less well known, however, is the peculiarly romantic rationale that lies behind the right to free expression, a right that has achieved common currency in the last 200 years. Indeed, the conflict between the purely aesthetic and the political emerged when composers and artists first found their freedom away from extra-artistic institutions. I have identified some of the ways composers in particular circumvented the conflict, notably those articulated by romantic theory.

Romantic theory continued to influence composers and theorists into the present century, though not always in the same way. Heinrich Schenker provided at the end of the last century what became a powerful argument in this one. He argued that a work's real meaning is not what it appears to be, but is something deeply hidden and purely musical. It takes a person highly trained in music to identify it. This argument sustained not only the formalist's cause but also the composer's general desire for freedom from extra-musical interference.

But the very idea that music could have hidden content was also to used to get composers into trouble. Richard Kraus recently described a view prevalent in the 1970s that resembles ones held earlier. Following the Cultural Revolution, performances of Western music were permitted in China. However, the authorities there remained suspicious of instrumental works that did not have 'programmatic titles' to identify their meaning. That such music, they said, 'came into being during...the establishment of capitalist production relations' suggested that it contained covert, 'bourgeois' meaning. It was not only titles that embodied social content, but the music as well. The authorities were particularly hard on Beethoven. The political content of his music— unwritten on its sleeve—must, they concluded, be extremely subversive.[27]

---

[26] Goldstein, *Political Censorship*, 62.
[27] *Pianos and Politics in China* (New York, 1989), 172–3.

Just as theorists sought reconciliation between the formalist and political significance of musical content in the last century, so theorists have in this one. Adorno articulated one solution. He maintained that music plays a political or 'critical' role in society—to emancipate and demystify it. This role is possible because music occupies a special and autonomous position within society. Instead of being functional as an ordinary tool is functional, music's function is 'to have no function'. In place of a function, music has a hidden and mysterious redemptive power, a power that resides in music's essentially musical and hidden form. What Adorno achieved was what romantic theory achieved earlier: he gave credence to the belief that music's hidden content could simultaneously be purely musical and political.[28]

VI

Romantic theory generated strategies for interpreting instrumental music that helped protect composers from the censors. Theories of transcendent and formalist meaning, as well as debates such as over absolute and programme music, provided composers with ways to articulate and endorse the double-sided provision of autonomy. The question remains whether theorists nowadays can maintain this provision without committing themselves to the often highfalutin and politically troublesome terms of romantic theory. I believe they can.

Suppose, by way of rejecting romantic theory, we claim that music is just another part of social, empirical reality and has no mechanism or grounds for separating itself from that reality. This conclusion would be unacceptable if it denied either music's ability to be beautiful, inspirational, and educative, or its 'critical' function in society. Regarding the latter, one wants to grant music some sort of autonomy, so that it can experiment with and create new 'political realities'. The question is what and how much we have to say about musical autonomy in order to accommodate that wish.

Freedom to experiment does not require the excessive degree of transcendence and detachment granted by romantic theory. Nor does it give composers grounds to abdicate political responsibility for what they have composed because they are somehow 'beyond politics'. Where there is music there can also be mischief. But freedom to experiment does give composers grounds, as it gives members of other academies, for refusing to serve the single 'Stalinist' role of expressing the overt ideologies of the age. This sort of freedom is guaranteed, however, not by music's retreat into the ivory tower, nor necessarily by asserting that music has redemptive power, but first and foremost by a society that allows genuine experiment, dissension, and divergence of thought.

[28] *Aesthetic Theory*, ed. G. Adorno and R. Teidemann, tr. C. Lenhardt (London, 1984), 322.

A society's political character is largely responsible for determining the terms of musical autonomy. Not only does it dictate the censor's creed, but it also encourages or discourages a composer's retreat into purism. Less directly, it bears responsibility also for the generation of aesthetic theories. Consider one socio-political force that helped motivate romantic transcendentalism and purism in the first place. Thus, romantic transcendentalism and purism were peculiarly late eighteenth-century responses to the thoroughly negative feelings that persons had come to bear towards the ordinary world. Put simply, so long as the world was being described in the derogatory terms of the common, humdrum, and mundane, why would anyone have wanted to see beautiful music as one of its constituent parts? Gabriel Fauré expressed the point succinctly in 1908: 'music exists to elevate one as far as possible above the ordinary world'.[29]

Were one to live in a better ordinary world, the impulse to leave it would lose its intensity. But changing the world is neither easy nor, perhaps, even the correct answer. Perhaps the answer does not require us to change the ordinary world, but only our attitude towards it—as it is. In doing this, we might find that nothing we wanted to preserve had been lost, that the need to take theoretical flight into the transcendent had lost its urgency, and, most importantly, that regarding music as one of society's parts no longer required us to ignore either its beauty, or its mystery, or its political dimension. Where there is mystery, there would also now be implicit preferences expressed for certain social, moral, and aesthetical values.

To bring music back into the world would not be to debase it. It would only be to describe music as it always must be. Demystifying music by showing its place in the ordinary world provides us, furthermore, with a modern, philosophical enterprise. This enterprise seeks to reveal the political dimension of a local domain—in this case, the music domain—without shedding the domain of its mystery. It would reveal the values endorsed by particular forms of musical production as well as the conditions of its beauty and power.

To engage in this enterprise could result, as romantic theory once resulted, in just the thing composers have been seeking so long: a justification for their practice conceived in their own terms and on their own terms. It could also provide composers with a range of ideas more powerful than those that once inspired romanticism. If, now, the censors came knocking at the door, composers would not need to claim that their music had no meaning to speak of. They could claim, instead, that the censor had misunderstood what was going on. For they would argue that their aim was neither to destroy arbitrarily whatever they disliked, nor was it to shirk political responsibility. They would argue that their aim was critically to (re)present, alongside other artists and scholars, all that is mysterious as well as brute, all that is good as well as bad, within society. They would not be claiming thereby that music could help

---

[29] Letter to his son, *Correspondance*, ed. J.-M. Nectoux (Paris, 1980), 275 (my translation).

make society perfect. But they would be showing that in their critical and reflective political role, performed in their unspoken and purely musical terms, they had a sophisticated defence against those with overbearing moralizing tendencies. Of course, admission of this sort requires an open ear. But that only proves my point further, that ideas about the nature and power of music—diffident or confident—are and always will be connected to those ideas that predominate in the society at large.

V

Notes on the Meaning of Music

ROGER SCRUTON

Music can have many meanings, depending on the use we make of it. In aesthetics we are interested in its meaning *as music*: the meaning that it has for the person who responds to its musical character. I shall call this *aesthetic* meaning, in order to distinguish it from the meaning that a piece of music has, for example, for the one who uses it as a signal, or a code. Theories of aesthetic meaning must satisfy three tests, which I shall call the 'semaphore test', the 'Frege test', and the 'value test'. The tests are closely related, and reflect an intuitive notion of aesthetic experience.

The semaphore test. Suppose John and Henry live at either end of a railway tunnel, and, sharing an interest in trains, send messages to each other about their common hobby. When a train enters the tunnel at John's end, he fires a semaphore rocket, so that Henry can prepare himself for the train that will soon emerge. This is an act of communication, which has the structure made familiar by Grice:[1] John intends Henry to understand that a train has entered the tunnel, by recognizing that this is John's intention.

The game develops, to the point where Henry can deduce, from the height, trajectory, colour, etc. of the rocket, a wealth of information about the expected train. Henry watches with awe and wonder as the rocket explodes in mid-air, showering the countryside with its multi-coloured sparks. His pleasure in watching this performance is an aesthetic pleasure: its object is the *appearance* of the exploding rocket, contemplated for its own sake. But Henry also feels a pleasure of anticipation: soon, he has deduced, a passenger express will hurtle from the tunnel in the vigorous way that always surprises and delights him. The two pleasures are in principle separable, and Henry might have enjoyed one without the other. Furthermore, Henry interprets the rocket: he assigns to the explosion a meaning—indeed, a 'non-natural' meaning in Grice's sense. This meaning is constituted independently of the aesthetic pleasure, being equally apparent to John, who takes no aesthetic interest in the rockets that he fires. Furthermore, the aesthetic experience is available both to Henry and to his neighbour who, not being part of the game, has no awareness of the meaning.

A theory that assigned meaning to music as Henry assigns meaning to John's rocket—without reference to the aesthetic experience—would not be a theory of musical meaning. Aesthetic meaning is available only in and through an aesthetic experience. To grasp the meaning of a piece of music is already

[1] H. P. Grice, 'Meaning', *Phil Rev.* 66 (1957), 377–88.

to respond to its aesthetic quality as music. Hence a theory which succeeded in providing rules of syntax and semantics for music would not yet be a theory of musical meaning. It would have to be shown that these rules were active in producing the aesthetic experience, and that the aesthetic experience was involved in applying them.

The Frege test. The meaning of a sentence is what you understand when you understand it. There are ways of *attaching* meaning to any object (pebbles on the sea-shore, scratches in a tree trunk, constellations of the stars). But these do not tell us what the object means. (Imagine someone who reads a text of Arabic from left to right, and succeeds in deriving a semantic theory that coherently interprets it. He would not be understanding the text, for his theory is not a theory of the language in which it is written.) To put the point directly, and in terms made familiar by Dummett,[2] a theory of musical meaning is a theory of what we understand when we hear with understanding.

We distinguish 'empty' music from music that means something. But the word 'meaning' is not forced on us; we might have spoken of 'expression', 'evocation', or 'correspondence'. Nor must we have words for the content of a musical utterance: indeed, to put it into words, we feel, is often to lose the musical character. Nor do we judge the content of music as true or false: the 'dimension of reference' is absent. Music differs, therefore, from those arts which we call representational or figurative. To put the matter simply,[3] representation involves what Frege called *thoughts*, which are identified by truth conditions. (The thoughts conveyed by representational works of art tend to be about imaginary worlds, but that does not affect the point.) Even if music resembles or imitates non-musical objects,[4] it does not represent them; which is to say that it does not tell a story about them which might be translated into another medium. There is no narrative in English which has the same truth conditions as a piece of music, as there is a narrative which has the same truth conditions as Titian's *Rape of Lucretia*. (You could *provide* such a narrative. But since the music could be understood by someone who was ignorant of the narrative, it would not be part of the meaning: that is what the Frege test implies.) This is the deep reason for saying that meaning in music is a matter of 'expression', rather than description.

The value test. Meaning in music is a part of aesthetic success. When we say that a piece has 'expression', we do not mean that it evinces a state of mind, whether real or imaginary. We mean that it is *expressive*; and music is expressive only if it invites us into its mental orbit. From the aesthetic point of view expressiveness is always a value, a reason for attending to the work that

[2] M. Dummett, *Frege: Philosophy of Language* (London, 1973).

[3] I have argued the point in 'Representation in Music', *Philosophy* (1976), repr. in *The Aesthetic Understanding* (Manchester, 1983).

[4] As is argued, for example, by Peter J. Kivy in *The Corded Shell* (Princeton, NJ, 1980), and *Sound and Semblance* (Princeton, NJ, 1984).

possesses it. A theory of musical meaning must therefore show why meaning is a value.

Croce and Collingwood believed representation to be of no *aesthetic* significance; in their view successful representation could accompany aesthetic disaster. Their concept of 'expression' was designed, by contrast, to pass the value test: expression was to be an intrinsic mark of aesthetic merit. Theories of musical meaning which rest their case in analogy characteristically fail the test. Those who argue, for instance, that musical expression is a matter of 'analogy' or 'resemblance' to human states of mind, must face the objection that you could (in that case) notice the expression while being aesthetically unaffected, and that a successful expression might be a worthless piece of music.

Someone might propose an amended version of the 'analogy' theory, arguing as follows. When we refer to analogies between music and our states of mind, we do not imply that these analogies can be noticed and appreciated independently of the musical experience. Music does not languish in the way that people do; it does not droop, revive, palpitate, and strain in the fashion of a human gesture, but in its own fashion. It is only through the musical experience that these features can be grasped. You have to hear the emotion *in* the music, and that means attending to the music, in an act of aesthetic interest.

The reply is also a capitulation. For it amounts to saying that the features we notice in expressive music are precisely *not* those we observe in the human psyche. If they were the same features, then we should not need this quite special experience (the appreciation of music) in order to notice them. We must hear these features *in* the music, by an act of musical understanding. And it is precisely this capacity, to hear emotion in music, that needs explaining. What does it mean, to say that we can hear our own emotional life in a sequence of inanimate sounds? To say that we 'hear resemblance' is either false (if it implies that the expression could be grasped without the aesthetic experience), or empty (if the resemblance has to be described in terms of the experience it was supposed to explain). The collapse of the analogy theory follows from the adoption of our three tests. In order to pass them, the theory must be so amended as to lose its specific content.

There is another, perhaps more interesting, reason for rejecting the 'analogy' theory. When we hear states of mind in music we do not merely notice analogies: we hear a distinctively musical process, in which human life is subjected to a kind of musical examination. The state of mind develops through the music, acquiring its character from the musical argument. Tovey begins his account[5] of the first movement of the Eroica in the following way:

---

[5] Donald Tovey, *Essays in Musical Analysis* (Oxford, 1981), i. 7.

After two introductory chords, the violoncellos state the principal theme. It is simply the notes of a common chord, swinging backwards and forwards in a quietly energetic rhythm. Then, as the violins enter with a palpitating high note, the harmony becomes clouded, soon however to resolve in sunshine:

And he adds: 'whatever you may enjoy or miss in the Eroica, remember this cloud: it leads eventually to one of the most astonishing and dramatic strokes in all music'. Tovey is here referring to the reappearance of the main theme at the end of the development, where the C♯ (all of music is contained in that C♯, said Wagner to Cosima) is used to throw the music out of the orbit of E♭ into F major and thence into D♭ major, before the home key of E♭ triumphantly reasserts itself. The implication is clear: the emotion belonging to the 'cloud' is part of a musical process, which catches our attention and our sympathy, leading us by musical means to see an entirely unexpected meaning in the hesitation from which it began. The meaning of the 'cloud' is provided by the great arch of musical argument which subsumes it.

Tovey gives only a rudimentary description of the content of Beethoven's movement. What is important, he implies, is the musical process, the alchemy whereby something is first given in the music, and then worked out, through a magnificent structure of paragraphs, until its character is shown in all its inherent richness, and all its comprehensive humanity. To describe this process in emotional terms is far less important than to identify the crucial transitions. At the same time, the success of the first movement is in part a *dramatic* success. It consists in the utterly unforced and sincere manner in which the little cloud of doubt is worked into the joyful dynamism that precedes it, and gradually taken through its musical paces, until finally hesitation is swept away, and the seed of doubt proves to be a seed of triumph.

In describing this musical process, I have used words which belong to quite another sphere—words like 'sincere', which do not merely describe a state of mind, but also convey a judgement on the character that lives in it. When it comes to the criticism of music such words seem unavoidable. Ask yourself, for example, what is really wrong with the last movement of Tchaikovsky's Sixth Symphony—what leads us, for all the movement's wonderful accomplishment, to stay at a distance from it. Do we not feel that the movement is in some way overdoing its display of grief, and, by overdoing it, not doing it at all? Here we come to the nub of the matter. If the description of music in terms of human states of mind were merely what so many philosophers say that it is—the making of analogies with this or that emotion, or with its 'logical form' or 'dynamic properties'—then it hardly seems credible that we should take the kind of intense moral interest that leads to such a judgement of Tchaikovsky's work, or that we should search in every phrase and every accent for the ring of truth. The forced climax, the sentimental cadence, the sugary harmony—these are defects in the *musical* nature of a composition, and at the same time faults of character, which turn us away (or ought to turn us away) from the thing that possesses them. The musical process is also a moral process, and our awareness of this is one of the reasons why music matters to us. (What I am saying here could be said of literature and painting too; but, as Hanslick pointed out, there is a difficulty involved in describing music in these terms: for music seems to divorce our states of mind from the intentional objects which would normally be required to identify them.[6])

Aristotle described music as an 'imitation' of character, which we in turn imitate through listening.[7] Since we acquire our own character by imitation, it is not surprising that we are alert to the 'bad habits' that could be picked up from music. Consider modern pop music, and compare it with New Orleans Jazz and Ragtime, and then with the folk music, African and American, from which both derive: you will see therein a tragic history of decline. Aggression and fragmentation have come in place of comfort and community. Does this not tempt you to agree with Aristotle, that a dreadful *example* has been set before the youth of our time, and that they are wrongly invited to imitate it? Aristotle's concept of imitation is, however, obscure. We do not know what it means to say that music 'imitates' character: to explain this relation in terms of analogies is once again to encounter the difficulties that I have mentioned. And when the listener 'enters into' the music, it is not the *music* that he imitates, but the character that he *hears in* the music. Surely it is this relation that most needs explaining: the relation between a listener, a piece of music, and a state of mind or character, which obtains whenever the listener *hears* the state of mind *in* the piece of music.

All the same, there is something appealing in Aristotle's idea. This becomes apparent when we ask how we might justify the application to music of terms like 'sentimental', 'honest', and 'obscene'. Consider sentimentality, which is a form of pretence. The sentimentalist lives in real situations as though they were make-believe, in order to bear witness to his own nobility. (Masaryk says somewhere that 'sentimentalism is egoism'.) At the same time sentimental pretence is a *substitute* for real emotion. The sentimentalist pretends that his wife is dead, in order to display his grief for her; in fact she *is* dead, and the sentimentalist also knows this. By imitating grief in the circumstance of grief, he strives to win the benefit of grief (the admiration and sympathy of others) without the cost (the suffering of real bereavement).

Sentimentality is a vice, according to the typology of vice given in Aristotle's *Nicomachean Ethics*. In sentimentality the ability to feel the right emotion towards the right object on the right occasion in the right degree is overcome by a habit of self-indulgence. Our happiness as rational beings depends upon

[6] Eduard Hanslick, *On The Musically Beautiful*, trans. G. Payzant (Indianapolis, 1986).
[7] See e.g. *Politics* (Oxford, 1948), viii, 5. 1340a.

interpersonal relations, which we can fruitfully enter only if we feel real and warm emotions, in which the other counts more than the self, and takes charge of our response to him. Sentimentality erodes that capacity, replacing other-directed emotion with a cold self-centredness.

Sentimentality in art is no different from sentimentality in life. The sentimental work invokes a 'great emotion', not in order to feel it, but in order to claim the credit of feeling it, without the cost of really doing so. Good taste, in art as in life, tells us to shun the company of those whose qualities we abhor. When Leavis, in his powerful analysis of 'Break, break, break . . .'[8] argues that Tennyson is mesmerized by a vast and vague emotion, from which the object has fallen away, he shows us sentimentality in action. He shows us the process whereby the subject of an emotion eclipses the object, occupying the foreground and confining the world to obscurity. While much is pretended in this process, little is felt. It is surely reasonable, therefore, to suppose that sentimentality in art is bad for us in just the way that *bad examples* are bad for us in the course of our moral education. This is surely what Aristotle was trying to get at, in his over-inclusive concept of *mimesis*.

Leavis's analysis is possible, however, because the poem represents an imaginary world, in which loss is described and also idealized. The critic's task and the moralist's task are here one and the same; identical concepts, identical arguments, and identical exhortations are invoked by both. Music, on the other hand, does not have the power to represent things; its world is a world of sounds only, organized by musical principles. So how could *music* be sentimental in the way that Tennyson's poem is sentimental?

The analogy theory of musical meaning, like the semantic theory, tries to identify a feature of music which is the bearer of meaning. We find, however, either that the feature can be explained without reference to the musical experience—in which case the theory fails the semaphore test—or that it can be understood only as the object of a certain experience (the experience of musical meaning), in which case the theory is vacuous. But, whatever our conclusion from this, we should at least take seriously the intuitions embodied in our tests, and turn our attention away from the music so as to focus instead on our response to it. What happens when we experience the meaning in a work of music? In what way is the 'character' of music modelled in our response to it? These, it seems to me, are the crucial questions for a theory of musical meaning.

The answer to them depends, I believe, on an account of sympathy. If you are afraid of a danger, and I too am afraid of it, then our feelings coincide: but neither is the work of sympathy. If, however, you are afraid of a danger, and I, observing your fear, come to share in it, then my fear is a sympathetic response. So too is my compassion, should this be my reaction to your fear.

[8] F. R. Leavis, 'Reality and Sincerity', in *Essays from Scrutiny* (Cambridge, 1969), ii, repr. in *The Living Principle* (London, 1975).

(Not all sympathy is empathy.) Sympathy may either approve or disapprove its object. And approving sympathy may range from the identification with another's joys and sorrows that is characteristic of love, to the mild tremor of compassion that is reserved for those whom we read about at the breakfast table. The importance of art derives largely from the fact that it can present fictional objects for our sympathetic feelings. I can identify wholly with a fictional object without, however, being exposed to any real predicament. This is the unique situation in which we are *free to feel*. Our emotions can therefore be educated through sympathy, without exposing us to the dreadful obligations of the real human world.

Our response to music is a sympathetic response: a response to human life, imagined in the sounds we hear. However, in the absence of representation, we cannot identify a precise *object* of sympathy. All we have is the musical *process*, the working through in music of states of mind and character to which the music gives no name.

Sympathy is not merely a matter of feeling things. There are sympathetic actions and sympathetic gestures. These gestures may arise in response to a real person, really feeling something—someone who needs help, encouragement, or reprimand; or they may arise, as in art, to things imagined, and so deprived of their natural urgency. Among gestures of this second kind none is more remarkable than dancing. In dancing I respond to another's gestures, move with him (or in harmony with him) without seeking to change his predicament or to share his burden. Even in the absence of music, dancing has an intrinsic tendency to become aesthetic: it involves responding to movement for its own sake, dwelling on the appearance of another's gestures, finding meaning in that appearance, and matching it with a gesture of one's own.

When Aristotle wrote of the character-forming nature of music, he had activities like dance in mind. When we dance to music we move in response to it, with the same dispassionate absorption with which we move to another's dancing. Dancing to music is an archetype of the aesthetic response—and our more 'civilized' habits in the concert hall are in many ways like truncated dances, in which our whole being is absorbed by the movement to which we attend, inwardly locked in incipient gestures of imitation. There is no doubt in our feeling that the object of this imitation is a human life, presented somehow through the music. We could not remove this thought from our response without destroying the whole place of music in our culture.

Why is it that people feel especially puzzled by music: why do they seek for an aesthetics of *music*, which is not merely a special application of principles that may be discussed in relation to any of the arts? One reason lies in the fact that music is a non-representational (abstract) art-form—a condition that other arts may aspire to, but which finds its paradigm instance in the art of sound.

For our purposes, however, there is a more important reason, which lies in the fact that there are so many different responses to the aesthetic character of music. You may listen to it, which is like looking at a painting or reading a poem. But you can also play it for yourself, perform it for others, 'sing along' with it and—last but not least—dance to it. All those are ways of engaging with a work's aesthetic character, responding to its meaning and attending to its intrinsic nature. (There is no such thing as 'painting along' with a work of visual art, and you can dance to it only in the oblique way in which you might try to 'capture' something in a gesture.) How can so many responses be ways of *understanding* a single aesthetic character? If we are to approach the mystery of music, it seems to me, we should not study listening, which has so much in common with reading and looking, but dancing, which places music in the very centre of our bodily lives.

Certain features of dancing bear on the questions that concern us:

1. When someone dances to music, he responds to the way it sounds. You could imagine someone being 'set in motion' by subdued music: but he would be dancing only if his movements involve an act of attention to the music. ('Dancing to' has the structure of an aesthetic response.)

2. The music does not move: the movement that the dancer hears in the music is no more really in the music than the face is really in the portrait.[9]

3. The dancer who moves with the music moves also with other dancers— and this is part of what he does, even when the other dancers are imaginary. Dancing creates a 'sympathetic space' whose meaning is corporate. (It is part of the pleasure of dancing that you are 'joining in'.)

4. A dancer may say, 'when I hear this music, I imagine a bird fluttering about its violated nest; that way I know how to dance to it.' On the other hand, he may simply say, 'This is how I dance to it,' and venture no interpretation of his gestures. Dancing, like music, hovers on the verge of representation, but without crossing it.

5. Dance is a close relative of gesture, and in particular of the formal gestures with which we encounter one another on special occasions—weddings, for instance, and funerals.

6. Consider the gesture of condolence: in performing this I *represent myself* to my grieving neighbour. The distinction is easily made between the sincere gesture of condolence and the sentimental gesture. We distinguish true compassion, which focuses on another's suffering, from the self-dramatizing gesture, which aims to display the 'beautiful soul' of the one who makes it. A sincere gesture of condolence is not an expression of grief, but an expression of sympathy for grief: its sincerity consists in its sympathetic concentration on another's predicament. Sincerity is therefore a matter of intention: does the gesture aim to comfort the victim, or rather to cast glory on the one who comforts him? Conventions emerge spontaneously, as David Lewis has shown,

---

[9] For a proof of this, see my 'Understanding Music', in *The Aesthetic Understanding* (Manchester, 1983).

from the complex intentions involved in communicating our states of mind.[10] The conventional gestures at a funeral make possible the sincere expression of condolence. In learning them you enter into a common culture with your neighbours.

7. There is no more difficulty in describing the gestures of a dancer as sincere or sentimental than there is in so describing the gestures of condolence at a funeral. In learning the steps of a dance you are learning how to represent yourself to others. And in dancing to music we respond sympathetically to an imaginary movement that is itself understood as a movement of sympathy.

We should think of the aesthetic response to music as a truncated dance. (Nietzsche was wrong to write of the 'birth of the tragedy out of the spirit of music'; but it would not be wrong to think of the birth of the tragic *audience* our of the spirit of dance.) All of the features noted above are easily attributed to the aesthetic response to music, when it is conceived in such a way. In responding to the meaning of a piece of music, we are being led through a series of gestures which gain their significance from the idea of a community that they intimate, just as do the gestures of a dance. As with a dance, a kind of magnetic field is created which shapes the emotional life of the one who enters it. We move for a while along the orbit of a formalized emotion and practise its steps. Our truncated movements are also acts of attention: we do what we do in response to the sounds that we hear, when we attend to them aesthetically. Hearing the meaning is therefore part of the aesthetic experience. For this reason, the theory proposed will pass the semaphore test and the Frege test.

But will it pass the value test? To put it another way: why is the 'experience of meaning' so important? And why does it reveal the *musical* value of its object? I shall conclude with a brief suggestion.

Music, like every art, exists in, and derives its life from, a continuous culture. Certain phrases, harmonies, timbres, and rhythms acquire a character, which adheres to them in whatever context they may appear. Consider the progression from the root chord of C major, with E above, to the seventh chord on F, with E♭ above and F below: the 'blues' character has become an immovable part of it. Or consider the rhythm of the tango, the 'folkish' character of the pentatonic scale, the timbre of the xylophone, the 'clenching' of the diminished seventh. Whenever we hear these details we are drawn by them into the little fragments of human life that they suggest. Yet we are drawn by the *music*. And if it is worth anything, the music does not leave us there, but leads us on, through its own powers of development. As we move with these elements, therefore, we are led by our sympathies into a wholly new totality: a musical bridge is created, spanning distant regions of human life, and teaching us that these regions may be connected in our feelings, and that

[10] D. K. Lewis, *Convention* (Cambridge, 1969).

the sympathetic response to one of them might be resolved, concluded, or questioned in another.

In Beethoven's Ninth Symphony, the listener is led through a gamut of tragic and resolute emotions, associated with the open fifth of D; he proceeds to a frenzied dance and thence to a calm meditation in double variation form. These three movements leave a memory of contrasted 'dances', in which our sympathies are stretched to their limit. And out of this, by purely musical means, emerge the lines of a recitative: phrases which take their meaning from the accent of human speech, and which lead, of their own accord, to the melody of the 'Ode to Joy'. This triumphant affirmation of community is not the cheap trick that it might have been: for it has received the stamp of musical inevitability. We are made to rehearse, in our extended sympathies, a particular movement of the soul. We return from private tragedy to public acceptance, and we feel this return as natural, even inevitable. Our over-whelming impression is that it is possible, after all, to explore the depths of human isolation, and still to re-emerge in joy. Beethoven's sincerity lies in the process, whereby we are led from tragedy to joy without a faltering or sarcastic step, without being called upon by the music to deny what has gone before or to turn away from it.

It is through such processes that the greatest triumphs of music are offered. The task of a theory of musical meaning is to show that these processes may be truly musical, and yet at the same time explorations of character, and invitations to sympathy. For it is through sympathy that music is understood.

Is There a Semantics for Music?

ROM HARRÉ

How do we succeed in making anything of a musical experience? I shall not tackle the question of how one picks out an auditory experience *as music*. Assuming that I am within the fuzzy boundary that demarcates music from all other auditory experiences, can any sense be made of the idea that the experience is in some way significant? Or points beyond itself? These questions can be animated by considering specific references such as the bird song in Beethoven's 'Pastoral' Symphony; but they might be animated by something more general such as the theme of death in the second movement of Mahler's Fourth. According to Mahler himself that theme is made manifest through the tuning of the solo violin. Who can doubt the cosmic significance of Bruckner's Eighth Symphony? But what of these 'significances' and 'references'? Couldn't Mahler's Fourth be a celebration of the Viennese tramcar network? (It is not hard to hear it that way once the idea has struck one!) And why should not Bruckner's Eighth be heard to display the essence of the mass production of steel? What about all those marching feet in Shostakovich's Seventh? Clearly there is something to be investigated here. I shall examine three attempts to characterize what it might be. I shall present each attempt as a reflection of one of the classical theories that has been offered to explain the general phenomenon of 'significance'. These are Augustinian nominalism, Saussurian structuralism, and Kantian constructionism. The first seems to underlie Urmson's 'representationalist' theory;[1] the second is what would be needed to give a complete structural theory in the manner of Langer,[2] while the third expresses the philosophical standpoint from within which Scruton's account[3] seems to me to develop.

1. Augustinian Nominalism

The 'inner' model for the general theory is the proper name and its bearer. Every meaningful word must denote something and that which it denotes is its meaning. As a general theory of linguistic meaning the name/bearer principle was pretty thoroughly demolished by Wittgenstein. His method of attack was two-pronged but very simple. It consisted in showing first that there are lots of

---

[1] J. O. Urmson, *Philosophy and the Arts* (London, 1973).
[2] S. K. Langer, *Philosophy in a New Key: A Study in the Symbolism of Reason, Rite, and Art* (Cambridge, Mass., 1963)
[3] R. Scruton, *The Aesthetic Understanding* (Manchester, 1983).

words about whose meaningfulness there could be no doubt when they were
made use of in some practical human activity, yet, even in simple cases, their
significance for their users could not be explained solely in terms of that to
which they referred. The second line of argument struck more directly at the
very idea of pure ostensive definition. One would not know how to take a
definitional act of pointing unless one already knew the sort of thing that the
word might mean, that is how to take the *sample*. Exemplars, to be used in
definitional demonstrations, are already inside the boundaries of language.

In the case of music both Hospers and Urmson have worked with the idea
of musical phrases etc. representing something outside the circle of the music
itself. I shall begin with the more simplistic of the two representationalist
theories, that of Hospers. He claims that 'the difference between programme
music and "pure" music is . . . one of degree'.[4] He seems to take it to be a
matter of empirical fact. He says that programme music is '*defined* as music
which evokes in most listeners the impression of specific objects . . .' but he
does not say whether this is achieved with or without the help of the hints in
the programme itself. If Mendelssohn told me that his composition was called
'Fingal's Cave' I would be hard put to conjure up a vision of anything non-
topographic. Hospers later weakens his thesis to the definition of representational music as 'music designed to invoke' some specific object or event as
referent. Suppose we find that a good many people do not have an impression
of a sea cave when they hear Mendelssohn's composition? According to the
first proposal the music after all failed to be programme music. But on the
second proposal it still qualified, but just did not work, as such. Its mode of
significance, if it had any, would be non-representational. By way of contrast
Hospers cites another kind of music exemplified by a Mozart concerto or
Haydn quartet. He claims that this kind of music does not evoke any specific
object 'for any of us'. It 'evoke[s] emotion but is unattached to any definite life
situation'.[5] 'Represent' according to Hospers 'means merely "to evoke the
impression of"'.[6] It is an empirical question whether or not some music is
representational and even whether, at some particular performance, it may not
come to be representational if it just happens to evoke a common impression
in the audience. As far as I can understand Hospers's position it follows that
music which does not as a matter of fact evoke such concrete impressions is
'pure' music.[7] Pure music, then, if all Hospers's proposals are put together,
evokes emotion but does not represent it. In short Hospers offers a causal
rather than a semantic theory of the emotional 'content' of music. Or to put
this another way—music has no emotional content, only emotional effects.

Before I go on to outline and discuss Urmson's view—which claims, like
Hospers's position, that there is both representational and non-representational music—I would like to cite some passages drawn verbatim from

[4] J. Hospers, *Meaning and Truth in the Arts* (Hamden, Conn., 1964), 45.
[5] Ibid. 44.   [6] Ibid. 49.   [7] Ibid. 45.

interviews with Messiaen. What are we to make of these remarks from the composer of *Des canyons aux étoiles*? He says 'my love of the mysterious, of magic, of enchantment, for these quotations from *Revelations* are extraordinary, extravagant, surrealistic and terrifying. Look at this one: "and to the star was given the key to the bottomless pit." This has allowed me to imagine such effects as the alliance of very low trombone pedal-notes to the shrill resonance of three clarinets and to the deep rolls of the tam-tam.'[8] I will return to comment on the crucial role of the double metaphor of high/low in this passage. And then there are these remarks: 'So I've tried to express in my work the colours mentioned in *Revelations* . . . the brass, dare I say it, should "play red" . . .'.[9] Can any of this be rescued and made sense of in some semantic theory?

Urmson begins with a consideration of the idea that music might be or contain representations of sounds.[10] There is a *musical* phrase in Beethoven's 'Pastoral' Symphony that can be interpreted as the call of a cuckoo because it resembles the sound that the cuckoo actually makes. There is an auditory likeness between the musical sound and the represented sound. But 'auditory likeness' will not do as an analysis of musical representation because, argues Urmson, while the former is reciprocal the latter is not. In the 'Pastoral' Symphony a musical phrase represents the cuckoo call but a cuckoo call in the springtime does not represent anything in the symphony. This argument does not strike me as wholly convincing. Might I not, during a walk in the woods, remark, 'Listen to that cuckoo. It is just as if a little bit of the "Pastoral" Symphony were being played'?

But Urmson does not leave the matter there. He elaborates the idea of representation and attempts to explain why it is asymmetrical by introducing musical intentions.

> *A* represents *B* if *A* is auditorily similar to *B* and *X* intends *A* to represent *B*.

There are several problems with this proposal. How is music as auditory representation to be distinguished from mere sound effects, since there is intention in both? 'Musician's intention' runs into the same difficulties that beset intention hypotheses generally—can we always be sure that we know what the composer's or the performer's intention was. If we cannot, must the music then lose representational significance? I suppose not.

It seems to me that Urmson has missed the crucial point about representation in music, namely that the imitative or resembling sound should be presented in a musical context. The reason that the remark about the cuckoo call sounds odd and a bit precious is that the call comes in the complete absence of a musical context. But in that context it would not matter that the

---

[8] C. Samuel, *Conversations with Olivier Messiaen* (London, 1967–76), 94.
[9] Ibid. 97.   [10] Urmson, *Philosophy and the Arts*.

call is imitated or whether we had a real cuckoo in a cage among the players to make the call at the right moment. We *could* have real cannon rather than mere maroons in the '1812'. Perhaps that has even been attempted. Hoffnung had real vacuum cleaners in his performances! If we are to countenance representation at all as one of the ways in which music can have significance and point beyond itself then I prefer some such proposal as the following:

> *A* represents *B* if *A* auditorily resembles *B* and *A* is produced as a proper part of a musical context.

The representation thesis is further weakened when programme music is examined more closely. For example, do the storm passages in the works of Rossini, Beethoven, or Mahler signify storms because they resemble the sounds of actual storms? It is easy to see that this cannot be the case, if we apply the substitution test as in the case of the maroons used in the '1812'. We could not replace the storm music by real storm noises, even if faithfully recorded, and preserve the significating mode of those works. Clearly some such notion as 'conventional sign' is needed here. Music of the romantic era is full of such conventional signs. Who can fail to understand the significance of the oft-repeated harp arpeggios which can mean nothing but raindrops?

Given that the representation relation is context bound and conventional the composer's intentions must drop out of our account. In *Fantasia* Walt Disney portrayed (what he took to be the significance of) the hard rhythms in Stravinsky's *Rite of Spring* as representing the vulcanism of the early Earth. We know that Stravinksy intended them to portray tribal dancing, via a familiar auditory suggestion. If we took composer's intention seriously for a semantics of representational music we would have to say that Disney's treatment of *The Rite of Spring* is in error. I cannot believe that anyone who has seen and heard *Fantasia* would be inclined to make that judgement.

Urmson carries his intentionalist theory of representation further by claiming the 'extra-musical evidence is normally necessary'.[11] By that he has in mind such extra-musical matters as the title 'Pastoral' Symphony or Mahler's gloss on the third movement of his First Symphony when we are encouraged, nay instructed, to hear the 'Dies Irae' as the funeral procession of the huntsman. But once we have disposed of the idea that representationalism requires composer intention, extra-musical evidence for that intention is also otiose.

However, there is another kind of extra-musical input that might indeed be relevant to the question of the nature of representional music. I have briefly alluded to it above. One might call it 'knowledge of the musical tradition'. *This*, indicating the relevant passage in the 'Pastoral' Symphony is how storms are done, and *this* , indicating the opening double bass solo of the third movement of Mahler's First, is how funerals are done. In acquiring one's competence as a listener (and a composer) one accumulates a repertoire of

---

[11] Ibid. 137.

musical devices, with, so to say, standard meanings in the culture. Having come to know a Beethoven 'storm' I am competent to recognize a Rossini 'storm'. I enclose the word 'storm' in quotes, since in neither case is stormy music auditorily related to the sounds of lightning (which silently rends the heavens), 'thunder, and the lashing of the rain in the way that the flute solos in *Siegfried* are related to birdsong.

So far the discussion has turned on such musical matters as melodic style, colour, and the like. Urmson also considers under the rubric of 'representationalism' what he calls 'formal correspondences'.[12] By that he has in mind such matters as rhythm and tempo. We hardly need the text to realize the representational significance of the 4/4 time signature and the marching tempo of 'Onward Christian Soldiers'. But what about the scherzo in Beethoven's Ninth? Why do I always think of horsemen? Again I think I am the victim (or perhaps the beneficiary) of a cultural tradition in which that particular rhythm is in numerous equine epics the accompanying score of horse riding. But does the *music* represent a troop of horsemen on the move? At this point I come up against a problem for which I have no clear solution. Perhaps I am the only one to experience that movement of the Ninth so naïvely but vividly. Am I wrong? As I might be if I thought that 'eschatalogical' meant 'lavatorial'? This problem cannot be settled by extending Wittgenstein's 'private language argument' to music since I would have no trouble at all in illustrating what the Ninth had come to mean to me by playing over the relevant movement juxtaposed to the theme music from *The Lone Ranger*. However, my intuition is that generally speaking the idea of an educated or sophisticated taste operates here as elsewhere in the arts. Communal agreement on the matter would override individual idiosyncratic interpretations however well founded they might be in cultural clichés.

2. Saussurian Structuralism

Those who attack representationalist theories of musical meaning often conclude that the failures of such theories to give a general account of musical significance show that 'music is not a language'. But that inference seems to me to go through only if one had presupposed an Augustinian account of meaning within one's a priori conception of language. To locate morphological theories of significance, such as S. K. Langer's[13] we need to open up the issue of linguistic meaning much further. The direction I want to take lies along the line of analysis proposed by Saussure.[14]

Linguistic meaning, according to Saussure, is the product of two systems of relations. A lexical item has *signifié* by virtue of the relations it has to some-

---

[12] Ibid. 138–9. [13] Langer, *Philosophy in a New Key*.
[14] F. de Saussure, *A Course in General Linguistics* (London, 1960).

thing extralinguistic. The details of Saussure's conception of extralinguistic meaning do not command much assent and need not detain us. It is the other set of relations, those that determine the *valeur* of a lexical item, that determine the internal structure of a language. The linguistic value of a sign is the totality of other signs which its presence excludes for the user of the sign system. These exclusions can be ranged along two dimensions. The syntagmatic dimension lies along the line of production of linguistic signs, for instance in speaking. The paradigmatic dimension contains all those signs that might have occurred where the sign in focus appears, but did not. Thus the linguistic value of the heard sign 'car' in an utterance about a journey has part of its meaning from the fact that as so heard it excludes the hearing of 'bike'. The formal properties of language can be expressed for both dimensions in the totality of exclusion rules for each and every sign.

Langer's theory of the meaning of music excludes any analogue of *signifié*. She asserts that 'Music is not a language because it has no vocabulary'. Yet it is significant. Significance must therefore somehow arise from musical form alone. That form seems to me to be able to be dealt with along lines that are very closely parallel to Saussure's conception of *valeur*. A single note in a melody is related positively to those notes that precede and succeed it both in time value and pitch. But it is also related to all those notes that are excluded at any moment by the presence of just this note. The same goes for the presentation of colour through orchestration, as is very clear in the remarks I have already quoted from Messiaen apropos of the orchestration of *Des canyons aux étoiles*.

However, music is a semantic enterprise, according to Langer, but of a radically different kind from speech or writing. Her general view can be expressed in the following: (*a*) it is false that a composer expresses emotions in the music, which then causes similar emotions in the hearer; (*b*) it is true that a composer expresses his or her knowledge of emotions in music, which is then understood (somehow) by the auditor. To anticipate, Scruton also holds that the deep question for philosophers is the nature of musical understanding, not the nature of any causal processes by which some aspect of that understanding might be mediated. Langer firmly rules out any recourse to a simple analogy with linguistic meaning. 'The analogy between music and language breaks down', she says, 'if we carry it beyond the mere semantic function in general, which they are supposed to share. Logically, music has not the characteristic properties of language—separable terms with fixed connotations, and syntactical rules for deriving complex connotations without any loss to the constituent elements. Apart from a few onomatopoeic themes that have become conventional, music has no literal meaning'.[15] Thus an elementary significant component of a musical 'object' is an 'unconsummated symbol' and does 'not assign meanings to specific forms'.

---

[15] Langer, *Philosophy in a New Key*, 232.

One of Langer's reasons for excluding the full language analogy is that she affirms the idea of a 'plasticity of musical meaning'. That is supposed to stand in contrast to language in which lexical signs have 'fixed connotations'. In the light of the criticisms of the use of the idea 'fixed connotations' in language use by such authors as Wittgenstein[16] and Harris[17] the contextuality of the significance of the musical sign is not enough sharply to distinguish language from music. It is also important to keep in mind the distinction between musical notation which is a language and the music which is produced at the behest of the commands that constitute the score. Goodman correctly identifies the score as a series of commands—do this! and then do that![18]

With these reservations and preliminaries in mind I can now turn to a critical exposition of Langer's structural theory of the significance of music as such. Langer's theory of musical meaning can be summarized in two principles.

1. Music has meaning by virtue of sharing a logical form with some aspect of human experience. 'Musical structures logically resemble certain dynamic patterns of human experience.'[19] And 'what music can reflect is only the morphology of feeling'.[20] While the notion of musical structure can be readily explicated in terms of melody, rhythm, and harmony the notion of a morphology of feeling is novel and in need of spelling out. That task is performed by Langer's second principle.

2. The 'inner life'—physical and mental—has formal properties, for example patterns of motion and rest, of tension and release, of agreement and disagreement. These formal properties are, claims Langer, similar to those of music. Quoting from Pratt she says, auditory characters are not emotions at all. They merely *sound* the way emotions *feel*.[21] But this account is not all as straightfoward and expository as it sounds. Scruton points to the striking role that unexplicated metaphors play in this account.[22] Of course, this is not necessarily a criticism or even a flaw. It may well be that here as in other fields of enquiry the use of metaphor is the only possible device by which attention can be drawn to some new insight. However, it is certainly the case that Langer's account cannot be assessed until the metaphors are analysed and their value and viability decided.

Already in my discussion of various accounts of the significance of music several unexplicated metaphors have surfaced. The concepts 'high'/'low' appear as doubly metaphorical in the remarks I quoted above from Messiaen. The first metaphor is so embedded in the language of musical commentary that we hardly notice that to speak of the bass as low and the treble as high is metaphorical. But the high/low contrast is also mapped onto the distinction

[16] L. Wittgenstein, *Philosophical Investigations* (Oxford, 1953).
[17] R. Harris, *The Language Makers* (Oxford, 1983).
[18] N. Goodman, *Languages of Art* (Indianapolis. 1968).
[19] Langer, *Philosophy in a New Key*, 226.   [20] Ibid. 238.
[21] Ibid. 244–5.   [22] Scruton, *The Aesthetic Understanding*.

between the sublime and 'lofty' (another metaphor) and the mundane, vulgar, and commonplace. But there are yet other twists to this cluster of metaphors. 'Low' can also mean despicable and evil, while 'high' picks out the praise-worthy and the good. So Messiaen's remarks about the pitch of trombones and clarinets contains a string of interconnected metaphors of altitude.

Returning to the metaphors suggested by Langer it strikes one how central is the idea of movement to most of her metaphors of structure. Indeed 'movement' is a ubiquitous concept in discussions of musical form in the sense that Langer is working from. Intercut with movement-concepts are various binary oppositions. Langer's system of structural metaphors seems to me to be Saussurian in just that way. Significant form is identified as a set of oppositions (exclusions) along various dimensions of metaphorical movement. Presumably there is movement in a 'turn' and rest in a dotted minim. A Plagal cadence creates a tension and then by resolving onto the tonic that tension is released. The structure can be generalized even further if we draw on the concept pairs difference/similarity and succession/stasis.

In short, given the general rightness that one feels with Langer's account, our analytic understanding can only advance through the detailed exposition and critical discussion, not only of her metaphors but of the metaphors through which the significance of music is generally portrayed. The analysis must go further than merely noticing the role of musical structure in the affective powers of music. The idea of such structure is not enough to account for the phenomenon of musical experience. There is structure galore in 'mathematically' conceived music. Why then do so many people find Berg's instrumental music so boring, so unmusical? And Bach's compositions intended as no more than practice routines for learners are experienced as music of profoundly satisfying aesthetic quality? There have been no lack of theories to account for this phenomenon. For instance Kepler (1595) in *Harmonices mundi* used a generally Neoplatonic cosmology to identify the truly satisfying musical harmonies and melodies (synchronic and diachronic structures of opposition respectively). Langer's second principle, which proposes an isomorphism between musical structure and structures of ex-perience, is necessary to account for the relative aesthetic quality of structures that are mathematically acceptable.

3. A 'Kantian' Account

Music reveals to us just exactly what we have put into it from our own resources. These resources, according to Scruton, come from our experience of ourselves. Choice of metaphors is explained in just the same way. 'It is our experience of ourselves, rather than any scientific representation of the world, which both prompts and explains the metaphors which we apply to music'.[23] We can see how this is supposed to work in three examples from Scruton's writing on the subject: 'movement', 'rhythm', and 'harmony'.

(a) 'Movement' as metaphor

The basic idea of movement is simple—'along' the time dimension and 'up' and 'down' in the dimension of pitch (these relative elevations themselves a metaphor). Rate of movement is also a simple concept at this stage of the analysis. It can be nothing but number of notes per bar in relation to the overall specification of tempo as andante, allegro, etc. But where does this system of metaphors and interpretative conventions come from? According to Scruton 'it is ourselves as agents—rather than any purely geometrical idea of space—which underlies our experience of musical movement'.[24] It seems to me that if this is right it entails that 'movement' ought to be a panhuman experiential aspect of movement, and also a ubiquitious metaphor wherever the quality and significant characteristics of music are discussed.

(b) Rhythm

Though there are rhythms in music and the concept is not metaphorical, yet, argues Scruton, 'the perception of rhythm involves imaginative transfer of the kind involved in metaphor'.[25] It is a transfer from our sense of ourselves to our perception of certain necessary qualities in music. We are enabled to perceive rhythm in music because we perceive it in ourselves. Our discovery of rhythm in music is a rediscovery of something we are already familiar with in the most direct and intimate way. But it is movement that is at the root of musical rhythm according to Scruton. 'When we hear a *rhythm* we hear sounds joining and diverging from one another etc. . . . in a manner familiar from our knowledge of human movement'. There is no doubt that as a matter of the history of musical form this observation is accurate. The 'movements' of early symphonic movements were just traditional dance forms, distinguished by their rhythms. But Scruton is surely proposing something deeper than that. Long before Haydn and Mozart appropriated the rhythms of the dance there were the dancers, who were themselves necessarily able to appreciate the rhythms that made the accompanying music the right music for this or that dance. It cannot have been the experience of the dance that made the appreciation of the musical rhythms possible. Dances are learned via the process by which the beginner comes to adjust and control his or her movements with respect to the rhythm already supplied by some external source. This seeming impasse is a familiar one. It is the impasse noticed by

---

[23] Scruton, *The Aesthetic Understanding*, 86. [22] Ibid. [25] Ibid. 90.

Wittgenstein in his discussion of rule-following. I can manage to follow a rule only if I already have the idea of a regularity in my behaviour. But many of the regularities of our behaviour seem to have had their origin in the following of some rule. In the end the possibility of normative institutions like rule-following must rest on certain natural regularities which we inherit as organisms. I think that Scruton's rhythms must have their source in something similar.

(c) Harmony

Musical harmony is not equivalent to the concord or discord of sounds. That phenomenon or group of phenomena are explicable in terms of the physics and physiology of sound vibrations and their detection. Scruton remarks that 'harmony belongs not to the material world of sound but to the intentional world of musical experience'.[26] Again the roots of musical harmony are to be found in something like 'movement'. Harmony appears in the 'tension, transition and resolution' to surrounding chords. It is a structural property of the diachronic development of music.

How does this view contrast with that of Langer? According to Scruton there is no relevant structure in music until we put it there in our way of hearing. The actual sonic phenomena provide the occasion for the musical phenomenon in something like the way that Kant thought that the empirical world, phenomena as we experience them organized into a spatio-temporally laid out world of causally active things, came to be by the schematization of the undifferentiated flux of sensation in accordance with the categories. On this view the laws of harmony must be akin to the most general laws of nature in Kant's scheme—synthetic a priori propositions. In Langer's scheme there are two structures, that of experience, for instance of emotional states, and that of music, which exists independently. In appreciating music we simply map them on to one another and at those moments in which we *discover* an isomorphism music is born. On Scruton's view the isomorphism is a product of the constructive (synthesizing) process by which we have, so to say, searched the music for something that has its origin, for us, in our experience of ourselves.

Two examples of 'programme' work may help to slant us in the direction of Scruton rather than Langer. Mahler went to considerable pains to explain why he felt it necessary to introduce words into his Second Symphony. By telling us how to hear it he effectively closes off the range of possible Scrutonian transferences from our given and presupposed (natural) experience. Recently the lead singer of the Moody Blues explained why pop music needed the visual images that have been introduced through the use of pop video. The audience is forced to contemplate, according to him, 'what the songs really

---

[26] Ibid. 93.

mean'. It is clear that these extrinsic pieces of advice on how to hear would be superfluous if the meaning resided unproblematically and unequivocally in the music independently of human thought. All this seems to lead in a now familiar post-modernist direction. There is certainly structure in music and it may be that Langer is essentially right in her view that structure becomes significant when it is isomorphic with structures of experience. But there are not two structures which somehow are glued together in the experiencing of sounds as of music. There is only one, which comes into being in and through the application to what is heard of those prior structuring procedures through which all signifying order is created. It is easy to slip into the illusion that that order is given in experience.

Goodman, Density, and the Limits of Sense Perception

DIANA RAFFMAN

I

According to Nelson Goodman, artworks and their scores, scripts, diagrams, blueprints, sketches, and even performances are *symbols*. The members of this eclectic group instantiate virtually every symbolic relation under the sun: they denote, refer, represent, notate, exemplify, express, describe. In his seminal and difficult book, *Languages of Art*,[1] Goodman undertakes to provide an analysis of these various relations, sharply segregating his theoretical concerns from merely 'applied' or 'practical' (e.g. psychological) ones. The following remarks are characteristic:

The ... stated requirements for a notational system are all negative and general, satisfiable by systems with null or even no [syntactic] characters. ... A good many other features that might be thought essential are not covered ... No requirement of a manageably small or even finite set of atomic characters, no requirement of clarity, of legibility, of durability, of maneuverability, of ease of writing or reading, of graphic suggestiveness, of mnemonic efficacy, or of ready duplicability or performability has been imposed. These may be highly desirable properties, and to some degree even necessary for any practicable notation; and the study of such engineering matters could be fascinating and profitable. But none of this has anything to do with the basic theoretical function of notation systems. (154)

In the limited space allotted me here, I shall try to show that Goodman's theoretical asceticism defeats his own analysis at certain places, blinding him to the fact that artworks and artistic activity in general are shot through with the 'practical limitations' of human *psychology*. In particular, I shall contend that Goodman's treatment of certain musical markings as *semantically dense* is hobbled by the finite character of auditory perception. At the end I shall offer a strategy for salvaging at least part of Goodman's account in an appropriately 'psychologized' form.

There are several vantage points from which the failing at issue can be sighted, but focusing on the musical markings will be effective for at least three reasons. First, and most important, the musical markings denote values

---

I thank Robert Kraut, George Schumm, J. J. Bharucha, Ivan Fox, Ruth Marcus, Jonathan Vogel, David Blinder, Barbara Scholz, Lee Brown, and Robert Batterman for many illuminating discussions.

[1] (Indianapolis, 1968). Page citations are to this edition throughout.

along *psychological* (specifically perceptual) parameters like pitch, loudness, and timbre. These latter are the so-called psychophysical correlates to acoustic properties of the sound stimulus: pitch correlates (more or less directly) with frequency, loudness with intensity, timbre with waveform, and so forth. Simply put, for an acoustic event to have a certain pitch (/loudness/timbre) is for it to be perceived—or, as is now commonly said, mentally represented—in a certain way. In at least some other cases, by contrast, Goodman seems to have wholly *non*-psychological properties of the art object in mind.[2] In his analysis of pictorial representation, for example, he selects the *height* of the image as his case in point:

Consider, for example, some pictures in the traditional Western system of representation: the first is of a man standing erect at a given distance; the second, to the same scale, is of a shorter man at the same distance. The second image will be shorter than the first. A third image in this series may be of intermediate height; a fourth, intermediate between the third and second; and so on. According to the representational system, any difference in height among these images constitutes a difference in height of man represented . . . (227)

We are given no indication that Goodman here means to refer to *perceived* or *apparent* height, a psychological property. It seems that any difference in the height of the image, *perceptible or not*, is relevant to its symbolic function. The disparity with the musical cases is striking: along musical dimensions like pitch and loudness, there are by definition no imperceptible differences. What I shall urge is that Goodman's troubles originate in his failure to heed a distinction between psychological properties of art objects, like pitch, loudness, and (arguably) colour, on the one hand, and non-psychological (presumably physical) properties, like acoustic frequency and height, on the other.

A second reason to take the musical markings as our exemplar is that they include clear cases of both dense and non-dense markings; hence just what the density consists in comes out clearly there. Third, the perception of music turns out to be importantly different from the perception of other artforms, and its psychological theory more fully developed; this will prove invaluable in our examination of Goodman's view.

II

We shall be concerned with the denotation of musical performances by musical markings; or, in other words, we shall be concerned with the com-

---

[2] For present purposes I am going to take for granted a rough and ready distinction between psychological and non-psychological properties of objects. The former are properties that objects have in virtue of being mentally represented in a certain way, the latter properties that objects have (as it were) mind-independently.

[3] Goodman would include tempos as tokens of the (metronomic) types '60 M.M.', '88 M.M.', etc., and metre and key presumably ought to enter in as well. However, for simplicity's sake I shall ignore those features here. Also, I am going to help myself to talk of tokens and types, but Goodman would surely disapprove; see e.g. p. 131 n. 3.

pliance of musical performances with musical markings. (Objects—here, acoustic ones—comply with the symbols that denote them (143–4).) On Goodman's view as I understand it, a musical performance is an acoustic object (a 'sound-event') that can be 'taken' in two ways, corresponding to its compliance with two different kinds of markings: on the one hand it can be 'taken as an instance of a work', while on the other hand it can be 'taken as a sound-event' (e.g. 237–8). Taken in the first way, the performance complies with the *notational* markings in the score; taken in the second, it complies with 'supplementary instructions, either printed along with the score or tacitly given by tradition, word-of-mouth, etc.' (237). Let me explain the distinction.

For Goodman, 'score' is a term of art referring exclusively to those markings that specify (what he takes to be) the definitive features of a work—essentially, pitches as tokens of the types A natural, B flat, C sharp, etc., and rhythms as tokens of the types quaver, crotchet, minim rest, etc.[3] These markings, together with their denotata, constitute a notational symbol system. That is to say, they are (*a*) syntactically disjoint: no token marking belongs to more than one syntactic type or 'character' (e.g. no token marking is both an A-natural marking and a B-flat marking); (*b*) syntactically differentiated: for any two distinct characters and any token marking that does not belong to both, it is theoretically possible to *determine* of at least one of the characters that the marking does not belong to it; (*c*) semantically disjoint: there is no intersection between the extensions ('compliance-classes') of any two distinct characters (e.g. no sound-event complies with both the A-natural marking and the B-flat marking); (*d*) semantically differentiated: for any two characters and any sound event that does not comply with both, it is theoretically possible to *determine* of at least one of the characters that the sound-event does not comply with it; and (*e*) unambiguous: no character has more than one compliance-class. For clarity I shall refer to the notational markings for a given piece as the 'Score', and take the liberty of using this spelling in the relevant places in citations from the Goodman text; by 'score' I shall mean the score in the ordinary sense of the word—that is, everything on the printed page. Goodman's claim is that the performance taken as an instance of a work (call this the 'performance (W)') complies with the notational markings that constitute the Score; in other words, it instantiates the sequence of pitch-time events prescribed by the Score.

Before we proceed further, a modification of the above criteria of notationality is in order. Specifically, Goodman's formulation of the differentiation requirements does not capture what must be—or at least ought to be—his true meaning. For example, according to Goodman a scheme[4] of vertical lines, densely ordered according to their lengths in fractions of an inch so that between any two is a third more similar to each of them than they are to each other, is syntactically undifferentiated. But requirement (*b*) above dictates otherwise: for any two characters L and L', and any line l that differs in length

---

[4] A scheme is a *syntax*; add a semantics and you have a *system*.

from (the length specified by) either L or L' (or both), it will always be theoretically possible to build a measuring device sufficiently fine-grained to register the difference. Hence if the vertical lines are to count as undifferentiated, the differentiation requirement will need to be strengthened. I propose the following: for any character C and any mark m, it is theoretically possible to determine whether m belongs to C. On the simplifying assumption that every mark belongs to one and only one character, we get the claim that for any mark m, it is theoretically possible to determine which character m belongs to. In somewhat more intuitive terms, a differentiated scheme will be one in which it is theoretically possible to uniquely type-identify any mark. For example, any pitch mark ('notehead') in the musical Score can be uniquely type-identified as an A-natural mark, or as a B-flat mark, or as a C-sharp mark, etc. With regard to the vertical lines described above, although we will be able to determine, of any given character to which a given line does not belong, that the line does not belong to it, we will not be able to determine which character the line does belong to. Analogous adjustments should be made to the semantic differentiation requirement: a semantically differentiated system will be one in which it is theoretically possible to determine the (unique) compliance-class of any object in the scheme's field of reference. From now on, when I speak of differentiation I shall have these revised senses of the term in mind.[5]

Thus far we have seen that the performance(W) complies with the Score, where the latter is a notational symbol—syntactically and semantically disjoint, syntactically and semantically differentiated, and unambiguous. In addition to the pitches and rhythms prescribed by the Score, a performance contains myriad fine-grained values, often called 'nuances', along its various dimensions. Du Pré's fortissimo may be a hair louder than Ma's; Tureck may sustain the first note of the *Goldberg Variations* a shade longer than the second; a violinist may raise the pitch of an A natural ever so slightly as the underlying harmony modulates from F sharp minor to A major. Indeed, every A natural the violinist plays in a given performance may differ slightly from every other; the category (the 'determinable') *A natural* subsumes many discriminably different pitches ('determinates'), just as the category *red* subsumes many discriminably different shades. Similarly, the category 'crotchet' subsumes events of many discriminably different durations, and the category *'forte'* subsumes events of many discriminably different loudness levels. These fine-grained values are, as Goodman puts it, 'nonconstitutive and may vary freely from performance to performance without affecting the status of any performance as a genuine . . . instance of the work' (237). Not prescribed in the Score proper, these nuances comply with 'supplementary instructions . . .

[5] There is ample textual support for such a recasting of the differentiation requirements; see e.g. pp. 134–6 of *Languages of Art*. After completing the present paper I have discovered that Kendall Walton noticed the same error in the Goodman text some time ago; see his 'Languages of Art: An Emendation', *Analysis*, (1971), 82–5.

either printed along with the Score or tacitly given by tradition, word-of-mouth, etc.' (237). For example, the score may call for a dynamic level of *fortissimo*, or a slow tempo, or the coach may instruct his student to play a certain A natural slightly higher (in pitch) so as to reflect an underlying modulation.

Now Goodman claims that the performance taken under its second aspect—viz. the performance taken as a sound event, or performance(SE)—complies with these supplementary markings. And therein he makes a crucial mistake. Admittedly, in one sense, the claim that the performance(SE) complies with the supplementary markings is trivially true. I say 'trivially' because the performance(SE) complies with all of the musical markings, not just the supplementary ones. It is sound-events that comply with the notational markings in the Score, too, as the following passage attests:

> If we consider piano scores alone, the language is highly redundant since, for example, the same sound-events comply with the characters for c-sharp, d-flat, e-triple-flat, b-double-sharp, and so on. (181)

What Goodman must mean, rather, in distinguishing the performance *taken as* an instance of a work from the performance *taken as* a sound-event, is that the *compliance-classes* of the supplementary markings are sound-event classes as such. But then the claim that the performance(SE) complies with the supplementary markings is simply false. The performance taken as a sound-event is the performance taken as an acoustic event, i.e. as a sequence of frequencies, intensities, attack envelopes, etc.[6] The supplementary markings, on the other hand, specify values along *perceptual* parameters—pitches, dynamics, articulations, and so forth. In short, Goodman confuses sound-event classes *as such* with perceptual-event classes, and wrongly identifies the former as compliance-classes of the supplementary markings. What complies with the supplementary markings is not the performance(SE) but rather what I shall call the 'performance taken as a sequence of nuances'—the 'performance(N)', for short. I shall say more about this construct as we go along; for now, suffice it to point out that the performance(N) is the performance taken as the sequence of all the fine-grained ('determinate') pitches, durations, speeds, timbres, and so forth that we actually hear in it.

Though syntactically disjoint and differentiated, the system of supplementary markings is, according to Goodman, semantically dense and undifferentiated: it 'provides for an infinite number of characters with compliance-classes so ordered that between each two there is a third' more similar to each of them than they are to each other (153), and there is no even theoretical possibility of determining which character any given sound event

---

[6] Later in the passage just cited, Goodman writes that 'In a violin score the characters for c-sharp and d-flat have no compliants in common', adding in a footnote that 'This may be disputed. I am told that a tone of, say, 333 vibrations per second is accepted for either character' (181–2). '333 vibrations per second' is a specification of acoustic frequency.

complies with. For example, 'since a tempo may be prescribed as fast, or as slow, or as between fast and slow, or as between fast and between-fast-and-slow, and so on without limit, semantic differentiation goes by the board' (184–5). Similarly, we may suppose, the pitch of a sound event could be prescribed as an A natural, or as a slightly high A natural, or as between an A natural and a slightly high A natural,[7] or as between an A natural and between-an-A-natural-and-a-slightly-high-A-natural, and so on without limit. As a result, there will be no even theoretical possibility of determining the compliance-class of any sound-event in a performance. Note that such a result obtains independently of the vagueness of expressions like 'fast' and 'slightly high'; in other words, if the compliance-classes of the supplementary markings are densely ordered, then those markings would be semantically undifferentiated even if they were non-vague. For example, even (relatively) non-vague supplementary pitch markings like, say, 'A natural(1)', 'A natural(2)', 'A natural(3)' . . . 'B-flat(1)', 'B-flat(2)', and so forth, or any other non-vague markings you like, would be semantically dense and undifferentiated. Indeed, later on we shall have occasion to adopt just such a numerical naming scheme.

With the distinction between performance(W) and performance(N) in hand, we are now positioned to evaluate Goodman's theory. From now on I shall run my arguments exclusively on the case of musical pitch, but any conclusions drawn herein are meant to apply to other relevantly similar perceptual dimensions. Also, in order to distinguish the compliance-classes of the supplementary markings from those of the Scored markings, I shall refer to the former as 'nuance pitch-classes' or 'N-pitch-classes' for short, and to the latter as 'chromatic' or 'C-pitch-classes'.

III

Goodman's treatment of the Score as a notational system is, it seems to me, straightforward and plausible; at any rate, I shall not contest it here. However, his treatment of the supplementary markings—in particular his claim that they are semantically dense—is an altogether different matter. As we have heard, pitches are perceptual creatures, and human perceptual systems, whatever their precise nature, are inherently limited: even the most sensitive ear can discriminate only finitely many steps of pitch difference across the audible range.[8] How then can there be a dense ordering of N-pitch-classes?

---

[7] Here, of course, I mean not 'between the *pitch category* A natural and a slightly high A natural' but rather something like 'between a "good" A natural (e.g. an A440) and a slightly high A natural'. In other words, both an A natural and a slightly high A natural are pitches *within* the pitch category A natural.

[8] An extremely sensitive ear can detect as many as 500 steps of pitch difference to the semitone (the smallest interval on the piano keyboard) under laboratory conditions. The average ear detects about 1,400 steps of difference across the audible range. See e.g. Carl E. Seashore, *Psychology of Music* (New York, 1967), ch. 5.

The answer may at first seem obvious. As Goodman explains, 'Semantic density requires only that a dense set of reference-classes be *provided for*, not that the field of reference be *actually* dense' (227). However, it seems reasonable to question even the mere theoretical possibility of a dense ordering of pitch classes. Different pitches are *discriminably* different: for sound events to be different (/identical) in pitch just is for them to sound different (/identical) to normal listeners under normal conditions, just as for objects to be different in colour is for them to look different to normal viewers. Therefore, the theoretical possibility of a dense ordering of pitches would seem to require the theoretical possibility of an infinitely sensitive discriminatory capacity, and *that* seems to amount to a 'change of subject'—we are no longer talking about perception, or about *human* perception anyway. One wants to say: a 'perception' *sans* discriminatory threshold does not merit the name. Note that appeal to an *indefinitely* sensitive discriminator—i.e. a discriminator such that, for any two distinct pitches, it could in theory be made sufficiently sensitive to detect the difference—is no help to Goodman here. As he himself warns: 'So long as the differentiation between [compliance-classes] is finite, no matter how minute, [the relevant determinations] will depend upon the acuteness of our perceptions and the sensitivity of the instruments we can devise' (135).[9]

It may be asked why we cannot theorize about infinitely fine pitch dis- criminations in the way that linguists sometimes theorize about the gram- matical generation of (e.g.) infinitely many sentences. Can't we appeal to an analogous idealization in the musical case?[10] No. The linguists' consideration of infinitely many sentences does not require even the theoretical possibility of an 'infinite understander'. Principles of grammatical sentence construction can be stated in a purely formal manner independently of any appeal to an understander, theoretical or otherwise. By contrast, pitch is an essentially psychological dimension: different pitches have got to be *discriminably* dif- ferent. And that makes theorizing about infinitely sensitive pitch discrimi- nation a different kettle of fish from theorizing about the generation of infinitely many sentences.[11]

At the root of Goodman's difficulties here, I suspect, is a mistake to which I

[9] I elaborate upon some problems with the idea of densely ordered pitches in my *Language, Music, and Mind* (Cambridge, Mass., in press), ch. 6.

[10] I thank Barbara Scholz for posing this question.

[11] One might further suppose that a dense ordering of N-pitches could be specified if the representation of pitch were identified with (or realized by, or otherwise correlated with), say, the voltage level of some cell assembly in the auditory system. Perhaps continuous variation in pitch could be identified with continuous variation in voltage, and pitch representations could then be densely ordered one-to-one with voltage values. Here I would respond by observing that, although it may be that states of the brain (e.g. voltage levels) can in theory be densely ordered, it is not plausible to identify *those* states with representations of distinct pitches. To repeat: different pitches are by nature *discriminably* different. Hence it is not enough that a system theoretically be able to occupy any of infinitely many (densely ordered) states; if those states are supposed to be (or otherwise underwrite) representations of distinct pitches, the system must furthermore be (theoretically) able to *discriminate* among them. And then we are back where we started, needing an infinitely sensitive discriminator.

have already alluded. In identifying the compliant of the supplementary markings with the performance taken as a *sound event*, Goodman illicitly transports features of the acoustic realm into the perceptual; specifically, he mistakes a dense ordering of frequency-classes for a dense ordering of pitch-classes. There is, I shall assume, no problem about a dense ordering of frequencies: between any two is a third more like each of them than they are like each other. However, what Goodman's analysis requires is not a dense ordering of acoustic frequencies as such, but rather a dense ordering of the *pitch*-classes of which (tokens of) those frequencies are members. And that, I submit, he cannot have.

Perhaps Goodman would object that our pretheoretic conception of 'different pitches' is overly narrow. Granted, he might say, the degree to which pitch-events can resemble one another *when considered pairwise* is highly limited: as any psychophysics text will tell you, the average listener can discriminate only about 1,400 steps of pitch difference across the audible range. Nevertheless, there may be the following 'indirect' route whereby pitches could be densely ordered. For any two distinct frequencies F_1 and F_2, there will always be some third frequency (indeed, infinitely many frequencies) F_3 such that tokens of F_1 are discriminable from tokens of F_3 but tokens of F_2 are not. (Just what F_3 is will vary both intra- and inter-subjectively, but some such frequency will always be specifiable.) To that extent, tokens of any two different frequencies are discriminably different; that is to say, they differ in pitch. The compelling intuition that pairwise indiscriminable frequencies are identical in pitch is simply mistaken; other, less direct though still perceptual evidence can be mobilized to map pitches one-to-one into acoustic frequencies in a dense ordering.[12]

This initially daunting picture does little to alleviate present difficulties. Whether or not the described individuation specifies a dense ordering of *perceptual* classes at all, it certainly does not specify a dense ordering of the kinds of pitch-classes invoked in Goodman's analysis. (What it specifies, I would contend, is a dense ordering of frequencies by appeal to their perceptual relations.) The relevant classes, recall, are those complying with the supplementary instructions for performance. And the point is, the teacher who asks his student for an A natural slightly higher than one just played will not be satisfied—his directive will not have been met—by a second A natural that is (pairwise) indiscriminable from the first. Slightly higher A naturals are *pairwise discriminably higher*, and a pitch 'between' an A natural and a slightly high A natural must be directly discriminably higher than the one and lower than the other.

If the preceding lines of argument are correct, there would seem to be no even theoretical possibility of a dense ordering of pitch-classes of the sort

---

[12] See the discussion of phenomenal qualities in Goodman's *Structures of Appearance* (Indianapolis, 1966), sections IX and X.

Goodman's analysis requires as it stands. Or at least, Goodman has given us no reason to believe that there is. Consequently, we have no reason to accept his further claim that the supplementary markings are semantically undifferentiated. Indeed, suppose we have established the array of N-pitch-classes (i.e. the array of all the pitches we can discriminate), starting at the bottom of the audible frequency range (around 15 Hz) and beginning a new pitch-class at the site of each successive just noticeable difference or JND.[13] (Analogously, we might array a series of colour chips in every visible shade across the spectrum.) And suppose we have set up an electronic tuning fork to produce on demand a tone at each of the relevant frequencies—in other words, to produce a token of any given N-pitch. Suppose furthermore, in the interest of minimizing any confounding effects of vagueness, that we have replaced our ordinary supplementary pitch markings (viz. 'slightly high A natural' et al.) with numerical names of the sort I suggested above—e.g. 'A natural(1)', 'A natural(2)', 'A natural(3)' . . . 'B flat(1)', 'B flat(2)', etc. Determining the compliance class of any given sound event could then consist in matching its pitch to that of one of the tones produced by the tuning fork, much as we might determine the compliance class of an object's shade by matching it to one of the chips in the colour chart (e.g. 'It's red(37)'). Some such scenario, anyway, seems plausible enough. The idea, then, is that such a scheme of supplementary pitch markings would be semantically differentiated in so far as it would be theoretically possible to uniquely determine, in something like the manner just described, the compliance-class of any given sound-event in a performance; that is, it would be theoretically possible to determine which supplementary pitch marking any given sound event complies with. So much the worse, in that case, for Goodman's analysis.[14]

It may be that not all is lost for Goodman, however. In the space remaining, I shall argue that it may be possible to 'psychologize' the theoretical property of semantic undifferentiatedness in a way that preserves much of the spirit of Goodman's analysis—as much, I think, as one could hope for in view of the aforementioned difficulties. To do this, I shall need to introduce some recent theory in the cognitive psychology of music.

---

[13] One can imagine various ways of individuating the audible pitches, but for present purposes those differences do not matter. The argument that follows will apply however the N-pitch classes are individuated.

[14] It may turn out that pitches cannot be type-identified in the way I suggest above (the non-transitivity of indistinguishability, among other things, may pose problems). If that is the case, then so much the better for Goodman, since the supplementary markings might turn out to be semantically undifferentiated after all. Rather, my point will be that even if we can type-identify pitches in the manner described above, it may still be possible to preserve the undifferentiatedness of the supplementary markings in a 'psychologized' form.

IV

Cognitivist theory has it that perception, among other things, is a matter of mentally representing the world in certain ways. On at least one popular view, perception consists roughly in the computation of a series of increasingly abstract mental representations of the external environment, proceeding from raw sensory responses to full-blooded conscious percepts.[15] With regard to the perception of tonal music, linguist Ray Jackendoff and composer Fred Lerdahl have hypothesized that the better part of this series is governed by the rules of a musical *grammar*.[16] The latter is thus envisioned as a component of the perceptual system that processes musical stimuli.

The situation is roughly, and crudely, this. The musical grammar is a set of analytical rules which you, the experienced listener, have stored unconsciously in your head. As you hear an incoming acoustic signal, you mentally represent it and analyse it according to the grammatical rules; that is, you compute a *structural description* of the signal. Essentially, the grammar takes as input a recovery of what we have been calling 'the Score' and yields as output a structural description of the signal as instantiating the structural elements specified in the Score—essentially, C-pitches and rhythms—as well as various higher order or more abstract structural features computed or 'inferred' from these fundamental two. It is *ex hypothesi* in virtue of representing the signal in this way that you have the musical experience you do, that you hear the signal *as* (a performance of) *a piece of music*, and not as an incoherent jumble of sounds.

Given present space limitations, I shall not have much to say here about the operations of the musical grammar. For our purposes the important point is that the grammar takes as input a recovery of the Score; call this input the 'mental Score' or 'M-Score' for short. The performance as represented by the M-Score is just Goodman's performance(W).

There is, of course, much more to a performance than what is captured in the M-Score. Recall that the musical grammar is supposed to be a *component* of the perceptual system that processes musical stimuli. Presumably, then, the structural description is only a component of the total mental representation constituting perception of a performance: by its very nature, the structural description fails to capture the *non*-structural phenomena. Intuitively speaking, it fails to capture what we have been calling the *nuances* of the performance. But of course the nuances must get mentally represented at some point; otherwise there would be no way to explain how we hear 'within-category' pitch phenomena like vibrato, slides, out-of-tune notes, and the myriad shades of pitch coloration in any expressive performance. In hearing vibrato

---

[15] Jerry Fodor, *The Modularity of Mind* (Cambridge, 1983). The above is a crude statement of Fodor's view; in particular, he takes pains to distinguish perception from so-called input processing; see e.g. p. 73.

[16] Lerdahl and Jackendoff, *Toward A Generative Theory of Tonal Music* (Cambridge, 1983).

and the rest we are hearing pitch differences *within* (i.e. more fine-grained than) the C-pitch categories notated in the Score. As is now familiar, while the Score can specify any of roughly 87 C-pitch-classes (corresponding to the roughly 87 keys on the piano), the performance typically contains many more than 87 different pitches. To come to the point, what all of this suggests is that the M-Score is inferred from a still shallower, 'raw' level of representation at which the many pitch nuances are recovered. As the psychophysical correlate to acoustic frequency (call it the 'P-correlate'), this raw pitch representation is presumably the shallowest level of mental representation of the signal to which the listener has conscious access. It will come as no surprise that the performance as represented by the P-correlate is just the performance(N).

To see how an undifferentiatedness might be reincarnated within this cognitivist framework, we shall need to understand how the inference from P-correlate to M-Score is accomplished. Recent psychological theory suggests that the music processing system generates the M-Score by mapping the P-correlate into long-term mental representations called 'schemas'.[17] These mental cubbyholes serve to reduce information load by organizing otherwise chaotic stimuli into various categories—here, categories corresponding to the C-pitches.[18] You can think of the C-pitch schemas as a kind of template or grid through which the P-correlate is passed. The grid is only as fine-grained as the C-pitches A natural, B flat, B natural, and so forth, so that incoming stimuli are categorized only that finely. The hypothesis is that the trained listener can classify (i.e. type-identify or recognize) heard C-pitches in so far as he has labels for them ('A natural', 'B flat', etc.) stored in the right places with the pitch information in the schemas. Crudely, it is as if each cubbyhole has a hook on which its appropriate label can be hung, so that sensory-perceptual and linguistic information are stored *together*. Classification of a sound-event as (e.g.) an A natural then consists in the activation, by the perception of that event, of the A natural schema.

In light of the foregoing considerations, it stands to reason that a classification of sound-events as tokens of *N*-pitch types would proceed via the activation of commensurately fine-grained schemas; that is, such a classification would require the activation of schemas as fine-grained as the pitch discriminations we can make. However (and here's the rub), the C-pitch schemas appear to be the 'narrowest' pitch schemas we have; in other words,

---

[17] Roger Shepard and Daniel Jordan, 'Auditory Illusions Demonstrating that Tones Are Assimilated to an Internalized Musical Scale', *Science*, 226 (1986), 1333–4, gives a good idea how this might go.

[18] Actually, given that most people lack so-called 'perfect' or 'absolute' pitch, the schemas probably correspond to Chromatic *intervals* or scale steps, not to pitches *per se*; see Diana Deutsch, 'Musical Recognition', *Psychological Review*, 76 (1969), 300–7, and W. J. Dowling, 'Scale and Contour: Two Components of a Theory of Memory for Melodies', *Psychological Review*, 88 (1978), 503–22. Since we need not worry about that distinction here, I shall keep things simple by speaking of C-*pitch* schemas.

we appear to have no mental categories sufficiently fine-grained to enable us to classify pitches more finely than as tokens of C-pitch types.[19] There is, of course, no incoherence in the idea that a great deal of practice should result in the acquisition of schemas more fine-grained than our present C-pitch ones. But even allowing for that remote possibility, it is overwhelmingly unlikely that we could, with any amount of training you like, acquire schemas as fine-grained as the pitch differences we can hear. In other words, it is overwhelmingly unlikely that we could acquire schemas sufficiently fine-grained to enable us to classify the sound-events of a performance as tokens of N-pitch types. Discrimination will inevitably outstrip recognition. Of course this is hardly surprising if the *raison d'être* of schemas is to reduce information load: what point would there be to a schema whose 'grain' was as fine as that of perception?

The import of this psychological story for Goodman's theory is as follows. Because the M-Score is structured as it is, the trained listener can (uniquely) classify heard sound-events as compliant with the C-pitch markings in the Score. Consequently, the C-pitch markings are semantically disjoint and differentiated even by Goodman's strict lights. On the other hand, given the design of our perceptual faculties, it is not possible to classify heard sound-events—by inspection alone, as it were—as compliant with the *supplementary* pitch markings. (Is it an A natural(17) or an A natural(18)? We are unable to say.) To that extent, I want to suggest, the supplementary markings are semantically undifferentiated: we cannot determine, by (auditory) inspection, which supplementary pitch marking any given sound-event complies with.

Now at first blush, this undifferentiatedness may seem a *merely* psychological or 'contingent' undifferentiatedness, not a logical or theoretical one; surely it is theoretically possible that we should be so designed as to have, or be able to acquire, schemas as fine-grained as the N-pitches we can discriminate. However, let me suggest the following line of argument as a possible response here. (For clarity's sake I'll state the argument in a very strong form; no doubt it may need to be softened.) Consider that our C-pitch schemas are responsible in large measure for the way tonal music sounds to us; they determine which pitch differences get noticed and which get ignored, they make acoustically identical events sound different and acoustically different ones sound identical, all depending on the current tonal context. For instance, it is apparently only because of the imposition of C-pitch schemas that we hear melodies as such; in other words, it is only because of the imposition of C-pitch schemas that melodies emerge out of the blooming and buzzing confusion of N-pitches in the P-correlate. By the same token, then, it seems reasonable to suppose that the activation of N-pitch schemas in our

---

[19] See e.g. Edward M. Burns and W. Dixon Ward, 'Intervals, Scales, and Tuning', in Diana Deutsch (ed.), *The Psychology of Music* (New York, 1982), 241–69.

perception of tonal music would radically alter the character of that perception. Indeed, it is not clear that we would perceive tonal music, *as such*, at all: among other things, if such schemas were activated, then every pitch in a performance would be *recognized*, and the melodies and harmonies we know and love would likely disappear in a sea of pitch details.

In particular, one might argue, if schemas as fine-grained as our pitch discriminations were activated in the perception of tonal music, there would be no N-pitches as such: nuances are within-category differences, and within-category differences, as such, are differences that do not get recognized or type-identified other than as differences *within* a certain category. But then if there were no nuances, the supplementary pitch markings would fail to refer: these markings denote pitch *nuances*, within-category differences. The difference between an A natural(16) and an A natural(17), *eo ipso* the difference between an A natural and a slightly high A natural, is a within-category difference, i.e. a fine 'shade' of difference within the C-pitch category A natural. *To that extent*, one might claim, there is no even theoretical possibility of determining, solely by ear, which supplementary pitch marking any given sound-event (in a performance of a tonal work) complies with. Any such determination would, in other words, entail a change of subject.[20] Such an undifferentiatedness, though still firmly rooted in the psychological realm, would be rather stronger (rather less 'merely contingent') than one might initially have expected.

The foregoing is at most a gesture in the direction a fully developed argument might take, and a great deal more would need to be said. One might object, for instance, that N-pitches could be recognized as such and yet still be heard as values within the C-pitch categories—still be heard, that is, as pitch *nuances*. No doubt our response here will depend to a large extent on what we think nuances are. I cannot explore these issues further at present, but I hope to have shown at least the possibility of psychologizing Goodman's notion of semantic undifferentiatedness in a way that preserves much of the spirit, if not the letter, of his analysis. It remains to be seen just how this revisionary picture would square with the rest of Goodman's theory of symbolism in the arts; but that endeavour too must await another occasion.

---

[20] Even if the perceptual recognition of N-pitches as such did not require schemas of the sort we actually employ, that recognition *by itself* would constitute a major transfiguration of musical experience; as long as the N-pitches are being recognized (type-identified) as such, one might contend, they are not being heard as 'nuance' differences within the C-pitch categories.

VI

Portraits in Music—A Case-Study: Elgar's 'Enigma' Variations

FRANCIS SPARSHOTT

There has been much discussion of whether music can really represent reality. But composers often do use their music to allude to the non-musical world, and there has been less discussion of the actual range and variety of means available to them. It is this last topic that is discussed here in relation to a single musical work: Edward Elgar's *Variations on an Original Theme*.

Elgar's original title-page is straightforward, and someone who hears the music played at a concert will simply hear a theme followed by fourteen variations.[1] Much in the music is wayward and whimsical, but no more than the theme-with-variations form allows for. Nothing in what one hears or reads hints that any aspect of the music alludes to anything. On reading the score, however, we find something else. On a separate page, the work bears a dedication: 'Dedicated to my friends pictured herein. Malvern 1899.'[2] And each variation carries a designation, usually in the form of initials, in parentheses after its number. The reader infers that each variation either is or somehow contains a 'picture' of the individual designated.

What does Elgar mean by a 'picture'? He does not say, but in general a picture of something is recognizable by anyone who is familiar with what it is a picture of and with the representational conventions employed. So if we knew the bearers of the initials and other designations we ought to find the portraits recognizable. But we are unlikely to know them, they are quite obscure people.[3] It is a very private mode of reference, then. The reader of the score learns only that there are meant to be 'pictures', that the waywardness of the music may be attributed partly to the pictorial aspects. The reader of the

---

[1] The title-page reads: '*Variations | on an Original Theme | for Orchestra* | composed by | Edward Elgar | (Op. 36) | Full Score | 9s. 3d. | London: Novello and Company, Limited. | Copyright, 1899, by Novello and Company Limited. | The Right of Public Representation and Performance is reserved. | Made in England.' The title-page of the manuscript full score reads: '*Variations | for orchestra* | composed by | Edward Elgar | Op. 36', and it is as '*Variations for Orchestra*' that the title appears on the front cover of my copy (miniature score). (The manuscript title-page, with the opening pages of the theme and of each variation, is printed in facsimile in *My Friends Pictured Within: The subjects of the Enigma variations as portrayed in contemporary photographs and Elgar's manuscript* (London, n.d.).)

[2] In the manuscript, as in the piano score (arranged by Elgar himself), this dedication appears at the top of the title-page.

[3] There were originally to have been variations for the famous composers Sullivan and Parry (Rosa Burley and Frank C. Carruthers, *Edward Elgar: The Record of a Friendship* (London, 1972), 121). Burley and Carruthers remark (93) that no one except the Elgars themselves is likely to have been acquainted with all the people portrayed.

score, but not the hearer in the concert hall, is then invited to speculate what sort of person in what sort of aspect is being portrayed. Such a reader has no means of telling whether Elgar is, or thinks he is, presenting some sort of true likeness, or is caricaturing, or is mistaken about the qualities he attributes to his targets; and, especially if the hearer knows nothing of any of the persons 'pictured', one does not know what allowance to make for Elgar's use of a private reference code or for limitations on his skill as portraitist.[4]

The reader of the score can see that nine of the fourteen variations are designated by initials, two pairs of them (VI and VII, 'Ysobel' and 'Troyte', IX and X, 'Nimrod' and 'Dorabella') by pseudonyms (though the former pair might be real names), and one (XIII, '***') by a parade of anonymity. The reader is not likely to know that the designation of XIV, 'E. D. U.', is not a real set of initials, but a disguised way of writing 'Edu', Elgar's wife's pet name for him; a reader who does know it, and knows also that the initials of the first variation are those of Elgar's wife herself, may suspect some underlying domestic theme.

What else does the reader see that the listener does not hear? Four of the sections of the score bear titles: the last one is 'Finale', so not merely another variation; Dorabella's variation (X) is called 'Intermezzo' and ***'s variation (XIII) is called 'Romanza', possibly suggesting two sentimental interludes in the portraitist's life; and at the beginning of the score, squeezed in between the title VARIATIONS and the first line of music, there is the word 'Enigma'.[5] By analogy, that should be a description of the theme; but it is not, like the other three section titles, a regular musical designation. What is it, then? And what is it supposed to mean? On the face of it, it is a mere mystification.

Anything else to be learned from the score? Only that in Variation XIII a thrice-repeated clarinet phrase is included within quotation marks, so it is presumably either a musical borrowing or a representation of what somebody said or sang—which, there is nothing in the score to show. For the rest, Elgar's directions to his players are musical instructions and not stage directions, and he writes nothing else in the score that might refer to any 'pictorial' aspects.

What a suitably competent person hears in performance and reads in the score determines what a work is. But when a new work is played a composer may provide an explanatory note for the concert programme, to explain to the audience what they should listen for. Later programme notes often incorporate part or all of this introduction. Such material is not itself part of

---

[4] Such a private code is likely, given Elgar's taste for cryptography. See Eric Sams, 'Elgar's Cipher Letter to Dorabella', *Musical Times*, 111 (1970), 151–4.

[5] Typographically, the word is on a par with such variation titles as 'Romanza' (as opposed to the initials, which are in small capitals). The extremely awkward spacing suggests that this was squeezed in as an afterthought. In the manuscript, the word 'Enigma' is written after the tempo indication, on the same line, in smaller and lighter letters. It was clearly an afterthought, but it was one that Elgar clung to. (The spacing is normal in the piano arrangement, published in the same year.)

the work of music; but it is not alien to it, since it is part of the package that is presented to the original audience for its understanding and appreciation, and hence indirectly to any subsequent audience. It has a certain authority, and if a later audience is not given this information there is something about the work that it does not know.

Elgar's *Variations* are an egregious example of this practice of packaging new works, to the extent that the note the composer provided for the first performance has attracted as much commentary as the work itself. His note does not tell us what to listen for in the music, nor does it (as in much 'programme' music) explain the articulation of the music by telling us a story that it may be taken to illustrate. Rather, it tells us about how the music is related to material that is not accessible to us and invites us to guess what that material might be. Elgar wrote:

It is true that I have sketched for their amusement and mine the idiosyncracies of fourteen of my friends, not necessarily musicians, but this is a personal matter and need not have been mentioned publicly. . . . The Enigma I will not explain—its 'dark saying' must be left unguessed and I warn you that the apparent connection between the Variations and the Theme is often of the slightest nature; further through and over the whole set another and larger theme 'goes' but is not played. . . . So the principal theme never appears, even as in some late dramas . . . the chief character is never on the stage.[6]

If it need not have been mentioned publicly, why was it?[7] It looks as if Elgar wants to tease, to insist both that the music is completely accessible as music and that we are to hear it *as inaccessible* in three separate ways: there are portraits we cannot recognize, there is an enigma we cannot solve, there is a theme (the *principal* theme!) we cannot hear. The piece is almost an essay in applied semiotics: no wonder it is customarily known as *The Enigma Variations*.

There is no guessing what may be going on in the head of a man so given to riddles, puns, japes, and ciphers as Elgar was, and we cannot tell how carefully he is expressing himself, so there is no way of solving the problems he seems to set us. The unheard theme could very well be 'love' or 'friendship', which are 'large' enough in all conscience, or it could be the tune of 'Auld Lang Syne' that in some unspecified sense ' "goes" ' 'through and over the whole set'.[8] As for the enigma, what Elgar says seems at first to be nonsense—if he explained it, it would not need to be guessed, and its being

---

[6] J.A. Westrup, 'Elgar's Enigma', *Proc. Royal Music Assoc.* 86 (1959–60), 81.

[7] Charles Barry wrote the programme note for the première from proofs of the printed piano arrangement, which said nothing about any 'enigma', but Barry had heard rumours and pressed Elgar for an elucidation. Elgar's explanatory note responded to this pressure (Jerrold Northrop Moore, *Edward Elgar: A Creative Life* (Oxford, 1984), 269).

[8] Arguments for 'Auld Lang Syne' may be found in Eric Sams, 'Variations on an Original Theme (Enigma)' (*Musical Times*, 111 (1970), 258–62), and Derek Hudson, 'Elgar's Enigma: The Trail of Evidence' (*Musical Times*, 125 (1984), 636–9). Hudson, like many others, thinks the hidden 'theme' is the same as the 'Enigma', but this equation, though it effects a desirable economy in mystery-making, is incompatible with what Elgar says.

unexplained looks like a reason for *not* leaving it unguessed. But perhaps what Elgar has in mind is that we do not know what the enigma is—is it the theme as a whole, or part of the theme, or something the theme stands for in some way?[9] Since we do not know what the question is, we cannot guess what the answer might be. The will to mystify is all we have. Elgar wishes us to know what we could not tell from the music alone, that he is a secretive man, that he and his music have hidden depths. But we cannot tell how important it is that we should know that, or why.

In the programme note Elgar says he has sketched the *idiosyncracies* of his friends, for private amusement. But in a letter to A. J. Jaeger, his contact man at his publishers, he had written (on 24 October 1898):

I've written the variations each one to represent the mood of the 'party'—I've liked to imagine the 'party' writing the var[iation] him (or her) self and have written what I think they wd. have written—if they were asses enough to compose—its a quaint idea & the result is amusing to those behind the scenes & won't affect the hearer who 'nose nuffin.'[10]

A mood is not the same as an authorial persona, and neither a mood nor a persona is the same as a sketchable idiosyncracy. What is Elgar actually doing in each case? Dora Penny, the 'Dorabella' of Variation X, who was in Elgar's confidence at the time of composition, published her recollections half a century later. Her memories and those of others, together with Elgar's own retrospective account, however unreliable, give us enough to ground our study of the resources of musical portrayal.[11]

The opening theme, presumably the 'Enigma', is not itself announced as one of the portraits. None the less, the theme is used in a later work to symbolize the loneliness of the creative artist;[12] the first four notes (repeated in slightly different versions) could represent 'Edward Elgar' in speech rhythm, and seem to be used in self-reference in a letter to Dora Penny in which she is referred to by a phrase from her variation.[13] The rests that punctuate the

---

[9] A statement in Elgar's hand, dated 'Torino, Ottobre 1911' and prepared for the programme of a concert there, reads: 'This work, commenced in a spirit of humour and continued in deep seriousness, contains sketches of the composer's friends. It may be understood that these personages comment or reflect on the original theme and each one attempts a solution of the Enigma, for so the theme is called' (Moore, *Edward Elgar*, 260). That is definite enough, but we cannot tell how much it owes to hindsight: the reference to the way the significance of the work changed in the course of composition is discouraging.

[10] Percy M. Young (ed.), *Letters to Nimrod: Edward Elgar to August Jaeger 1897–1908* (London, 1965), 27.

[11] Mrs Richard Powell, *Edward Elgar: Memories of a Variation* (London, 1937; 3rd edn. 1949). Mrs Powell was formerly Dora Penny, the 'Dorabella' of Variation X. Elgar's notes were written in the 1920s to accompany the pianola rolls issued by the Aeolian Company, and are reprinted in *My Friends Pictured Within*. Burley sums up her recollections in Burley and Carruthers, *Edward Elgar*, 116–29. These sources will be cited hereafter as 'Powell', 'Burley', and 'Elgar'.

[12] In *The Music Makers* (1912). In a letter to Ernest Newman, Elgar wrote: 'It expressed when written (in 1898) my sense of the loneliness of the artist... and to me, it still embodies that sense...' (Moore, *Edward Elgar*, 259).

[13] Michael Kennedy, *Portrait of Elgar* (London, 1968), 59.

theme give it a tentative air. But, historically, only one enigma deserves the name, and that is the Sphinx's riddle to which the answer is 'man'. So perhaps the man Elgar, privately conceived as lonely artist, is alluded to through a quasi-cipher of his name and presented as hesitant, to be fulfilled by his friends and fleshed out as 'E. D. U.' in the finale. (In the theme itself, the two 'Edward Elgar' passages (the first marked 'molto espress.') flank a sinuous tune, in which I find no extra-musical significance—but we shall see in discussing the finale that another view is possible.)

In short, the way the theme itself is handled throughout the work stands in an indeterminate fashion for the way his friends accompanied and supported him in his musical career and self-discovery. But the work neither contains nor implies any narrative or description of this career: it is a 'theme' that is not heard.

So much for the theme on which the portraits vary. How is the portrayal to proceed? Elgar's resources, we shall see, are various. The most direct resource is what is audible, and, since many of Elgar's friends are musicians, we find them portrayed through the music they make—the instruments they play and how they play them, their musical preferences. They are shown through their speaking voices: the way they converse, the timbre and lilt and phrasing of what they say. We hear them laughing and whistling and stammering. We hear social occasions in which they figured, doors slamming and people discussing them. We hear the way they move, dancing or bustling. Their shapes may be referred to in the shape of the music. Gentleness and nobility imputed to their characters is alluded to in the gentleness and nobility Elgar tried to impart to the music he dedicated to them. One 'sitter' is evoked by way of the sounds and movements his dog makes; another (it is said) by the machine he rides; a third by the evoked atmosphere of the house she lived in. A friend on a sea voyage is evoked by a complex allusion to the voyage itself. In one or two cases, we are told that 'likenesses' were recognizable though no one could say how.

These are the means that we will find Elgar using. Perhaps not everything he purports to do can really be done. But that hardly matters if he can try to do them and succeed well enough that his friends can recognize, with suitable prompting, that he has done so. But we may well wonder, since essentially the same standard musical resources are used throughout, whether it will always be possible to recognize which code is being used in a given passage.

C. A[lice] E[lgar], the first variation, is Elgar's wife, to whose support he owed everything except his talent; Powell allows it to be a portrait and says it is actually *like* her in some unspecified way. Elgar himself says this music was 'a prolongation of the theme with what I wished to be romantic and delicate additions; those who knew C. A. E. will understand this reference to one whose life was a romantic and delicate inspiration'. So the music is supposed to have certain named qualities that the sitter for the portrait also has. It does not matter whether music can be delicate in the way people are delicate: what is relevant, Elgar's language implies, is that music and person are appropriate bearers of the same name. We note that the gaps in the 'Edward Elgar' motto music have vanished, filled in by sustained notes; and the whole variation is pervaded (on oboes and bassoons) by the phrase which Edward habitually whistled to tell his wife he was home.[14] So perhaps the music shows us how the wife completes the husband, and how important to him was her continued presence. If so, it does this by altering the shape of a self-reference previously established, and by the way it iterates a private sign.

The only representational aspect alleged for the second variation is that it presents its object (H. D. S[teuart]-P[owell]) as pianist, the semi-quaver passages simulating the figure with which he warmed up his hands before playing (in the piano trio of which he and Elgar were members); this is 'humorously travestied', Elgar tells us, because it is more chromatic than H. D. S.-P. would have liked. So here a musician is presented in the most direct possible way, through his musical practice; not by the music he makes, however, but through the procedures of his musicianship, partly by likeness, partly in teasing contrast.

The third variation is more complex. It alludes to a theatrical performance in which the subject, R. B. T[ownshend], proved unable to sustain the vocal quality his part required. Powell also tells us that the opening bars mimic his 'curious didactic way of speaking', and that at four bars before no. 10 we hear his habitual impatience with people who were unimpressed by his travellers' tales ('The growing grumpiness of the bassoons is important,' says Elgar). So here the subject is presented through three aspects of his speaking voice, caricaturing his manner rather than representing his character. Incidentally, he used to ride a tricycle—Powell says we can hear that, too.

In the fourth variation it is not clear what code is being used. Powell says that W. M. B[aker] was a 'small, wiry man, very quick and energetic. He had an incisive way of speaking—and of laying down the law sometimes'. The music principally conveys the quickness and energy, by being itself quick and energetic; perhaps also the tone of voice. Elgar tells us that we hear an occasion when he '*forcibly* read out the arrangements for the day and hurriedly left the music-room with an inadvertent bang of the door' (just before no. 13), after which his guests (the woodwinds) discuss him. If so, the music gives us his characteristic movement style, aspects of his speaking voice, and perhaps audible aspects (slamming, chattering) of an episode involving him. Elgar tells us that the subject was 'a country squire, gentlemen and scholar', but does not say whether these aspects of him contributed to the portrait.

In the fifth variation, by contrast, we are told that it is R. P. A[rnold]'s

---

[14] In the piano arrangement, both here and in the Finale, the tune for solo bassoon that continues and elaborates on this call is written in on a small supplementary stave over the main stave. Since a pianist could hardly include this passage in a performance, its inclusion shows that Elgar thought it conceptually but not musically essential. I do not know why this is.

character ('pleasant, scholarly' says Powell) that is conveyed, rather than his manner, together with his way of talking—'His serious conversation was continually broken up by whimsical and witty remarks,' says Elgar, and this is shown in the way the solemnity of the theme in the basses is contrasted with 'light-hearted badinage' among the winds. But Powell (106) remarks on how we also hear in the woodwind his funny, nervous little laugh, '*Ha* ha ha, ha ha *ha* ha ha'—a vocal sound, then, neither linguistic nor musical. At the beginning, the theme on bassoons and low strings is counterpointed against a flowing tune largamente on the violins. This sounds as if it should mean something, but one cannot tell what—there is nothing to tell us what code, if any, is being used.

The sixth variation again presents a musician through music. 'Ysobel'— Isabel Fitton—learned viola to help out at Malvern. Elgar himself says that 'The opening bar, a phrase made use of throughout the variation, is an "exercise" for crossing the strings—a difficulty for beginners,' so once more the musician is presented not through the music played but, in a teasing mode, through aspects of her musicianship. (Unlike H. D. S.-P., Ysobel is 'got at' not through what she did but through what it was hard for her to do—Elgar is as it were setting her an exercise.) The wide intervals in the viola part are also said to allude to her extreme tallness;[15] if so, it is the first time in these variations that musical spatiality has been used as a metaphor for actual space. There is no evident reference to any aspect of the subject's character, personality, or manner, though Elgar describes the movement itself as 'pensive and, for a moment, romantic,' which presumably he wishes us to think relevant.

When Elgar played the seventh variation for Powell he said, 'What do you think of that for the giddy Ninepin?'—'Ninepin' being his nickname for E. Troyte Griffith, 'Troyte'—but Powell could not see it. Elgar is said to have said that the cross-rhythm on the drums alludes to the subject's habit of saying unexpected things (Powell (107) quotes someone who called him a 'refreshing but highly argumentative Harrovian'), but the pianola notes say that 'the boisterous mood is mere banter' and that the strong rhythms in the lower strings represent his maladroit attempts to play the piano, corrected by the composer. Powell says we can hear the subject's shout of laughter somewhere. If all this is true, we have here another example of satire on musical amateurishness, and a use of musical rhythm as metaphor for what one might call mental rhythm. But Elgar may have had something more in mind which he failed to communicate. The inner circle of Elgar's friends were not being given information, but were expected to recognize and relish a likeness, the evident fitness of which would itself suffice to show what code was being used. This would not work for someone who knew the subjects in a different aspect from that which Elgar relied on. One author says that Troyte

---

[15] A. E. B. Smith in *Music and Letters*, 16 (1935), cited by Westrup, 'Elgar's Enigma', 94.

was 'quiet and seemingly aloof', so that his variation is 'the antithesis to his personality'—but is this the Troyte Elgar knew as 'the giddy Ninepin'?[16]

The 'gracious personality' of Winifred Norbury, the subject of the eighth variation, is 'sedately shown', according to Elgar, though Powell finds the music to be at odds with her 'rather determined and persistent character'. But the music is really about her ambience—specifically her eighteenth-century house. Elgar says her way of laughing is also alluded to—Burley says it is 'unmistakably... denoted by the arching little arpeggio figure'. We observe that Elgar thus repeatedly takes advantage of the fact that laughs are among the most distinctive sounds that humans emit; it may also be relevant that the composition of the variations was, by all accounts, pervaded by laughter.

A. J. Jaeger, the 'Nimrod' of the ninth variation, is said to have worn himself out on Elgar's behalf, as his publisher. The music was thought to be at variance with Jaeger's personality and with his jocular and voluble manner, but Elgar is representing not his manner or his personality, or even his character, but the core of his being as Elgar divined it. In a letter of 13 March 1899, he wrote: 'I have omitted your outside manner and have only seen the good, lovable honest SOUL in the middle of you!';[17] and again, on 4 November 1900: 'What a jolly fine tune your Variation is:... it's just like you—you solemn, wholesome, hearty old dear.'[18] So I suppose the music represents him by being itself solemn, wholesome, and hearty. The letter continues: 'I *could* give another side of your character but won't (musically) just yet', and in the pianola notes Elgar says that 'something ardent and mercurial' would have been necessary to portray his 'character and temperament'.

Elgar begins his note by saying that not all the variations are portraits: some represent moods, others recall incidents. This variation is one of the last kind. Elgar's account is reticent, but according to what Powell says Elgar told her, the opening reference to the initial measures of the second movement of Beethoven's Sonata Op. 13 alludes to an occasion when Jaeger tried to move Elgar from a fit of depression by citing Beethoven's example, quoting the introduction and first allegro of that sonata as expressing Beethoven's indomitability. If so, this is the first time when a musician is alluded to through the actual music made; though the allusion is indirect, via the occasion of the music's performance.

The tenth variation 'suggests a dance-like lightness', says Elgar, and its subject, Dora Penny, in fact used to accompany Elgar's playing of his own pieces by quasi-dances in the manner of Maud Allen.[19] But a recognizable and characteristic sound rhythm, halfway between a manner of speech and an

---

[16] Percy M. Young, *Elgar OM* (London, 1955), 281.

[17] Young, *Letters to Nimrod*, 42.

[18] Ibid. 113.

[19] Moore, *Edward Elgar*, 24. Maud Allen's way of dancing was to move from one graceful pose to another; this pattern of movement can perhaps be discerned in the interrupted line of Elgar's melody, where it is combined with the 'stammer' effect.

impediment in speech, plainly alludes to her stammer, and perhaps more generally to her speech rhythms. The music may also enshrine a sentimental view of her personality—he was 40, she was 20; and perhaps this is implicit in Elgar's drawing our attention to the 'inner sustained phrases at first on the viola and later on the flute'. But the stammer and the dancing lightness are unmistakable, once we know they are relevant.

Elgar insists that the referential aspect of the eleventh lies in its representation of G. R. S[inclair]'s bulldog Dan falling into a river, paddling up and down, and barking on landing—an episode which the owner challenged Elgar to set to music. So the subject is presented by way of an animal associated with him, the animal itself shown partly through its characteristic sound and partly through the rhythm of its movement and the sequence of its movements on a particular occasion. Powell says Elgar habitually wrote 'moods of Dan' phrases in its owner's visitors' book, including the growl; one could easily compose a set of 'dog' pieces, differences in the music corresponding recognizably to differences in size, shape, and temperament of dog, as well as to different things dogs are well known to do—provided that the hearer knew beforehand that was what one was doing. Is it relevant that in photographs Sinclair looks rather like his dog—a likeness his contemporaries remarked on? Commentators note that the 'dog-paddle' movement (which persists throughout the variation) would give the organist Sinclair something to do with his pedals.[20] But Elgar denies that any such reference is intended, and the illustration of the dog incident itself is equally far from sketching the subject's idiosyncracies and from showing how he would compose music were he to compose any.

B. G. N[evinson], of the twelfth variation, was the cellist of the piano trio Elgar played with, and the variation features a juicy part for solo cello. That seems to be all. Elgar says it is 'a tribute to a very dear friend whose scientific and artistic attainments, and the whole-hearted way they were put at the disposal of his friends, particularly endeared him to the writer', but there is no suggestion that we are meant to *hear* any of that.

With reference to the thirteenth variation, Elgar writes: 'The asterisks take the place of the name of a lady who was, at the time of composition, on a sea voyage. The drums suggest the distant thud of the engines of a liner, over which the clarinet quotes a phrase from Mendelssohn's "Calm Sea and Prosperous Voyage."' Nothing is conveyed about the subject portrayed, not even the fact (attested in a letter from Elgar to Jaeger in May 1899) that she was 'pretty'; the only evident allusion is to the fact of travel itself, and this is mainly conveyed by the title of the musical work quoted—the work is not named in the score, but the Mendelssohn phrase is put in quotation marks.

---

[20] Westrup ('Elgar's Enigma', 90–1) remarks that there is no contradiction between the 'dog in river' and the 'organ pedal' interpretations of Sinclair's music, since Elgar often made use of music previously composed for the dog.

Moore points out that the programme notes to a concert Elgar had attended in 1889 mention a suggestion that the Mendelssohn phrase was originally 'intended to embody the accents of love, fulfilling itself as the goal of the prosperous voyage approached'; it is not impossible that Elgar had this in mind, as adding an esoteric significance to the variation.[21]

The 'E. D. U.' of Variation XIV is hardly a recognizable portrait of 'Edu'. Whatever composers compose both reveals their idiosyncracies and shows how they would compose if they were to compose, so that both Elgar's descriptions of his aim are vacuously fulfilled. This 'Finale', which Elgar calls 'bold and vigorous in general style', simply presents the composer triumphant, in contrast with the initial 'loneliness of the artist'. Elgar's whistling call to his wife makes a dramatic appearance at no. 72, and Jaeger's 'Nimrod' theme reappears in a grandiose version, so we end with Elgar flanked by his chief personal and professional supporters—Elgar says that their presence is 'entirely fitting to the intention of the piece'—with the rest of his portrayed friends left behind. Since Elgar says that the piece was 'written at a time when friends were dubious and generally discouraging as to the composer's musical future', their absence here is no doubt deliberate. The present inflated ending was added after the first performance, at Richter's suggestion and on Jaeger's insistence; the original ended more neatly, soon after no. 76.[22] So the new ending (which presents Elgar posturing as extrovert, to me his least engaging persona) is unlikely to have extra-musical significance. Moore, however, finds in this conclusion the final and convincing solution to the problem of how to reconcile the conflicting sections of the original theme, a metaphor for the real subject of the whole work, the 'creation of a self in music', the imperfect solutions in the other variations representing unsuccessful experiments in character building.[23]

So much for what Elgar does in portraiture. But how, in general, *can* anything be represented in musical sound? Let us recapitulate and expand our initial analysis.

In some cases, representation relies only on what any hearer with the appropriate competence can hear; in other cases, it depends on the composer's

---

[21] Moore, *Edward Elgar*, 140. The two sentimental variations, the 'Romanza' and the 'Intermezzo', are those of which it is denied that there is any connection with the theme (Diana M. McVeagh, *Edward Elgar* (London, 1955), 159; Burley, 124–5). Can this be coincidence? I doubt if it is even quite true. In the 'Intermezzo', of which Dora says that Elgar said there was 'only a trace' of the 'Enigma' theme 'which no one would be likely to find unless he knew where to look for it', it seems to me that the opening B–D–G and fall in the first two bars sound like an echo of the thematic phrase at bar three of the 'Enigma'; and in the 'Romanza' the rocking bass at the 'Meeresstille' quotation is a clearly audible transformation of the drum rhythm that opens Variation VII, itself of course a transform of the rhythmic movement of the first part of the theme. It is the *sound shapes* that do the work. But, of course, the 'theme' to which allusion is denied might in any case be not the musical phrases but the 'enigma' itself, something personal to Elgar; it is hopeless to expect clear solutions to any of these muddy riddles.

[22] See Michael Kennedy, *Elgar Orchestral Music* (London, 1970), 27, for facsimile.

[23] Moore, *Edward Elgar*, 259.

announced intention; in yet other cases, it exploits an agreement prevailing within the appropriate community as to what represents what. Without such announcement or agreement, the homogeneity of musical means makes it hard for the uninitiated to tell what code is being used. In the present case, the portraits are not supposed to be recognizable as such to strangers. The game was that those who knew the person portrayed and who knew that a portrait was intended should recognize the likeness and see how it was brought off.[24] The last point is significant: in discussing his own compositions, Elgar always shows most pride in the ingenuity of his methods as a technician. In the case of these variations, then, the composer's intention is crucial. The problem is that we do not always know who was intended to be able to recognize the portrait—in some cases it may have been no one but Elgar himself; in the uncompleted Parry and Sullivan variations, it would have been any educated musician.

People can be represented either through their characteristics, or by way of events involving them. Variation IX is about Jaeger, and also refers to an incident involving him.

People can be represented directly, as themselves, or indirectly, through contexts including them (Variation VIII) or events caused by them. They can be represented less directly still, by how others react to them (Variation IV).

The most straightforward way of musically representing things or people, since music is sound, is by way of the sounds they make. Sounds may be emitted by a thing's internal motions, or caused by the interaction of a thing with something else.

Of sounds emitted by a living thing, some are parts of a communication system and some are not; and sounds of the former kind may be proper parts of the system (utterances) or incidental to it (inflections).

Human communication systems may be expressive sounds of the social animal, such as grunts and sighs (what Aristotle called 'voice');[25] or they may be articulate language; or they may be music itself, which is a system *sui generis*; or they may be ambiguously related to these systems.

The most direct musical representation must be by music portraying music. This could be the very music that we hear (Variations IX, XIII); or it could be different music, some of the features of which are presented or alluded to in what we hear (Variation XII, perhaps). The musical sounds alluded to could be actual music made in performance (Variations VI, VII, XII); or sounds made deliberately but peripherally to performance (tuning, practising— Variation II); or sounds made incidentally or accidentally in music-making. Except in the first case, the person portrayed would be represented not as a practitioner of the art of music, but as a person going about the business of making music.

[24] Burley (117) says that Elgar was 'constantly challenging me to *guess* whom they represented' (my emphasis). Only the Enigma, we recall, was to be left 'unguessed'.
[25] Aristotle, *De Anima*, II. 8.

People can be represented through their use of language, which is the most conspicuous medium of human communication. Music can use translation systems to encode linguistic content in a musical medium (composers like to use encoded spellings of their names in this way); or it can convey a linguistic medium by using the recognizable cadence of a familiar phrase (the Theme). And it can represent a tone of voice or linguistic mannerism, expressive of mood or character (Variations III, IV, V—though this may come more under the heading of 'voice'); or a recognizable quirk of utterance, not language itself but a feature of an individual's delivery of language (Variation X).

'Voice' in human beings is mostly absorbed into tone of speaking voice or musical utterance; but sighs, groans, and especially modes of laughter (Variations V, VII, VIII) belong here. Many sounds we utter are indeterminate in placing, being spontaneous parts of our vital activity. Elgar's self-announcing whistle (Variations II, XIV) is in itself a musical phrase (tuned and timed), but would be typical of 'voice' if it were a spontaneous emission rather than a deliberate signal. It actually functions, though, as a linguistic item, like a rebus.

Representation through accidentally emitted sound (snores, belly-rumbles, and such) is a possibility, but not one Elgar uses; besides being impolite, it would not contribute to a portrait. Unlike Cromwell's warts, which were a part of what he looked like and hence of what he was as a portrayable person, the sounds our bodies accidentally emit are no part of what *we* sound like as representable people. Representation through sounds made by our passage through the world are possible where there is a repeatable sequence of knocking and frotting, or an episode with a recognizable pattern. There is little opportunity here for a composer, because such recognitions are unreliable—except in the interface between musical performers and their instruments, which we treated as a special case. Powell says we can hear R. B. T.'s tricycle in Variation III—but can we?

People can be portrayed otherwise than through the sounds they make. Such portrayal is less direct, but recognition may be no harder. Least indirect is representation through movement patterns, characteristics of which are shared by musical movements with other movements.[26] And, since music is made by people, we can expect that significant differences in human movement (awkward, graceful, abrupt, hesitant) will often be paralleled by significant differences in musical movement. But without a very strong 'caricatural' quality or anecdotal support we can seldom be sure whether a movement quality in the music we hear is to be referred to a movement quality of the person depicted, or to that person's personality, or to something quite different—or whether it has no referential significance at all.

---

[26] This is a main theme in Eduard Hanslick's *On The Musically Beautiful*, trans. G. Payzant (Indianapolis, 1986), and forms the basis of Susanne K. Langer's theory of musical meaning in *Feeling and Form* (New York, 1953).

Physical characteristics can be musically conveyed. A ponderous person may be given heavy music. Wide intervals in a part may allude to the player's gawkiness (Variation VI)—but unless we knew that the performer was tall we would not even suspect an allusion. Analogies between physical and musical forms may be definite once their relevance is ascertained, but are unlikely to be detailed enough to be recognizable without a hint.

Whatever external features a person has may be thought expressive of a personality (a style of conducting one's life) or character (morally relevant qualities), to which we have no other access. But musical representation may go directly to someone's personal qualities, without it being clear to composer or hearer just how these are conveyed. Thus C. A. E.'s portrait (Variation I) is said to be generally 'like her': graciousness, strength, supportiveness, humour, and so on can be conveyed without any systematic reduction being possible. The composer simply bears the person in mind and creates something that 'sounds like' her. Others who share the identical culture and know the person can perceive the likeness with equal directness. But again there can be problems. People who knew Dora Penny as a rather obstinate young woman did not hear her in Variation X, which sounded dainty and charming. Perhaps that was the way she danced, or the way she looked—at least, to Elgar. We can easily hear that the objections were right; but we cannot hear whether or not they were relevant.

When we turn from personality to character (or 'soul'), we find Elgar acknowledging that Variation IX does not portray Jaeger's manner and personality. The portrayal seems to be carried by labels: the tune is grand, simple, noble, and implies that Jaeger's soul has the characteristics those words connote.

People can be represented through the way of life they typify (Variation VIII). This can be done with 'national' traits, and with such contrasts as bucolic versus urban, aristocracy versus peasantry (and, in architecture, 'Queen Anne' versus Bauhaus), for which we have a large repertoire of reliable musical stereotypes and analogies. As with the portrayal of personality, it may not be clear either to composer or to listener just what devices are being used.

People may be represented by the reactions they evoke—sounds of applause or derision, perhaps. In Variation IV, the way the subject is discussed suggests that his manner is found amusing and endearing rather than annoying—a fact that has a direct bearing on his actual personality.

Some depictions go almost entirely to events involving the friend rather than the friend in person. Variation XIII says nothing about its seafaring subject except that its tenderness suggests that she is a proper object of tender feeling.

A special case is Variation XI. What is alluded to directly here is an episode involving the subject's dog—vividly portrayed—but indirectly this presents the owner as notorious dog-lover; and, less directly still, the relationship between Elgar and the dog-owner implied in the practice of composing 'moods of Dan' for the visitors' book.

What is one to say of the phrase in the theme that seems to bear the cadence of the name 'Edward Elgar'? Clearly this refers to Elgar through his name. But is anyone uttering the name? Apparently not. The name, and through the name its bearer, is simply proposed as a subject for discussion.

Another semantic oddity is the quotation from the Beethoven sonata in Variation IX. This refers to Jaeger's playing another part of that sonata on an occasion of deep significance to Elgar, and hence to the quality of soul Jaeger shows in playing it. But as Jaeger played it it referred to Beethoven's perseverance as a composer, and hence to the comparable perseverance that Jaeger wished to encourage in Elgar, and hence to the entire scheme of the *Variations* as a sort of *Heldenleben*.[27]

Variation XIV remains a problem. What is the element of portraiture here? A difficulty is that we would not expect to share Elgar's view of himself, cannot guess what code or codes he might here be using at any more recondite level than that of the direct allusions mentioned above. Perhaps the main point is that for the most part it is just music, the rousing conclusion to a set of very varied variations: the Elgar we are offered is simply the complete and accomplished musician.[28] The other variations represent something other than musical music, music made by or about people who are really thinking of something else. Elgar, as a professional musician, just makes music. But here, as in all the other variations, any number of allusions could be intended that we know nothing about; and we cannot tell how many of those would actually have been recognizable if we had the relevant biographical knowledge.

What does all this suggest by way of a conclusion about musical portraiture? Painters show people as being what they are and as doing what they do by what you can see them being and doing. Musical depiction is not in the least like that. Granted, Elgar's *Variations* are a special case, using a special repertory of effects, because so many of his subjects are musicians with whom he shared his music-making. Even so, what is going on is not like portraiture.

---

[27] Strauss's *Ein Heldenleben* appeared the year before Elgar's *Variations*, but presumably not before the plan of the latter was formed. Elgar first heard the work in 1902 (Young, *Letters to Nimrod*, 172), and there is nothing to show that he knew the work previously. The *Heldenleben* aspect alleged here is not known to have been in Elgar's mind at the time. The origin of the work is traced to a domestic evening in which Elgar casually improvised on a theme, 'playing it in the different ways his friends might have done had *they* thought of it. "Surely you are doing something that has never been done before?" asked Alice. And so was born the idea of the *Enigma* Variations' (McVeagh, *Edward Elgar*, 25). However, if the theme that evening was the 'enigma' theme itself, and if Elgar already attached a deep personal significance to it, the anecdote is misleading. Elgar would not in any case have taken Strauss for a model: 'S[trauss] puts music in a very low position when he suggests it must hang on some commonplace absurdity for it's very life' (Young, *Letters to Nimrod*, 238, from a letter of 1904).

[28] According to the subject of Variation VII, 'Elgar intended the original ending to mean "Well, we have had a very pleasant evening. I am glad to hear what you all think about it. Good night"' (Michael Kennedy, *Portrait of Elgar* (London, 1968), 61 n.).

We use our eyes to see the world as it is and to find our way in it. We use languages with extensive but limited vocabularies, with elaborate and determinate grammars, to share our beliefs and wishes. Portrayal and narration can exploit these prepared information systems quite straightforwardly to show and tell things about the world. But our ears convey only movement, they tell us nothing about a motionless world, and audible movements are normally informative only in a context of other knowledge. So neither painting a picture nor writing a story or a description could be a good analogue of what goes on in Elgar's *Variations* or in any auditory representation that eschews language. What we have seen Elgar doing is much more like *telling* a story.

A raconteur certainly uses verbal skill in narrating and describing, and a whole range of constructive skills in arranging the sequence of disclosure, pacing, emphasis, affective tone of voice, postponement, flash back and flash forward, secondary narrations and so on. But a story well told includes more than that. It is eked out with gesture, quotation, mimicry, sound effects. It is a multi-media operation, both auditory and visual, in which anything is legitimate that will get the story across and keep the audience entertained and attentive. A musical narrator follows the same rule and enjoys a comparable licence, except that everything must be audible and carried out by *musical means*—the import of that restriction being determined by what is acceptable in the practice to which composer, performers, and audience subscribe. So the medium is restricted, but that medium is made the field for a free-ranging communicative intelligence, very unlike the systematic developments of representational painting or discursive narrative. Whatever will actually convey or suggest a connection to a comparably alert and imaginative listener who is in a position to know that the connection exists and is a possible subject for allusion is equally legitimate.

Ingenuity, variety, and wit in the use of means to convey what may be quite unexpected meanings are of the essence. For Elgar, given to 'japes' and conundrums and verbal distortions and ingenuities of all kinds, this would be and evidently was an occasion to test what people could catch on to. But the fact that the world is inaudible to us in its deep structures means that musical depiction must always tax a composer's resourcefulness.

Aesthetic Decomposition:
Music, Identity, and Time

JOANNA HODGE

a picture held us captive ...

Wittgenstein

There are two sets of issues addressed in this chapter. First, there are issues emerging out of the parallel, drawn by Wittgenstein, between understanding sentences in language and understanding musical themes. Secondly, there is the relation between aesthetics and the philosophy of art, and a suggestion about how the distinction between them might be understood. These issues are addressed by disrupting the presumption that there is one theory of art, which can be applied with minor modifications to all the art media. There are two ways of disrupting this model: by exploring Wittgenstein's parallel between language and music; and by concentrating analysis on the characteristics of art, which are especially marked in music. These characteristics are the relation of artworks to time, their temporal duration, their temporal structure, and their historical contexts. For the purposes of this chapter, the view to be disrupted will be referred to as that of 'classical aesthetics', and it consists in a combination of Plato's theory of art with eighteenth-century analyses of taste and judgement.

This disruption opens the way to distinguishing between philosophy of art, which allows for plurality; classical aesthetics, which is here taken to presume a single theory of art; and a post-classical aesthetics, reflecting on the consequences of disrupting the classical version. The chapter consists of three parts. The first two provide a discussion of the parallel between understanding musical themes and understanding sentences in a language; and a discussion of the relation between aesthetics and the philosophy of art. In the third section, the two sets of issues are connected up, to suggest a further parallel, between the appreciation of artworks and the formation of individual identity. The chapter concludes by outlining the possibility of a contribution from aesthetic theory, to the analysis of personal identity. It suggests how this contribution helps explain the importance to human beings of art, since art

I am very grateful to Dr Bojan Bujic, who suggested I write the chapter in the first place; to his seminar in Oxford, at which an early draft of this chapter was discussed; to the departmental seminar at the University of Stirling, who gave it a sympathetic second hearing; and to Dr Terence Diffey, of the University of Sussex, who made a number of shrewd criticisms.

provides a model for understanding the relation between human identity and temporality.

1. Understanding Sentences, Understanding Tunes

The remark in the *Brown Book*, referred to in the opening section of this chapter, runs as follows:

What we call 'understanding a sentence' has in many cases a much greater similarity to understanding a musical theme than we might be inclined to think. But I don't mean that understanding a musical theme is more like the picture which one tends to make oneself of understanding a sentence; but rather that the picture is wrong, and that understanding a sentence is much more like what really happens when we understand a tune than at first sight appears. For understanding a sentence, we say, points to a reality outside the sentence. Whereas one might say 'Understanding a sentence means getting hold of its content; and the content of the sentence is in the sentence.'[1]

Here, then, is the problem of content, and Wittgenstein sets up two opposed accounts of how the content of a sentence is to be understood.

There is here first of all the pictorial account, whereby the content of a sentence is taken to be a picture of some reality outside the sentence. There is, conversely, the parallel with the content of a theme, which is nothing but that theme, taken as a construct of the elements contained within it, whose values are a function of the possibilities of music making in which that theme occurs. In this second view, the theme, or sentence, works as a construct of elements, made available by a certain style of music making, or language use, and the theme itself is understandable by contrast to other actual and possible sequences of such elements. It is not to be made sense of by reference to some second domain of other kinds of element, to which the sentence or theme 'points', and to which the elements of the sentence or theme are supposed in some way to connect.

The point of the epigraph is to invoke Wittgenstein's objections to supposing picturing to be the right view of how language works. It is then possible to go on to criticize the view that picturing is the right metaphor for construing an understanding of art and of music. The picture of picturing holds the understanding captive. This is even more the case, when the concern is with art and aesthetics. Aesthetic theory has been dominated by images drawn from those artistic practices, which construct a realist relation between what is produced in the artistic practice and the world of experience. Making music central to an understanding of art, and to aesthetic theory, disrupts the picture of picturing as the dominant image through which to develop an understanding of art, and leads to the required decomposition of a certain image of aesthetics.

---

[1] Ludwig Wittgenstein, *Blue and Brown Books: Preliminary Studies for the 'Philosophical Investigations'* (1933−5) (Oxford, 1958), 167.

In the *Philosophical Investigations*[2] Wittgenstein suggests that philosophical problems arise as a result of thinking in accordance with a misleading picture of a particular process, which then blocks the development of a more adequate understanding of that process. A picture can hold us captive all the more so if we should not be using the image of a picture at all. The example of understanding a musical theme as a competitor to the picture theory of meaning, disrupts this obstacle to understanding how language works. It is tempting to suggest that a conception of habit should be mobilized to displace this notion of a picture holding us captive. It might be less inhibiting to think in terms of habits, formed and breakable.[3] Certainly the conception of picturing as the model for understanding is a generalized version of the picture theory of meaning, which the musical example is supposed to disrupt.

The aim here is to extend this disruption, displacing obstacles in thinking about aesthetics, to the understanding of art. The parallel between understanding music and understanding language suggests a further parallel between the relation of words to a sentence, consisting of those words; and the relation of sounds, or notes, and a tune, consisting of the notes. Both relations make reference back to a system of conventions, a particular natural language or system of symbolization; a musical notation, a harmonic system, in terms of which the well-formedness of the sentence or tune can be made out. The wrong picture of meaning is the picture whereby words and sentences are taken to represent a reality lying outside that sentence. Similarly, the wrong view of what is happening in music would be to take sounds or tunes to be representing processes external to the music. While occasionally there may be a tune which reproduces the sound, for example, of a cuckoo, this is the exception, not the rule, for the construction of musical meaning. Occurrences of such cases stand out in contrast to the rest of the musical context. The parallel for language would be the thought that meaning in language is derivable from its occasional onomatopoeic effects, reproducing, for example, the impression produced by waves breaking regularly on a beach.[4]

The notion of music as deriving its meaning and structure primarily from imitating sounds naturally occurring in human experience is not particularly plausible. The view that the primary meaning of music is a function of its role in expressing and representing human emotion is much more common and less obviously false. Again there is a parallel with a mistaken view about meaning, that sentences somehow reproduce a pregiven private meaning,

---

[2] Wittgenstein, *Philosophical Investigations* (Oxford, 1953).

[3] This could involve an appeal to David Hume on habit and association as a supplement to Wittgenstein on thinking about aesthetics.

[4] In the 18th century there were accounts of meaning in language, in a parallel with such accounts of music, that of J.-J. Rousseau for example, which put forward the hypothesis that the imitation of natural sounds and processes and the expression of human emotion were the primary processes through which meaning in language is determined. These accounts according to the present argument are incorrect both with respect to language and with respect to music. See Rousseau, *On the Origin of Language* (1777).

constituted in a domain other than the domain of words and sentences. The wrong parallel to set up would be that of musical themes and of sentences expressing some internal inscrutable processes in human beings, emotion for music, thought for language. As is well known such explanation, by reference to a private meaning and emotion, which only becomes available for inspection at the moment when it is put into that music and sentence, sets up a highly unsatisfactory and implausible model. Something which cannot be inspected is supposedly serving as an explanation for something which can. This is the point of Wittgenstein's critique of private languages. Neither private meaning nor emotion can be identified in advance of their external manifestations, and so neither can be used as elements in the explanation of those very external manifestations, in which they first become identifiable.

Music, then, and indeed art in general, is often taken to reproduce, represent, or express some occult humanity, or occult value, which is produced in some other domain, and then transposed into publicly accessible form, in sentences, or music, or artworks. However, not only has this reference back to an occult domain absolutely no explanatory power, since the explanation is offered in terms of a domain which remains, inevitably, occult. It furthermore substitutes for and blocks off the possibility of beginning to give an account of what is actually in process in the production of meaningful language, the composition of music, and more generally in the production of artworks. Appeal to a meaning and value transcending the medium in which they are articulated is a barrier to understanding, and functions as a central myth, both assigning value to art and philosophy, and disempowering them from any substantive contribution to understanding what it is to be human.

This notion of a transcendent meaning or value, which is then realized in particular practices, artistic or linguistic, is derived from the platonic account of art and of its secondary status, as an imitation of an imitation, developed in the *Republic*.[5] The platonic view presumes that there is a given set of ideals, meanings, and musical possibilities, which then artists, language users, and composers attempt to reproduce in their practices. The musical possibilities are defined according to this model in terms of a set of emotions, with which human beings are equipped and which they strive to articulate. This model suggests that the structure of human emotion and the standard of beauty and harmony are invariant, providing a set of timeless possibilities, which particular historical agents realize.

The contrasting, constructivist model abandons these timeless ideals, setting out the parameters for artistic and linguistic practice, and instead construes meaning, music, and art as simply a function of whatever contingent possibilities are available, and of whatever conventions have been adopted, without reference to some standard above and beyond the practice and

---

[5] I am here adopting the convention of using lower case for views emerging out of the writings of Plato, reserving the upper case for views I would wish to acribe to Plato.

conventions in question. Meaning and value, beauty and harmony thus become terms whose values themselves are to be determined immanently within those practices and conventions. Audibility and articulability are construed not as timeless fixed spheres of possibility, but as functions of the systems of convention within which they occur. Thus, on this model, what can be said and heard within European languages and musical systems is quite different from what can be said and heard in some other set of conventions about language and music. European grammar, classical harmony, and indeed the twelve-tone system make available a set of articulations, simultaneously excluding a whole range of other possibilities. To try to make sense of what can be said and heard in these different systems by reference to some system above and beyond these enabling conditions cuts loose from those very systems of convention which make the saying and hearing interesting or over-conventional, challenging, or banal.

These two, the platonist and the constructivist view of art, are versions of the two views of sentence meaning and musical themes set up by Wittgenstein in his remark in the *Brown Book*, as the picture theory and the internalist theory respectively. The platonist theory of art is a version of the picture theory, since artworks are taken to imitate or represent a true original, in Plato's case the unchanging idea, in the case of the empiricist the reality depicted. The internalist account is a version of constructivism. The suggestion here is that Wittgenstein's disruption of the picture theory of meaning can be taken also to disrupt platonizing views of how art works. The next section goes on to examine the upshot of this disruption.

2. Aesthetics and the Philosophy of Art

In this section, these considerations are developed into a questioning of the model offered by classical aesthetics. The central issues are the supposed timelessness of the standards of judgement and of the sensibility used in judgement; and the supposedly unchanging nature of the ideas and emotions, which are depicted and reproduced in art media. The timelessness of the one requires the timelessness of the other; and requires the independence of the artwork both from this process of production and from the process of forming a sensibility and capacity for judgement. Once these can be shown to interact, then the standards of taste and the ideals striven for in artistic practice cannot be supposed to be invariant, except at a very general level of analysis.

There are two things wrong with this model: first, the supposition that there is just one all-inclusive system of sensibility for judging all artworks is assumed not argued; secondly, the conception of the artwork as constituted independently of the system of sensibility is implausible. If the above remarks about the relation between convention and saying or hearing are right, then sensibility is not one and the same in all contexts, but in fact variable, as a function of what systems of convention are in operation. The objects judged, similarly, are not constructed in accordance with timeless values and principles of constitution, but are a function of those very conventions which play a role in the formation of the sensibility made use of in producing judgements of them.

The classical model takes the process of producing artworks to be irrelevant to the status of the artwork as an artwork. The artwork is taken in isolation from its producer and from its context and process of production. Similarly, the critic, the artist, and the artwork are taken to be constituted independently of each other. Thus the model seeks to provide a general theory, in terms of a single account of sensibility and of a transcendent value of beauty, for all artworks in all contexts. The philosophy of art by contrast becomes the study of the specificities of particular art media, their particular constraints and deviations from this general model. The artwork is not necessarily taken in isolation from its producer and context of production. The suggestion is that analysis in the philosophy of music generates deviations which cannot be contained in the general model.

The general theory, then, while presented as providing a model equally relevant for all art media, is in fact closely connected to the specific constraints of particular art-forms, of so-called realist writing and of realist painting which, for reasons not to be investigated here, became the dominant forms of practice in those two media in Europe at the turn of the eighteenth century.[6]

At the same time as what is here called the classical conceptualization of aesthetics was being reaffirmed, highly disruptive, experimental, and non-realist forms of artistic practice were also in evidence. Examples of these are the highly artificial conventions out of which the music of Mozart and his contemporaries emerged; the experiments with novel form of Sterne and Diderot; the highly artificial conventions of so-called realist painting, which sets up the point of vantage from which the picture is viewed as static, not in motion. Indeed the classical model of the non-participating critic of art is itself a highly artificial construct, resulting from convention not nature. The model of non-participatory appreciation, with a passive spectator, not playing any role in the constitution of the pattern viewed, is an invention, not an obvious and natural way of considering the relation between art and appreciation.

At this time Kant's attempts to construct connections between a naturalistic epistemology and a naturalistic aesthetics result in problems of inconsistency between the two, revealed in the introduction to *The Critique of Judgement*.[7]

[6] It would, however, be worth considering the role which aesthetic theories produced in the course of the 18th century had in confirming that dominance; and, conversely, worth analysing the shared historical conditions of possibility for the production both of realist art practices and for the reaffirmation of classical aesthetics at that time.

[7] Immanuel Kant, *The Critique of Judgement* (1790) (Indianapolis, 1987).

Different, incompatible functions are ascribed to the imagination in the two accounts. More crucially his theory of aesthetics, while presented as naturalistic, emerges out of and depends on a highly sophisticated convention of enquiry. There is thus a gap between the image of critical philosophy and of this revised classical aesthetics as somehow the natural and obvious way to set up the appreciation of art, and the highly conventional, theoretically sophisticated artistic practice and theory, through which that model is produced. While classical aesthetics is supposed to set up a general theory of art appreciation and of artworks, it is in fact an account specific to a certain limited kind of artistic practice. It is thus philosophy of art, in the sense set out above. There is then room for some other account of the general significance of art, in the place left open by the displacement of this supposedly general but in fact partial aesthetic theory.

Such generalizing views of art can be made to look more or less plausible depending on choice of art media and of practice within those media. There are those which reproduce the platonist prejudice that philosophical enquiry must set up general models as timeless unaltering truths, as the result and point of departure for theory, irrespective of the interpreter. The narrator, artist, and theorist are then to be construed as standing outside the domain of artworks, and of objects to be represented in art. They are construed as unaffected by that domain and by the process of representation. The artwork is set up as somehow external to the world, and the more it approaches excellence, the more external to the world and to the temporal processes of the world it becomes. The criterion of excellence becomes the degree to which an artwork approaches the status of the timeless, eternal value, of which according to the theory it is an imitation.

This external relation between artwork and world establishes a relation of mimesis or representation between world and artwork. Realist and idealist conceptions of art can thus be shown to share a single mistaken notion of art imitating a domain of entities outside its own sphere. The realist version supposes that artworks imitate natural entities and occurrences; the idealist version that these artworks imitate transcendent values. Constructivism by contrast is opposed to both of these, since for constructivism the mode of working, sensibility, the artwork and ways of looking at the world are simultaneously constituted, not independently produced structures. The two treat time and historical context very differently; for the classical view they are irrelevant; for the constructivist view they are all important.

These relations of independence between artist, artwork, world and its temporal structure are put in doubt by two aspects of musical practice. They are put in doubt by the importance of time to musical structure, which will be discussed in the next section. They are also put in doubt by the relation between musical appreciation, performance, and composition, which are not necessarily distinct functions, taken up by different kinds of individual. The model of performance, composition, and appreciation as functions of one and the same group of people, as opposed to distributed between three distinct groups, is one shared by eighteenth-century musical practice and by the proliferation of different forms of music making in the twentieth century. A division of labour, signalled by Adam Smith's political economy, is certainly true of some nineteenth-century European practices of music, in the public space of huge symphonic works, but not of all musical practice, even in Europe in the nineteenth century.

The division of function between critic and artist rests on a distinction between grasping the point of breaking with an existing set of rules and inventing a new one, and actually producing that break. While it is clearly a distinction, with enormously significant consequences, it is difficult to see how these two capacities could in fact be anything other than closely associated. To understand what has been heard or said is to be able to continue the sequence in a relevant way, be it continuing to add two to the sequence 2, 4, 6, 8, or the ability to fill out a harmonic progression, a jazz improvisation, or a twelve-tone sequence. Understanding and appreciation then could be construed as the capacity to continue, or follow the continuation, of the series, not the ability to judge correctness according to some occult external standard. Only with the latter model is there a clear basis for distinguishing between the contribution of an artist and the contribution of a critic to the constitution of artworks as artworks.

In *The Critique of Judgement*, Kant argues that the invention of a rule, of a pattern to be imitated by other artists, is the sign of genius in art:

What this shows is the following: (1) Genius is a talent for producing something for which no determinate rule can be given, not a predisposition consisting of a skill for something that can be learned by following some rule or other; hence the foremost property of genius must be originality. (2) Since nonsense too can be original, the products of genius must also be models, i.e. they must also be exemplary; hence, though they do not themselves arise through imitation, still they must serve others for this, i.e. as a standard or rule by which to judge. (3) Genius itself cannot describe or indicate scientifically how it brings about its products, and it is rather as nature that it gives the rule.[8]

To recognize the invention of a rule and to grasp that a rule is being followed is here set out as a feature of the capacity to appreciate art.

Thus Kant recognizes the importance of invention for art, and does not emphasize a relation between art and some timeless standard. He is then potentially a critic of the platonizing view of art, and, while affirming the possibility of detachment and invariance in judgement, nevertheless accepts the possibility of change in artistic practice itself. He thus disrupts the classical view of art as the imitation of pregiven models. However, he does not go on to criticize conceptions of timeless standards, indeed he implicitly

---

[8] Ibid. 175.

endorses them, even though the invention of a rule in art is not far removed from the invention of a rule in art criticism. Kant's theory is undecided between two options: between the view that art reproduces an already existing reality, and art making available new ways of constituting our sense of reality. The second option breaks with the representational view of art, and makes it possible to claim that Dickens made fog an identifiable feature of experience, and that Van Gogh made sunflowers visible.

The naturalism and the realism presupposed in the classical model for aesthetics is completely inappropriate for non-realist, non-naturalist artistic practices. Art in the mode of surrealism, and symbolism, impressionism, and expressionism makes us see the world differently, produces a different world. It makes clear that naturalism and realism make available a specific range of experiences and perceptions and play a role in affirming a particular kind of conception of what the world is like. Shifts in the dominant practices of painting make it easier to identify that music does not fit into the general model put forward by the classical view. It is even possible that this lack of fit prompted the production in the nineteenth century of theories of music as expressive of human emotion, for they more nearly conform to the pattern set up by the general model.

The degree of shift possible in forms of artwork leads Heidegger in his paper 'The Origin of the Artwork',[9] to argue that artworks make identifiable a variability in the relation between human beings and the spatio-temporal frame in which they exist. Epic poetry and Greek temples set up one such relation; modernist functionalist architecture and television another. This is a different order of construction, in which the entire spatio-temporal frame of experience is revealed as transformed between epochs. This is a radicalization of Kant's view that the spatio-temporal frame of human experience is a projection of human sensibility. Kant argues that there is only one such frame. Heidegger suggests that the frame alters, and that the alteration can be identified through careful attention to artistic practice. This suggests that classical aesthetics, then, far from providing a general theory of artworks, in fact draws on a restricted domain of artworks, presupposing a naturalism and a realism about entities and about the relation between artistic productions and what there is in the world. The separations of the classical model work only for a certain form of sensibility and a certain kind of artistic practice, in which an understanding of the artwork is made separate from an understanding of what the artist is doing. The model takes as standard what is in fact historically specific: a division of labour between an active artist and a passive critic, the capacities of the latter being taken to be fixed and the capacities of the former taken to be inexplicable. In the next section, the possibility of theorizing a simultaneous constitution of artwork, artist, and

[9] Martin Heidegger, 'The Origin of the Artwork', in *Poetry Language Thought*, trans. and ed. Albert Hofstadter (New York, 1971).

standards of taste will be opened out, by criticizing the relation between aesthetics, the artwork and time, which the classical model presupposes.

3. Art, Time, Transcendence, and Identity

According to the picture of artistic work, which is to be rejected, a reality external to the artwork is taken up and transformed into an image approaching timelessness. Artistic activity is supposed not to play a part in constituting our sense of reality and therefore it is possible to detach the product from the world in which it takes place and to measure it against a non-worldly, non-temporal standard. By positing a reality existing independently of the artwork, it becomes possible to detach the artwork from the temporal structure of that reality. Classical aesthetics then seeks to neutralize temporal process. Philosophizing about particular art-forms and particular artworks cannot do this, because individual works have their own temporal structure, having a place in a sequence of historical development and individual production. Thus there opens up a difference between philosophy of art and aesthetics, as a result of their different relations to time and to history.

Music poses the centrality of time to the artwork itself, with a particular urgency. Time is central not just to the formation of the conventions and the development of the individual artist's capacities, required to produce or perform the work in question. A relation to time, to temporal sequence, and to temporal structure is internal to music itself. This disrupts the attempt to set up aesthetic values as timeless and to presume that time and temporality are irrelevant to artworks, and to judgements about them. The function of time within music sets up a contrast to the form of temporality, which predominates in everyday experience. There the most obvious temporal structure is that of causal sequence, with effects following on from temporally previous events. Time is the frame in which tasks have to be accomplished. Music by contrast offers a site for identifying a difference between those everyday preoccupations with time as causal and as providing opportunities for accomplishing certain tasks, and the function of time as making structure available. Temporal sequence is not just a frame in which music occurs, but the very structure of its articulation, as is demonstrated by the possibility of playing the same piece of music in shorter and longer periods of time. Time is intrinsic to the internal construction of music, not simply a frame in which it occurs.

The contrast between time as a frame within which effects follow causes, or in which purposes are accomplished, and time as an integral part of the entities in question, sets out a different notion of transcendence from the notion of aesthetic values transcending time. Analysis of music suggests a transcendence of the time of preoccupation, without making the claim to transcend temporality altogether. It therefore sets out differences between conceptions of time and transcendence, which turn out to have striking equivalencies to the relation to time experienced by human beings, in questioning their own identities. To grasp a piece of music as a single structure, it is necessary both to grasp its temporal structure and to suspend the fragmentation which extension through time tends to impose on the process thus extended. The appreciation of and suspension of temporal process required to grasp the coherence and unity of a piece of music is the same process as is required to grasp the coherence and unity of a single life, whereby a sense of individual identity can be constructed. Aesthetics then can become a study of different temporal structures and of transcendence as the suspension of an understanding of time, as simply the temporal structures of causal sequence and purposiveness. Aesthetics can become again the study of the relation between understandings of spatio-temporal frameworks and the objects contained within those frameworks, as set out by Kant at the beginning of *The Critique of Pure Reason*.[10]

There is an oscillation in the status of artworks between an immanent materiality and a transcendence of spatio-temporal specificity required to grasp that work as a single entity. This oscillation is reproduced in the double status of artworks as social facts and autonomous entities. Adorno states this duality in his *Aesthetic Theory* thus:

Art's essence is twofold: on the one hand it dissociates itself from empirical reality and from the functional complex that is society; and on the other, it belongs to that reality and to that social complex. This comes out directly in the particular aesthetic phenomena which are always simultaneously aesthetic and *faits sociaux*. Aesthetic autonomy and art *qua* social fact are not the same; moreover each calls for a different kind of perception.[11]

For Adorno the task is to analyse the differences between these different statuses of artworks and to show how different kinds of response are elicited depending on whether the artwork is considered as one, or as the other, or as both.

The suggestion to be made here is that this oscillating structure is shared by artworks and by human identity. Thus understanding the conditions of possibility for identity in artworks can contribute to an understanding of the conditions of possibility for identity in human beings. The parallel structure between the role of temporality in music and the role of temporality in the constitution of human identity is repeated in the parallel between the appearance of timelessness in a painting and the appearance of timelessness in the passive sensibility used to judge it. This timelessness, however, is wholly spurious, and makes sense only as an artificial abstraction from the processes through which the painting is presented to the critic, and the critic comes to be standing in judgement over it. It appears plausible because it matches a

---

[10] Kant, *The Critique of Pure Reason* (1781) (London, 1929).
[11] T. W. Adorno, *Aesthetic Theory* (London, 1984), 358.

common philosophical prejudice in favour of eliminating or reducing the effects of time on the objects to be studied.

The juxtaposition of the time of causal sequence, the temporal structure internal to music, and the suspension of temporality required for grasping a piece of music as whole makes available to human beings a differential conception of time. There is an everyday taking for granted of time, and a puzzle about its divergent functions. There is the time of causal sequence, the time of particular actions and the suspension of temporal process required for grasping the coherence and unity of a single life. Aesthetics could be set up not as the denial of the importance of time, but rather as the investigation of the effects of temporal structure, of which that denial would be one version. By affirming a connection between music and time, as Kant's form of inner sense, rather than with emotion, the disruptiveness of music with respect to classical, platonist views of art can be opened out into an analysis of parallels between understanding art and understanding human identity. By analysing the effects of different temporal structures in the domain of producing and admiring artworks, it becomes possible to develop an analysis of relations between human identity, human experience, and the temporal structures in which they occur, thus advancing understanding of personal identity.

Understanding Humour and
Understanding Music

KENDALL WALTON

All of a sudden I wonder why I have to tell this, but if one begins to wonder why he does all he does do . . . why when someone has told us a good joke immediately there starts up something like a tickling in the stomach and we are not at peace until we've gone into the office across the hall and told the joke over again; then it feels good immediately, one is fine, happy, and can get back to work.

Julio Cortázar, 'Blow-up'

Anthony is an anthropologist doing field-work on Mars. He notices that Martians laugh on occasion. They emit from time to time, out of the opening in their bodies from which they speak, a kind of staccato melisma. (I shall not enquire into how Anthony identifies this behaviour as laughter.) Anthony does not understand why they laugh when they do; he does not see what is funny. So he sets about trying to find out. He takes careful notes on the circumstances in which they laugh and those in which they do not. When necessary, he arranges experiments, setting up various situations to see which ones elicit amusement from the natives. Eventually, Anthony is able to predict when Martians will laugh. He knows, for instance, that if Martha, or any other mature Martian from the upper socio-economic class, sees a yellow square shape moving horizontally from left to right across a movie screen, and if she has not seen such a phenomenon previously, she will break out in peals of hysterical laughter. For the sake of argument, let us make the enormously unrealistic assumption that Anthony's predictions are perfect.

Not only does Anthony predict successfully when Martians will laugh, he knows what makes them laugh. He knows, for instance, that part of what makes Martha laugh is the fact that the movement of the square is from left to right; he has experimented with squares moving from right to left and observed that they elicit nothing but bored stares from Martians like Martha. And he knows that the size of the squares does not matter, because he has observed that varying their size does not change Martians' responses.

But there is a sense in which Anthony still doesn't *understand* why Martha laughs. It is a mystery to him why she should find a yellow square moving

This is a revised version of a paper presented at the meetings of the Society for Music Theory in Austin, Texas, in October 1989. I am indebted to Marion Guck for many helpful suggestions.

from left to right amusing. So Anthony renews his grant and goes back to work. Perhaps he investigates Martian physiology or neurology, or the architecture of their logic boards. He knows what changes the moving squares produce in Martians' sensory receptors, and can trace the electrical and chemical effects of these changes in other parts of their bodies, and he knows how all of this leads finally to the up and down bouncing of their laughter. Or perhaps Anthony comes up with a psychological explanation of a more or less mechanistic sort. He discovers somehow or other, after painstaking research, that it is because members of the upper classes have a slight sense of guilt about their position in society, along with feelings of superiority, that they laugh at yellow, right-moving squares—they would not laugh if they did not feel the guilt or the superiority—and that the experience of observing the squares relieves or lessens their guilt. Or maybe he discovers that their amusement depends on their realization that Mars is smaller than Venus. Now Anthony can explain in much more detail why Martha laughs when she does. But he still does not understand. He does not see what is funny about the yellow squares, even to her. It is still a mystery to him why she laughs.

The point is not that Anthony is not amused himself, that *he* does not laugh. One need not laugh oneself in order to understand, in the sense in which Anthony does not, why others laugh. I may not be amused, when others are, because I am in a bad mood, or tired, or because I have heard the joke too often previously, or because I am offended by its racist or sexist undertones, or because I have outgrown that kind of humour. Yet I may *understand* perfectly well what is funny about it, why other people find it funny.

One must 'get' the joke, at least, in order to understand why others laugh. It is possible to get a joke even if, for one reason or another, one is not amused by it. But getting the joke, in one sense anyway, is not enough. It may consist in being aware of a pun or an obscure allusion, or in possessing a crucial piece of information. (For example, Duchamp's *Mona Lisa*: 'LHOOQ'.) I am supposing that Anthony has all of the relevant information of this sort; he knows what the Martians know. But he is still mystified by their laughter.

Notice that it is possible to understand why someone laughs, in the sense in which Anthony fails to understand why Martha does, even if one lacks experimental data of the kind Anthony has. I may not realize that a comedian's speeding up his rate of delivery would ruin his joke, for example, or that it plays on my repressed Oedipal feelings, or gives me relief from guilt. I may be utterly unable to predict what sorts of things will cause me and others with senses of humour like mine to laugh. Yet when we do laugh I understand why we do, in the sense in question. The kind of explanation Anthony is able to give of Martha's amusement is no more necessary than it is sufficient for this kind of understanding.

Anthony's observations and experiments are insensitive to a crucial distinction—the distinction between what *makes* Martians laugh, and what they laugh *at*. Anthony knows what *causes* Martha's amusement but not which of the causes are also *objects* of it. What makes me laugh when a comedian tells a joke may be, in part, the timing of his delivery. But I do not laugh *at* his timing. Television producers know that laughter on the sound-track encourages viewers to laugh, but it is not the sound-track laughter that viewers find funny. It may be only after I have had a beer, or only after I have successfully completed a difficult project and so am in a relaxed mood, that I laugh in a certain situation. But it is not the beer or my completion of the project or my relaxed mood that I am amused by or find funny. These are *causes* but not *objects* of my amusement. Amusement is an intensional experience, an experience which is *of* something. It is not a mere twinge or tickle in the stomach that one feels as a result of hearing a good joke.

The kind of understanding Anthony is unable to achieve involves an awareness of what it is that Martha laughs *at*. This is a little like knowing a person's reasons for doing something, not just what causes him to do what he does. It may be misleading to say that Martha has reasons for laughing, however; this may imply that her laughter is deliberate in the way in which many of our actions are. Knowing what Martha laughs at is more like knowing why a person is angry (or jealous, or feels guilty) in the sense of knowing what he is angry at or angry about, not just what causes him to be angry. If we call these his *reasons* for being angry, this need not imply that his anger is deliberate. To understand a person's anger one must know his reasons for being angry in this sense. And to understand Martha's amusement Anthony must know what she is laughing at or amused by, what her reasons are, in this sense, for laughing.

Knowing this is not sufficient for the kind of understanding Anthony is after, however, nor is knowing what a person is angry about sufficient for understanding his anger. Suppose Martha is fully aware of the objects of her amusement and tells Anthony what they are, and suppose that he knows she is not mistaken and is not lying. It may still be a mystery to him why she laughs at what she laughs at. Anthony needs to *understand* Martha's reasons for laughing; knowing what they are is not enough.

What Anthony lacks is a kind of understanding some have called *Verstehen*, one that involves an ability to 'empathize' with Martha when she laughs. But what is that? I think we can say at least this much: understanding what it is like to be amused as Martha is related to an ability to imagine being amused oneself, to imagine the experience of being amused in the situation in question and by whatever it is that amuses Martha. (I do not mean simply an ability to imagine *that* one is amused, or to suppose that one is.) One can imagine being amused without actually being amused, of course. But imagining this does involve—and here I will have to be rather vague—exercising one's own sense of humour. To imagine being amused in the way that Martha is and thereby to understand her amusement Anthony would have to have and make use of a sense of humour that is in relevant respects like hers. Anthony's observations and experiments do not provide him with this sense of humour, and they do not enable him to engage in the relevant imagining. Nor does anything Martha might tell him about what features of the situation are objects of her amusement explain to him how to imagine being amused by those features.

I am sure you have guessed by now that I will be interested in what analogies there might be between understanding a joke and understanding a musical composition.

To say that in analysing a piece of music theorists attempt to understand how and why it *works* is not to say very much, but it is fair enough, I suppose, as far as it goes. This characterization of analysis is not entirely non-committal. An interest in how a piece works is an interest in how it works *on* or *for* *listeners*. One does not merely try to explain the events of the piece, how they happen to have come about or what they are like in themselves, as one might try to explain, for instance, the birth of a star or the formation of Yosemite valley. (Or anyway, I will not be concerned with analyses that do only that, ones that do not also seek to explain how compositions work on or for listeners.) But to be interested in how a piece works is not to be interested just in listeners' experiences, construed merely as experiences they have as a result of listening to the piece. Their experiences are experiences *of the music* and to understand them one must understand what they are experiences of—the music.

This, incidentally, argues against the identification of pieces of music with listeners' experiences, as some have proposed.[1] It is in the nature of these experiences to be experiences *of the piece*; the distinction between the experience and the piece is given in the experience itself. (Part of one's experience is a sense of a difference between what one finds *in* the piece, and what one imposes on it or does with it.)[2] In focusing on the experience one will have to recognize the piece that it is an experience of.

What makes a composition work is (to quote Kerman) 'what general principles and individual features assure the music's continuity, coherence, organization or teleology'.[3] What makes a given composition work may include its key structure, inversions and retrograde relationships, melodic augmentations and diminutions, regularities and irregularities of metre and rhythm, relationships among pitch-class sets, qualities of timbre and texture and changes in them, and so on. It is the job of music theorists, not philosophers, to decide what characteristics are important in what instances, and I will not

[1] John Rahn, 'Aspects of Musical Explanation', *Perspectives of New Music*, 17, No. 2 (Spring–Summer, 1979), 205, 217, 218.

[2] To insist on recognizing the piece as an entity distinct from one's experience of it is not to deny that the piece is a cultural construct of some sort, rather than something existing independently of people or human institutions.

[3] Joseph Kerman, 'Analysis, Theory and New Music', in *Contemplating Music* (Cambridge, Mass., 1985), 61.

presume to intrude. My interest now is not in the answers to such questions but in the methods by which one might arrive at them.

How does one discover what makes a composition work? Shall we run a series of experiments, altering characteristics of the piece one at a time and asking competent and experienced listeners, after each change, whether it still works (or whether it still works in a particular way)? Will we eventually, after many such experiments, succeed in isolating the characteristics that make it work?

This will not be an easy task, for obvious reasons. There are an enormous number of distinct variables in even a simple piece—probably infinitely many of them; in any case more than one could hope to check out even in a lifetime. The experimenter will have to make a lot of guesses about which variables are worth testing. And many of the variables are not independent of each other. The melodic shape of the bass line cannot be changed much without altering the piece harmonically. So how will we set up an experiment to ascertain whether it is the melody's shape or the harmony that helps to make the piece work? This is not an unfamiliar problem in the experimental sciences, and there are, in principle, ways of getting around it. One would have to devise a much more sophisticated and complex experimental procedure than the one I sketched, and the data would be less direct evidence for the conclusions. One might start by modifying melodies in ways that have only slight harmonic implications, in order to establish generalizations about what kinds of effects melodies with certain sorts of shapes tend to have. These generalizations might then ground inferences concerning what part of the effect of melodic changes which do involve significant harmonic changes is attributable to the former.

But is any procedure of this sort what we want, even assuming that it can be carried out? Music theorists rarely undertake anything like the kind of experimentation I have described (although psychologists of music do). Could it be that although this experimental method would be the ideal one, it is simply not feasible; the difficulties of carrying it out are overwhelming. So theorists work informally, sloppily, unsystematically, in effect guessing at what the results of such experiments would be? I do not think so. Even if this kind of experimentation were feasible, it would be unsatisfying in the way that Anthony's research on the Martians' sense of humour is unsatisfying. It would tell us what it is about the music that makes it work, what causes it to work, but it would not, not by itself anyway, enable anyone to *understand*, in the way that I think most analysts want to understand, why or how the music works, why it moves us.[4]

An indication of this is the fact that the experimental procedure I

---

[4] Wittgenstein argues for something very much like this point, in his *Lectures and Conversations on Aesthetics, Psychology, and Religious Belief*, ed. Cyril Barrett (Berkeley, Calif., n.d.), 19–21. Frank Jackson tells stories that are in some respects like my Martian story in 'Epiphenomenal Qualia', *Philosophical Quarterly*, 32 (Apr. 1982), 127–36.

outlined—both the simple one and more sophisticated variants of it—do not require the experimenter to exercise his musical intuitions; indeed he need not even have any. A Martian anthropologist with no musical sense at all, or none relevant to our music, could in principle conduct the investigation, using native listeners as subjects, just as Anthony might investigate Martian humour in the manner I sketched earlier without engaging his own sense of humour. The Martian anthropologist may be at a practical disadvantage in one respect. One would want to exercise one's musical intuitions in choosing which hypotheses about what makes a piece work are worth testing. But maybe Martian anthropologists live for thousands of years, or the Martian anthropologist might be lucky and accidently pick the right hypotheses early on. In any case, one might in principle succeed in carrying out this investigation and learn what it has to teach without exercising any musical intuitions at all.

This point can be obscured by the fact that the subjects of the imagined experiments do use their musical intuitions; they have to tell the experimenter whether a piece or a variant of it works. And the experimenter might use himself as a subject, even as his only subject. The experimenter may think of his task primarily as that of explaining what makes the piece work for him. In that case he is the obvious subject to use. Ideally, then—if only it were possible—he will sit down at the piano and alter the piece bit by bit, asking himself at each step whether it still works. Eventually he comes up with a list of the features that make it work for him.

Now I do think that engaging in this process might help the appreciator to understand how the music works for him. But this understanding does not consist simply in accepting the results of the experiments, in being able to specify the relevant features. The experimenter could employ subjects other than himself and, using ordinary experimental safeguards, extrapolate the results to himself with at least some degree of confidence. (Compare testing the effects of a drug on a limited population and extrapolating the results to others.) The experimenter's own musical intuitions need play no role in this procedure, and it is clear that he might accept the results, the list of features which make the composition work for him, without achieving any particular understanding of how it works. There is still a gap between knowing what features make the music work and understanding how and why it works.

But if the music does work on me, don't I already understand how it does? If I find a joke funny myself don't I see what is funny about it? Yes, in a way. I may not know the mere causes of my experience, of course, but that is not what we are usually after anyway. What we are after is an understanding of the character of the experience, not how it happened to have come about. A full description of an experience need not mention its causes, but must specify its objects, its intensional content. I do not fully understand what a person is feeling if I know merely that he is angry, or jealous; I must know what he is angry about or whom he is jealous of. I need not know, however, that his feeling angry or jealous is (in part) a side-effect of a drug he is taking, or (in part) a result of a chemical imbalance in his brain, or that it results (in part) from such and such early childhood experience. The feeling itself might have been the same had it been caused differently. But it would not have been the same feeling if what the person is angry about were being passed over for a promotion, for example, rather than an insult from a fellow worker.

When I am moved by a musical composition I, presumably, have some sort of awareness of the content of my experience, the particular features of the music that it is an experience of. But I may not be able to specify in much detail what they are. To specify them, to articulate them, is to achieve a better understanding of how the music works for me (as well as, possibly, to make it work better for me). This, I believe, is a large part of what many music theorists do when they analyse a composition: they spell out the intensional objects of their musical experiences (and of the experiences of other listeners as well, to the extent that others experience the music in similar ways—or come to do so under the influence of the analysis). The method is not the experimental one I described, since that method does not separate mere causes from objects of the experience. And in any case the theorist has his own vague awareness of the content of his experience to start with.

The process of articulating the content of one's musical experiences is not unlike that of becoming fully aware of the content of other intensional states—coming fully to realize what exactly one is angry about or worried about or articulating for oneself why one has qualms about pursuing a certain course of action, as when a person is able to say, 'Now I know why I have always disliked him—it is his pretense of humility.'[5] I do not have in mind so much what a person might do on the psychiatrist's couch, as more ordinary and everyday reflections on the content of one's intensional attitudes. (There would seem to be nothing corresponding to Freud's notion of *repression* which must be overcome to achieve a realization of the content of one's musical experiences.) We might also compare the experience of having a word on the tip of one's tongue, and then trying to decide what it is, and, of course, the process of determining why we laugh when we do—not just what makes us laugh, but what exactly we laugh at.

The primary means by which one uncovers the content of one's intensional states is 'introspection'. I am favourably disposed to Boretz's observation that 'introspection is the crucial testing-ground' for 'the kind of personally interested musical experience [his] work has addressed and cultivated'.[6] I am not taking introspective data as data on which an empirical scientific theory is built, however (in accordance with Hempel's deductive-nomological model, for instance). My point is rather that achieving the introspective results is itself our objective, or a large part of it. We seek to explain our musical experiences

[5] Arnold Isenberg, 'Critical Communication', in *Aesthetics and the Theory of Criticism: Selected Essays of Arnold Isenberg*, ed. William Callaghan *et al.* (Chicago, 1973), 171.
[6] Benjamin Boretz, 'The Logic of What?', *Journal of Music Theory*, 33, No. 1 (1989), 113.

in the sense of specifying, spelling out, *what they are like*, not in the sense of saying why they are as they are, or how they came about. (If one wants to say that explaining what something is like is actually a kind of *description*, I will have no objection.)

There is still room for explanations of other sorts, however. It certainly may be of interest to know what kinds of sound event people (or certain people) hear in what kinds of ways—which ones provoke experiences with what intensional content. And to discover this would I suppose constitute at least part of an explanation of how it happens that we hear sound events in the ways we do. If (as I assume) objects are also causes, to discover by means of whatever empirical investigation might be relevant the causes of my musical experience may at least give me clues as to what the objects of the experience might be, and may thereby contribute to the introspective task I just described.

The result of this introspective task—the task of articulating what I am angry about, or what my musical experience is an experience of—is not a mere piece of information. I do not merely acquire the knowledge that what I am angry about is the subtly insulting tone of someone's remark, or that what worries me about so-and-so's heading a certain organization is (let's say) his tendency to ignore certain kinds of advice. I could in principle acquire this information about myself by being told by someone I trust—a psychologist or a friend I believe to be perceptive; I might take someone's word for it. Or I might read and believe a study that concludes that when people like me are angry or worried in circumstances like the one I am in, that is what they are angry or worried about. The result of my introspection is rather a recognition, an acknowledgement that that is indeed what I am worried or angry about. Now I *see* that that is so. (It is not easy to say what this means.) Of course, being told by a trusted friend might help me to see this, to acknowledge it. But seeing it goes beyond merely concluding that what the friend says is true. Recognizing, finally, what the word on the tip of my tongue was is more than just knowing what it was.

Likewise, the introspection that may attend devising an analysis of a piece or examining someone else's analysis leads ideally to a recognition or acknowledgment that such-and-such features of the music are included in the content of one's musical experience, a recognition or acknowledgment that goes beyond acquiring information about what features are part of the content of one's experience. I might acquire this information about myself simply by taking the word of a theorist I admire and whose way of hearing I have reason to expect will be much like my own, without engaging in any introspection at all. But upon introspection I 'see' for myself that my hearing of the piece corresponds to the analysis, I come to *understand* my experience as being an experience of the features in question.[7]

---

[7] See Nicholas Cook, 'Music Theory and "Good Comparison": A Viennese Comparison', *Journal of Music Theory*, 33, No. 1 (1989), 128.

The kind of understanding Anthony fails to achieve in his study of the Martians' sense of humour is the understanding of acknowledgement or recognition. We now see that it has two aspects. One might, in the first place, 'see' the humour of a situation. One does this when one acknowledges or recognizes one's own amusement. (I am not sure one ever is amused without acknowledging that one is.) It is harder to say what exactly one recognizes or acknowledges when one sees the joke but is not actually amused—perhaps a blocked or inhibited or potential reaction of amusement. But it is clear that the understanding does not consist simply in possessing the information that one would laugh if one were not tired, or jaded, or offended by the joke's racism, or whatever. The understanding consists in experiencing and acknowledging a certain response to the joke, if not one of actual amusement.

It is a further step, beyond seeing the humour, to articulate just what it is about the situation that is funny, to recognize or acknowledge the objects of one's amusement. When one does this one understands more deeply why the situation is funny, why those who laugh at it do so (assuming, of course, that they laugh for the same reasons).

Music theorists investigating music of their own culture usually possess an understanding of the first sort to start with, a recognition or acknowledgement that the music works (not just acceptance of the fact that it does). Much of their effort, I suggest, goes to deepening this understanding in the way I described, recognizing or acknowledging, and articulating, the content of their musical experiences. In many cases this makes the experience itself more satisfying. (My anger may be more satisfying after I have fully articulated what I am angry about, even if what I am angry about has not changed.)

My suggestions so far will help clarify the issue of whether only what is or can be *heard* in a piece of music is musically significant, and whether the analysis or explanation of a composition ought to be restricted to specifying features of it that listeners do or might hear.[8]

I urge that we avoid a narrow conception of what one hears. We are sometimes angry or jealous without being able to articulate fully what we are angry or jealous about. We also, even more frequently perhaps, laugh without being able to say in much detail what it is that we are laughing at. (It might be essential to our amusement, in some cases, that we not be able to specify its objects very precisely.) So the content of a musical experience may include features of the music the experiencer cannot specify. There may not always be a good way of ascertaining what the content of any of these intensional states includes, of acquiring the capacity to articulate them in their entirety. When possibilities are suggested, we may recognize or acknowledge them as indeed among the objects of the experience (as having been so all along). But failure to make such an acknowledgement cannot be taken as conclusive proof that they are not objects of the experience. Recognition does not always come easily.

---

[8] See Cook, 'Music Theory and "Good Comparison"', 117–41.

So analyses are probably, more often than one might have thought, specifications of what we hear. The possibility is open that even the Schenkerian deep structure of a piece, or the fact that the foreground and middle ground are elaborations of the deep structure, is in fact an unacknowledged part of the content of musical experiences even of ordinary listeners. Listeners' inability to specify the tone row of a twelve-tone piece is not sufficient to establish that they do not hear it. An analysis of a piece may amount to a *speculation* about what might be in the unacknowledged content of the analyst's or other listeners' experiences. In arriving at such speculations, the analyst may depend more on general impressions of what sorts of things are likely to be heard in what ways than on introspection of his own musical experience, even if they are speculations about the character of his own actual experience.

The objective of analysis is not always or only to explicate how listeners in fact hear pieces, however. Many analyses are designed to explain and encourage new ways of hearing. The obvious way of doing this is by specifying the intensional content of the new hearing. (The information in the analysis does not by itself enable one to hear the composition in the new way or even to understand that kind of hearing in the sense I have been concerned with, but it may help.) But the distinction between explicating a current way of hearing and pointing to a new one is not clearcut. Even an analysis consisting entirely of specifications of what a listener already hears in a piece is likely to change the way he hears it.

We have already observed that coming to acknowledge the content of one's musical experience makes for a change in the experience. Being angry and fully aware of what one is angry about is not the same as being angry without realizing exactly what it is that one is angry about. The experience of hearing one melodic line as an inversion of another while being aware only of a vague similarity between them differs from the experience of *noticing* that the one melody is the inversion of the other. (To notice something is, approximately, to perceive it while acknowledging one's perceiving of it.) So an analysis which, by specifying what I hear in a piece, helps me to acknowledge what I hear in it, changes my experience at the same time that it enhances my understanding of it.

There is much more to a musical experience than hearing certain features of the music and noticing some of them. Musical experiences are multi-faceted and multi-layered complexes of many intensional states, including expectation, surprise, satisfaction, excitement, recognition, admiration, and even humour, as well as hearing and noticing. (Some of the constituent intensional states take others as objects, as when, in noticing features of the music, one acknowledges the fact that one hears them.) Rather than comparing the experience of listening to music to that of laughing at jokes, we will do better to compare it to the larger experience of 'appreciating' a comedian's routine, also a multi-faceted, multi-dimensional experience involving not just humour but various other intensional attitudes as well. Achieving an awareness of the cause of one element of either a musical experience or an appreciation of a comedy routine often makes the cause part of an object of another element of it, and in this way alters the experience.

In addition to laughing at a joke, one may come to notice how the laugh was achieved, how the timing of the comedian's delivery, for example, contributed to its effect. One may then admire the elegant or masterful means by which the laugh was elicited, take delight in the artistry that went into it. The manner in which the timing of the delivery helps to induce one's laughter may surprise or impress the appreciator (or for that matter, disappoint or bore him). The timing is just a cause, not an object of humour, but it becomes part of an object of the larger appreciative experience.

Likewise in music. A modulation may be surprising partly because of its 'timing', because of certain rhythmic features of the passage in question, even if it is just the modulation, not the rhythmic features, that listeners are surprised by. Accents or dynamic qualities may contribute to recognition of one passage as an elaboration of another. If we come to notice either of these causal relationships, we may relish or admire the elegant manner in which the surprise or the recognition is effected. And the relishing or admiration, as well as the surprise or recognition, is part of the musical experience.

I assume that the causes are features we heard in the music all along but did not notice. Once we notice them, acknowledge our hearing of them, we are in a position to notice how our surprise or recognition depends on them, and hence to appreciate the way the surprise or recognition is brought about. One function of an analysis specifying what we hear in a piece may be in this way to induce awareness of causes of certain elements of our musical experience in order to incorporate them in the content of other elements of it. The analysis at one and the same time explains the listener's experience and extends it.

Analysing musical compositions is not a matter of standing back from one's musical experiences to investigate 'objectively' the compositions or how they work on us. Analysis is continuous with appreciation, and explaining or understanding how it is that one hears a piece is not to be separated from the experience of hearing it. Although an analysis might, coldly and matter of factly, inform someone—a musicologist from a different planet, for instance—of certain facts about a way of hearing a piece, analyses are usually meant to induce the recognition or acknowledgement that constitutes *understanding* of that way of hearing, understanding that goes beyond accepting what the analysis explicitly says and involves exercising one's own musical intuitions. What one comes to understand may be either the kind of musical experience one previously enjoyed, or a new one. In either case the understanding is likely, in the ways I have described, to deepen and enrich one's subsequent hearings of the piece.

Theoretically Informed Listening

MARK DeBELLIS

Peter Kivy's recent book on musical experience begins with this epigraph:

It will be generally admitted that Beethoven's Fifth Symphony is the most sublime noise that has ever penetrated into the ear of man. All sorts and conditions are satisfied by it. Whether you are like Mrs. Munt, and tap surreptitiously when the tunes come—of course, not so as to disturb the others—; or like Helen, who can see heroes and shipwrecks in the music's flood; or like Margaret, who can only see the music; or like Tibby, who is profoundly versed in counterpoint, and holds the full score open on his knee....[1]

It is the difference between Mrs Munt and Tibby that interests me, and with which this chapter will be concerned. Why should we, finding ourselves in the position of Mrs Munt, aspire to that of Tibby? What are the benefits to a listener of having a technical knowledge of music? It is of course a basic premiss of the programme of aesthetic education behind music appreciation classes that this sort of progress is worthwhile, but how and why is it so?[2]

This chapter will be concerned in particular with the cast on these issues rendered by recent discussions of the *explanatory* status of music theory. In recent years there has been revived debate over the nature of theory, its claim to being a scientific enterprise, and its role in shaping musical activity and experience. In my view these discussions have tended to polarize the functions of theory as explanatory on the one hand and as contributing to the listening experience on the other, and laid insufficient stress on the way those functions interact. I shall argue here that the value of hearing music in theoretical terms sometimes derives from their explanatory potential, and shall describe one way in which this can occur.

In their recent article, 'The Scientific Image of Music Theory', Matthew Brown and Douglas Dempster frame their discussion of the nature of music theory in the following way:

If music theory is to be taken seriously, and we think it should, then it must clarify the nature of music and thereby guide our musical activities, whether they be performance,

---

[1] Peter Kivy, *Music Alone* (Ithaca, NY, 1990), p. vi; the passage is from E. M. Forster's *Howards End*. This chapter grew out of a response to *Music Alone* read at the American Society for Aesthetics annual meeting in Austin, Texas, October 1990. I am grateful to Kivy for his comments on that and other occasions, and for having helped me to recognize many of the issues addressed here.

[2] The question is interesting partly because those able to listen to music analytically sometimes choose not to, but my topic here will be the benefits of theoretically informed listening, not why we might sometimes choose to do without them.

composition or historical research. Music theory must also be a rational pursuit. By
'rational' we mean . . . that theory helps us illuminate, elucidate, understand or explain
music . . . Some [theorists] believe that music theory ought to model itself on the
sciences; they claim that it can and should aspire to the rigorous methods and
precise terminologies that have made science so successful in accounting for the world
around us. They insist that it is only by applying scientific paradigms to well-defined
phenomena, that music theory can be truly explanatory.[3]

Brown and Dempster thus, at the outset, point out two distinct roles or
functions of music theory: as an enquiry into music and 'musical activities',[4]
and as something that contributes to those activities. They go on to defend a
conception of music theory as a scientific enquiry which aims at discovering
laws of musical phenomena and providing Hempelian deductive-nomological
explanations of those phenomena.[5]

Kivy devotes a chapter of *Music Alone* to the topic of music theory's claim to
scientific status. His target in this chapter is the project of thematic analysis
advanced by Rudolph Reti and invoked, sometimes implicitly, by other writers.
The aim of thematic analysis, as stated by one proponent, is to 'explain the
musical as well as the psychological feeling of unity sensed in the great works
of Mozart, Haydn, Brahms, Beethoven'.[6] This is undertaken by reference to
hidden, or at any rate non-obvious, thematic or motivic resemblances. Kivy
compares this to the scientific goal of explaining the gross properties of matter
in terms of its microstructure (125).

Using Reti's analysis of Beethoven's Ninth Symphony as an example of the
approach, Kivy argues that it fails as science since there are no clear constraints as to what is to count as a relevant thematic resemblance. Kivy
goes on to suggest that such analyses are better understood along the lines
of interpretation than as explanation: as 'open[ing] up to us heretofore
unperceived and unappreciated features of the works they treat of for us to
contemplate, understand, enjoy,' in distinction to 'explanations of [art works]
qua natural phenomena' (144).

Kivy's criticism may well be on the mark for the case he cites. Nevertheless,

---

[3] Matthew Brown and Douglas Dempster, 'The Scientific Image of Music Theory', *Journal of
Music Theory*, 33 (1989), 65.
[4] I assume the relevant 'musical activities' include listening, though Brown and Dempster do
not explicitly say so in the quoted passage.
[5] Brown and Dempster, 'Scientific Image', 96. They point out certain ways in which the
schema would have to be modified in order to accommodate music-theoretic explanation, but
their overall conception is in the spirit of Hempel's D-N model.
[6] David Epstein, *Beyond Orpheus: Studies in Musical Structure* (Cambridge, Mass., 1979), 3,
quoted in Kivy, *Music Alone*, 129. In *The Thematic Process in Music* (London, 1961), Reti remarked
that the 'existence [of the unity of a work may] be felt beyond a doubt,' though 'it may be difficult
to prove' (355). This feeling of unity consists in, or is related to, the recognition that 'we cannot
produce a convincing musical composition by taking a group or a section from one work and
linking it to that of another—even assuming an affinity of key, rhythm, and tempo' (348). It was
Reti's assumption that although such unity is felt, its basis had not yet 'enter[ed] the general
musical consciousness' (5)—whence his study.

Ex. 1

I want to suggest that music-theoretical terms typically do have a certain kind of explanatory status, and that the value of hearing music in those terms sometimes derives from that status.

Let me illustrate the kind of explanatory connection I have in mind.

1. Closure is explained by motion to the tonic. In the main theme of Haydn's Symphony No. 104, first movement (Example 1), the melody is relatively open or incomplete at certain points (e.g. on the second half of bars 20 and 24), relatively closed at others (the beginning of bar 32). This is explained, in part, by the *scalestep positions* of the pitches. The tonic (scalestep 1 or *doh*) generally sounds stable, the dominant (scalestep 5 or *soh*) unstable. Hence motion to the tonic helps to explain closure, motion to the dominant a lack of closure.

2. A change in emotional tone is explained by a change in mode from minor to major. At the beginning of the fourth stanza of Schubert's song 'Gute Nacht', there is a change in the mood of the song which might be described roughly as one from despair to nostalgia. This is explained in part by the change of mode.

3. Unity is explained by motivic repetition. In a study paradigmatic of thematic analysis, David Epstein calls attention to, among other things, the constant repetition of the ♩ ♩ ♩ rhythm in the Haydn movement just cited (see Example 2).[7] It seems to me that even if some thematic analyses ought to be dismissed as pseudo-explanation, the present case is different. The rhythmic recurrence does help to explain the unity or coherence of the movement, even as it sounds to a naïve listener who does not attend to

---

[7] Epstein, *Beyond Orpheus*, 143–8. Epstein points out all the instances shown in Ex. 2 except for bar 48.

Ex. 2

the recurrence. Or, at any rate, it is a plausible hypothesis that it does, a hypothesis that cannot easily be dismissed.

What I want to argue is that in cases such as this, the value to a listener of perceiving music in the relevant theoretical terms stems in part from their explanatory power. For us to see how this is so, we must first enquire into what is being explained in terms of what, and into what the nature of the explanatory link is.

One possibility is that what is explained in these cases is a psychological state of the listener, or the event of his coming to be in that state. We might understand closure, on this account, to be a state marked by a lack of expectancy or a feeling of satisfaction. The relevant sort of explanation would then be a causal one, an explanation of how the music works on a listener.[8]

Surely there can be causal explanations of listeners' responses. But I want to suggest that for the cases in question another account is preferable.[9] For

---

[8] I am assuming that scalestep properties belong to the music, and that their status is unproblematic.

[9] Kendall Walton suggests that music theory might be subsidiarily concerned with such causal explanations, and considers how someone can appreciate the way in which an artwork, or the telling of a joke, works on him, in 'Understanding Humour and Understanding Music', elsewhere in this volume. I do not rule this out, but shall explore a different option.

what is explained here seems best understood not as states or properties of listeners, but as properties of the music: one perceives the music as coming to a close, not oneself as having this or that expectation. Hence if the phenomenology of musical experience is to serve as our guide here (as I shall allow it to do), we should understand the object of explanation to be the presence of a certain property in the music.

Let me suggest, moreover, that the explanatory relation here is not a typical causal one where cause and effect are distinct, but one in connection with the *reduction* of a property such as closure to theoretical properties such as scalestep position. This follows Kivy's analogy of a microstructural reduction, such as that of heat to the motion of molecules. On the present account, then, the presence of closure is identified with some complex structural condition in terms of scalestep properties and the like. The explanation, on this account, depends on an *explication* of closure, an account of what it consists in.

Call this the 'reduction' model of the explanatory connection, as distinguished from the causal model given earlier.[10] In my view, the reduction model is more plausible than the causal model in the present cases because the *explanans* and the *explanandum* are simply not distinct (or, at any rate, not wholly distinct). The event of a passage's coming to a close is not just something brought about by the motion to the tonic, but to some extent consists in that motion. The brightening in emotional tone of the Schubert passage is not just an effect of, but resides in, the change of mode. The unity of a passage is not separable from, but consists in, the various sorts of coherence that inhere in the passage: rhythmic, thematic, and so on.

The sort of explanatory power relevant to the present discussion, then, is that of explication and reduction—the reduction to theoretical properties of other properties that music has. And the central issue will be what this means for the listener. But first I want to address briefly two questions that arise about explanation and the status of music theory. The first is a sceptical worry about whether we have any reason to believe in such explanations; the second has to do with what role such explanations play in the music-theoretic enterprise.

On the first point, it might be argued that we do not have explanations unless we have laws; laws are exceptionless generalizations; and no one can actually state an exceptionless generalization linking, for example, closure and scalestep properties. Motion to the tonic is certainly not *sufficient* for closure, since the tonic can occur in the middle of a phrase; and it would not be hard to find examples showing that it is not necessary either. It would be difficult, in short, to formulate laws of closure.

---

[10] In his discussion of microstructural explanation Kivy cites John Searle's view that a 'surface feature [can be] both *caused by* the behaviour of micro-elements and at the same time . . . *realized in* the system that is made up of the micro-elements' (*Minds, Brains, and Science* (Cambridge, Mass., 1984), quoted in Kivy, *Music Alone*, 125). I am not sure I understand this, but at any rate the reduction model does not exclude causation.

But this does not show that we have no reason to believe that motion to the tonic has an explanatory link to closure. We can have reason to think a certain dependence exists without being able to state laws that govern it: we can see that the rock's striking the window caused it to break, even if we cannot say precisely which materials would break under what conditions. Of course, it takes *something* to justify such beliefs, but I would contend that experienced listeners have this, at least for the first two examples (I am in some doubt about the third).

The second question is whether it is a central task of music theory to provide such explanations and to discover laws that would support them. Now, if the causal model were correct then it would seem the relevant laws would be outside the domain of music theory. It is the psychology of music that is properly concerned with discovering laws of human responses to music, and we should no more conflate music theory with that discipline than we should conflate theories of linguistic structure with the psychology of language.[11]

On the reduction model, on the other hand (which we have adopted), it seems that music theory would have to be concerned with the discovery of the relevant identifications (assuming they are not obvious, so there is something to discover). If this is not the business of music theory, then of what theory? But it would still remain to be seen how important the discovery of such identifications would be, as tasks for music theory go. I shall not attempt to answer that question in this paper, except to indicate later on how an interest in such discovery may or may not be relevant to a listener's understanding.

Let me now ask what all of this means for Tibby. In regard to the first example, I assume that Tibby, by dint of diligent practice in ear training, hears each pitch of the Haydn theme as having the scalestep position in D major that it in fact has. This means he can reliably identify the scalestep positions of the pitches he hears in this and unfamiliar tonal passages. Moreover, different pitches sound different to him in a way that is correlated systematically with their scalestep position. The pitch A has, for Tibby, the quality associated with *soh* in a D major context; it does not have this quality in an E major context, whereas B, the fifth scale degree in that context, does.

Mrs Munt's experience, I take it, lacks this aspect. Hence Tibby's experience has a content that is in some sense richer than hers. However, it is worth pointing out that this does not mean that the content of Tibby's perceptual experience is more *determinate* than Mrs Munt's, in the sense that the truth conditions of Mrs Munt's experience are wider, that it is satisfied by more possible situations, than Tibby's.[12] It may well be that Mrs Munt's experience is just as restrictive in this sense as his. For Mrs Munt's experience of the

---

[11] Jerrold J. Katz, 'An Outline of Platonist Grammar', in Katz (ed.), *The Philosophy of Linguistics* (Oxford, 1985), 203.

[12] Saying that a perceptual experience is satisfied by a possible situation is equivalent to saying that it would be veridical in that situation.

melody may in fact be a rather precise representation of it: she may be able to detect flaws in intonation and other mistakes. The important difference between her experience and Tibby's is that the latter has a conceptual dimension absent in hers. Someone might have a visual experience of a jagged mountaintop that represents it as having a certain irregular shape without possessing concepts to specify that particular shape. That perceptual experience would be one with a highly determinate 'analogue', as opposed to conceptual, content.[13] Likewise, Mrs Munt's analogue content might well be rich enough to determine the pitch content of the melody, on which the pitches' scalestep positions would supervene. Tibby's experience would then be better thought of as involving a kind of conceptual overlay on features already represented in Mrs Munt's experience, than as a more restrictive specification of how things are.[14]

But with this clarification noted, the question remains: of what benefit is this conceptual level of hearing to Tibby? Let me say that the benefits in which I am interested are those of musical understanding and enjoyment. I am concerned, then, with describing how the explanatory status of theoretical terms is related to the understanding and enjoyment of someone who hears music in those terms. (That is not to rule out other possibilities for understanding and enjoyment.)

Here is one possible answer. Tibby knows that closure is explained by reference to scalestep properties. Hence, not only does he hear the music coming to a close, and hears the arrival of the tonic, but he hears the closing with an appreciation of the way it depends on the tonic's arrival. For this reason, his intentional object has a coherence not present in the experience of someone who is unaware of the connection. This coherence, moreover, leads to understanding and enjoyment: he understands the music better in virtue of hearing it with an appreciation of the explanatory connection, and this issues in a more satisfactory, more pleasurable experience than he otherwise would have.

I believe this answer has plausibility. But two important objections can be made to it.

The first is that it is not clear why we ought to count the understanding Tibby derives from knowing the explanatory connection as an understanding *of the music* rather than an understanding of what the music *is* or how it *works*. Clearly, not everything that counts as a way of understanding an artwork in the latter sense is an aesthetic understanding, or counts toward the aesthetic appreciation of that work. While a sensitivity to consonance and dissonance, for example, is surely essential to musical understanding, it is doubtful that a

---

[13] See Christopher Peacocke, 'Analogue Content', *Proceedings of the Aristotelian Society* Suppl. Vol. 60 (1986), 1–17. The example is his, in 'Scenarios, Concepts, and Perception', in T. Crane (ed.), *The Contents of Experience: Essays on Perception* (Cambridge, 1992).

[14] I investigate these issues further in *Music and the Representational Content of Experience* (Cambridge, forthcoming).

knowledge of their physical basis in frequency ratios is essential. We need some reason to count Tibby's understanding as an aesthetically relevant one.[15]

The second objection goes as follows. If our aesthetic posture toward a work consists in appreciating the way feature A depends upon feature B, it had better be the case that one really does depend on the other. It is an important attribute of aesthetic pleasure that it is not merely hedonic, but has an aspect of being justified or grounded.[16] A pleasure taken in the supposed way one feature depends on another, when it does not, would be a false pleasure, and would entail no kind of understanding. (This would not be appreciation, but a kind of pseudo-appreciation.) Moreover, it is part of the aesthetic point of view that we should avoid such false pleasures or misunderstandings. Now if, as appears to be the case, theoretical identifications of the relevant sort are not obvious, then they would be appropriate topics for enquiry.[17] Hence it seems as if the aesthetically appropriate attitude would include having an interest in being well informed about the results of such enquiry.

To put the point another way, theoretically informed musical pleasure, on this account, is subject to a certain defeasibility. Were we to learn that a given rhythmic repetition does not explain coherence, a pleasure taken in that supposed connection would be shown to be in a certain sense unjustified.

The problem is that the aesthetic posture taken in theoretically informed listening does *not* require this interest or involve this defeasibility. A concern with confirmation and disconfirmation—arguably central to science—does not play a comparably important role *vis-à-vis* the listening situation. (The point is not that we do not take this interest when perhaps we should, but that such an interest is not demanded by the aesthetic situation.) The pleasures derived from thematic analysis, for example, are immune from defeasibility, as they would not be if the above picture were correct. The criticisms Kivy makes of Reti *qua* science are true, but somehow irrelevant. Kivy recognizes this, of course, and I take it that this is part of the reason why he regards thematic analysis as interpretative rather than explanatory. But I hope to find a different way out of this box, one that captures the relevance of the explanatory aspect to the interpretative.

We might be led to a better account of Tibby's enjoyment and understanding if we consider the way the coherence of his experience was characterized earlier. One might, from the above account, think of his experience as consisting in an awareness of phenomenally distinct features that are, as it were, connected. By 'phenomenally distinct' features I mean ones that are

---

[15] This is, I take it, a point made by Kivy in his oral response to my comments on *Music Alone*: he questioned whether on my account Tibby's enjoyment is an enjoyment 'of the music' or 'of the explanation', linking this to the traditional problem of 'aesthetic or artistic "relevance"' ('Comments on Comments on *Music Alone*', Austin, October 1990).

[16] I shall not attempt to give a theory of such justification.

[17] The point does not depend on this, but in my view the relevant theoretical identifications would be necessary a posteriori and the relevant enquiry would be empirical.

qualitatively different and introspectively distinguishable, such as the colour of a patch from its shape, or the timbre of a sound from its pitch. It is, I want to suggest, an important fact about Tibby's intentional object that the relevant features are not phenomenally distinct in this way. The coming of a passage to a close, and the motion to the tonic pitch, are not separable aspects of Tibby's intentional object. Rather, the motion to the tonic, as he hears it, just is part of closure, as he hears it. Let me call this property of Tibby's intentional object, whereby the appearance of one feature is not (wholly) distinct from the appearance of another, *fusion*.

The present point is distinct from the basic tenet of the reduction model that the properties themselves (e.g. closure and motion to the tonic) are intimately related. The point is, rather, one about their modes of presentation to Tibby, and consists in a stronger claim. For one might be presented with what correspond to the two sides of a theoretical identification via distinct modes: one might, for example, see in an electron microscope the motion of molecules that is the heat one feels. What is important about the musical case is that this sort of phenomenal separation does *not* occur: the intimate relation between the properties themselves is mirrored in the fusion of their modes of presentation.

Leibniz wrote, 'the pleasures of sense are reducible to intellectual pleasures, known confusedly'.[18] Theoretically informed listening, if I am right, is not always in the direction of decreasing confusion. Perhaps it often distinguishes what should be kept distinct, but sometimes it fuses what ought to be fused: as closure consists partly in motion to the tonic, so the appearance of closure, for Tibby, consists partly in the appearance of motion to the tonic.

I speculate—though it is a psychological question I am not prepared to investigate—that this fusion of qualities in Tibby's intentional object is sometimes a result of the fact that his perception is theory laden. The more strongly someone believes that all and only As are Bs, the more the distinction between that person's seeing something as an A, and as a B, is blurred. It may be that a beginning theory student can identify motion to the tonic as such, and hear closure, without hearing one as part and parcel of the other. It may be necessary that one believe that motion to the tonic is connected with closure, and allow this belief to infiltrate one's auditory perception, for fusion to occur. That is the interesting case, so I will assume this applies in what follows.

With the notion of fusion in mind, let me now make a revised suggestion about what is distinctive and valuable in Tibby's experience. Tibby hears closure for what it is. It is not the acquisition of an understanding of connections among distinct features he hears, but a deepened perception of a property for what it is, that is central to his increased appreciation. And with this comes a deepened pleasure in the music.

[18] 'Principles of Nature and Grace', cited by Kivy, *Music Alone*, 38.

In the space that remains, I want to consider how this account fares against the two objections considered earlier. First, why should what I have described count as a deepened understanding *of the music*? I cannot offer a theory, from scratch, of what makes a way of listening to music an instance of musical understanding. However, it does seem that if the perception of a certain property is already recognized as basic to musical understanding, then hearing it in a deepened way is apt to count as an extension of that understanding. And closure and other properties explicated by music theory are typically basic to musical understanding. Of course, not any extension of perception based on a theoretical identification will do. Watching waveforms on an oscilloscope would not add much to the experience of pitch or timbre, or such is my intuition. But I want to suggest, though I cannot prove, that fusion is relevant here: it is the fact that we have an enrichment and extension of the experience of closure, rather than its supplementation by a different sort of experience, that makes theoretically informed listening particularly valuable.[19]

Let us turn now to the question about confirmation and defeasibility. On the present account, Tibby's pleasure is not one *taken in* the awareness of explanatory connections, even if it causally depends on a belief in such connections. This, I think, does something to defuse the second objection since, even if Tibby's belief is false, it does not follow that he is appreciating, or pseudo-appreciating, what is not the case. So the interest we ought to have in avoiding such pseudo-appreciation is irrelevant, on the present account.

Still, since on this account the way Tibby perceives a passage depends causally on his having certain theoretical beliefs, doesn't his aesthetic posture require an interest in being well informed about the truth or falsity of those beliefs, and isn't his pleasure defeasible? Suppose, for example, that he believes that the unity a naïve listener senses in the Haydn is brought about by the rhythmic repetition, and that this belief (*inter alia*) causes him, when he attends to the rhythmic repetition, to have a coherent and satisfying experience of the piece. Wouldn't the discovery that the rhythmic repetition has nothing to do with unity thus sensed rob his pleasure of a certain justification?

In my view, the answer is negative. By the time Tibby has reached the point at which his listening strategy is coherent and satisfying, his enjoyment is likely to be aesthetically sound for many reasons unrelated to any such false belief. It may be, for example, that even if the rhythmic repetition has nothing to do with unity as the naïve listener senses it, it has much to do with *Tibby's* experience of unity, since he has paid so much attention to it. The falsity of a theoretical assumption that plays a causal role in someone's arriving at a certain aesthetic situation will not undermine the situation, I suggest, if there

---

[19] As to why this leads to greater pleasure, I do not have a general account. It seems to me that the story in any given case would be parasitic on why the perception of the explained property is relevant to understanding and enjoyment.

are independent reasons for which it is to count as genuine appreciation. And this is, I think, usual in theoretically informed listening. For the listener, such assumptions are a ladder that might be kicked away; hence it would be beside the point for Tibby to worry about their truth or falsity.

Index of Names